T0373215

THE AMERICAN INDIAN
AND THE END OF THE CONFEDERACY,
1863–1866

The American Indian and the End of the Confederacy, 1863–1866

BY

ANNIE HELOISE ABEL

atque ubi solitudinem faciunt, pacem appellant.—Tacitus, *Agricola*, cap. 30.

*Introduction to the Bison Book Edition
by Theda Perdue and Michael D. Green*

University of Nebraska Press
Lincoln and London

Introduction copyright © 1993 by the University of Nebraska Press
All rights reserved
Manufactured in the United States of America

First Bison Book printing: 1993

Library of Congress Cataloging-in-Publication Data
Abel, Annie Heloise, 1873–
[American Indian under Reconstruction]
The American Indian and the end of the Confederacy, 1863–1866 / by
Annie Heloise Abel; introduction to the Bison book edition by Theda
Perdue and Michael D. Green.
p. cm.
"A Bison book."
Originally published: The Amerian Indian under Reconstruction.
Cleveland: Arthur H. Clark Co., 1925.
ISBN 0-8032-5921-2 (pa)
1. Indians of North America—Indian Territory—History—19th cen-
tury.   2. Indians of North America—Confederate States of America—
Government relations.   3. Indians of North America—Confederate
States of America—Slaves, Ownership of.   4. Indian Territory—His-
tory—Civil War, 1861–1865.   5. Reconstruction—Indian Territory—
History—19th century.   6. Indians of North America—Indian Territory—Treaties.   7. Indians of North America—History—Civil War,
1861–1865.   I. Title.
E78.I5A24   1993
973.7—dc20
93-17686   CIP

Reprinted from the original edition titled *The American Indian under
Reconstruction* and published in 1925 by the Arthur H. Clark Company,
Cleveland, Ohio

∞

TO
THE MEMORY OF MY MOTHER

CONTENTS

INTRODUCTION
by Theda Perdue and Michael D. Green

The close of the Civil War found the southern Indians politically divided, economically devastated, and socially dis-
rupted. Many Cherokees, Creeks, and Seminoles who opposed the Confederate alliances of 1861 fled to Kansas, and
federal invasions after 1862 forced Confederates from
these nations into the Choctaw Nation and even into Texas.[1]
In North and South, refugees faced the end of the war far
from home and often apart from their families.[2] Those who
had remained in their nations also experienced disruption.
Frequently victims or perpetrators of bushwhacking and
vigilante justice, the wartime residents of the southern Indian nations lived in fear and seethed with hatred toward
their opponents. Even among the relatively unscathed
Choctaws and Chickasaws, the end of the war brought
dread of a future in which their slaves might not only be
free but also citizens of their nations.[3] Indeed the impending end of slavery among the five southern nations promised profound change, but so did their new relationship
with the federal government. Their alliances with the Confederacy meant that the United States now regarded them
as vanquished foes, and they were in no position to resist the
demands of the victor. In the third, and arguably best, volume of Annie Abel's *Slaveholding Indians*, she examines the
Confederate defeat and the process of reconstructing the
Confederacy's Indian allies.

Abel wrote in the era when William Dunning and his followers dominated Reconstruction scholarship.[4] Replete

with racist assumptions about the inferiority of African Americans, these works focused on the failure of Reconstruction and laid the blame for that failure squarely on the corruption of "radical" white politicians and philanthropists and the incompetence of blacks foisted into the political arena. Abel's own choice of adjectives for describing Native peoples—"the inoffensive Nez Perces, the aggressive Poncas, and the noble Cheyennes"—certainly places her in the company of those historians who wrote in racial stereotypes. On the other hand, Abel had no interest in marshalling her scholarship to the cause of segregation and racial oppression in the South. Her interests lay in the West, and she wrote about the reconstruction of the southern Indian nations in the context of western expansion, "territorial growth," and the "displacement of the aborigines."

For the purposes of this book, Abel defined reconstruction as "political re-adjustment." The treaties of 1866 that reestablished relations between the "five tribes" of Indian Territory and the United States accomplished this, she believed, and thus the book ends where modern historians would assume it should begin. With her focus clearly fixed on the political and diplomatic elements of the story, she left untold the "too painful" effects of the readjustment she details here.

Abel is not bashful about assigning blame for the pain. The United States government abandoned the Indians of Indian Territory in 1861 when it reassigned troops to other areas and virtually invited the Confederacy to take over. Then, after the five tribes had signed treaties with the Confederate government, the United States failed to alleviate the suffering of the Indian refugees who fled to Union Kansas. Worse, federal civilian and military officers colluded in the theft of hundreds of thousands of head of Indian-owned livestock, thereby magnifying the certain difficulty of postwar economic recovery. Meanwhile, U.S. Senator James Lane and Congressman S. C. Pomeroy, both of Kansas, won legislation in Congress to invalidate all previous treaties that defined and protected the land rights of the five tribes and authorize the removal of other Native peoples from Kansas into Indian Territory. And finally, Iowa Senator James Harlan prepared legislation that would formally organize Indian Territory as a federal territory complete with governor and legislature, in effect denying the sovereignty of the five tribes.[5] Combined, this list of oppressive measures adds up to a massive campaign to strip the nations of Indian Territory of their political independence, their land, and natural resources, and when coupled with the further requirements to free their slaves and admit the freedmen to full equality, to reduce their citizens to poverty and dependence.

The culmination of this story occurs in the negotiations of the so-called Reconstruction Treaties of 1866[6] Orchestrated by a trio of rapacious, expansionist, anti-Indian Iowans—former Senator (now Secretary of the Interior) Harlan, Commissioner of Indian Affairs Dennis N. Cooley, and Elijah Sells, head of the Southern Superintendency—these treaties reflected the principles of the Lane-Pomeroy legislation and the Harlan bill and went beyond to include grants of land for railroad construction through Indian lands. Although Abel singles out the Cherokee treaty for detailed analysis, she makes clear that all the negotiations rested on a single policy of expansion and development at the expense of the Indians.

Abel wrote this book, as she did the first two volumes in her trilogy, before organization of the National Archives. Her extraordinary research took her into previously unused government records which were so scattered and in such disarray that her bibliographic essay reads like the instructions for a scavenger hunt beginning with a search for a garage on the corner of 24th and M Streets, NW, and requiring the scholar to do battle with General Ainsworth, who guards the documents with such zeal as "almost to pre-

clude thoroughgoing historical research." Perhaps this is
the reason she filled her footnotes with transcripts of key
letters and reports.

Important contributions in their own right, the special
significance of Abel's books probably lies in the fact that
they are the first to explore the questions contained in the
history of the Civil War in Indian Territory. Historians who
have built on her work have followed two major lines of inquiry. The first concerns the fate of freedmen in the southern Indian nations. The interest in black history spawned
by the modern civil rights movement led a number of
scholars to examine the treatment of former slaves by the
Indians who had been their masters.[7] Two book-length
studies by Daniel F. Littlefield, Jr., demonstrate the complexity of relations and the diversity of solutions. In *The
Cherokee Freedmen: From Emancipation to American Citizenship*,[8] Littlefield traced the freedmen problems that arose
from the Cherokee Treaty of 1866. Given only six months
to establish residency and citizenship, many Cherokee
freedmen who had been removed from the Nation during
the Civil War failed to meet the deadline, and the Cherokees sought to exclude them. Federal agents, however,
proved more lenient, and in their recognition of the freedmen's claim to citizenship, they made "perhaps the most
profound inroad on Cherokee autonomy in the post–Civil
War period."[9] Despite their problems, Cherokee freedmen
probably fared better than those former slaves of Chickasaws whom Littlefield described in *The Chickasaw Freedmen:
A People without a Country*.[10] Periodically demanding total expulsion of their former slaves, the Chickasaws never
adopted the freedmen nor extended citizenship rights to
them.

The second line of scholarly inquiry that has emerged
from the Reconstruction experience of southern Indians
focuses on economic development and, in particular, the
construction of railroads. The subtitle of M. Thomas
Bailey's *Reconstruction in Indian Territory: A Story of Avarice,*

Discrimination, and Opportunism[11] pretty much captures the essence of the story, but H. Craig Miner's work more accurately reveals its complexity. In *The Corporation and the Indian: Tribal Sovereignty and Industrial Civilization in Indian Territory, 1865–1907*,[12] Miner explored the ramifications of Reconstruction treaties that forced the southern nations to grant railroad rights of way. This action dramatically enlarged the cast of characters in Indian country and gave some people already there new roles. With self-interested Indians on their payrolls, corporations joined land-hungry whites to challenge Indian sovereignty and demand allotment in severalty. Although Abel did not reach beyond 1866, she suggested and others have demonstrated that Reconstruction Indian policy opened a new chapter in United States expansion.

Annie Abel was born in England in 1873[13] At the age of twelve, she emigrated with her family to Kansas. She received her undergraduate and master's degrees from the University of Kansas and studied for a year at Cornell. In 1893 she became the first woman to receive Yale's Bulkley Fellowship; Yale awarded her the Ph.D. in 1905. Her dissertation, "The History of Events Resulting in the Consolidation West of the Mississippi," appeared in the *Annual Report* of the American Historical Association in 1906.[14] In that year, she moved from her first job at Wells College to Women's College of Baltimore, now Goucher College, where she remained until 1915. While she was living in Baltimore, Abel had easy access to Indian Bureau records in Washington. She began to investigate the role of Indians in the Civil War, and published an article on the subject in 1910.[15] In 1915, the year the first volume of *Slaveholding Indians* appeared, Abel moved to Smith College. There she developed an interest in British policy toward Native peoples, and in 1921 she went to Australia on her sabbatical to research aboriginal policy. Abel married while she was in Australia and resigned her position at Smith. She used her husband's name, Henderson, but after they separated permanently in 1927 she adopted a hyphenated surname, Abel-Henderson. Returning to the United States, she taught briefly at Sweetbriar College and the University of Kansas before retiring in 1930 and moving to Aberdeen, Washington, to live with her sister. When she died in 1947, Abel left a substantial body of work on Native peoples. In addition to her studies of southern Indians, she meticulously edited the records of travelers, fur traders, and Indian agents.[16]

Abel's major legacy, however, is her trilogy, *Slaveholding Indians*. In this work, she charts the diplomatic maneuvers that led to a Confederate alliance, the participation of Native soldiers in military operations that brought devastation to Indian Territory, and the impact of Confederate defeat on the peoples that had repudiated their treaties with the United States in favor of a Confederate alliance. The story is a tragic one, but leaving it untold would be a greater tragedy. Native southerners shared the experience of civil war with other Americans, and their involvement in that upheaval had as profound an effect on their subsequent history.

NOTES

1. Abel detailed these experiences in her two earlier works in this trilogy, *The American Indian as Slaveholder and Secessionist* (1915) and *The American Indian in the Civil War* (1919), both reprinted by the University of Nebraska Press in 1992. For other accounts, see Morris L. Wardell, *A Political History of the Cherokee Nation, 1838–1907* (Norman: University of Oklahoma Press, 1938), pp. 142–207; relevant chapters in William G. McLoughlin's forthcoming *After the Trail of Tears: The Cherokees, 1839–1880* (Chapel Hill: University of North Carolina Press); Edwin C. McReynolds, *The Seminoles* (Norman: University of Oklahoma Press, 1957), pp. 289–312; and Angie Debo, *The Road to Disappearance: A History of the Creek Indians* (Norman: University of Oklahoma Press, 1941), pp. 142–213.

2. For problems of the refugees specifically, see Dean Banks, "Civil-War Refugees from Indian Territory in the North, 1861–1864," *Chronicles of Oklahoma* 41 (1963): 286–98; Wiley Britton, "Some Reminiscences

of the Cherokee People Returning to Their Homes, the Exiles of a Nation," *Chronicles of Oklahoma* 6 (1928): 163–77; Edmund J. Danziger, Jr., "The Office of Indian Affairs and the Problem of Civil War Refugees in Kansas," *Kansas Historical Quarterly* 35 (1969): 257–75: and Angie Debo, "Southern Refugees of the Cherokee Nation," *Southwestern Historical Quarterly* 35 (1932): 255–66.

3. Angie Debo, *The Rise and Fall of the Choctaw Republic* (Norman: University of Oklahoma Press, 1934), pp. 80–109; Arrell M. Gibson, *The Chickasaws* (Norman: University of Oklahoma Press, 1971), pp. 259–78.

4. William A. Dunning, *Essays on the Civil War and Reconstruction* (New York: Macmillan Company, 1898) and *Reconstruction, Political and Economic* (New York: Harper and Brothers, 1907). This line of thought reached its height with Claude G. Bowers, *The Tragic Era* (Cambridge, Mass.: Houghton Mifflin Company, 1929). Historians gradually began to challenge the interpretations of the Dunning school. Among the first were Francis B. Simkins and Robert G. Woody, *South Carolina during Reconstruction* (Chapel Hill: University of North Carolina Press, 1932) and W. E. B. DuBois, *Black Reconstruction* (New York: Harcourt, Brace & Company, 1935). The most recent comprehensive study is Eric Foner, *Reconstruction: America's Unfinished Revolution, 1863–1877* (New York: Harper and Row, 1988).

5. The Harlan bill never passed. The five tribes considered territorial government in 1870 as a consequence of the reconstruction treaties of 1866, but Congress rejected the measure and no nation ratified the proposed constitution. "The Ocmulgee Constitution: A Step towards Indian Self-Determination," *Chronicles of Oklahoma* 58 (1980): 264–81.

6. Charles J. Kappler, *Indian Affairs, Laws and Treaties* (5 vols., Washington: Government Printing Office, 1904), 2: 910, 918, 932, 942.

7. For example, Thomas F. Andrews, "Freedmen in Indian Territory: A Post Civil War Dilemma," *Journal of the West* 4 (1965): 367–76; Parthena Louise James, "Reconstruction in the Chickasaw Nation: The Freedman Problem," *Chronicles of Oklahoma* 45 (1967): 44–57; Walt Willson, "Freedmen in Indian Territory during Reconstruction," *Chronicles of Oklahoma* 49 (1971): 230–44; Harold Martin Troper, "The Creek Negroes of Oklahoma and Canadian Immigration," *Canadian Historical Review* 53 (1972): 272–88; Tim Gammon, "Black Freedmen and the Cherokee Nation," *Journal of American Studies* 11 (1977): 357–64; Gary R. Kremer, "For Justice and a Fee: James Milton Turner and the Cherokee Freedmen," *Chronicles of Oklahoma* 58 (1980–81): 377–91; George O. Carney, "All-Black Towns," *Chronicles of Oklahoma* 69 (1991–92): 116–233.

8. (Westport, Conn.: Greenwood Press, 1978).

9. Ibid., p. 103.

10. (Westport, Conn.: Greenwood Press, 1980).

11. (Port Washington, N.Y.: Kennikat Press, 1972).

12. (Columbia: University of Missouri Press, 1976). Also see Miner's "The Struggle for an East-West Railway into the Indian Territory, 1870–1882," *Chronicles of Oklahoma* 47 (1969): 560–81 and " 'A Corps of Clerks': The Bureaucracy of Industrialization in Indian Territory, 1866–1907," *Chronicles of Oklahoma* 53 (1975): 322–31.

13. This biographical sketch is condensed from Harry Kelsey, "A Dedication to the Memory of Annie Heloise Abel Henderson, 1873–1947," *Arizona and the West* 15 (1973): 1–4.

14. 1 (1908) 235–450.

15. "The Indians in the Civil War," *American Historical Review* 15 (1910): 281–96.

16. *The Official Correspondence of James S. Calhoun While Indian Agent at Santa Fe and Superintendent of Indian Affairs in New Mexico* (Washington: U.S. Government Printing Office, 1915); "The Journal of John Greiner," *Old Santa Fe* 3 (1916): 189–243; *A Report from Natchitoches in 1807 by Dr. John Sibley* (New York: Museum of the American Indian, 1922); *Chardron's Journal at Fort Clark, 1834–1839* (Pierre: South Dakota Department of History, 1932); *Tabeau's Narrative of Loisel's Expedition to the Upper Missouri* (Norman: University of Oklahoma Press, 1939); "Indian Affairs in New Mexico under the Administration of William Carr Lane; from the Journal of John Ward," *New Mexico Historical Review* 16 (1941): 106–32, 328–58.

PREFACE

The present is the concluding volume of the Slave-holding Indians series. Its title may be thought somewhat misleading since the time limits of the period covered by no means coincide with those commonly understood as signifying the Reconstruction Period of United States History. In that history, the word, *reconstruction*, which ought, etymologically, to imply the process of re-building and restoring, has attained, most unfortunately, a meaning all its own, a meaning now technical, nothing more nor less, in fact, than political re-adjustment. It is in the light of that meaning, definite and technical, that the limits of this book have been determined.

The treaties made with the great southern tribes in 1866 were reconstruction treaties pure and simple and this volume, therefore, finds its conclusion in their negotiation. They marked the establishment of a new relationship with the United States government; but their serious and far-reaching effects would constitute too long and too painful a story for narration here. Its chapters would include an account of tribal dissensions without number or cessation, of the pitiful racial deterioration of the Creeks due to unchecked mixture with the negroes, of the influx of a white population outnumbering and over-reaching the red, and, finally, of great tragedies that had for their theme the compulsory removal of such tribes as the inoffensive Nez Percés, the aggressive Poncas, and the noble Cheyennes.

In recent years, an increasing interest has been aroused in the course of the westward movement so-called and, little by little, the full significance of American expansion is being appreciated.   In less than a century of time, the United States has extended itself over the vast reaches of this continent from the Atlantic to the Pacific and its territorial growth has necessarily involved the displacement of the aborigines.   Its treatment of them is bound to concern very greatly the historian of the future, whose mental grasp will be immeasurably greater than is that of the men, who now write and teach American history in the old conventional way with a halo around New England and the garb of aristocracy enveloping Virginia.   It is in American History rightly proportioned that the present study will have its place.

ANNIE HELOISE ABEL

Washington, D.C., March, 1920

I. OVERTURES OF PEACE AND RECONCILIATION

The failure of the United States government to afford to the southern Indians the protection solemnly guaranteed by treaty stipulations had been the great cause of their entering into an alliance with the Confederacy and it was also the primary cause of their persisting in their adherence to its fortunes.   From first to last military conditions and events determined political and it is certainly no exaggeration to say that had a time ever come after the opening twelvemonth of war when the Federals could have shown themselves in unquestioned possession of the Indian country the treaties with the South would, one and all, have been immediately abrogated even by such initial and arch offenders as the Choctaws and Chickasaws who, alone of all the slaveholding tribes, had attached themselves, originally and in a national way, to the Secessionists because of a frankly avowed sympathy with the "peculiar institution."   Success wins support everywhere, at all times and under all circumstances. Occasionally a very little of it is necessary, the glamor of the mere name being all-sufficient. It had taken next to nothing to call back the Cherokees to their allegiance to the North, the embodiment of the power with which all their other treaties had been made, and, just as the Confederate victory of Wilson's Creek, or Oak Hills, had terminated the neutrality that they had hoped, Kentucky-like, to maintain, so the penetration of their country by a Union force in the summer of sixty-two saw the last of their inclusion as a tribe within the southern league.

During 1863 the example set by the Cherokees was frequently followed, never by tribes, it is true, but by groups of Indians only, large or small. Individuals, families, clans could pass with impunity within the Federal territory whenever such passing appeared to promise a fair degree of personal security. It was contrariwise with nations, the Unionist fortunes of war being as yet too fluctuating for nations to care to take additional risks. None the less the time seemed reasonably opportune for friendly advances to be made to repentant tribes and so thought several of the generals in the field, among them Schofield and McNeil.[1] In November, the former emphatically asserted that terms of peace might with propriety now be offered and the latter, having already reached the same conclusion, proposed the appointment of a special agent, clothed with plenary power to treat.[2] For reasons difficult to enumerate at this juncture no really serious attention was given to the matter by Washington officials until a new year had dawned. Confessedly, the main reason was, the continued inability of the Federals to prove military occupancy of the Indian country. Without military occupancy it was worse than useless to make promises of protection. So firmly convinced

---

[1] For an estimate of McNeil's understanding of and sympathy with frontier conditions, see A.G.O., Old Files Section, *Personal Papers of John McNeil*. McNeil had asked for service in the frontier [S. H. Boyd, Benjamin F. Loan, Joseph W. McClurg to Stanton, March 11, 1864, *ibid*]. He had strong political backing and men like John W. Gamble, J. B. Henderson and J. R. Winchell found justification for even his summary execution of guerrillas at Palmyra. [*ibid.*]

[2] Schofield to Halleck, November 12, 1863, A.G.O., Old Files Section, *B 1013, V.S. 1863, Jacket 2 of 15*; Usher to Stanton, February 19, 1864, *ibid.*

of this was Commissioner Dole that, in January, he quite scouted the idea of its being feasible to do much towards reorganization before something more than forts and posts was in Federal possession.[3]

While taking this stand, as caution dictated it was only right he should, Dole was willing to admit that the facts as alleged by Schofield and McNeil were correct and that Union sentiment among the Indians was very perceptibly on the increase. So excellent an opportunity, however, for recalling to the minds of congressmen and cabinet officials the remissness of the War Department and of the army from the very outset of the war was not to be lost. It was a case, if there ever was one, where reiteration, bold and constant, did no harm. The time was approaching and would soon be here when the United States government and all in authority under it would do well to remember where the blame for Indian defection really lay. Shirkers of responsibility have proverbially short memories.

Yes, Unionist sentiment among the Indians was on the increase[4] and it was on the increase because the spectre of eventual Confederate failure was looming up ever larger and larger in the distance. The Choctaws, stanchest of allies once, were now[5] wavering in their devotion to the South but not many of them were as yet fully ready to unite with Abolitionists and *Black*

---

[3] Dole addressed himself, under date of January 25, 1864, to Congressman Boyd of Missouri who, from his position on the House Committee of Indian Affairs, had recommended (O.I.A., General Files, *Southern Superintendency, 1863-1864*) a man named Sullivan as an eminently fit person to negotiate with the slaveholding Indians (O.I.A., *Letter Book*, no. 73, pp. 54-55.)

[4] Commissioner of Indian Affairs, *Report*, 1863, pp. 26, 182, 208, 209.

[5] The first signs of their wavering had appeared long since (Abel, *The Indian as a Participant in the American Civil War*, p. 220) and were subject for detailed comment by Dole in his annual report the preceding year (Commissioner of Indian Affairs, *Report*, 1863, p. 26).

Republicans. Their *interests* were still, as Commissioner Scott had defined them, *all southern.*[6] Their laws were largely derived from the statutes of Mississippi,[7] whence most of them had come. They were a wealthy people, and largely of the planter class. Race prejudice was strong among them as was also repugnance to any race mixture that entailed their own assimilation with inferior blood. In this characteristic they resembled the haughty Anglo-Saxon and differed radically from the Gallic Frenchman and, strange to relate, from their own kith and kin, the Creeks, who mingled Indian blood with African freely. All but about three hundred[8] of the Choctaws had gone over to the Secessionists and the tribe had numbered approximately eighteen thousand before the war.[9]

The first stage in the Choctaw re-tracing of steps would seem to have been marked by the desire for inactivity, the convenient pose of a neutral, and the second, by a plan to organize an independent Indian confederacy.[10] The principle of self-determination, not christened yet, was dominant throughout the South. It lay back of all secessionist action and ought logically, reasoned the Choctaws, to work as well for red men as for white. Its *reductio ad absurdum* as the principle of anarchy *par excellence* naturally never suggested itself to anyone. Possibly, all cogitation was

---

[6] See Address to the Choctaws and others, quoted in Dole's Report for 1863, p. 226.

[7] Commissioner of Indian Affairs, *Report*, 1859, p. 160.

[8] *Ibid*, 1863, p. 25.

[9] August Wattles to Secretary Smith, March 4, 1862, O.I.A., General Files, *Central Superintendency*, W 528 of 1862; I. D., *Register of Letters Received*, "Indians," no. 4, p. 517; Wm. P. Dole to Smith, March 17, 1862, O.I.A., *Report Book*, no. 12, p. 335.

[10] Report of Colonel W. A. Phillips, February 16, 1864, *Official Records*, first series, volume xxxiv, part i, p. 107; Phillips to Dole, February 24, 1864, O.I.A., General Files, *Southern Superintendency*, 1863-1864, p. 143.

time-serving in character. The discouraged and disgusted Indians dallied with ideas of independent
sovereignty because it was altogether too early yet for
leading Choctaws, prominent half-breeds mostly, to
join forces with the detested North. Besides, the Indian was loath to abandon his erstwhile friend; for the
Indian is fundamentally loyal. He keeps faith so long
as and often longer than faith is kept with him. Let
the Confederates give some evidence of disinterested-
ness of motive, of genuine concern for Indian welfare
and all might yet be well. Their martial prowess was
undoubted, their star of fortune seemed occasionally
still in the ascendant; but rally their forces they must.
There could be no surer way to a restoration of confidence.

The general Indian council that had been regularly
meeting at Armstrong Academy was the political body
before which to propound the independent confederacy
project and it was while that body was holding a session
in February [11] of 1864 with the object of assisting the

[11] The inception of the movement was much earlier and is indicated in
the following letter addressed by Jackson McCurtain to General McNeil,
December 16, 1863. McNeil had suggested that McCurtain come in person
to Van Buren, his headquarters, and discuss the situation in the Choctaw
country. McCurtain's absence would have aroused suspicion and he offered
as his substitute, "Mr. Thomas Edwards, a citizen of the Choctaw Nation
and of Sugar Loaf Co.," where unionist sentiment was slowly germinating.
The letter reveals how timorously men like McCurtain were advancing on
the return journey to their allegiance to the United States government. It
reads as follows:

"We had a meeting on last Saturday, when I proposed to the people
that was now camped in the mountains to return to their former homes
and not molest or take up arms against the U. S. forces upon condition that they would not molest our lives or property. I told the
people that I would try and make some arrangement for them to
remain at home and be protected, and that no man or citizen of this
County to go into the Bush for the purpose of bushwhacking the
U.S. forces as they pass through this Nation, and moreover I told
them that it was of no use of us following the Confederate States

Army any longer. For they have left us to fight for ourselves and I thought it quite time that we ought to come to some terms of agreement with the Federals . . . and that I had not the least doubt, but the Gen¹ at Fort Smith would reply to our wishes, and it was the wish of the people to form themselves into a home Guard to protect their homes and property against Jay Hawkers and marauding parties who is now in our Country. If this wish meets your approbation and Gen¹ it is for you to form your own judgement in regard to a treaty with our Government, as it is out of our power to do anything with a treaty.

"Though I firmly believe as soon as the U. S. forces begin to march through our Country that the Choctaws from all the other Counties will follow the example of this County, and by so doing it will be the means of stiring our Government up to come to terms of a treaty. As we dont wish to be divided like other Nations if we can be saved any other way. As we all come out together and we should all like to come in together. As it never was the wish of the Choctaws at the commencement of this war to take up arms and fight against the U. S. forces, but we were compelled to do so being surrounded by Seceded States and our lives and property taken from us which was threatened. But so long as the Southern forces is in the nation it is impossible for the Choctaws to turn over at the same time, but by working the thing slowly it will succeed in time for it is well known with the people that we can not sustain ourselves without the aid of some other power. Gen¹ I wish for you to give me a protection paper and from that paper I can issue to the people of this County or any other County that may submit to my views a ticket with the words (Home Guards) and (Home Protection) upon so that your forces will know who is soldiers. For every man that belongs to this Guard will have his ticket to show and those that has not is a Enemy to our cause, or any other mode that you might suggest, and Gen¹ if it is necessary that you might want to see me, I will try and come out to see you, but as they have got a suspicion upon us in this County, and watching us it is almost impossible to come out at present.

"And Gen¹ I am sorry to have to inform you that your last scouting parties plundered a deal of property from our people which they was greatly enraged against, and I hope Gen¹ that after these remarks that you will not allow it to proceed but if so we will have to bear it. For it is the means of men turning Bushwhackers and that is a thing I greatly opposed." (A.G.O., Old Files Section, *Consolidated Indian Home Guards Papers*, B 1013, V. S., 1863).

If Jackson McCurtain was the same as Jock McCurtain, it would seem from the following letter that he was one of those Cooper counted upon. His own guilty conscience must have made him feel that he was under suspicion. He was still on the Confederate side in 1865.

"Col.

"I have to acknowledge the receipt of your letter of the 18th inst.

Confederates in the rallying of forces [12] that certain
Choctaws, who had irretrievably lost confidence in the
South and despaired of any course being practicable
that did not presuppose the resumption of old-time
relations with the United States, attempted to organize
an opposition element and to secure an expression
of opinion favorable to the immediate repudiation
of the Confederate alliance. Calling themselves
the Choctaw Nation, *de facto* and *de jure*, they met
in mass-meeting at Doaksville; but dispersed again
on realizing that they were there too near the enemy
forces. They re-convened betimes at "Skullyville,
twenty miles from Fort Smith," where the Federals
were now holding sway.[13] · Not far from Skullyville
was New Hope Academy, a female seminary, which,
in the late fifties, had been successfully conducted under the auspices of the Methodist Episcopal Church

and enclose special order, No (?) from these Hd. Qrs ordering an
election for Brigadier Gen. of (?) Indian Brigade.

"I always knew you would be firm & true. The Grand Council of
the Allied Indian Nations has been ordered to assemble on the 10th
day of June at Armstrong Academy & until they determine what
must be done we must keep the Federals out of the country. You can
make requisitions on Col. Walker and draw ammunition for your
command.

"The Delegates to the Wild Indian will report to the Grand Council
on June 10th.

"It would be well to notify the Federals to keep their troops out
of the country until the Grand Council can determine what course to
pursue. We do not want any fight with them, under existing circumstances, but if they disturb any one of the Indian Nations, all will
unite in war against them." (D. H. Cooper to Col. Jock McCurtain,
May 24, 1865, A.G.O., *Confederate Archives*, chap. 2, no. 258, p. 36.
See also a reference to McCurtain in Cooper to Scott, May 14, 1865,
Official Records, vol. xlviii, part 2, p. 1303).

[12] Abel, *Indian as a Participant in the American Civil War*, p. 323.

[13] Perkins to Dole, April 18, 1864, O.I.A., General Files, *Choctaw, 1859-
1866*, P 166; Perkins to Usher, April 18, 1864, I. D. Files, Bundle no. 52
(1864); Abel, *The Indians in the Civil War, American Historical Review*,
vol. xv, p. 295, note.

South. It now presented itself as a convenient and safe meeting-place and at New Hope, on March fourteenth, a convention of disgruntled Choctaws took drastic action indicative of their weariness of the war and of all that it involved. The following resolutions [14] were unanimously adopted:

Whereas, In entering upon the reconstruction of our Government in this Nation, we believe that the government of the United States has been an infinite blessing to all parts of this country, and especially to our own Nation, and,

Whereas, Certain portions of the United States have set up their individual rights in opposition to the Federal Government, *Be it resolved*,

First, That we the citizens of the Choctaw Nation, as well as of the United States, knowing that the Government of the United States must be maintained supreme over the so-called rights of any portion of this country, do, on the part of the Choctaw Nation, utterly disclaim any pretensions to any so-called rights which may be subversive of the rights of the Federal Government, and hold that our primary allegiance is due to the Government of the United States.

Second, Resolved, That we, Citizens of the Choctaw Nation, desire the authority of the United States to be vindicated, and the people brought back to their allegiance.

Third, Resolved, That the following named citizens be appointed a committee to select proper men for Provisional Governor of the Nation, Sec. of State, *pro tem.*, subject to the future vote of the people of the Nation, and a Delegate to represent our Nation at Washington,

(Committee)   Jeremiah H. Ward [15]
               J. G. Ainsworth
               John Hanaway
               William P. Merryman
               J. H. Jacobs

---

[14] O.I.A., Land Files, *Choctaw, 1846-1873*, Box 38, E 48.

[15] The prominence of Jeremiah Ward as a repentant Choctaw and the effect of the Red River disaster upon his tribesmen are indicated in a communication from Agent Colman, September 1, 1864 [Commissioner of Indian Affairs, *Report*, 1864, pp. 313-314].

Fourth, Resolved, That the thanks of the Convention be and hereby are tendered to Lt. Lindsay and the escort under his command.

WM. F. STEPHENS, Pres't of Convention
THOMAS EDWARDS,[16] Sec.ᵗ

The nominating committee retired and later offered the name of Thomas Edwards for governor, of George W. Boyd for secretary of state, *pro tem.*, and of Edward P. Perkins for delegate. Its report was accepted and the nominations confirmed by the convention.[17] Whereupon, the men selected began without further ado to exercise the functions of their respective offices. Ten days subsequently Governor Edwards issued a proclamation [18] outlining the new policy.

PROCLAMATION

To the Choctaws, and the Citizens of the Choctaw Nation:

At a Convention held at New Hope, C.N., on March the 14th, 1864, by the loyal citizens of your Nation, a preamble of Resolutions were adopted to secure to you the rights and suffrages which you are entitled to from the Government of the United States.

The last Treaty between the United States and your Nation, which was ratified in 1855, guaranteed to you on the part of the United States Government "protection from domestic strife and hostile aggression," [19] (Treaty 1855, Article xiv) is the only agreement in that treaty wherein the United States has failed to fulfill for the time being her part of the compact; and though three years have elapsed since the "stars and stripes" was struck down in the Garrison, erected for your defence, by a rebellious and misguided people, that flag again waves in triumph over your fortress, and the Government which it repre-

[16] Edwards was the man that McCurtain had sent as his substitute to McNeil. See McCurtain to McNeil, December 16, 1863, *op. cit.*

[17] O.I.A., Land Files, *Choctaw, 1846-1873*, Box 38, E 48.

[18] The proclamation as here given is copied *verbatim* from a printed hand-bill found with Perkins's letter of April 18, 1864.

[19] Kappler, *Treaties*, p. 710.

sents is HERE in full force and power to keep her word and offer you its protection.

The Government of the United States is well aware of the sophistry and eloquence brought to bear upon the minds of your people, by such men as Douglass H. Cooper and Albert Pike to delude you into a treaty with the rebellious confederacy, of which they were the agents; and can excuse you to a certain extent for an alliance formed when despotism and treason were in your midst. But now that the Government holds indisputable possession of near four-fifths of your country, it calls upon you to return with truthful allegiance to your natural protector.

The same rights offered to the rebellious subjects of the States by the late Proclamation [20] of the President is guaranteed to you. Three years of strife, misery and want, should at least convince you that the unnatural alliance which you have formed with the enemies of the United States has been one of the heaviest calamities that ever befel your Nation. They made you brilliant promises, but never fulfilled them. What is your condition to-day? The enemy after having swept ruin through your entire land, brought starvation to your very doors, and spread a scene of utter degradation and suffering in your families; have been lying for months on the extreme southern border of your Nation, listening to the first roar of Federal artillery, to flee away and leave you alone. A delegate has been appointed by the Convention to represent your Nation at Washington. Every effort is being made to secure for you your ancient privileges and customs. Citizens of the Choctaw Nation, it now devolves upon you to do your part. You were once possessed of the most beautiful country between the Arkansas and Red River. – It can again be yours. Not only your present generation, but your posterity demands that you make a quick and speedy return to that Government which has protected you for over half a century, and secure in the future for yourselves and children what you have lost in the past three years for as-

[20] It was not surprising that the Indians readily conceived their case as covered by the amnesty provisions of President Lincoln since neither the original proclamation of December eighth, 1863 nor that of March twenty-sixth, 1864, supplementary and interpretative in character, expressly confined those provisions to white men.

sociating with one of the most accursed foes that ever polluted your country.

Citizens, not only your fertile valleys and beautiful hills invite you to the homes which you have deserted, but the Government from which you must ever after look to for succor, bids you come. I take this method, in this, my first proclamation, to say to all of you who are desirous of possessing the homes which you have abandoned, and re-uniting your allegiance to the Government, that has ever been your friend, now is your time. You have nothing to fear – and the former blessing which you have derived through a friendly intercourse with the United States Government, will again be renewed.

THOMAS EDWARDS, Provisional Governor Choctaw Nation
FORT SMITH, ARK., March 24, 1864

The governor's proclamation merits no word of praise. Its spirit is the spirit of the self-seeking, of the abjectly craven, and calls, not for commendation, but for execration. By virtue of its issue, Edwards and his associates put themselves into the position of rats that leave the sinking ship. General Thayer presumably sympathised with them and condoned their act since he appears, in the following December, to have honored the governor's requisition for transportation needed for the refugees, who were about to be removed to Fort Gibson;[21] but not so Colonel Phillips. It was not that the doughty Scotchman was averse to what, from his Republican point of view, might be regarded as the political regeneration of the Indians. None had worked harder to reclaim them than had Phillips. He had personally distributed[22] among the rebellious tribes copies of President Lincoln's amnesty proclamation,[23] notwithstanding that he seriously doubted its

[21] Special Orders, no. 225, issued at Fort Smith, December 27, 1864. Apparently, the restored Choctaw and Chickasaw refugees were consolidated with the New Hope conventionalists.

[22] *Official Records*, vol. xxxiv, part i, pp. 109, 110, 111.

[23] Richardson, *Messages and Papers of the Presidents*, vol. vi, pp. 213-215.

strict applicability to the Indian country.   Pioneer and hardy frontiersman though he was, the ex-newspaper correspondent was usually found to be magnanimous where Indians were concerned.   Maugre that, he hesitated not to disparage the work of the New Hope convention, contemptuously disposed of Delegate Perkins, protested against the acceptance of his credentials, and ridiculed the authority from which they emanated.   In his opinion, the Choctaw Nation was yet *de facto* rebel and deserving of severest chastisement.[24]   The minority at New Hope had no official status and were nothing but politic opportunists.[25]

Anticipated chastisement was the open sesame, the cue to all that had transpired.   Because of the prompt and wholesale character of their defection, the Choctaw had been a tribe especially singled out for condign punishment.   It was its funds more particularly that had been those diverted to other uses by act of the United States congress.   Recognized as a powerful foe and by many denounced as a treacherous enemy, the Choctaws had virtually none to state their case except traducers.   Few there were among western politicians and army men that had the slightest inclination to deal mercifully with them and Colonel Phillips was not of

[24] Phillips to Dole, March 22, 1864, O.I.A., General Files, *Choctaw, 1859-1866*, p. 154.   The same letter, with some slight verbal inaccuracies, is to be found in Commissioner of Indian Affairs *Report*, 1864, p. 328.   Mrs. Eaton seems to find in this letter of Colonel Phillips the origin of the sequestration policy of the government (*John Ross and the Cherokee Indians*, p. 199, note).   Her opinion is scarcely warranted by the facts.   In April, Phillips reported to Curtis that the Confederate Indians were determined "to try the effect of resistance once more." [*Official Records*, vol. xxxiv, part 3, p. 53].

[25] The United States Senate, however, took cognizance of their action. See Doolittle to Usher, April 28, 1864, enclosing a copy of Senate Resolution, April 20, 1864, relative to the return of the Choctaws to the protection of the Federal government (O.I.A., *Choctaw*, D 407 in I. D. Files, Bundle, no. 52 (1864).

that few. His animosity expressed itself in no uncertain terms in connection with his denunciation of the New Hope convention; but, perhaps, that was accountable to a sort of irritation caused by the fact that, as he himself reported, the Choctaw was the only Indian nation yet refractory. For the Creek, the Seminole, and the Chickasaw, the war was to all intents and purposes over.[26] Governor Colbert of the tribe last-named was in Texas. He had fled there "on learning of the defeat at Camp Kansas."[27] Into Texas, by the way, there was now going on "a general stampede." "That a handful of men about Scullyville would like to be the 'Choctaw Nation'" was very "probable and that a portion" who had "not fled from the northern section might be willing to accept an assurance of Choctaw nationality, and pay for acting as militia to expel all invaders" was "also probable;" but, all the same a much larger element, meeting in council above Fort Towson, had not even, so far as Phillips could learn, "made up their minds to accept peace."[28]

All plans for the chastisement of recalcitrant Indians took one direction, the direction pointed out by economic necessity, by political expediency, call it what one will, *land confiscation*. This was the direction most natural and most thoroughly in accord with historical development; but, none the less, it had some special causes. Kansas wanted to divest herself of her Indian encumbrance, from the viewpoint of her politicians the reservation system having most signally failed. Never in all history, so it would appear, has the insatiable land-hunger of the white man been better illus-

---

[26] Report of Colonel W. A. Phillips, dated Fort Gibson, February 24, 1864, *Official Records*, first series, vol. xxxiv, part i, p. 108.

[27] Phillips to Curtis, February 14, 1864, *ibid*, p. 330.

[28] Phillips to Dole, March 22, 1864, *op. cit.*

trated than in the case of the beginnings of the sun-
flower state. The practical effect of the Kansas-
Nebraska Act had been to lift an entail, a huge acreage
had been alienated that before had been sacred to Indian claims; white men had swarmed upon the ceded
lands; and the Indians had retired, perforce, to diminished reserves. A few short years had passed and now
those selfsame diminished reserves were similarly
wanted for the white man's use; but the question was,
Where next was the Indian to go?   South of the thirty-
seventh parallel the southern tribes were in possession
and they were in possession of a glorious expanse as
hermetically sealed to other Indians as it had proved to
be to southern projectors, railway and other, before the
war. Originally conferred by the United States government upon the Five Great Tribes as a sort of indemnity for the outrageous treatment accorded them
east of the Mississippi, it had been conveyed by patent
in fee simple and was now held under the most solemn
of Federal guarantees. It was to be so held exclusively
and inviolably forever.

Prior to the formation of the Indian alliance with
the Confederacy, that Federal guarantee of exclusive
and inviolable possession had been an insuperable obstacle to outside aggression but now all might be
changed if only the United States government could be
convinced that the great slaveholding tribes had legally
forfeited their rights in the premises. In and out of
Congress middle-western politicians harped upon the
theme but were suspiciously silent on the concomitant
theme of Federal responsibility in the matter of rendering to the Indians the protection against domestic and
foreign foes, pledged by treaties. Strange as it may
seem they never undertook to consider the question of

Indian culpability in the light of that rather interesting and additional fact.

It was a fact, indisputable, however, and one that Commissioner Dole liked to insist upon, although even he finally succumbed to the arguments in favor of forcing the southern tribes to receive other Indians within their choice domain.   Dole's change of front came subsequent to his visit to Kansas in 1863.   On the occasion of that visit it was doubtless borne in upon him that Kansas was determined to accomplish her purpose,[29] willy-nilly, and would never rest until she had forced the northern tribes across the interdicted line.   Their aversion to removal was somewhat of an impediment; but that she might overcome by persecution.   Persecute them she accordingly did and chiefly in the old familiar southern way, by the taxing of their lands, notwithstanding that it was a procedure contrary to the terms of her own organic law.

In his annual report for that year of his western visit, the Commissioner of Indian Affairs advised a concentration of the Indians since they seemed not to flourish on small reserves.   For the man who had always heretofore apologised for the conduct of the Indians this was a sort of opening wedge to a complete change of view.   By April of 1864 the change had come and Dole had then the conscience to say that he was "unwilling to renew the treaties with those people (the rebellious tribes) especially the Choctaws and Chickasaws without first securing to the Government a portion of their country for the settlement of other Indian

---

[29] In all fairness it should be said that Dole claimed to have seen much to make removal of the Indians advisable on their own account. Proximity to the whites was proving, as always, exceedingly detrimental to their morals. For particulars, as pointed out by the Commissioner, see his *Report*, for 1863, p. 6, and for 1864, p. 5.

tribes which we are compelled to remove from the States and Territory north of them." [30]   The confession was made to Phillips, a Kansas settler, a Kansas politician, if you please, who, in his letter of March 22, had invited it. [31]   Upon Schofield's ideas [32] of identical

[30] Dole to Phillips, April 6, 1864, O.I.A., *Letter Book*, no. 73, p. 434.

[31] Phillips had written, "Of course the government understands its necessities and purposes here. The Indian nation being really the Key to the southwest makes me respectfully urge that guarantees be not given that we may have to break. Our necessities here are not of a character to force us to steps that may be prejudicial."
and again
"Having a clear view of what seems to me the government necessities I have been cautious about promising these rebels anything save what the *mercy* or *generosity* of the government might give them. I have thought that to sweep out the Choctaw country of rebels would leave *very little*, and *that fragments*, and that these countries south of the river might, if it was desired, be open for settlement. This would leave the Cherokee and Creek – weak as they are – almost in the shape of Reserves, and I have always felt that a proper policy could make a majority of these vote for a more secure *organisation* and *community*. . ." (Extracts of letter from Phillips to Dole, March 22, 1864, *op. cit.*)

[32] Schofield's letter has wider application than the present discussion calls for and is worth quoting almost entire. Its tone is sane throughout. –
"The hostile Indians in southwestern Arkansas and the Indian Country are manifesting a strong disposition to treat with the Government and General McNeil suggests that full powers should be given to some person to settle with them the terms of peace. There are some important facts connected with this matter which should not be lost sight of. The wealthy Indians, landholders mostly, nearly all joined the rebels, and are now among those suing for peace. The feeling of hostility on the part of the loyal Indians towards these rebels is intense. I believe the feud between them is of longer standing than the present rebellion.
"It will, I believe, be practically impossible for the disloyal Indians to return and occupy their lands. They would all be murdered by the loyal, or "poor," Indians. It is an important question whether the lands owned by the disloyal Indians should not be all declared forfeited to the Government. Also, if forfeited, whether they should be given to the loyal Indians or be held by the Government with a view to the ultimate extinction of the Indian title to a portion of territory which must before many years be required for the use of white men.
"I presume the question of forfeiture is the only one which need be decided soon. My present information leads me to believe the lands

tenor and better-reasoned basis, made some months
earlier and referred to him,[33] Dole had not seen fit to
so much as lightly comment and he had repeatedly discouraged congressional action looking to the same end.

The mistrust of the Choctaws manifested by Colonel
Phillips was fully warranted. The papers, inclusive
of President Lincoln's amnesty proclamation, which he
had caused to be distributed among the southern tribes,
had had their effect and were the direct occasion for
the calling of a general council to meet at Tishomingo,
March 16 and therefore almost simultaneously with the
convention at New Hope. "Seven delegates," reported
Superintendent Coffin, "from each of the following
rebel tribes," Choctaw, Creek, Seminole, Cherokee,
Caddo, and Osage, were summoned.[34] Presumably all
attended.[35] Full and fierce discussion of all points involved was inevitable for the times were critical. Some
of the delegates argued for immediate submission, some
for continued loyalty to the South. Finally, the in-

owned by the hostile Indians should be declared forfeited and that
they should not be permitted to return among the loyal. Their future
peace seems to require that they be kept separate. This will of
course embarrass very much any negotiations for peace. Yet I see
no way of securing peace among the Indians on any other terms.

"My personal knowledge of these matters is too limited to justify
the expression of a very decided opinion as to what policy should be
adopted. I desire simply to call your attention to what seem to be
important questions to be decided and to ask for instructions.

"I believe there is no civil officer of the Government now in that
Territory, empowered to treat with the Indians." (Schofield to Halleck, November 12, 1863, *op. cit.*)

[33] Halleck to War Department, November 18, 1863, *ibid*; Usher to Stanton, February 19, 1864, *op. cit.*

[34] Coffin to Dole, March 16, 1864, O.I.A., General Files, *Southern Superintendency, 1863-1864,* C 824; Cox to Coffin, March 16, 1864, Commissioner
of Indian Affairs, *Report,* 1864, pp. 331-332.

[35] Phillips, in reporting the meeting, omitted mention of the Cherokees
(Phillips to Curtis, March 17, 1864, O.I.A., Land Files, *Southern Superintendency, 1855-1870,* W 412; Commissioner of Indian Affairs, *Report,*
1864, p. 329).

fluence of Generals Maxey and Cooper, exerted from the outside, prevailed for the Confederacy and the ultimate resolution was, to make one more stand on Red River. Beyond that the council refused positively to commit its constituents; for the sight of the distressful body of refugees stretching all across the country was enough to shake the fortitude of the strongest. Near the eastern boundary line, under the shelter of the garrison at Fort Smith, were those Choctaws, mostly refugees,[36] who had gathered at the New Hope convention, now dissolved; but other refugees, fearfully impoverished, were "clustered in great numbers from Washita River up Red River and on Washita below Fort Washita." Even the Indians of the least depleted resources and of the most pronounced secessionist persuasion were discouraged. Many were running their slaves, their only remaining tangible wealth, to the Brazos for safety.

The summer of '64 brought no return of good fortune to the Trans-Mississippi Department. Much had

---

[36] A letter written to the Indian Office, February 22, 1865, by a man who signed himself Wm. T. (F.?) Stephens and who was present at the convention, throws light upon its personnel, also incidentally upon the tribal status of Delegate Perkins and his notion of discharging his duties. It reads as follows:

"A part of our people are in a state of rebellion against the U. S. but the other part are loyal and are refugees at this post, and are in a destitute condition having left their homes and property in consequence of their political sentiments. The Choctaws that are at this place held a convention (or rather a Mass meeting) at New Hope, Choctaw Nation, on the 14th day of March 1864, and appointed E. P. Perkins to act as a delegate and represent their interest at Washington City, D.C. Said delegate is a white man who recently married a member of the Choctaw tribe of Indians; he is also an officer of the U.S. army. Said delegate proceeded to Washington City as I suppose but on his return did not give any satisfaction concerning the business upon which he was sent. Please inform me whether E. P. Perkins was recognized by the department . . ." (O.I.A., General Files, *Choctaw 1859-1866*).

been hoped for but little realized and, as a consequence, the distress and dissatisfaction of the Indians had grown apace. Apparently, they had given up all thought of making their peace with the North. In an excess of recovered zeal for a doomed cause, they had allowed the moment for a possible reconciliation to pass and the Federals had made no new overtures. The Indian alliance was now a desperate case, yet there was no talk of abandoning it. Desperate remedies had to be applied and foremost among them was a reversion to savagery. Irregular warfare of the most deplorable and destructive kind was now the ordinary thing, particularly where the Cherokee champion, Stand Watie, led. For such as he, there could be no surrender. For him, utter despair was out of the question. Ready he was to risk everything, at any moment, in one last throw.

Another possible remedy, involving, perhaps, the essentials of the first, was an alliance with tribes that in happier days the highly-civilized southern would have scorned. This was something more than the Indian confederacy that the Choctaws had earlier projected. To consider its possibilities a general council was arranged for and invitations extended to all of their own group, to the indigenous and emigrant tribes of Kansas,[37] and to the wild tribes of the plains. At the

---

[37] Agent H. W. Martin reported upon this to Dole, September 11, 1864, as follows:

"Through Keokuk, Che-kus-kuk, and Pah-teck-quaw, chiefs of the Sacs and Foxes of Mississippi and the most reliable men connected with the tribe, I learn that messengers from the Rebel Indians have been sent to many of the Indian tribes in Kansas, inviting them to meet in a grand council to be held in the Creek Country in or near the rebel lines the last of October next. These messengers are sent from the Comanches, Creeks, and other rebel tribes in the southwest. I am informed that the *"Tobacco,"* as they term it, has been sent to the Big Hill Osages, Little Osages, Black Dog's Band of Osages,

moment not much success attended the movement, owing to the promptness with which Superintendent Coffin and others organized a counter one.   They assembled representatives of all the tribes [38] they could reach

Sacs and Foxes, and, I have no doubt, to the Pottawatomies, Kaws,
Kickapoos and all other tribes that they can reach.

"They proclaim that they will kill, *clean out*, all the whites to the
Missouri River and occupy the country themselves. Now while I
believe that the Sacs and Foxes, as a tribe, are as loyal to the Government of the United States as any other Indian tribe in Kansas, yet
I have good reason to doubt the loyalty of two or three former
leaders of what we call the Wild, or Prairie Band. For the good
of the country and the Sac and Fox tribe, I would respectfully suggest the propriety of arresting and confining at Fort Leavenworth
the parties referred to until the close of the war.

"The evidence that led me to this conclusion, I received from the
above named chiefs, whom I have had watching this matter for the
last six weeks. I can not give you the details so as to make it satisfactory. If I could see you, I think I could satisfy you that a grand
effort is being made to involve all the Kansas Indians in this outbreak.

"If the proposition to confine two or three of the doubtful Indians
referred to meets your approbation, telegraph me Leavenworth, care
of Carney & Stevens. . . " (O.I.A., General Files, *Sac and Fox
1862-1866*, M 371).

[38] Among the Indians present at the Council were, Chickasaws, Creeks,
Seminoles, Senecas, Quapaws, Shawnees, Osages, Western Miamies, Pottawatomies, Weas, Peorias, Kaskaskias, Piankeshaws, and Sacs and Foxes
of Mississippi. The Kaws were not able to appear; but their trustworthiness
was not to be doubted. Their chiefs empowered Agent Farnsworth to
attach their names to the declaration of loyalty (Farnsworth to Dole, January 9, 1865, O.I.A., Land Files, *Kansas 1863-1865*, Box 80, F 204). Some
slight aspersions had, indeed, been cast upon the Kaws; but their agent
thought he could easily establish their innocence. His report sounds
plausible,

"As soon as the annual payment was made, I obtained protection
papers from the general commanding this District and all this tribe,
with very few exceptions, left for the buffalo country. Last month I
heard from different sources that the Kaws were not behaving well
and were having friendly intercourse with tribes hostile to the U.
States. In December I made a visit to all their camps on the Smoky
Hill river, Sharps Creek, Little Arkansas, and Big Turkey. The Kaws
have lost a few men and some stock, taken from them by hostile
tribes, but I could not get the slightest evidence of any friendly feeling
existing between these tribes. On the contrary, when I was among
them, a large war party was absent after the Cheyennes to avenge
their losses. The conduct of the Kaws towards the Whites has in-

in a "Grand Council" [39] at the Sac and Fox Agency
between the fifth and ninth of October and secured
from them an expression of unswerving loyalty to the
government of the United States.[40] Meanwhile the
southern tribes, desperately in earnest, so continued
and redoubled their own efforts that constant vigilance
was necessary in order to circumvent them.

Towards the close of the year, the best plan of all
for defeating the purpose of the secessionists was
devised by the Cherokees. Had it been put into operation, it might, not only have counteracted what Coffin
called "the infamous machinations of the rebel hordes
in the southwest," [41] but likewise have prevented the
depredations on the Colorado line that, unchecked,
grew to such astounding proportions in the decade after
the war had closed. It might, moreover, have recalled,
though tardily, the secessionists to their allegiance and
ended the tribal estrangements that were to result so
disastrously in the adjustments at the peace council.
The plan was outlined in a memorandum, addressed to
President Lincoln by Lewis Downing, Acting Principal Chief of the Cherokees. It bore date, December
20, 1864.[42] It is here given: –

variably been friendly, and upon examination, all unfavorable reports
were found to be without good foundation . . ." (Farnsworth to
Dole, January 9, 1865, O.I.A., General Files, Kansas 1863-1868,
F 202).

[39] Of the council, Agent Martin had much that was interesting to say.
See particularly Martin to Dole, October 10, 1864, O.I.A., Land Files,
Indian Talks, Council, etc., Box 3, 1856-1864, M 388: Commissioner of
Indian Affairs, *Report,* 1864, p. 362.

[40] The formal declaration of loyalty accompanied Agent Martin's letter
and is on file with it. Its receipt was duly acknowledged by Dole in terms
that revealed how much importance he, like others, was disposed to attach
to the action of the council (Dole to Martin, November 7, 1864, O.I.A.,
Letter Book, no. 75, p. 397; Dole to Coffin, same date, *ibid,* p. 396).

[41] Coffin to Mix, Acting Commissioner of Indian Affairs, February 1,
1865, O.I.A., General Files, *Southern Superintendency, 1865,* C 1209.

[42] — *Ibid.*; Interior Department Files.

We, the undersigned for ourselves and as the representatives of the Cherokee People, feeling an intense interest in maintaining perpetual harmony and good will among the various tribes of Indians mutually, as well as between these and the people and government of the United States, beg leave, very respectfully, to lay before your Excellency a few facts and suggestions relating to this important subject.

We deem it a matter of vast moment to the Cherokees, Creeks and Seminoles, and to the State of Kansas and to Nebraska, as well as to the Whole Union, that the perfect friendship of the wild tribes be secured and maintained, while our friendship is of paramount importance to the said tribes; and it is with the deepest regret that we hear of and observe acts of hostility on the part of any Indians. It is our firm conviction that southern rebels are, and have been, instigating the wild tribes to take part in the present rebellion against the Federal Government. The depredations recently committed by portions of some of these tribes on emigrants crossing the western plains, we are forced to regard as the result of such instigations on the part of the rebels.

There are also indications that these tribes are forming into predatory bands and are engaged in stealing stock in connection with wicked white men who are first loyal and then rebel as best suits their purposes of stealing and robbery.

As the war progresses and the rebel armies are broken into fragments, the rebels will doubtless scatter among these tribes and will make every effort to *organize them into banditti—*. Then, when the strength of the rebellion is broken and peace is formally declared and we are off our guard, they will fall upon defenseless neighborhoods of loyal Indians, or whites, and plunder and kill unrestrained.

The highways to the Pacific States and to the gold regions of the West, they will infest, to harass emigrants and merchants and endanger their property and lives. To keep down such depredations by force of arms will require many men and a vast expense.

In our opinion no pains should be spared to gain the friendship of these people by peaceful means and thus secure their help against the rebels and in favor of the public peace.

In the year 18—, a general convention of Indian Tribes was held at Tahlequah in the Cherokee Nation which convened at the call of the Cherokee National Council. Representatives from the Cherokees, Creeks, Seminoles, Chickasaws, Delawares, Shawnees, Osages, Senecas, and twelve other nations attended this convention and participated in its deliberations. It was a harmonious, pleasant and profitable meeting of Red men of the West. Friendship and good will were established and a league was entered into by which the most friendly relations were maintained among the various tribes for many years. Arrangements were made for the punishment of crimes committed by the citizens of any nation on those of any other.

Many years have passed away since the said convention of tribes. Men who were then young now occupy prominent positions and are the rulers of their respective nations, yet they know but little of the harmonious feeling and the amity established among their fathers.

The long continuation of the present war, together with the lies and machinations of the rebels, operating on these ignorant tribes, have shaken the confidence of some of them in the government of the United States and, to some extent, made the impression that the Cherokees, Creeks, and other nations who are in alliance with the Federal Government, are the enemies of these wild tribes and that the enemies of the Government are their friends.

In view of this state of things we propose that the nations, who are fighting under the banner of the Union, invite all the tribes of the Southwest and as many others as possible to meet in general convention and re-establish their league of amity and re-assert, in solemn council, their loyalty to the Federal Government. Let them there, in the presence of the *Great Spirit,* give mutual pledges to maintain the peace among themselves and with their white brethren, to abstain from all acts of theft, robbery, murder or violence, and to do all in their power to bring to justice any persons, either Indians or whites, who may be guilty of such acts, or may incite others to commit them under any pretex whatever.

Let them there league together to crush out the rebellion and put an end to the war throughout the country.

We propose that the said convention of tribes be held near Claremore's Mound, on the Verdigris River, in the Cherokee Nation and that it convene in the early part of next June.

We all desire very respectfully to request President Lincoln to send a talk signed with his own hand and sealed with the great seal of the United States to this convention. Let him also send a white pipe, and with tobacco and a white flag and the Book of God containing the talk of the *Great Spirit* to men. Let all be wrapped in the flag of Union and let him send some suitable person to deliver this talk, and on behalf of the President to smoke the pipe of peace with these nations of Indians beneath the waves of these flags.

We would also ask that the President give to military commanders orders to afford proper protection to such convention and to the delegates both in going to and returning from said convention.

In view of the fact that the war has so desolated our country that the Cherokees cannot, as in former times, provide for the feeding of such a council, we, very relucktantly, ask that such provision be made by the United States.

II. THE RETURN OF THE REFUGEES

The existence of Indian refugees was the best indication that all projects, made while the Civil War was still in progress, for the removal southward of Kansas tribes and for the organization of Indian Territory were decidedly premature and altogether out of place. For a season, indeed, they were almost presumptuous. Disaster followed disaster and it seemed wellnigh impossible for the Federals ever to regain what they had so lightly thrown aside in 1861. At the very moment when the removal policy was being re-enacted there were upwards of fifteen thousand Indians living as exiles and outcasts solely because the United States government was not able to give them protection in their own homes. Nevertheless, with strange inconsistency and the total ignoring of most patent facts, its law-makers discussed in all seriousness, as is the habit of politicians, the re-populating with new northern tribes the very country that the army had abandoned and had not yet recovered. Meanwhile, as if to add to the incongruity of the whole matter, three full regiments of Indian Home Guards, composed largely of the legitimate owners of the territory in question, were fighting on the Union side.

The earlier misfortunes of the Indian refugees have been described with fullness of detail in the preceding volume of this work. A large proportion of the first Indians, who had fled for safety across the border, had been conducted, at vast expense, with much murmuring, and some show of resistance, to the Sac and Fox Agency. There they were yet, the old men, women, and children, that is; for the braves were away fighting. They included Creeks [43] who had accompanied Opoethleyohola in his flight, a few Euchees, Kickapoos, and Choctaws, about two hundred and twenty-five Chickasaws,[44] and about three hundred Cherokees.[45] At Neosho Falls, were the refugee Seminoles, some seven hundred and sixty, not counting the enlisted warriors.[46] On the Ottawa Reservation, were the non-fighting Quapaws and the Senecas and Shawnees,[47] while, encamped on the Verdigris and Fall rivers, in the neighborhood of Belmont, were almost two thousand Indian refugees from the Leased District.[48] They had come there following the outbreak that had resulted in the brutal murder of Agent Leeper. Beyond them and beyond the reach of aid, as it proved, at the Big Bend of the Arkansas, were Comanches, one band, and scattering elements of other wild tribes.

At the opening of 1863, the great bulk of the Cherokees were in southwestern Missouri, exposed to every conceivable kind of danger incident to a state of war. They were the larger part of those who, when the Con-

---

[43] Perry Fuller asserted that the Creeks at the Sac and Fox Agency exceeded five thousand in number. It was doubtless an outside estimate, which had taken account of the braves, absent with the Home Guards, as well as of the more helpless members of the tribe. It was at this time that Fuller succeeded in having himself made attorney for the Creeks (Fuller to Dole, March 21, 1863, O.I.A., General Files, *Creek*, 1860-1869) and likewise for the Chickasaws, Choctaws, Quapaws, and Leased District Indians (Same to same, April 15, 1863, *ibid., Southern Superintendency*, 1863-1864, F 35; Same to same, April 18, 1863, *ibid.*, F 37).

[44] Coleman to Coffin, September 2, 1863, Commissioner of Indian Affairs, *Report*, 1863, p. 184.

[45] Harlan to Coffin, September 2, 1863, *ibid.*, p. 179.

[46] Snow to Coffin, September 4, 1863, *ibid.*, p. 185.

[47] Coffin to Dole, September 24, 1863, *ibid.*, p. 174.

[48] — *Ibid.*, p. 177.

federates successfully invaded and occupied the Nation, had escaped to the Neutral Lands, a portion of their own tribal domain but within the limits of Kansas, and had been discovered, in October of 1862, settled upon Drywood Creek, about twelve miles south of Fort Scott. The Indian Office field employees had ministered to their needs promptly,[49] if not efficiently; but, towards the close of the year, to the great surprise [50] and financial embarrassment of Superintendent Coffin and under pretext of restoring them immediately to their homes,[51] the army, ordered thereto by General Blunt, had removed them, bag and baggage, to Neosho.[52] There they had remained, their position in-

[49] Coffin to Dole, September 24, 1863, Commissioner of Indian Affairs, *Report*, 1863, p. 175; Coffin to B. T. Henning, December 28, 1863, *ibid.*, pp. 192-193.

[50] Coffin to Mix, August 31, 1863, O.I.A., General Files, *Southern Superintendency*, 1863-1864, C 466.

[51] Blunt entertained grave suspicions of the probity of Coffin and his subordinates and he feared that unless something were soon done to remove the refugees beyond the reach of their graft the service would be eternally disgraced. Moreover, it was high time some attempt were being made to keep the promises to the Indian Home Guard. A letter of Blunt's, written after his first indignation had exhausted itself, and he had been reconciled to Coffin may here be quoted in part.

"... it was a military necessity that something should be done immediately to save the Indian regiments from demoralization and quiet the apprehensions of the other refugees. I had to act and act promptly. Certain parties who were interested in keeping the Indians in Kansas complained that I was interfering with that which was not pertinent to me and no doubt made representations to Col. Coffin relative to my acts that were false and which led to the writing of the letter by Coffin to me – which I thought was impertinent and uncalled for – Language that I made use of in that report – and which I learn has been construed into specific charges against Col. Coffin – was not so intended but was intended to apply more particularly to the cormorants & peculators who hang around every Dept. of the Government. . . " (Blunt to Secretary of the Interior, January 25, 1863, I. D. Files, Bundle, no. 51 (1863); O.I.A., *Southern Superintendency*, B 61).

[52] The southern superintendency continued to supply them with necessaries as best it could (Coffin to Harlan, December 29, 1862, Commissioner

creasingly precarious and their condition, because of the desolateness of the region and its inaccessibility to adequate supplies, increasingly miserable, until March, 1863.[53]

By that time, General Blunt had made his peace with Superintendent Coffin [54] although he had failed to keep his promises to the Indians, who, as a result of un-realized hopes, were becoming daily more fractious, both the refugees and their kin in the Indian Brigade. Colonel Phillips of the Third Indian Regiment, which was wholly Cherokee, sympathised with them; for only too well he knew the lack of consideration shown the loyal Indian and the secondary place he was forced to occupy in the public estimation. Despised, disappointed, discouraged, the Indian Home Guards were getting mutinous. Moreover, southwestern Missouri, if not "a perfect den of rebels," as Coffin, in his chagrin and indignation had described it, was no fit place for helpless women and children.

With the first indication of the breaking up of winter, Colonel Phillips recommended, in strong terms, the resumption of the task of refugee restoration [55] and solicited, for it, the assistance of the southern superintendent, heretofore ignored. Coffin responded with secret elation; for, by appealing to him, the military authorities had tacitly acknowledged the ineptitude of which he constantly accused them. Agents

of Indian Affairs, *Report*, 1863, pp. 193-194; Harlan to Coffin, September 2, 1863, *ibid.*, p. 179). Its efforts to relieve their distress were supplemented by those of the military.

[53] Coffin to Dole, January 5, 1863, *ibid.*, p. 192.

[54] Blunt to Secretary of the Interior, January 25, 1863, I. D. Files, Bundle, no. 51 (1863); *Register of Letters Received*, Jan. 2, 1862 to Dec. 27, 1865, "Indians," no. 4, p. 175.

[55] In the opinion of Phillips, it was imperative that the removal should take place in March " and not impracticable" (Phillips to Proctor, February 17, 1863, Commissioner of Indian Affairs, *Report*, 1863, pp. 196-197).

Justin Harlan and A. G. Proctor were detailed to conduct the expedition and early in April the majority of the Cherokee refugees were again in their own country.

Before departing from Neosho, Harlan had come to an understanding with Phillips by which the two had agreed that the reconstruction work should begin on the Tahlequah side of the Arkansas, where beeves and milch cows were yet to be had. Seeds had been provided by the Department of Agriculture [56] and gardening implements by that of the Interior, so all was in readiness; but Phillips with the vacillation, which seems to have been his crowning fault, changed the plan at the last moment and without seeking further advice from his fellow in authority. He crossed the line at about the same time Harlan's company did and at once issued an order for the establishment of six different posts, or points of distribution.[57] As a result, the refugees scattered in all directions. The problem of protecting them became a serious one. The Confederates were still lingering in the country. No attempt had been made to oust them before undertaking the return of the refugees. No expected accretion came to swell Phillips's command. Indeed, before very long he was in danger of having to fall back into Kansas; for Blunt's troops were nearly all being drawn off "for the purpose of re-enforcing General Herron in Missouri." [58] The Indian Brigade, Phillips in command, intrenched itself at Fort Gibson [59] and there,

---

[56] This is inferred from Dole's letter to Phillips, February 25, 1865 (O.I.A., *Letter Book*, no. 70, p. 97). Phillips had made an early application for the same (I. D., *Register of Letters Received*, "Indians," no. 4, p. 421, January 23, 1863).

[57] Harlan to Coffin, May, 26, 1863, Commissioner of Indian Affairs, *Report*, 1863, p. 204.

[58] Coffin to Dole, May 2, 1863, *ibid.*, p. 199.

[59] A. G. Proctor to Coffin, July 31, 1863, O.I.A., General Files, *Southern Superintendency*, 1863-1864, C 466; Same to same, August 9, 1863, *ibid.*

too, the now doubly disappointed refugees eventually huddled so as to profit by the protection of its garrison, their range limited, scarcely any farming possible. It was most vexatious, since, if the original plan had been carried out, a force of about two hundred men might have been ample to protect Tahlequah.[60]   Harlan was beside himself with indignation and especially so when its own meagre resources exhausted, the brigade had to borrow [61] from the produce intended for the subsistence of the refugees.   The replenishment of supplies was something no one dared count upon with any certainty.   There was nothing to be obtained south of Fort Scott; for the country intervening between that place and Fort Gibson was totally uncultivated.   It had been devastated over and over again and was now practically denuded of everything upon which to support life.   Moreover, it was infested with bushwhackers, who roamed hither and thither, raiding when they could, terrorizing, murdering.   And then, not one of them but like unto them, there was Stand Watie, Cherokee chief of the Ridge faction, staunch Confederate, who, insatiably bent upon vengeance, harrowed the country right and left or lay in wait, with his secessionist tribesmen, for any chance supply train that might be wending its way towards Gibson.[62]

As the summer advanced, the wants of the restored refugees grew apace and proportionately their despair. So pitiable was their state, mentally and physically, with no prospect of amelioration that the most hard-

[60] Henry Smith to Coffin, July 16, 1863, Commissioner of Indian Affairs, *Report*, 1863, p. 212.

[61] Borrowing was not invariably the mode of procedure; for the military authorities, complained Coffin, sometimes forcibly seized the supplies meant for Indians. (Letter to Mix, August 31, 1863, *ibid.*, pp. 216-218).

[62] Coffin to Dole, September 24, 1863, Commissioner of Indian Affairs, *Report*, 1863, pp. 175-176.

hearted of the onlookers was moved to compassion. Rumors were afloat that they were to be sent back to Kansas,[63] since military protection, poor as it was, might at any moment have to be withdrawn. Such a confession of failure was unavoidable under the circumstances. The situation was most perplexing. As late as June, Blunt was not able to furnish large enough escorts for supply trains, so depleted was his army, and recruits had to be sought for from among the refugees at Belmont.[64] The turn in the tide came, fortunately, soon afterwards and Phillips received his long-looked-for re-enforcements. Local conditions were not much improved, however, and stories about the necessity of forcing another exodus still continued to circulate. They had their foundation in fact and Coffin was in agreement with Phillips that return across the border might be advisable for the winter months.[65] In southern Kansas, provisions were plentiful and cheap, while supply trains were a costly experiment and a provocation to the enemy.[66]

[63] —*Ibid.*, pp. 203, 211, 213.

[64] Coffin to Dole, July 11, 1863, *ibid.*, p. 210.

[65] *Report*, Coffin to Dole, September 24, 1863, *ibid.*, p. 176.

[66] Published with Dole's annual report for 1863, are various letters that show, in one way or another, how difficult it was to get the supply trains through. There were dangers besetting them from start to finish. When one train, for instance, was about to leave Emporia, in May, the country all around was excited over the presence of jayhawkers (Coffin to Dole, May 26, 1863, *ibid.*, p. 201). The following gives some illustration of the variety of difficulties attending transit:

"Mr. Dole leaves today for Kansas and I improve the opportunity to communicate to you.

"I arrived safely at Fort Gibson on Friday the 24th and crossed the train on the ferry next day. I received no reinforcements from Gibson . . . All but eight or ten of our Indians had left us as soon as there was danger of our being molested.

"We were ordered by messenger from Gen¹ Blunt to cross at Ross' ford and move on to Tahlequah, as the families were to be moved there. Grand River was however impassable so I moved the train

Superintendent Coffin expressed exasperation at the whole proceeding. "The contrariness and interference manifested by the military authorities" [67] had annoyed him exceedingly and he rated restoration under their auspices as at the maximum in impudence and at the minimum in accomplishment. If they would but do their rightful part, clear the country of Confederates and render it safe for occupancy by the defenceless wards of the nation, the remaining refugees, those living miscellaneously in Kansas, might be returned.

With effective military protection as a prerequisite, he accordingly recommended their return. That was in September, when he made his annual report. [68] His prerequisite was a large order; for it was most unlikely that the War Department would arrange its affairs with reference to Indian comfort and safety as matters for primary concern. It had never thus far been overzealous to co-operate with the Indian Office. As compared with the great needs of the nation, in times so critical, the welfare of aborigines was a mere bagatelle. It might be thrown to the winds; they, in fact, annihilated and no thought taken.

The reasons for expediting refugee restoration were many and more than balanced, in importance at all events, the elements of previous failure. They were chiefly of two kinds, financial and personal. The cost of maintenance had been a heavy charge upon tribal funds, both regular and diverted. The expenditure of relief money had given satisfaction to nobody unless,

down to Gibson and crossed there to save time. Moved from Ft. Gibson Sunday & train started for Kans. Tues. accompanied by Judge Harlan." (Proctor to Dole, July 31, 1863, *Southern Superintendency,* C 466 of 1863).

[67] Coffin to Mix, August 31, 1863, O.I.A., General Files, *Southern Superintendency,* 1863-1864, C 466.

[68] Commissioner of Indian Affairs, *Report,* 1863, p. 178.

possibly, to contractors. The estimates had mounted every quarter. To Coffin, Dole had conceded a large discretion. He probably knew his man and his own conduct may not have been impeccable.[69]   At any rate, from the official point of view, Coffin greatly abused the trust reposed in him and, even if not guilty of positive dishonesty as charged by his enemies,[70] was not always wise in his decisions. To Dole's disgust, he spent refugee relief money for resident Kansas tribes, temporarily embarrassed, although they had large tribal funds of their own and, in individual cases, were really well to do.[71]   At the same time, he grumbled because he was forced to stint the true refugees, his allowance not being nearly enough, and he begrudged any portion of it to the Cherokees in Indian Territory,[72] who, though ostensibly restored, were in a most distressful state, wretchedly poor.

[69] Dole's participation in the bidding for the sale of the Sac and Fox trust lands, while not exactly criminal, transgressed the ethics of the public position which he filled (Abel, *Indian Reservations in Kansas and the Extinguishment of Their Titles*, Kansas Historical Society *Collections*, vol. viii, p. 101).

[70] Blunt's suspicions returned in force. How strong they were may be inferred from his request, August 1, 1863, that "if a special agent be sent to investigate Indian affairs in Kansas," "an honest man be selected who is not engaged in Indian contracts." (I. D., *Register of Letters Received*, "Indians," no. 4, p. 178). Acting Secretary Otto instructed Dole, September 2, 1863, to have the "matters referred to by General Blunt" investigated (*ibid.*, *Letter Press Book*, "Indian Affairs," no. 5, p. 140). See also J. W. Wright to Usher, September 6, 1863, *ibid*, Files.

[71] Dole to Coffin, June 18, 1863, O.I.A., *Letter Book*, no. 71, pp. 50-51; Commissioner of Indian Affairs, *Report*, 1863, p. 206. The *Neosho Files* of the Indian Office reveal a state of destitution among the New York Indians in 1862 and 1863. They were Kansas immigrants. Coffin distributed relief to them, nevertheless. The Wyandotts, whom he likewise assisted, were immigrants and, in normal times, wealthy.

[72] The suggestion that the Cherokees be disconnected, in a fiscal way, from the other refugees and subsisted "from the appropriation accruing to them from their trust fund interest" came originally from Dole, it would seem (Coffin to Dole, June 8, 1863, Commissioner of Indian Affairs, *Report*, 1863, p. 205).

The Indians in all localities were dissatisfied. They were tired of privation, tired of changed habits of life, and they were homesick. "The strange attachment of these Indians," wrote P.P. Elder, "to their country and homes from which they were driven, and their great desire to return thither, continue unabated."[73] Elder wrote thus of the insignificant Neosho Agency tribes; but what he said might have applied to any. The Seminoles, who at Neosho Falls were more comfortable than most of the refugees, suffering less,[74] put up a pitiful plea. Their old chief, Billy Bowlegs, well-known to the government because of his exploits in Florida, was away with the army at Camp Bentonville; but he wrote sadly of his own hope of return to the country that he had not set foot in since the war began.[75] That country was endeared to him, not because it held the bones of his ancestors but simply because it was home. Home recovered would mean re-union with his family. He envied the Cherokee soldiers, who were now in close touch with their women and children. He admitted there was great confusion in the Indian Territory; but he had noticed empty houses there, deserted, in which he was childishly confident his people might find shelter.[76] His communications fired the

[73] Elder to Coffin, September 20, 1863, Commissioner of Indian Affairs, *Report*, 1863, p. 187.

[74] Snow to Coffin, September 4, 1863, *ibid.*, p. 185.

[75] Billy Bowlegs to Commissioner of Indian Affairs, March 2, 1863, O.I.A., General Files, *Seminole*, 1858-1869, B 131. A copy of this letter was forwarded to Coffin, March 24, 1863 (*ibid.*, Letter Book, no. 70, p. 208). On the thirteenth of May, Bowlegs wrote to Dole again (*ibid.*, General Files, *Seminole*, B 317 of 1863), expressive of his confidence that the United States power could, if it would, clear the Indian country of Confederates. The Seminole part of it was being held by disloyal Seminoles and Texans. Bowlegs signed himself, "King of the Seminoles and Captain of Co. 'F', 1st. Ind. H. G.," and he asked for the replacement of a gun which he had lost in a tussel with a bushwhacker, who had run away with his horse.

[76] Billy Bowlegs, Fos-huchee-ha-jo, No-ko-so-lo-chee, Koch-e-me-ko to

enthusiasm of those same people and they begged their
Great Father to send them back. They would go, no
matter what impediments athwart their way and they
would go that very fall.[77] Agent Snow doubted their
being able to maintain themselves in their devastated
country during the winter;[78] but the thought did not
deter them. They had known a scarcity of food in
Kansas the preceding year and might fare better farther south. Anyhow, they could burn green wood as
they pleased, which they had not been allowed to do
on the white man's land. They had taken everything
into consideration and where the Great Father's energy
ended theirs would begin.

The homesickness of the refugees was due to a variety of causes and not of least consequence was the en-

Oak-to-ha and Pas-co-fa, dated Ft. Blunt, C.N., September 4, 1863, O.I.A.,
General Files, *Southern Superintendency*, 1863-1864.

[77] "We have got a letter from Billy Bowlegs and others . . . and
from what we hear in this letter we think we can go home with safety.
We know it will be impossible for the Government to haul provisions
all the way down there for us. We have taken all this into consideration. We know that we will live hard this winter, but we want to
go home on our own land. We must be there this fall if we expect to
plant in the spring. Corn must be put in there in March. Fences
must be built, houses repaired, farms improved and this must all be
done before we can expect to raise a crop . . .

"We are here on the white man's land – we cannot cut green wood
to burn and when we got word from Billy Bowlegs that we can get
in our own country, we are anxious to go where we can burn green
wood as we please. And we would ask you to help us to move down
before cold weather sets in. Our dear Father, if you can only get
wagons, we want you to get all you can to help us back to our
homes . . . And if you *can't* help us then we will try what we can
do in moving ourselves. We expect that the rebels have destroyed
all of our property, but we think if we can get to our Brothers the
Cherokees we could get enough of them to live on, untill we could
raise something for ourselves . . . " (Pas-ko-fa, Seminole, Tus-
ta-nuk-e-mantha, Creek, Robert Smith, Cherokee, Lewis, Chickasaw,
to Wm. P. Dole, dated Neosho Falls, Kansas, September 14, 1863,
ibid.).

[78] Snow to Dole, September 14, 1863, *ibid.*

forced change in their habits of living. Let it be remembered that they had come from homes of comfort and plenty. In Indian Territory, they had lived in up-to-date houses and had fed upon fruit and vegetables and abundantly upon meat. In Kansas, cast-off army tents were their portion and frequently damaged grain their diet. The tents had not been enough to protect them from the inclemency of the weather, their clothes were threadbare,[79] their bodies under-nourished. The mortality among them had been appalling and only very recently on the decline. Moreover, they were apprehensive of what was being charged against their account; for they, from long experience, had no illusions as to the white man's generosity. The whisperings of graft and peculation were not unheeded by them and their mutterings echoed political recriminations. They were conscious that they had outstayed their welcome in Kansas, that citizens, who were not profiting from the expenditure of the relief money, were clamoring for them to be gone. On the Ottawa Reservation, and to some extent on the Sac and Fox, their red hosts had ceased to be sympathetic.

Practically, all of the agents in the southern superintendency with the exception of Harlan [80] advised the return of the refugees to Indian Territory and they advised that it be undertaken early. Coleman apparently seconded the urgent appeal of his charges that they be sent home "the earliest practicable moment."

---

[79] The clothing distributed among the refugees at the Sac and Fox Agency allowed a part of a suit only to each individual (Cutler to Coffin, September 5, 1863, Commissioner of Indian Affairs, *Report*, 1863, p. 181). It must have been of extraordinarily poor quality; for, within ten months, it was almost worn out.

[80] The plight of those already removed constituted a warning against being over-sanguine and Harlan refrained from endorsing the advice given by his fellow-agents (Harlan to Coffin, December 7, 1863).

A return in the autumn or the winter would permit
them to "gather cattle and hogs sufficient to furnish
meat, and at the same time prepare their fields for a
spring crop, thereby obviating the obligation of the
government to subsist and clothe them." [81] The Creeks
were, however, afraid to venture before assurance was
forthcoming that their enemies had certainly been
cleaned out. Were that assurance to come, it would
bring conviction of another thing, that secessionist Indians, now despondent, had returned to their allegiance
to the United States government. There were many
indications that they were wavering in their adherence
to the Confederacy.[82] For their return, as for refugee
restoration, military protection would have to be a preliminary provision and it would have to extend beyond
the confines of Fort Gibson and southward as well as
northward of the Arkansas River. That river ought
to be opened to navigation. Were transit once rendered safe, the Indians would haul their own supplies;
but they wanted more than the Cherokee country
cleared and protected.[83] The Chickasaws, for instance,
could not go back until such time as Forts Washita and
Arbuckle had been seized and garrisoned. A small
incompetent force in Indian Territory was worse than
none at all. It simply invited attack and, if not augmented, should be withdrawn.[84]

The wheels of governmental action turn slowly and

[81] Coleman to Coffin, September 2, 1863, Commissioner of Indian Affairs, *Report*, 1863, p. 184.

[82] A "strong Union element" was reported existing among the Chickasaws and Choctaws. Union leagues were forming and the secessionists waiting for a Federal force to appear before breaking away from their alliance with the South (Commissioner of Indian Affairs, *Report*, 1863, p. 26). Secession-ist Creeks were resorting to Fort Gibson and enlisting with the Home Guards (*ibid.*, p. 182).

[83] — *Ibid.*, p. 184.

[84] Harlan to Coffin, September 2, 1863, *ibid.*, p. 180.

the winter months of 1863 came and went with no forward movement for refugee restoration. In January
of the next year, the agitation for it reached Congress
and, on the twenty-seventh, the Senate Indian committee, through its chairman, called upon Usher for
his opinion as to whether "the state of affairs" would
not allow a return to Indian Territory in time for the
raising of a crop.[85] On the fifth of February, Dole
consulted with General Blunt,[86] who was then in Washington and who might be presumed to possess some
expert knowledge of the subject. Blunt replied [87] to
the effect that the refugees ought most assuredly to be
reinstated in their own country to prevent demoralization among them; but that the serious obstacle to the
carrying out of so desirable a policy was the lack of
military protection. "Since the creation of the Department of Kansas all the troops heretofore serving in the
District of the Frontier, except three Regiments of
Indian Home Guards at Fort Gibson (very much
decimated) are reporting to General Steele in the
Department of Missouri." The Indian country was
somewhat removed from all convenient sources of sup-

[85] Doolittle to Usher, January 27, 1864, I. D., Files, Bundle, no. 52 (1864).
[86] "Knowing that you have lately been in command of our forces in
the vicinity of Forts Smith and Gibson and are familiar with the
condition of the Indian Country south of Kansas, I respectfully request you to furnish me with a statement of your views as to the
propriety of an immediate return of the Refugee Indians now in
Kansas to their homes, and, especially as to whether the military
forces now in the Indian Country and vicinity are adequate to afford
such protection to these Indian Refugees as would enable them to
remain at, and cultivate their farms in that Country, without constant
danger of being driven therefrom, their growing crops destroyed,
and they compelled to seek the protection of the Forts, and further
as to the practicability and means of subsisting them in that country
while raising a crop." (Dole to Blunt, February 5, 1864).
[87] Blunt to Dole, February 5, 1864, O.I.A., General Files, *Southern Superintendency*, 1863-1864, B 656; Commissioner of Indian Affairs, *Report*,
1864, pp. 322-323.

ply, the Arkansas was closed to navigation, and stores had to be transported long distances over interior lines. It "required a large portion of the small military force there to protect the trains." The difficulties in the way of obtaining supplies were the main reasons why the Federals were occupying so small a section of the Indian country. Blunt's recommendation was, a reorganization of the western departments so as to give to General Curtis, in command of the Department of Kansas, the control of the "two western tiers of the counties of Arkansas" and most certainly of Fort Smith, the supply depot of Indian Territory.[88] Sufficient troops must be furnished to permit of "successful operations both defensive and offensive."

Possessed of this additional information, the Senate carried its inquiries to the War Department and ascertained from its secretary that no reason was known there why the refugees should not return. Accordingly, on the third of March, James H. Lane introduced a joint resolution calling for their removal from Kansas.[89] He gave their number as ninety-two hundred and the monthly cost of their maintenance as sixty thousand dollars. The resolution was referred to the Committee on Indian Affairs. On the twenty-second, he sent to Dole a paper,[90] signed by members of the Indian committee of each house, earnestly recommend-

---

[88] Blunt pointed out that Fort Smith, captured by the Federals, September 1st, 1863, had been peculiarly placed by the departmental reorganization. In the Department of Kansas, was "the military post . . . through which (the garrison) runs the line dividing the state from the Choctaw Nation, and separated from the city by a single street, the city being in the Department of Missouri." The arrangement was exceedingly disadvantageous since Fort Smith was necessarily "the Depot and base of all military operations in the Indian country and also the Depot for supplying the Indians . . . "

[89] *Cong. Globe,* 38th cong., 1st sess., p. 921.

[90] General Files, *Southern Superintendency,* 1863-1864.

ing an immediate return to Indian Territory so as to make the putting in of a crop that season possible.[91] Congress appropriated the requisite funds.[92]

How Secretary Stanton, with all the facts before him, the facts alleged by General Blunt and true, could have conscientiously conveyed the impression that he did convey to the Senate Indian committee is a mystery. The restored Cherokees had not been sent back to Kansas as at one time proposed.   Their own feelings would have been against such a move had it ever been seriously contemplated; but for reasons, military and economic, not to say political, they had been retained in Indian Territory.   More and more their numbers were in one way added to and in another taken from.   Malnutrition, overcrowding and bad hygienic conditions generally offered fertile soil for diseases.   Small-pox alone carried the refugees off by hundreds.   Medical aid, reported by Agent Cox as "indispensably necessary," [93] was not to be had and military protection was even less of a factor in the alleviation of misery than it had been.   Guerrillas raided and robbed at will.   It was

---

[91] It was scarcely necessary to urge this upon Dole; for earlier, on February 25th, he had himself informed Usher that immediate action must be taken if the refugees were to be removed to their homes the coming spring (O.I.A., *Report Book*, no. 13, pp. 316-317).

[92] On March 25, 1864, Senator Doolittle introduced a bill (S 198) to aid the refugees in returning home.   It was referred to his committee (*Cong. Globe*, 38th cong., 1st sess., p. 1274).   It passed the House of Representatives in due course (*ibid.*, pp. 2016, 2050) and became law, May 3rd.

[93] Cox to Coffin, December 5, 1863 (O.I.A., *Cherokee*, C 633).   This letter is quoted in full in connection with the subject matter of Chapter vii.   The census roll of the Cherokees which accompanied it has more than statistical value and is here given.   Its file mark is, *Cherokee*, C 647.   Coffin's letter of January 25th, 1864 — he wrote it from Fort Leavenworth — refers to Cox's census as but temporary and promises the transmission of Harlan's as soon as it is completed.

TABULAR STATEMENT OF CENSUS OF THE CHEROKEE NATION
J. T. Cox, Sp. Ind. Agt.

CLASSIFICATION	Classes	Males	Females	Totals	REMARKS
ADULTS					
Number of Men Over 60 Years of Age, and infirm under that Age	291	291		291	4 Per Cent of the Registered Population
Number of Widows	977		977		13¼ Per Cent of the Registered Population
Number of Married Women	1100		1100		15 Per Cent of the Registered Population
Number of Single Women	835		835		11¼ Per Cent of the Registered Population
Total Number, Male and Female		291	2912	2912	44 Per Cent of the Registered Population
Total Number of Adult Females					40 Per Cent of the Registered Population
Of the Whole Number of Adult Females				2912	33⅓ Per Cent are Widows
Total Number of Adults	3203			3203	
CHILDREN					
Number of Boys, Orphans	564	564			
Number of Girls, Orphans	455		455		
Total Number of Orphans				1019	14 Per Cent of the Reg'd Population
Of the Whole Number of Children					25 Per Cent are Orphans
Number of Boys Fatherless, the Mother living	671	671			
Number of Girls Fatherless, the Mother living	580		580		
Total Number of Fatherless				1251	16 Per Cent of the Registered Population
Number of Boys whose Parents are living	1022	1022			
Number of Girls whose Parents are living	785		785		
Total Number of Children whose Parents are living				1807	About 24 Per Cent of the Registered Population
Total Number, Male and Female		2257	1820		
Whole Number of Children				4077	
Whole Number of Adults as Shown Above		291	2912	3203	
				7280	
To this Number Add Boys over 15 Years				300	Capable of Self Support, Not extended in Register
To this Number Add Men under 60				200	Capable of Self Support, Not extended in Register
Add Soldiers of Two Cherokee Regiments				1500	Not extended in Register
Probable Number resident, yet to Enroll				800	Not extended in Register
Probable Number at Sac & Fox Agency				300	Not extended in Register
Total Population				10380	

only directly under the guns of Fort Gibson that life
and property were at all secure.[94]

Late in the autumn, the Cherokee authorities, taking
cognizance of all such facts and fearing lest longer
delay might result in unmitigated woe to the nation,
resolved to make one last desperate appeal [95] for effective military aid.   The National Council, therefore,
authorized [96] the appointment of a deputation that
should call upon General McNeil and acquaint him
with all the circumstances of the case.   The special

[94] Letters from agents furnish abundant evidence of this. Two in
particular from Justin Harlan, both of date, December 7th, 1863, are worth
noting. Coffin's letter of transmittal (O.I.A., *Southern Superintendency,*
1863-1864), dated from Washington, January 22, 1864, will be found to be
an excellent introduction to Harlan's (*ibid., Cherokee,* C 633) as well as
a summary of other communications.

[95] Another kind of appeal was made at intervals to the Indian Office.
December 17, 1863, Dole reported to Usher news that he had received from
the Cherokee delegation then in Washington, Downing, Jones, and McDaniel,
all to the effect that there was absolute destitution in the Nation (O.I.A.,
Report Book, no. 13, p. 262).

[96] "*Be it enacted by the National Council,* That the Principal Chief be
and he is hereby authorized to appoint a deputation of three persons
whose duty it shall be to visit the General commanding the 'District
of the Frontier,' and lay before him a full statement of the present
condition of the Cherokee people. It shall be their duty to set forth
the services tendered by the Cherokees in the Army of the United
States, the painful destruction of life they have sustained from the
many casualties incident to war and the heavy loss of property they
have been forced to bear from the waste and depredations committed upon them by various persons under one pretext or another.

"And they are directed to assure the General . . . of the un-
shaken loyalty of the great mass of the Cherokee people . . . and
of their unwavering fidelity to the stipulations of the treaties existing
between said Government and the Cherokee Nation.

"The said deputation are further directed to request the General
. . . to adopt such stringent measures as will abate the evils complained of and to make such disposition of the forces under his command, & particularly of the Indian troops, as will enable them to
hold the Indian Country, protect their homes & families and repel and
punish Rebel forces making raids . . .

"And finally to ask authority to raise a Regiment of native troops
to be officered by themselves and mounted, equipped and supported

boon asked of him should be, either such a disposition of the Indian Brigade as would be a defence in actuality or permission to raise a real Home Guard. In course of time, news of the mission reached Washington [97] and its object was brought through the instrumentality of General Canby [98] to the attention of the

by the United States for duty more particularly in the Indian Country & whose term of service shall be three years or during the war.

Ketoowha, C.N., Nov. 17th, 1863

JAMES VANN, Prest. *Pro tem*, Nat¹. Comᵗ.

(Signed)

J. B. JONES, Clk. Nat. Committee, Concurred

ALLEN ROSS, Clk. Council   TAH-LAH-LAH, Speaker of Council

Approved,

SMITH CHRISTIE, Actᵍ Prin¹ Chief."

[97] The deputation submitted to Colonel Phillips "a statement of their views and wishes," which Representative A. C. Wilder referred to the Indian Office, February 10, 1864 (O.I.A., General Files, *Cherokee*, 1859-1865, W 332). The Reverend Evan Jones endorsed the application (*ibid.*, J 401). He was associated with Lewis Downing and James McDaniel as a special delegate from the Cherokees. Under authority from General Blunt, these three men, all of the Indian Guard contingent, Jones as chaplain, 1st I.H.G., Downing as lieutenant-colonel, 3rd I.H.G., and McDaniel, captain, 2nd I.H.G., had come to Washington in the spring of 1863 to present the Cherokee cause to the authorities. The War Department resented their coming and Secretary Stanton ordered that their expenses should be charged against Blunt's command –

" . . . the nature of their business and the necessity for the absence of these officers from their commands is not known by this Department. The action of Major General Blunt in sending them was disapproved and his pay was ordered stopped, until it was ascertained that the Government was not involved in any expense by that action . . . " (Letter to Usher, January 10, 1864). The foregoing was sent in reply to an inquiry from Senator Lane, whom Blunt had interested in his claim (A.G.O., Old Files Section, B 1340 of 1863; B 2133 (V.S.) 1863). Apparently, the matter did not end there and the regimental pay of the delegates was withheld. Blunt and Curtis both urged payment; but the case hung fire for some time (*ibid.*, B 1013 (V.S.) 1863, Jacket 3 of 15; C 13, 16, C 16, C 405, W 1390, W 3239, A 478, J 575 (V.S.) 1864; S 1040, W 178 (V.S.) 1865, Jacket 4 of 15).

For Dole's hearty endorsement of the Cherokee petition, see his report to Usher, March 7, 1864, Commissioner of Indian Affairs, *Report*, 1864, pp. 325-326.

[98] General E. R. S. Canby transmitted, January 10, 1864, to the General-in-Chief of the Army a copy of the resolutions of the Cherokee National Council, his sympathies having been aroused by the very evident distress

War Department. The official comment to the effect that the commander of the Department of Kansas would no doubt afford protection to the restored refugees was almost ironical in view of the fact that, by general orders of April seventeenth, Indian Territory was detached from that department and given to General Steele, commanding the rival one of Arkansas [99]. Of so little account had been General Blunt's intimation that a part of Arkansas should be added to Curtis' command if anything really remedial were in contemplation for the refugees, restored or to be restored.

The expeditious removal of a horde of human beings, more or less helpless by reason of sex, age or condition, was not the easy undertaking some people thought it. Anticipatory of congressional action, Superintendent Coffin prepared, in February, to transfer his office to Fort Smith by April first;[100] but at that point his activity halted. Kansas food contractors were interested in the further detention of the refugees and they had one unanswerable argument, the same that Thomas Carney advanced in a letter [101] of April twelfth to Dole,[102] that it was already too late in the season to re-

of the refugees. The following indicates in what spirit his communication was received:

"While it is not deemed expedient to grant the authority for raising such a regiment, the Department (of War) appreciates none the less the unfortunate condition of these Indians . . . Commander of the Dept of Kansas will no doubt afford protection." (A.G.O., Old Files Section, B 1013 (V.S.) 1863, Jacket 2 of 15).

[99] For popular criticism of the transfer of Indian Territory to the Department of Arkansas, see (Leavenworth) *Daily Conservative*, April 19, 23, 26 and July 10, 1864.

[100] — *Ibid.*, February 24, 1864.

[101] O.I.A., General Files, *Southern Superintendency*, 1863-1864.

[102] On the day following, the thirteenth, Dole referred to Usher a letter that he was proposing to send to Coffin containing instructions for immediate removal. The bill appropriating funds had then passed the Senate and was before the House.

move prospective agriculturists. In Indian Territory, the spring opens in March. The law, appropriating the necessary funds, was not enacted until May. Nevertheless, the senatorial advocates of removal persisted in prodding the Indian Office and, on April fourteenth, a resolution was passed requesting the president " to communicate to the Senate the reasons, if any exist, why the refugee Indians in the State of Kansas are not returned to their homes." [103] The response, which Dole communicated to Usher, May 11, 1864, ought to have been disconcerting to more than one department of the government since it was a plain statement of discreditable facts that funds had not been forthcoming and that the same causes that made the southern Indians refugees still operated, their country being exposed perpetually " to incursions of roving bands of rebels or hostile Indians." [104]

The shortcomings of the military arrangement that had separated Indian Territory from Kansas became startlingly obvious when Coffin applied for an armed escort and found that Curtis could furnish him with one to the border only. General Steele was far away " at or near Shreveport " and therefore Coffin telegraphed [105] to Dole, hoping that he might be able to get an order for troops direct from the War Department. The Red River expedition was in progress and it was not to be wondered at that Steele, absorbed in affairs of great import, affairs that were to terminate so dis-

---

[103] *Congressional Globe*, 38th Congress, 1st Session.

[104] O.I.A., *Report Book*, no. 13, pp. 408-409.

[105] April 21, 1864, O.I.A., General Files, *Southern Superintendency*, 1863-1864. With the same object in view, Coffin telegraphed once more on May tenth and again May thirteenth. His transportation was all ready and the only thing lacking was the assurance of military protection. Secretary Usher advised his not being too premature in moving the refugees; but allowed him to act upon his own responsibility and judgment.

astrously,[106] was inattentive to Coffin's call. The superintendent's preparations went on notwithstanding, the obstacles in his way multiplying daily; for the refugees, informed as to the military situation, were averse to courting new and untried dangers,[107] small-pox raged among the Seminoles,[108] and he had little latitude in the expenditure of funds, Congress having so hedged its appropriation about with restrictions.[109] He still pleaded for an additional armed force and his prayer was eventually answered. On May twenty-sixth, Stanton notified Usher that General Steele had been directed to furnish an escort from the Kansas border onward.[110]

The getting of the refugees ready for removal was, to Coffin's mind, the most difficult job he had ever undertaken. The Leased District Indians refused point-blank to go. Fort Gibson was not in the direction of home for them and they preferred to hazard subsisting themselves on the Walnut, where antelope and buffalo

[106] On May 11th., the Senate called for an investigation of the Red River disaster [*Cong. Globe*, 38th cong. 1st sess., p. 2218].

[107] Coffin to Dole, May 22, 1864, O.I.A., General Files, *Southern Superintendency*, 1863-1864; Commissioner of Indian Affairs, *Report*, 1864, pp. 338-339.

[108] Small-pox had appeared at Neosho Falls as early as September, 1863 and then had disappeared for a time. In the following spring, it broke out again with terrible virulence. "Great consternation at once seized and preyed upon the minds of these superlatively wretched exiles," wrote the attending physician, "offering large vantage-ground to the extension of the fearful malady. All were immediately vaccinated; but unfortunately the virus, though reported good, proved inert, and the next supply but partially succeeded . . . " (A. V. Coffin to W. G. Coffin, August 25, 1864, Commissioner of Indian Affairs, *Report*, 1864, p. 307). The disease spread to Belmont and in many cases proved fatal (*ibid.*; Gookins to W. G. Coffin, October 20, 1864, *ibid.*, p. 319).

[109] Coffin to Dole, May 14, 1864, O.I.A., General Files, *Southern Superintendency*, 1863-1864; Commissioner of Indian Affairs, *Report*, 1864, pp. 337-338. The money was not to be spent in Kansas. See Dole to Coffin, May 7, 1864, *ibid.*, pp. 336-337.

[110] O.I.A., General Files, *Southern Superintendency*, 1863-1864.

ranged, to journeying thither.[111] For a time it seemed impossible to procure enough teams.[112] The Indians were " very fearful." Some of the Creeks had to be left behind sick at the Sac and Fox Agency and quite a lot of the Seminoles [113] at Neosho Falls [114] No attempt was made, on this occasion, to lure the Quapaws and their neighbors from the Ottawa Reservation. Their home not being even passably safe,[115] they were to remain north, for a period, with Agent Elder, their differences with their hosts being no longer cause for uneasiness.[116] The procession, when it finally started,

[111] Henry Smith, Coffin's clerk, to Dole, May 28, 1864, *ibid.*, C 877. For an estimate of their number, see Coffin to Dole, March 21, 1864, *ibid.*, C 754. Their faithful agent, E. H. Carruth, died April 23rd. and Coffin appointed temporarily in his place, John T. Cox (Coffin to Dole, April 27, 1864, *ibid., Wichita*, 1862-1871).

[112] "Nearly three hundred teams were required . . . and these had to be secured and gathered up through the country wherever we could get them." Coffin to Dole, September 24, 1864, Commissioner of Indian Affairs, *Report*, 1864, p. 303).

[113] Bowlegs had died recently and Long John, who succeded him as head chief, appealed for help to President Lincoln, March 10, 1864 (O.I.A., General Files, *Seminole*, 1858-1869, S 291). Pas-ko-fa, the second chief, seconded the appeal, basing his claim to assistance upon the indisputable fact that his people had been loyal to the United States in the face of desperate odds, while the few who had gone with the South had been taken unawares by Pike (*ibid.*).

[114] In June, Smith reported their number as 550; but, in September, Agent Snow placed it at 470 (Commissioner of Indian Affairs, *Report*, 1864, p. 317).

[115] "These Indians could not be returned to their homes this summer, as their country lies just south of the south line of Kansas, and in the worst district of country for guerillas and bushwhackers west of the Missouri river, and cannot be occupied by either Indians or whites who are in the least suspected of loyalty, until a military post, or stockade, or fort is established there to hold the country against the marauding bands that have infested it for the last three years. It is there where our supply trains are so frequently attacked, and where General Blunt's body-guard and brass band was captured and murdered in cold blood . . . " (Commissioner of Indian Affairs, *Report*, 1864, pp. 304-305).

[116] Apparently some of the ill-feeling between them and the Ottawas had been allayed. They were now on the Ottawa allotted lands and Agent Elder reported, "There has been no uneasiness or complaint on the part

58   *The Indian Under Reconstruction*

included nearly five thousand refugees [11] and, by the end of May, it had reached, without molestation, the Osage Catholic Mission. There it awaited the coming of the supplementary escort.[118]

Meanwhile, affairs were in bad shape at Fort Gibson. There was discord everywhere, between white and red people and between civilians and soldiery, and the food contractors were responsible for most of it.

of the Ottawas in consequence of such occupancy, except such as has been engendered by the counsels of whites who have a prospective interest in the future disposition of their lands." (*ibid.*, p. 315)

[117] Before starting out with his refugee train, Coffin attempted to secure the Creek consent to the Senate amendments to the treaty of 1863 and he called a council at the Sac and Fox Agency for the purpose. The mooted point was, the claim of the loyal Creeks about which Dole had consulted with Senator J. H. Lane in January (Dole to Lane, January 27, 1864, O.I.A., *Report Book*, no. 13, pp. 287-291). The loyal Creeks claimed national status an untenable position according to those, who, like Lane, wanted to force a cession in order to accommodate the Kansas tribes when removed. The Senate amendment to Article 4 of the treaty deprived the secessionist Creeks of all claims to the tribal lands (Resolution, March 8, 1864; Usher to Dole, March 23, 1864, O.I.A., Land Files, *Treaty*, Box 3, 1864-1866.

Concerning the council that Coffin held with the Creeks at the Sac and Fox Agency, the account, gleaned from the Leavenworth *Daily Times* and from the St. Louis *Globe Democrat* and published in Commissioner of Indian Affairs, *Report*, 1864, pp. 339-340, is sufficiently explicit. The Creeks resisted all blandishments and, as a matter of fact, never did accept the Senate alterations in their treaty. The treaty, in consequence, remained unratified although its binding force was occasionally subject for inquiry for many years afterwards. In illustration, see Byers to Lewis V. Bogy, February 7, 1867, O.I.A., General Files, *Creek*, 1860-1869, B 94. Undoubtedly, there were many people, who fain would have had the government proceed as if it were a fully negotiated and finished treaty; but the Creeks were too wary. They would have none of it and yet, except for the objectionable amended fourth article, they deemed it a *good* treaty (Oc-ta-hasa Harjo and others to Dole, December 9, 1864).

While the treaty was pending in the Senate, "loyal Africans from the Creek Nation," through Israel Harris of the American Baptist Home Missionary Society, asked that they be "guarantied" "equal rights with the Indians." All of their "boys" were in the army and ought to be remembered (Mundy Durant to Dole, February 23, 1864, O.I.A., General Files, *Creek*, 1860-1869, D 362).

[118] Coffin to Dole, June 3, 1864, *ibid.*, *Southern Superintendency*, 1863-1864, C 895.

Those were the days when cattle-stealing became a public scandal but more of it anon. The discord between white and red people existed both inside and outside the army. Inside the army, it was a matter as between officers and men and was most apparent when Colonel Phillips took the Indian Brigade on an expedition towards the Red River early in the year. The bickerings that arose between the white officers and the Indian rank and file soon grew notorious and were chiefly caused by the disputed ownership of ponies.[119] Litigation succeeded altercation and there was no end to the bad feeling engendered. Fortunately, the Indian plaintiff had friends at court in the person of government agents [120] and the brigade commander, Colonel Phillips standing well the test of "earnest and substantial friend." [121]

---

[119] J. T. Cox to Dole, February 5, 1864, Commissioner of Indian Affairs, *Report*, 1864, p. 321.

[120] Besides Special Agent Cox, there was with the expedition Special Agent Milo Gookins of Attica, Indiana, who had, in the preceding August, been sent by Coffin "to accompany the Indian regiments now with the Army of the Frontier, under command of Blunt, during their campaign in Indian Territory." (Coffin to Mix, August 31, 1863, O.I.A., General Files, *Southern Superintendency*, 1863-1864, C 471). Coffin had instructed Gookins to "enquire carefully into the loyalty of all the prominent Indian chiefs, headmen, & braves, and keep a correct & full record of all their acts, standing & position towards the Federal Government . . . " (Coffin to Gookins, August 19, 1863, *ibid.*). It was not a promising outlook and yet, in the spring of 1864, Gookins was disposed to be most magnanimous in his attitude towards the recalcitrants. On March 23rd., he wrote to Dole,

"I see by the papers that steps are being taken in Congress for the appointment of Commissioners to examine and adjust claims against the Government for losses sustained by the war, embracing all the States. I presume it will not have escaped the notice of the Interior Department, the Indian Bureau, or the Cherokee delegation that a similar bill for the Indian territories should be more liberal in its provisions, embracing hundreds, who by force of surrounding circumstances, and under compulsion, might have *appeared* to be, and probably to *act* disloyal, when in fact and in truth they were not so" (*ibid.*).

[121] Cox to Dole, February 5, 1864, *op. cit.*

The troubles caused by the contractors were more widespread and of more lasting effect. They grew out of peculations and the delivery of inferior goods. Flour furnished for the refugees, when inspected,[122] was found to be worthless as far as its food properties and appetizing qualities were concerned. "Some of it was nothing but 'shorts,' the rest, the poorest flour manufactured." Agent Harlan accepted it only because "the Indians had been over 30 days without bread," and he knew, if he rejected it, that "they would get none until spring."[123] T. C. Stevens and Company were contractors in this affair and the only circumstance that Coffin could offer in extenuation of their conduct was the great difficulty always "experienced in obtaining a good article of flour in southern Kansas . . . in consequence of the inferior character of the mills in that new and sparsely settled country . . ."[124] Similar complaints were made of the firm of MacDonald and Fuller.[125] Was it any wonder that the

---

[122] "I am informed by good authority from Kansas that some fourteen hundred sacks of flour has been condemned by a military tribunal in Kansas as worthless – that the flour was delivered to the Refugee Indians on a contract of Stevens & Co.

"I am further informed that the evidence in the case with samples of the flour has been forwarded to you. I propose to have that evidence & samples before the Indian Committee that they may fully realize with whom they are dealing in Kansas. I trust that you will retain the samples until the Indian Committee meets . . ." (J. H. Lane to Dole, March 14, 1864, O.I.A., General Files, *Southern Superintendency*, 1863-1864, L 313).

[123] Usher to Dole, March 7, 1864, communicating the statement of the inspectors, *ibid.*, I 467.

[124] Coffin to Dole, March 10, 1864, *ibid.*

[125] The criminality of this firm was exposed later and with more publicity. For a copy of its original contract, see Coffin to Dole, April 13, 1864, *ibid.*, C 778. Of the rival firm, Thomas Carney was a principal member. He had come from Ohio [Connelley, *Standard History of Kansas and Kansans*, pp. 764-768] and had early gained an unenviable reputation in business dealings. His friend and associate, Robert S. Stevens, was notorious for sharp practices, in the location of land warrants for eastern people, the

refugees felt themselves neglected, abused, and out-raged?

The advance guard of Coffin's refugee train reached Fort Gibson June 15.[126] Its progress had been ham-pered by minor vicissitudes, cattle thieves and thunder-storms, all natural to the region.[127] The condition of affairs north of the Arkansas was at the time most un-satisfactory; for the Federals had military control of Forts Smith and Gibson only and "everything," so complained the superintendent, "done out of range of the guns of the forts has to be done under an escort or guard." The Creeks, who comprised the major por-tion of the refugees, could not be taken to their own country unless General Thayer should consent to erect a military post within its limits. For the time being they were, therefore, to remain with the Cherokees, a bad arrangement.[128] The Chickasaws were to go east-

building of Indian houses, and the like. He had emigrated from New York and, in combination with S. N. Simpson and Charles Robinson, had inter-ested himself in the construction of the road that was "the beginning of the railroad troubles in Kansas [Robinson, *Kansas Conflict*, pp. 419-420.].

[126] Coffin to Dole, June 16, 1864, O.I.A., General Files, *Southern Su-perintendency*, 1863-1864, C 922.

[127] — *ibid.*; same to same, June 7, 1864.

[128] Old Sands, who was then head chief of the Loyal Creeks, would give Phillips no peace until he consented to lay the complaints of the Creek refugees before the department (Phillips to Usher, June 24, 1864, I. D. Files, Bundle, no. 52). Usher communicated the facts to the War Department, August 16, 1864. The leading chiefs, including Sands, addressed themselves July 16th to Dole as follows:

"We did not get here in time to raise anything for ourselves. We are therefore destitute of everything. Months intervene between the arrival of each train and the supplies they bring are barely sufficient to keep us alive from day to day . . . There are at least twenty thousand persons here to feed, all of whom will have to depend on the trains for *all* their subsistence except beef, and this winter when the trains must necessarily have to stop, our sufferings will be terrible in the extreme. Last winter the refugees who were here were re-duced to almost absolute starvation, so much so, that they were glad to hunt out the little corn that *fell from the horses & mules* of the mil-itary. Then there were large fields of corn south of this post, belong-

ward to Fort Smith where they would be a trifle nearer home than would be the case were they to remain at Gibson. Their own country, though, was considerably far to the westward, beyond the Choctaw. It was now too late to put in regular crops and consequently subsistence would have to be furnished as before and at a far greater cost. Coffin estimated the number of refugees at close upon sixteen thousand and the expense, he feared, would "be truly enormous." The Indians would have to be put at once "on the shortest kind of rations." Coffee, sugar, vinegar, condiments and everything else that could by any manner of means be dispensed with would have to be "cut off altogether." The prospect was not encouraging and Coffin, almost at his wit's end, despairingly wrote that "the military have most wonderfully changed their tune."

There was soon occasion for more particular criticism of army practices. In April, General Blunt had issued an order, well-intentioned no doubt, restraining the Indians from selling their stock. He had likewise ordered the seizure of certain salt-works, "salines," the value of which to the Indians can be calculated only by reference to the prominence given in all early records to the salt-licks used in turn by buffalos, aborgines, settlers.[129] In the case of each of Blunt's orders, the immediate object in view was the benefit, not of pri-

---

ing to the rebels, which our soldiers took and gathered; now there are none; the whole country is a waste, and the suffering must be much greater next winter than it was last, unless the most prompt and energetic steps are taken to procure and transport supplies to this place.

"It was a terrible mistake that we were not brought down here in time to raise a crop for ourselves . . . " (O.I.A., General Files, *Creek*, 1860-1869).

[129] Hulbert, *Historic Highways*, vol. i, p. 106. Phillips seconded Smith Christie's appeal that the salt-works be restored (June 3, 1864, I. D. *Register of Letters Received*, C, p. 423) and Usher favorably recommended the matter to the attention of the War Department, June 15 and again

vate individuals, but of soldiers. Moreover, as the Indian crops matured, those same soldiers helped themselves freely to grain and other produce, the outcome of the labour of "helpless women and children," and they did it quite regardless of Indian needs. A real grievance existed and the intervention of the War Department was besought for its redress.[130] Things went from bad to worse. Illicit traffic in Indian cattle added its nefariousness to the general disorder and the conduct of the military authorities was deemed as iniquitous as that of the contractors. Phillips himself did not pass muster. He was as unpopular with one set of men as Blunt was with another. Before long Indians, too, came to share in the cattle-driving. The Wichita Agency tribes [131] were the chief offenders and they stole

August 15, 1864 (*ibid.*, D., p. 284; *Letter Press Book*, no. 6, pp. 90-92; *Letter Book*, no. 5, p. 20).

[130] There were, perforce, some extenuating circumstances. Blunt was short of both men and food (Blunt to Curtis, April 6, 1864, *Official Records*, vol. xxxiv, part 3, p. 69). He was quite unable to meet the necessities of Phillips's command (Phillips to Curtis, April 5, 1864, *ibid.*, pp. 52-53), which at first had recourse to the grain fields of the upper Canadian. The old question of the relationship of Indian Territory to Arkansas from the military point of view was still being bruited. On the sixteenth of April, Grant asked that their union be urged upon the president (Grant to Halleck, April 16, 1864, *ibid.*, p. 178) and he gained his point immediately. Blunt was then ordered back to Curtis (*ibid.*, p. 192). The need of a restraining order to protect the Cherokee produce developed very shortly thereafter and continued unabated throughout the summer (Harlan to Dole, July 30, 1864, Coffin to Dole, August 8, 1864, O.I.A., General Files, *Cherokee*, 1859-1865, C 987, Commissioner of Indian Affairs, *Report*, 1864, pp. 345-346; Mix to Usher, August 15, 1864, *ibid.*, pp. 344-345, Indian Office *Report Book*, no. 13, p. 507, I. D. *Register of Letters Received*, D, p. 284; Smith Christy to Coffin, September 7, 1864, O.I.A., General Files, *Cherokee*, 1859-1865, C 1045; Harlan to Dole, September 30, 1864, *ibid.*, H 956 of 1864).

[131] The Wichitas turned to cattle-stealing to relieve their necessities. Sickness had prevented many of them from going out on the usual fall hunt (Coffin to Dole, October 27, 1864, O.I.A., General Files, *Wichita*, 1862-1871, C 1094; Gookins to Dole, April 24, 1865, *ibid.*, G 258 of 1865). Milo Gookins, who had taken charge of these Indians in July (Secretary of the Interior to the Commissioner of Indian Affairs, July 22, 1864), reported

from the Creek country mostly; but they also made excursions into the Cherokee and down into Texas. White men went frequently with them. It was commonly supposed that few of such raiders ever returned alive; but the profits were worth the risk. And there was raiding in other directions. Supply trains preferred to go unescorted; for the military guard had more than once been a raiding party in disguise. Everything conduced to confusion.[132]

that settlers paid liberally for the gathering up of other people's cattle and were the prominent men of the vicinity. He wrote from Butler County, Kansas (Gookins to Coffin, November 14, 1864, *ibid., Southern Superintendency*, 1863-1864, C 1143). Coffin was inclined to condone the cattle-driving when it was confined to "Texas and that part of the Indian Territory exclusively under rebel control and where the stock all falls into the hands of rebels and is used to prolong the war . . . " (Coffin to Gookins, December 3, 1864, *ibid.*). Gookins' relations with Colonel J. H. Leavenworth, Special Agent for the Kiowas and Comanches, were not amicable. He came to suspect Leavenworth of stirring up disaffection among the Wichitas (Gookins to Sells, October 31, 1865, *ibid., Wichita*, 1862-1871, S 827) and he highly disapproved of a plan, credited to Leavenworth, for settling the Comanches, so recently hostile, on the Arkansas (Gookins to Coffin, November 25, 1864, *ibid., Southern Superintendency*, 1863-1864, C 1143). The Wichitas were still miserably destitute in 1866 (Cooley to Harlan, June 23, 1866, O.I.A., *Report Book*, no. 15, p. 334. See also pp. 388, 487, 495).

[132] The following documents illustrate the point:

(a) "Stand Watie has captured government train at Cabin Creek, three hundred troops and two hundred fifty teamsters. Have troops sent to Gibson at once. All demoralized on the border. Something must be done or Indians will cause trouble. Our loss sixty thousand dollars." (Telegram from Perry Fuller to Dole, dated Leavenworth, September 20, 1864). There were those who unfavorably contrasted the Federal treatment of the Indians with the Confederate, the Confederate, that is, as instanced in the elevation of this same Stand Watie to a brigadier-generalship (John W. Stapler to Usher, dated Philadelphia, June 22, 1864, O.I.A., General Files, *Cherokee*, 1859-1865, S 389).

(b) " . . . I have just come in from the train with despatches to Col. Blair &c. All is confusion. The soldiers are regularly organized into a mob and swear no train shall go down. We shall start in the morning anyhow. I take back despatches from Col. Blair. Night before last the sutlers were robbed. Fuller lost heavily. They went through me. I lost six thousand dollars worth of tobacco. Last night they made another attack on Fuller's train, took one box worth

Moreover, there was suffering nearly everywhere.
Positive destitution made its appearance in July. It

six hundred dollars. The Indians pitched into them and drove them
back. Had a nice little fight. The Indians swear they will fight
for the train to the last. Sent this morning for the Indians from
Gibson to come on and meet us. Capt. Anderson is here from the
Indians. Our escort swear they will not fight if they meet the
enemy. Dennison refuses to send any troops to our assistance. Blair
gives up, says he can do nothing. The only redress is to stop the
pay of the escort. It is one of the most high-handed outrages ever
committed. Will you see Gen. Curtis and see what can be done in
the matter?

"Vail's teams have turned back from Coxe's Creek. I stopped them
and then went back to the escort for assistance in making them go on.
Capt. Anderson came out and tried to get them to come back, made
them all kinds of offers. But as he was not in command of the escort
and as Capt. Ledger had gone back to Ft. Scott for assistance he
could do nothing. Blair says to make them go back but they are now
too near Ft. Scott to make the connection. I would not pay him one
cent for he has acted the dog. It is true the mob went up and stole
all their outfit, blankets, clothes, provisions and even whips. But Capt.
Anderson offered to furnish them with everything and we made them
all kinds of offers. The soldiers do not take because they want the
property only, but they destroy all they can lay their hands on, took
600 pounds of soda and scattered it all over the prairie, also 200
pounds of matches. Last night they tried to burn up the train. Our
only hope is in the Indians. I would write more but am in a hurry
to start back. Don't know the extent of the loss but must be thirty or
forty thousand dollars. I think you may count on this train not getting
through . . . " (Cutler to Coffin, November 24, 1864, O.I.A.,
General Files, *Southern Superintendency*, 1863-1864, C 1138).

(c) ". . . I have just returned from Fort Scott by way of Hum-
bolt & the Neosho Valley. We have succeeded in getting off a train
of supplies for the Indians at Fort Gibson under most discouraging
circumstances. After making the propositions of which I advised
you to furnish flour and corn, Carney and Stevens declined and Fuller
& McDonald are trying to comply. With what aid I could give them,
we had secured about six thousand bushels of corn and two thousand
sacks of flour. We had engaged transportation enough to take it all,
but just as we were to commence loading on the 9th and 10th of November there came one of the severest rain, hail, and snow storms ever
known in this country, which entirely disheartened and backed out
more than half our teams. We succeeded in getting teams enough to
load all the goods you and Harlan purchased in New York which were
a month overtime in getting here.

"After loading all the teams we could procure at Baldwin City with

was then that Coffin resented the expenditure of money for the support of John Ross and the rest of the Chero-

corn, I went immediately to Fort Scott and succeeded in detaining the military train and escort one week for our teams that were behind to come up, but owing to the extreme bad road and bad weather more than half of them did not reach there in time and we were compelled to unload and discharge them at Fort Scott, and part of them returned. After joining the train as you will see by the enclosed letter from Major G. A. Cutler and Mr. Vail, the troops that have been in are still escorting trains from Fort Scott to Forts Gibson and Smith and have become demoralized that there is no longer any safety in sending trains under them. They commenced robbing the wagons in open daylight before they left the camp near Fort Scott, and openly declared they would not suffer a loaded wagon to reach Fort Gibson. (It is due candor to say, those troops belong to General Steele's department, no difficulty of the kind has been incurred with troops under General Curtis, who I am bound to say has always coöperated with me and has at all times promptly given us all the aid and assistance in his power, with the limited means and number of troops at his command. His district only extends to the southern boundary of Kansas just where danger begins.) It is most exceedingly unfortunate that General Curtis' district does not include the Indian Territory. Had such been the case the last year I am very sure that the results of our Indian operations would have been very different.

"I have just learned from Gen'l Curtis that our train is halted at Hudson's Crossing of the Neosho, from a report that a large rebel force had crossed the Arkansas above Fort Gibson and were marching towards the train. They had sent out scouts to ascertain the truth and were waiting the result. I very much fear the train will have to return which will entail upon us a very heavy expense, and what the Indians will do in the mean time, it is hard to foretell. I greatly fear they will all be back in Kansas again before the country can be sufficiently cleared to enable us to send down another train.

"Immediately on starting the train from Fort Scott I commenced getting up another train and have secured four thousand bushels of corn and four hundred sacks of flour in addition to what was left at Baldwin City and Fort Scott and have now engaged about one hundred and fifty teams and am engaging all that can be had.

"Should the present train get through safe and another start in two or three weeks I fondly hope to be able to get enough breadstuff down to prevent suffering till supplies can reach them by water.

"But from all the facts now before us I am constrained to say, that unless some more efficiency can be infused into the military operations in the Indian Territory all our efforts to supply those unfortunate Refugees must end in failure, for no prudent men would take their teams and property under the escort of what practically amounts to

kee delegation in Washington.[133] The Commissioner of
Indian Affairs tried to get Choctaw bonds diverted to
refugee relief.[134] When the autumn came, clothing and
blankets [135] were solicited as well as food. Appealed to
for the amelioration of an all too-evident distress,
President Lincoln gave his approval to the making of
purchases on credit.[136] In Kansas, conditions among
the Indians were equally bad. The Seminoles at
Neosho Falls were reported naked and famishing in
August.[137] Earlier yet a cry of want had come from the
Weas, Peorias, Kaskaskias, and Piankeshaws, whose
lands were on the Missouri border and subject to raids
and whose funds had not materialized during the war.
They had been invested in interest-bearing stock by the

an organized band of paid and fed robbers." (Coffin to Dole, December 1, 1864, *ibid.*).

[133] I. D., *Register of Letters Received*, D, p. 282.

[134] At the suggestion of the Indian Office, the Secretary of the Interior opened up a correspondence with the Treasury Department, August 11, 1864, with that end in view (*ibid.*). For later stages of the proposal, see the history of Senate Resolution, no. 85, *Cong. Globe*, 38th cong., 2nd sess., pp. 967, 1336, 1420. Senator Doolittle, June 11, 1864 (*Cong. Globe*, 38th cong., 1st sess., p. 2869) had moved an amendment to the pending Indian appropriation bill which was substantially a confiscation of Indian annuities for the relief of refugees. The recommendation was no new thing and the use of secessionist Indian funds for such a purpose had been authorised much earlier.

[135] Harlan to Dole, September 30, 1864 (O.I.A., General Files, *Cherokee*, 1859-1865, H 957); Cutler to Dole, October 3, 1864, (*ibid., Southern Superintendency*).

[136] See Lincoln's endorsement on the department letter of October 1, 1864, "Understanding that persons giving credit in this case will have no strictly legal claim upon the government, yet the necessity for it is so great and urgent, that I shall most cheerfully urge upon Congress that such credit and claims fairly given and made shall be recognized and paid." (I. D., *Register of Letters Received*, D, p. 293). Agent Harlan was instructed to buy on credit in New York thirty thousand dollars worth of clothing and Coffin in Kansas one hundred and seventy thousand dollars worth of food (Otto, Acting Secretary of the Interior, to Dole, October 1, 1864).

[137] Snow to Dole, August 8, 1864 (O.I.A., General Files, *Seminole*, 1858-1869). The account of Carney & Stevens against the Seminoles alone was $7563.21. See Snow's voucher for the same (*ibid.*).

United States government and, in some mysterious way and without consultation with the Indians, had been converted, just previous to the outbreak of hostilities, into stock of the secessionist states. There were those in Congress who repudiated every idea of responsibility resting upon the government for the substitution and, while senators quibbled over whether relief should be furnished as of right or as a matter of charity, the despoiled and too-trusting Indians starved.[138]

A disposition to shirk responsibility did not reveal itself in connection with the matter of the substituted stocks only but came out again in the Senate debate on the condition and treatment of the restored refugees, restored only in the sense that they had been taken back into the Indian country. An item in the annual Indian appropriation bill carried seven hundred and fifty thousand dollars for their relief. It was no mean figure and it was based as much upon past expenditures as upon present needs.[139]   Senator Brown considered that the

---

[138] *Cong. Globe*, 38th cong., 1st sess., pp. 1154, 1207, 1454, 2050, 2405, 2869-2870, 2873, 2874-2875, 2877, 3219, etc. The obligation of the government to stand surety for investments of Indian trust funds was debated in 1854 (*ibid.*, 33rd Cong., 1st sess., pp. 1026-1027).

[139] On January 11, 1865, Doolittle called upon Usher for complete returns as to the expense of removing, subsisting, and protecting refugees (I. D. Files, Bundle, no. 53). March 28th, Dole applied to Coffin for more statistical information (O.I.A., *Letter Book*, no. 76, p. 497). As it happened, Coffin sent some such the very next day but it was entirely based upon the accounts of the last December (*ibid., Southern Superintendency*).

Cherokee	Justin Harlan, Agt.
1. Now drawing rations	9,900
2. To draw rations when mustered out of Guards	2,000
Creeks and Euchees	G. A. Cutler, Agt.
1. Now drawing rations	6,000
2. To draw rations when mustered out of Guards	1,500
Seminoles	under care of Creek Agt.
1. Now drawing rations	300
2. To draw rations when mustered out of Guards	100
Choctaws and Chickasaws	Isaac Smith, Agt.
1. Number drawing rations	900

Indians had less claim upon the generosity – if that be
what it should be called – of the government than had
the people of Missouri, his constituents, or than had the
unpaid soldier everywhere.[140] Doolittle disputed the
point by recalling the circumstances of the abandonment by the United States, the consequent exposure
to intimidation and attack, and the expulsion from
home with all its attendant miseries. The terrible
havoc wrought in the Cherokee country he expatiated
upon with vigor, contending that the argument put up
by the opposition to the effect that the spoliation,
desolation, destruction were the work of Indians, guilty
of defection, only made the matter worse for the
government and the consequent obligation resting upon
it all the greater; since the United States had sworn to
protect against both foreign and domestic foe.[141]
Brown's concluding charge that three-fourths of the
"donation" would, in his belief, "go in the shape of

Coffin's accompanying remarks are of interest as showing how rapidly the
Indians were deserting the Confederate cause. In June only about seventy
Choctaws and Chickasaws were receiving rations at Fort Smith. Coffin
anticipated that the number might swell to five thousand by July.

The congressional appropriation as made fell very far short of needs and
expectations (Usher to Dole, March 20, 1865). The alarm of the field
employees can be deduced from an unofficial letter that P. P. Elder sent to
Dole from Ohio City, Kansas, March 18, 1865. He had been subsisting his
charges on credit and he feared that, as a result of the meagre appropriation,
"a squabble will ensue who is to be paid first." For further information
about the condition at Neosho Agency, see *Neosho*, W 896 of 1865 and S 714
of 1865.

For a list of the people to whom rations were distributed at Fort Gibson,
April, 1865, see A.G.O., *Fort Gibson* File-box, 1864-1868.

140 *Cong. Globe*, 38th cong., 2nd sess., p. 1299.

141 Proof of this promise, variously phrased, is to be found in the following extracts from treaties: The list is not exhaustive.

"The United States are obliged to protect the Choctaws from
domestic strife and from foreign enemies . . . " (Treaty of
Dancing Rabbit Creek, 1830, article v, Kappler, vol. ii, p. 311);

" . . . they also agree to protect them in their new residence,
against all interruption or disturbance from any other tribe or nation

fraudulent contracts," it was not so easy to refute and Doolittle discreetly ignored it. Like Banquo's ghost, however, it was bound to reappear; for charges against the contractors [142] and their accomplices or abettors were constantly being insinuated if not formally lodged. The whole matter would have to be threshed

of Indians or from any other person or persons whatever." (Quapaw Treaty of 1833, article ii, Kappler, vol. ii, p. 396).

" . . . hereby consent to protect and defend them against the inroads of any other tribe of Indians, and from the whites; and agree to keep them without the limits of any State or Territory. The Chickasaws pledge themselves never to make war upon any Indian people, or upon the whites, unless they are so authorized by the United States. But if war be made upon them, they will be permitted to defend themselves, until assistance be given to them by the United States, as shall be the case." (Chickasaw Treaty of 1834, article ii, Kappler, vol. ii, p. 418).

" . . . The United States agree to protect the Cherokee nation from domestic strife and foreign enemies and against intestine wars between the several tribes . . . " (Treaty of New Echota, 1835, article vi, Kappler, vol. ii, p. 442).

"The United States shall protect the Choctaws and Chickasaws from domestic strife, from hostile invasion, and from aggression by other Indians and white persons not subject to their jurisdiction and laws; and for all injuries resulting from such invasion or aggression, full indemnity is hereby guaranteed to the party or parties injured, out of the Treasury of the United States, upon the same principle and according to the same rules upon which white persons are entitled to indemnity for injuries or aggressions upon them, committed by Indians." (Treaty of 1855, article xiv, Kappler, vol. ii, p. 710).

Exactly the same provision as the one immediately preceding is to be found in the Creek and Seminole Treaty of 1856, article xviii [Kappler, vol. ii, p. 762].

[142] The firm of McDonald and Fuller was continually under fire of criticism and the ill-feeling between its members and Colonel Phillips was most pronounced and bitter. When the Creeks complained of the kind and quality of goods furnished them, McDonald and Fuller charged that Phillips was at the bottom of the whole matter, he being, so they claimed, a secret partner in the Ross sutler business (McDonald and Fuller to Coffin, March 11, 1865; Coffin to Dole, March 13, 1865; Cutler to Coffin, March 13, 1865, O.I.A., General Files, *Southern Superintendency*, 1865, C 1279). Ewing and Browning, attorneys for the Cherokees, asked, March 18, 1865, that "a requisition from W. G. Coffin now pending at the Treasury be suspended until they can have an opportunity to prove that the claim of McDonald and Fuller and others is fraudulent" (*ibid., Cherokee*, 1859-1865, E 70). John

out, investigated thoroughly, ere many moons had passed.

The abuses of the system, supposing that the way the refugees were provided for can be distinguished by so dignified a name, were all the time creeping out. Charges and countercharges against individuals as responsible for the abuses were of disgusting and appalling frequency and, even if large allowance be made for personal malice, tribal animosities, trade rivalries as well as for the old Indian distrust of white men and for the old jealousy between civil and military authorities there was yet enough to merit the strongest opprobrium then and now. The money was going and yet there was absolutely no visible alleviation of misery. There was much of truth in Senator Sherman's observations that " if we could protect them (the Indians) from our own race, if we could leave them alone without a dollar, with no white man, woman, or child within fifty miles of them, they could take better care of themselves than we could with all our appropriations for them. Their troubles have grown out of their contact with white men . . . I do not know but that we had better bring these fifteen thousand Indians to the city of New York and send them to the Astor House or some other comfortable place and take care of them. The same rule applied to the support of all

W. Wright wrote to Usher in similar wise, March 18th, "I do know that the claim of McDonald & Fuller for which it is proposed to place money in the hands of W. G. Coffin is an outrageous swindle.

"That corn to the amount of 10,000 bushels was purchased of the Cherokees at less than $3 per bushel and immediately turned out at $12 to other Cherokees . . .

"That 7/8 of the beef furnished refugees was stolen from the Indians . . . " (*ibid.*).

Usher called in the vouchers preparatory to an investigation (Usher to Dole, April 7, 1865, *ibid.*) and shortly afterwards the accused parties attempted a defense by recriminations against Phillips. See particularly H. E. McKee to Coffin, April 20, 1865, *ibid., Southern Superintendency.*

the people of the United States would ruin us as a nation in six months . . . " [143]

A particular instance of the mismanagement and shortsightedness of the powers that were is to be found in the very location of refugees other than Cherokee.[144] The Creeks were detained near Fort Gibson and, in the dead of winter, were encamped on the west side of the Grand River in a low wet swamp within two or three miles of their own boundary.[145] The pretext for their detention was that the government could not protect them far from the fort. Within sight of home,[146] precariously sustained by what was, in popular ignorance dubbed charity, they yet had the mortification of knowing that their country was being denuded of its cattle and that very cattle sold by contractors to the government for refugee consumption. Military authorities regarded the cattle as contraband, not so the Indians.[147] It was their opinion that all property left in the Creek country ought rightfully to belong to that part of the Nation that had remained loyal.[148]

[143] *Cong. Globe*, 38th cong., 2nd. sess., p. 1300.

[144] January 30, 1865, Coffin forwarded to Dole a letter from Agent Harlan (O.I.A., General Files, *Southern Superintendency*, C 1197 of 1865) loudly protesting against the policy of congregating the refugees within the Cherokee country where they were not and could not be, in the very nature of things, safer than in their own or so well provided for.

[145] Ok-ta-hasas Harjo to Dole, January 11, 1865, O.I.A., General Files, *Creek*, 1860-1869.

[146] Just after this complaint was made, Chief Sands and some of his people crossed the Verdigris River into their own country and there started a sort of colony, the "further bound" of which was the Tallahassee Mission (Presbyterian), some twelve miles distant, where Phillips stationed a military outpost. His command had by that time been reduced to Indians alone (Phillips to Dole, February 27, 1865, O.I.A., Land Files, *Creek*, Box 45). Phillips solicited seed corn for their use (Dole to Coffin, March 24, 1865, *ibid., Letter Book*, no. 76, p. 469), probably some of that that the Indian Office expected to purchase at twelve dollars a bushel (*Cong. Globe*, 38th cong., 2nd. sess., p. 1300).

[147] See Creek petition transmitted by Ross to Lincoln, February 15, 1865, O.I.A., General Files, *Southern Superintendency*.

[148] Ok-ta-hasas Harjo to Dole, January 11, 1865, *op. cit.*

III. CATTLE-DRIVING IN THE INDIAN COUNTRY

Much of the dissatisfaction existing among the restored refugees was attributable to cattle-stealing which, since 1862,[149] had become a regular frontier industry, participated in by civilians, more or less respectable, and by soldiery. Viewed in its proper light as a gross infringement upon the property rights of the Indians, it represented practices altogether criminal, incompatible with ever so loose an interpretation of treaty guarantees, yet tacitly condoned and, at times, even connived at and shared in by agents of the United States government. By 1865, it had reached such scandalous proportions that right-thinking people took alarm for well might its longer continuance prove inimical to the future maintenance of law and order. To sane and sober private citizens north of the line, as to certain army leaders south, it began to seem incredible that the government dared to put itself in the position of one compounding a felony.

In ante-bellum days, Indian Territory had been well-stocked. The individual slaveholding tribes, without exception, were rich in cattle, swine, and ponies; but particularly so in cattle. The passing of southern troops across their domain had offered the first occasion for spoliation, the hog-pens being pretty generally plundered.[150] It was the fortune of war, the price that

---

[149] Blunt to Harlan, May 16, 1866, I. D. Files, Bundle, no. 56.

[150] Carruth and Martin to Coffin, July 25, 1862, Commissioner of Indian Affairs, *Report*, 1862, p. 160.

had to be paid by a helpless people for strategic position and the Indians, although they felt their losses keenly, accepted them stoically. Their flourishing bacon trade soon showed diminishing returns and, finally dwindled almost to nothing. Then came the time when, after a period of hesitancy, the Cherokees had joined forces with the Confederacy. The whole of Indian Territory was thenceforth virtually in the hands of the South and the material resources of the region at its disposal. In consequence, Indian live-stock was regularly requisitioned. Not only the geographical position but the grain and the stock and the countless other needful things that the Indian country abounded in made the securing of it desirable and the alienation of it unthinkable. It was not to be marvelled at, therefore, that the resources when once made available, in virtue of the alliance, were immediately drawn upon to the fullest possible extent. The Indians acquiesced. It was still the fortune of war.

The Federal troops reached Tahlequah, July 1862. After a duration of about ten months all told, the Cherokee alliance with the South was, so far as the Principal Chief and the full bloods were concerned, at an end, notwithstanding that the treaty was not at once abrogated [151] and that the Ridge faction, led by Stand Watie and his nephew, E. C. Boudinot, continued loyal to its promises. Divided interests and divided councils worked as always great havoc. The Cherokee country became the legitimate prey of both armies, Cherokee cattle the victims of constant marauding.[152] The freed

[151] The treaty was abrogated officially, February, 1863, *ibid.*, 1863, p. 227.
[152] " . . . The rebel army, bushwhackers, and guerillas are not the worst enemies the Indians have. While the rebels, bushwhackers, and guerillas have taken horses, cattle, hogs, corn, and other crops – all they wanted – white men, loyal, or pretending to be so, have taken

blacks had a share, too, in the general robbery. They were reported by the Federals as pillaging "indiscriminately, as well from the Union Indians as from the rebels." [153] Beyond the Arkansas lay the country of the Choctaws and Chickasaws, allies of the South. Their property the Federals regarded as legally contraband; but even if so it ought not to have been subject, as it regularly was, to individual reprisal. [154] The private citizen acted as if he had as good a right to it as the government.

For the seizing of the live-stock, white men employed irresponsible parties, usually Indians, [155] the

five times as much, and all kinds of stock has been driven north and west, and sold . . . " (*ibid.*, 1864, p. 309).

[153] Carruth and Martin to Furnas, July 25, 1862, *ibid.*, 1862, p. 161.

[154] (a) " . . . This I consider very decidedly less objectionable than when they were taking them from a country comparatively loyal. And as all my efforts and those of the military authorities have utterly failed to stop, or even check the traffic, I have, on consultation with General Curtis, adopted the policy of granting permits to a few respectable and responsible men to purchase cattle of the Indians, under all the restrictions and liabilities enforced by the United States laws regulating trade and intercourse with the Indian tribes, and requiring them, in addition thereto, to take bills of sale of the stock purchased . . . " (Coffin to Dole, September 24, 1864, *ibid.*, 1864, p. 306).

(b) " . . . The contraband portion of these cattle belong either to the loyal Indians of the respective Territories, or to the general government, and certainly no one individual has a permanent right over another to take them and convert them to his own private use, and any discrimination in that way, by raising ambition in others, I think is calculated only to make matters worse . . . " (Gookins to Coffin, October 20, 1864, *ibid.*, p. 320).

[155] Among the Indians employed were Shawnees, Kickapoos and others [Carruth to Coffin, September 6, 1863, Commissioner of Indian Affairs, *Report*, 1863, p. 186.] besides the Leased District tribes. The Shawnees involved were presumably the so-called *Absentees*, who were the Missouri as distinguished from the Ohio Shawnees. It was mainly with the latter that the Manypenny treaty of 1854 (Kappler, vol. ii, pp. 614-618) had been made (Senate Doc., no. 269, 59th cong., 2nd. sess., serial no. 5072), notwithstanding that the former had had the prior and the better title to the Kansas lands coveted and ceded (Abel, *Indian Reservations in Kansas*, pp. 7, 22).

less-civilized of the Leased District,[156] forsooth, or

The Absentee Shawnees had wandered southward and, failing to return within the time most unfairly set by the treaty, had been held, by presidential proclamation in 1863, deprived of their title. Naturally, legal procedure of the sort was incomprehensible to them and they were now in defiant mood. The Kickapoos were similarly in the position of an aggrieved party. Their troubles antedated the outbreak of the war, some of them being due to the fact that they had preferred to have established among them the Methodist Episcopal Church South and had had their wishes thwarted by Walter Lowrie, the indefatigible agent of the Presbyterian Board of Foreign Missions (O.I.A., *Schools*, B 64 of 1859; B 150 of 1860; R 1013 of 1860; S 258 of 1860). In 1862, Agent Charles B. Keith had negotiated with them a treaty of cession and of contemplated removal to the country south of Kansas. It was charged that he had used coercive means and had worked in the interests of the Atchison and Pike's Peak Railway Company. He was succeeded by Abram Bennett as agent and meanwhile the treaty was held up. Many parties had solicited the suspension of its execution (Benj. F. Loan to Dole, March 29, 1864, O.I.A., General Files, *Kickapoo*, 1855-1865) and W. W. Guthrie, Attorney-General of Kansas and a director of "Jeff. Thompson's old Rail Road Co." reorganized, had journeyed to Washington to secure its annulment. He was in the pay of citizens of St. Joseph, Missouri and of the northern tier of Kansas counties and was opposed by Congressman S. C. Pomeroy (*ibid.*, P 64 of 1863). At the time of the Kickapoo emigration from Indiana, some of the tribe separated from the main band and went on beyond the thirty-seventh parallel (Edward Wolcott to Dole, December 15, 1864, *ibid.*, *Kickapoo*, 1855-1865, W 748). Those radically averse to the Keith treaty joined forces with them (*ibid.*; Annual Report of Superintendent Wm. M. Albin, October 1, 1864, O.I.A., Land Files, *Central Superintendency*, 1852-1869, Box 10, A 865). The malcontents were estimated at fully one-half of the tribe. A small group, as anxious to get away from the Kansans as the Kansans were to get rid of them, prepared to start off with the untrustworthy Keith, in the late spring of 1864, to select a new home (Loan to Dole, March 29, 1864). These or other hapless wanderers were soon accused of "being engaged with other Indians in their murderous raids in western Kansas. . ." (Wolcott to Dole, August 20, 1864, O.I.A., General Files, *Kickapoo*, 1855-1865, W 603; Bennett to Albin, September 20, 1864, Commissioner of Indian Affairs, *Report*, 1864, p. 373). The charge was quite unfounded; but there was some reason to think that an effort was being made "to involve all the Indian tribes in Kansas in a war with the Government." (Wolcott to Dole, August 20, 1864).

[156] The Reserve Indians seem to have been early engaged in the traffic; but Agent Carruth, by the fall of 1863, thought he had influenced them against it (Commissioner of Indian Affairs, *Report*, 1863, p. 186). The death of Agent Carruth and the delay of his successor, Milo Gookins, in taking office (*ibid.*, 1864, p. 319) apparently caused their dispersion and, to some extent, their resumption of pernicious practices.

wandering Kickapoos,[157] Shawnees, and Delawares, none of whom had any compunctions in the matter but treated it as sport and as a gainful occupation. Most of them had no property of their own to lose, being homeless, and some had a grievance of long-standing against the Choctaws and Chickasaws. Some of the stock was driven north into Kansas [158] and there disposed of; some, the army applied to its own needs;[159] but by far the largest portion went into the hands of contractors, who sold it to the government for the use of the refugees [160] and at a most exorbitant figure. Profiteering on so enormous a scale and conducted with such shameless audacity had surely never before been known in that locality or anywhere on the frontier. After a time the pillagers grew bolder and laid violent hands upon the stock of the loyal Cherokees and Creeks.[161] To capture the Creek stock undisturbed was

---

[157] The Kickapoos engaged themselves in the nefarious business very early. In the summer of 1862, they were reported as bringing in at one time about a thousand head of horses and ponies, which the Creeks claimed were stolen (*Daily Conservative*, June 19, 1862, quoted from the *Fort Scott Bulletin*).

[158] Commissioner of Indian Affairs, *Report*, 1864, pp. 309, 312.

[159] The army was accused of wastefulness and utilized the butchered cattle very much as white hunters utilized the buffalo. Travellers record that the prairies were sometimes strewn with the carcasses of buffalo slaughtered just for sport, the more dainty morsels like the tongue of the cow having been the only portions used. In 1863, Agent Proctor reported on the army use of cattle thus:

"Cattle are yet abundant in the nation, although the consumption of the army has been enormous as well as wasteful. I have known a small party of our scouts to shoot down a large fat ox *for a few slices of steak*, and leave the rest for the wolves . . . " (*ibid.*, 1863, p. 224).

[160] In making his estimates for the subsistence of the refugees, Coffin had counted upon the Indians using their own meat (*ibid.*, 1864, p. 323).

[161] *Ibid.*, 1863, pp. 186, 197; 1864, p. 316. The following letters illustrate the despoiling of the Creeks as reported by agents to the Commissioner of Indian Affairs:

(a) "About the 16th ult. Major Colman and myself, together with

not a difficult undertaking since the Creeks, removed
from Kansas, had not been suffered to go to their own
homes to look after their possessions. Fully aware that
they were being sold at the very highest of prices their
very own cattle, they were yet obliged to linger in the
Cherokee country, the pretext of their guardian being
that in no other way could they be protected. Their
indignation, their resentment, and their consciousness
of intolerable wrong can easily be imagined.

From time to time, through the years just passed,
complaints, made their way to Washington and, be-

---

a large number of our Indians, started for Humboldt, Kansas, the
headquarters of the Military in southwestern Kansas, to recover, if
possible, some cattle belonging to the Southern Refugee Indians, which
we had understood were at that place.

"We found, on reaching there, that a large amount of cattle, variously estimated from five hundred to a thousand head, had been
driven from the Indian Country by irresponsible persons, the greater
portion of which, it was thought, had fallen into the hands of speculators. Major Colman and myself succeeded in recovering one
hundred and thirteen head of cattle at that place which we turned
over to our Indians, the owners . . . " (Cutler to Dole, June 30,
1863, O.I.A., General Files, *Southern Superintendency*, 1863-1864,
C 360).

(b) "Hearing that a large number of cattle belonging to the
Southern Refugee Indians had been brought from the Indian Territory to southern Kansas, by irresponsible parties, claiming them as
Sesech cattle, a portion of these cattle was seized by the military
authorities at Humboldt, Kansas. Major Cutler and myself with a
portion of the Indians under our charge went to Humboldt where we
called on Captain Doudna Commandant of the Post and filed a
descriptive list of the cattle claimed by our Indians. We then in
company with Captain Doudna took the Indians to the herd to examine
the cattle. They selected one hundred and thirteen head, all of which
was branded with the brand of the respective claimants. We then
turned them over to the Indians. They drove them to this place,
[Sac and Fox Agency] where they herded them a few days and then
sold them, each owner selling his cattle or retaining them for milch
cows, at his option. We heard of another drove of the same description of cattle going north. We followed them to Clinton and found
a few head belonging to the Creek Indians. The owner of the drove
paid them for their cattle." (Coleman to Dole, July 12, 1863, *ibid.*).

ginning with 1864, were of so serious a character that they could no longer be safely ignored. Army men, although one-time offenders themselves and still so on occasion, professed to be horrified at the extent of the illicit traffic. Their sensitiveness may, in the original instance, have been kindled by personal antipathy to certain contractors who had encroached upon the preserves of the army sutlers; but their moral sense developed with their honest appreciation of the righteousness of the cause which they had espoused. They impugned the motives of government officials of all ranks; they implicated particular persons of high position in a general charge of wrong-doing, while most of their own offences they were able satisfactorily to account for.

The autumn of 1864 found things in a bad way in the Indian country. The backwardness of the spring, the summer drought, swarms of grasshoppers, chinchbugs and innumerable other insect pests had all affected the Kansas crops [162] upon which those entrusted with the care of the refugees had expected to place their chief reliance. The Red River expedition, conducted by Generals Banks and Frederick Steele, had ended in egregious disaster. Its failure had dealt a terrific blow to refugee restoration under Federal auspices.[163] Furthermore, it had obviously prevented a rather general stampede of secessionist Indians from the Confederate ranks.[164] On the eve of its being undertaken, they were about to desert in a body; for they were disgusted with and greatly affronted by the treatment that had been accorded them and were not only dubious but actually

[162] Commissioner of Indian Affairs, *Report*, 1864, pp. 312, 348, 354, 386.
[163] — *Ibid.*, p. 314.
[164] — *Ibid.*, p. 313.

despairing of the eventuality of a Southern victory. They staked their dice on one last throw and the almost undreamed-of success justified an entire change in their plans. Their spirits were buoyed up anew. Not surprising, is it, that Colonel Phillips thought them – they were chiefly Choctaws and Chickasaws – absolutely unreliable and that he, in consequence of their fluctuating tendencies and their flouting of his friendly advances, grew vindictive and advised [165] against making any terms with them until they had been made to rue their own original defection? As already narrated, he vehemently objected to a favorable reception of the New Hope conventionists; for he was not willing, as was the just and magnanimous president, whose amnesty proclamation he had been industriously circulating,[166] to build a new structure upon the basis of a loyal minority.[167] In the punishment to be meted out betimes to the Red River tribes he, a Kansan by adoption, saw the possibility of relief for Kansas, relief, that is, from her Indian encumbrance. The forfeited and confiscated Choctaw and Chickasaw lands would afford excellent accommodation for the tribes whose knell as property-holders in the region consecrated to freedom had been sounded when the Kansas-Nebraska Bill with

---

[165] Phillips to Dole, March 22, 1864, *ibid.*, p. 328.

[166] On Phillips' own confession, it is known that he circulated the proclamation with political intent among the recalcitrant Choctaws and Chickasaws. He hoped it would "help to demoralize them, and prevent them from organizing as large a force of Indians against me as they otherwise would." (*idem.*)

[167] This is, of course, generally conceded to have been President Lincoln's policy. For an exposition of it, see McCarthy, *Lincoln's Plan of Reconstruction*, p. 193; Rhodes, *History of the United States*, vol. v, pp. 55-56; Nicolay and Hay, *Complete Works of Abraham Lincoln*, vol. ii, pp. 672-675; Richardson, vol. vi, pp. 189-191. Had the tragedy of April Fourteenth, 1865 never occurred it is highly improbable that Harlan and Cooley would have been permitted to consummate their iniquitous designs against the misguided Indians.

what a noted Kansan has so pertinently called its "glittering generalities" [168] had passed to its enactment. A successful termination to the Red River expedition would have meant a return of peace and security to the whole Indian Territory.[169] The refugees would then have ceased to fret at their inchoate restoration. As it was, they remembered only too well that their unalleviated sufferings [170] of the previous winter bade fair to be repeated and they dreaded that repetition. Their grain fields and their vegetable gardens were at that very moment being despoiled. Under the circumstances, what of hope and trust had they to build upon? They murmured at the miserable incompleteness of their restoration and they chafed under the restraints that reduced them to penury. In Kansas, the tribes chafed likewise. Farm products were exceedingly scarce and their regular buffalo hunt had, because of the hostilities of the tribes of the plains, been peremptorily forbidden.[171] It was General Curtis' intention to start a vigorous campaign against the Kiowas and raiders in complicity with them and he wanted, so he affirmed, to run no risks of confounding friends with foes, hence his order that peaceful hunters should stay at home, hungry though they might be, on their barren reservations. Their absolute dependence upon the hunt

[168] Gleed, Charles S., *The Kansas Memorial*, p. 143.

[169] *Cong. Globe*, 38th cong., 2nd sess., p. 1299. For what it might have meant to the whole Confederacy, see Taylor, *Destruction and Reconstruction*, p. 189. Taylor, p. 196, says, "The Red River campaign of 1864 was the last Federal campaign undertaken for political objects, or intrusted to political generals."

[170] For an account of the circumstances conditioning those sufferings see Smith to Coffin, July 16, 1863, Commissioner of Indian Affairs, *Report*, 1863, pp. 211-213; Gookins to Coffin, October 17, 1863, *ibid.*, p. 222; Harlan to Coffin, September 30, 1864, *ibid.*, 1864, pp. 309-311.

[171] Farnsworth to Dole, August 11, 1864, O.I.A., General Files, *Kansas, 1863-1868*, F 158; Commissioner of Indian Affairs, *Report*, 1864, p. 369.

for a livelihood he chose to ignore. Their sufferings were a matter of indifference to him. Against the shortsightedness and arbitrariness of his order the Indian Office protested, but in vain.[172] Military expediency won the day but military effectiveness did not rid the country of the raiders.

While Agent Carruth was yet alive and caring for the Wichitas and other Leased District Indians, the accusation was first made that they were serving as "go-betweens," or middle-men, in the cattle-stealing enterprise. Late in July, 1864, Milo Gookins succeeded to the post made vacant by Carruth's decease, a circumstance rather fortunate, in a way, inasmuch as Gookins professed to be peculiarly competent to lift a goodly share of the responsibility for cattle-driving from Indian shoulders. Previous to his selection as Wichita agent, he had been on duty, under appointment from the Indian office, with the Army of the Frontier. At Fort Gibson he was a special agent and in a position to make correct and interesting observations of men and events. To a considerable degree he undoubtedly merited the confidence reposed in him; but he early developed the traditional animus of the civilian against the military chief and consequently a strong bias seems always to have vitiated most of his findings for the Indian service.

The cattle-driving business of the Indian country became the subject of official inquiry in the spring of 1864 and continued so at intervals thereafter for a period of several years. It would seem that it was mainly upon the complaint of Milo Gookins [173] that the origi-

[172] Dole to Usher, August 19, 1864, *ibid.*, pp. 369-370.

[173] Others had undoubtedly made complaints also; for, on February 16, 1864, Usher transmitted to Stanton copies of communications from Agent Justin Harlan "in relation to the conduct of the military officials in the

nal inquiry was started and he made his complaint [174] while he was still occupying his post of observation. Early in February, Colonel Phillips with detachments of the Indian Brigade had started out upon his expedition in the direction of Red River, the expedition upon which he carried President Lincoln's amnesty proclamation and made his appraisement of the existing Indian disposition. On the return march, his force separated and each contingent pursued a different route. That under Major Foreman passed through a section of the Creek country that had been previously traversed and gathered up as it went between four and five hundred head of stray Indian cattle, from which, upon the arrival at Fort Gibson, the brigade quartermaster, Captain Chester Thomas, who was making up an ox-team for Fort Scott, selected about eighty head. Euchees, possibly Creeks, of the First Indian Home Guards being privileged to watch the proceedings, recognized the cattle as their own and laid claim accordingly. The evidence consisted of private brands and so they had no great difficulty in establishing, to the satisfaction of the bystanders, their ownership. Thomas issued vouchers in acknowledgment of government indebtedness; but, on one pretext or another, as Gookins in *ex parte* fashion reported it, delayed and ultimately refused payment. As a matter of fact, he had good ground for his refusal and was supported in it by both Foreman and Phillips; for he had discovered that Perry Fuller, the contractor, was figuring as Indian counsel, a self-constituted Indian claim agent,

region of country referred to." (A.G.O., *Old Files Section*, B 1013, V.S., 1863, 2 of 15). Usher claimed that President Lincoln and he knew Agent Harlan personally and could vouch for his intelligence and reliability.

[174] Letter to Dole, March 8, 1864, O.I.A., General Files, *Southern Superintendency*, 1863-1864, G 121; *Letter Book*, no. 13, p. 351.

and had induced his unsuspecting clients to make over to him one-half of the requisitioned and identified cattle.[175]   Large fees of the sort become scandalous when public attention is called to them; but they have ever been but a mere phase, an incident only, of the white man's exploitation of his red brother.

The charges against Perry were the prelude of many to follow; but, in this instance, they were lodged only when the government took cognizance of Gookins' worse than innuendoes against army officers. Reported in regular sequence to Dole, to Usher, and to Stanton, those innuendoes, along with others from like sources and of like character, were finally referred to General Curtis for investigation and report.[176]   The die had been cast.

---

[175] Chester Thomas, Captain and A.G.M., U.S. Vols., to Captain M. H. Insley, Chief Q.M., Dept. of Kansas, dated Ft. Leavenworth, May 7, 1864.

[176] The burden of Curtis' report was to the effect "that the information, communicated to your (Usher's) Department, was erroneous, and the charges made against the officers of the United States Army entirely unfounded." (Stanton to Usher, May 26, 1864). Although Phillips was undoubtedly exculpated along with the rest, this fact is worthy of insertion here: In August, 1865, Daniel Childress, a Creek, made affidavit that he was detailed in February and March of 1864 by Colonel Phillips to drive cattle from the Indian country to Iola, Kansas (General Files, *Southern Superintendency*).

It was about the time that this investigation was going on that Phillips, disgusted with the whole course of events, resolved to retire from the service. His resignation was refused acceptance, however. Note the following letter:

"I have the honor to acknowledge the receipt of your endorsement of the 28th ultimo, referring for acceptance the resignation of Col⁰. W. A. Phillips, 3d Indian Regiment.

"In reply, I am directed to inform you that the resignation was referred to Major Genˡ Curtis, U.S. Vols., for his recommendation, who returns the same with the following endorsement:

'Col⁰. Phillips is a good officer and I think he ought to remain in his present Command. I cannot approve of his resignation'."

(A.A.G. to S. C. Pomeroy, April 26, 1864, A.G.O., Old Files Section, *Personal Papers of W. A. Phillips*).

Not until June 10, 1865 was Colonel Phillips officially discharged (*ibid.*).

The cattle stealing was a form of the very general evil of peculation and most unfortunately there stood insuperable obstacles in the way of its eradication. The chief of them was the existence of a political force behind the cattle thieves, a political force that radiated from Kansas and that had its stronghold in the army, in the Indian Office, and in the United States Senate. There were two sets of contractors and each had its own supporters in the public service. The set that Colonel Phillips was to take such exception to, the McDonald [177] and Fuller firm, was the set that Blunt, when once restored to his old command, February twenty-seventh, had immediately endorsed and there is much reason to believe as did his detractors that it was its special interests that he was seeking to subserve when he issued, on April sixteenth, just prior to his own removal from Fort Smith back to Fort Leavenworth, the notorious military order, No. 7, notorious because of the opprobrium which the objections of influential Indians and of Phillips' adherents called down upon it. The order [178] restricted the sale of Indian produce and brought within military jurisdiction emanating from Fort Smith the absolute disposal of Indian cattle. Among the Indian objectors were prominent men like John Ross [179] and Smith Christie,[180] the former assuredly enough of a patriot to make the insinuation that he

---

[177] McDonald was a brother of Alexander McDonald, who was United States senator from Arkansas, 1868-1871.

[178] The great injustice of the order, as viewed by its opponents, is best set forth in a letter from W. L. G. Miller, a Cherokee by adoption, to Usher, April 23, 1864 (O.I.A., General Files, *Southern Superintendency*, 1863-1864, M 271; I. D., *Register of Letters Received*, no. 4, p. 373). A copy of the order is filed with it in the Indian Office. The letter is too long for insertion here. It was referred to the Commissioner of Indian Affairs, May 17, 1864.

[179] John Ross and Evan Jones to Usher, July 29, 1864, I. D. Files,

protested only because he had investments in the Ross sutler's store, against which Blunt's order discriminated, seem at this distance of time utterly absurd. Despite the protests the order continued in force long after Blunt's authority had been removed. General Thayer, who had no reason to approve of its author, he being the one who had given Thayer what Curtis described as a "terrible castigation",[181] pronounced in its favor,[182] extolling its merits. Finally, early in August, opposition to it took a new form and resolutions [183] purporting to have been unanimously adopted by the "Pin League" were given wide circulation through the newspapers. The rift in the lute was at last apparent; for they attempted no concealment of the differences existing between Blunt and Phillips and openly charged the former with having been guilty of class legislation. The acting Cherokee agent, A. G. Proctor,[184] inquired of Chief Downing as to their genuineness

Bundle, no. 52. See also letter from the Secretary of the Interior to the Secretary of War, August 16, 1864.

[180] Dana to Usher, September 2, 1864, O.I.D., General Files, *Southern Superintendency*, 1863-1864.

[181] Curtis to Blunt, April 17, 1864, *Official Records*, vol. xxxiv, part iii, p. 199.

[182] Report of John M. Thayer, dated Fort Smith, August 10, 1864. Blunt's restrictive order covered also certain salines within the Cherokee country. The Interior Department, June 15, 1864, urged its modification out of deference to Indian wishes; but both Thayer and Halleck reported adversely (O.I.A., General Files, *Cherokee*, 1859-1865, W 615). Smith Christie had protested earnestly against the salines being taken possession of by the military authorities for the uses of the army. For criticism of Blunt's order, other than Indian, see *Official Records*, vol. xxxiv, part 3, p. 213.

[183] The resolutions, dated Fort Gibson, August 9, 1864, are on file in the Indian Office both in manuscript form and as printed in the newspapers. They represent a strong endorsement of Phillips and an equally strong denunciation of Blunt and the contractors. (O.I.A., *Southern Superintendency*).

[184] On July 11, 1864, Coffin wrote to Dole, asking his approval of the appointment of A. G. Proctor of Emporia, Kansas as Special Agent to

and received information that confirmed his own suspicions;[185] for presumably no one belonging to the Nation knew anything about them. Proctor's own predilections stood revealed when this most re-assuring news he communicated without semblance of delay to McDonald and Fuller.[186]

Throughout the summer and autumn of 1864 recrimination and counter-recrimination remained the order of the day. Almost coincident with the issuance of the "Pin League" resolutions, Phillips personally redoubled his efforts towards the suppression of the McDonald-Fuller influence. August second he addressed Usher, strongly urging the expulsion from the Indian country of a certain Henry McKee, an agent of the firm.[187] The firm itself he would have ordered out also and its license cancelled on account of gross abuse of privilege and the betrayal of public trust. He enlisted the services of General Thomas Ewing to the same end and Ewing informed Dole that Phillips ought by all means to be supported in his endeavors "to expose and put down the robbers of the Indians."[188] Instead of support, however, he had received, August fifth, an order to turn over his command to Wattles and

assist Harlan, Cox having resigned (*ibid., Cherokee*, C 952 of 1864). John T. Cox was also a Kansan, from Coffey County. The specific reason for his resignation is not divulged; but, in September, 1864, he was presiding as chairman of the Kansas State Republican Convention, the convention at which Crawford was nominated for governor and Sidney Clark for congressman (Crawford, *Kansas in the Sixties*, p. 200). Proctor resigned as Special Agent in September and Coffin then asked for the approval of the appointment of W. A. Harlan (O.I.A., *Cherokee*, C 1044 of 1864); but Proctor was still officiating late in the autumn, but as acting agent only.

[185] Lewis Downing, Acting Principal Chief, to Proctor, October 28, 1864 (*ibid., Southern Superintendency*).

[186] Proctor to McDonald & Fuller, November 30, 1864, *ibid.*

[187] Phillips to Usher, August 2, 1864, I. D. Files, Bundle, no. 52; *Register of Letters Received*, "Indians," no. 4, p. 425.

[188] Ewing to Dole, dated Headquarters, St. Louis District, September 1, 1864 (O.I.A., Land Files, *Southern Superintendency*, 1855-1870, I 711).

to report himself at Fort Smith. Phillips believed the
contractors to be at the bottom of even that action.[189]
Energetic in their own interests they obviously were.
Their devotion to their friend, Blunt, instigated an attack upon General Steele. They adjudged it wrong to
detach Indian Territory from Kansas and they begged
that Blunt might be put in command at Fort Gibson.
His presence alone would be worth two thousand
men.[190] There were Indians, on the other hand, who
had had enough of Blunt and wanted no more of him.

Opposing Phillips and exerting all possible influence in behalf of the contractors were the field employees of the Indian Office and yet nobody knew better than they that abuses existed and that the cattle-
thieving business was flourishing unchecked. It was in
all parts the same. The Confederates [191] had it to contend with as had the Federals and yet everywhere were
the indigents [192] and the suffering refugees. The whole
situation was deplorable.

---

[189] Phillips to Ewing, August 17, 1864, *ibid.*

[190] Perry Fuller to Usher, September 22, 1864 (*ibid., Southern Superintendency*, 1863-1864). Fuller accused Steele of inefficiency and his
troops of demoralization. The *National Union*, October 15, 1864 had this
to say in eulogy of Steele,

"There is no officer in the army who is more free from the breath
of suspicion in regard to speculations or using his position as a
means of acquiring wealth . . . "

[191] "Major Gen¹ Maxey directs me to write to you in relation to
captured mules & now being carried to Texas. On the march from Perry-
ville to this point many of the men of Gano's Brigade left the command
without permission and are said to have driven off mules, branded U.S. and
other brands placed on sutlers' mules captured from the enemy at Cabin
Creek. In some instances it is reported that the brands had been obliterated
by burning or cutting the hair. Of course this property will be claimed by
the Government and belong to this District . . . " (Portlock to Inspector-general, Bonham, Oct. 13, 1864, A.G.O., *Confederate Archives*, chap.
2, no. 259, no. 81, p. 64).

[192] P. P. Pitchlynn to Maxey, December 29, 1864 (*Official Records*, vol.
liii, supplement, p. 1035; Maxey to Boggs, December 31, 1864, *ibid*, p. 1034).

In the course of time, Phillips, still without command, filed formal charges against the contractors and, in a document, dated November 30, 1864, they attempted an answer in rebuttal.[193] The case hung fire, so to speak, all through the winter; but Phillips went on amassing his evidence while Coffin and other government agents made a feint of rooting out the illicit traffic in Indian cattle.[194]

With the beginning of 1865, a strong reaction against the evildoers set in. Phillips was again in control at Gibson[195] and for once the commander there and at Fort Smith were on a co-operative basis. Simultaneously almost they issued restrictions[196] upon trade

[193] O.I.A., General Files, *Southern Superintendency*, 1865, M 485.

[194] Coffin to Dole, September 12, 1864 (*ibid.*). Coffin averred that he had had, since May 1, 1864, a detective at work ferreting out information, which he would report upon later. The detective was apparently George A. Reynolds (Coffin to Dole, April 14, 1865, *ibid.*, C 1328). Coffin secured the co-operation of General Curtis. On this same general subject, see Office Letter of September 5, 1864.

[195] Concerning his return to command, Phillips had this to say, when writing to General Herron, January 16, 1865 (*Official Records*, vol. xlviii, part i, pp. 542-543).

> ". . . The order to proceed to Wahington I did not receive, but late one night 1 was summoned to General Thayer's headquarters and received orders to resume command of the Indian Brigade. They were reticent, and I sought to know no more than they thought proper to communicate. I assumed command on the 29th ultimo . . . "

The Indians had begged for his restoration. See petition of the successor of Opoeth-le-yo-ho-la, dated December 23, 1864. (O.I.A., *Southern Superintendency*, 1865). It was transmitted by John Ross to President Lincoln, February 15, 1865.

[196] The restrictions issued by Phillips were comprehended in General Orders, no. 4, dated from Fort Gibson, January 14, 1865. They are to be found in I. D. Files, Bundle, no. 53, and in *Official Records*, vol. xlviii, part i, pp. 516-519. In reporting upon his order to General Canby, February 16, 1865, Phillips said, " . . . I, however, desired to secure through you sufficient protection from the department above to stop the nefarious system which appears to have a thorough organization in the State of Kansas . . . The case of the Indian Nation is peculiar. The Secretary of the Treasury decided that 'it was not a State in rebellion,' and consequently sends no Treasury agents here. The question as to what is con-

operations. Rigorously they enforced a rule of the Treasury Department "allowing only three thousand dollars to be introduced per month inside of the line of Rebel States," and against that action McDonald and Fuller filed their protest [197] Phillips soon renewed his charges against them,[198] definitely this time implicating agents of the Indian Office whom he accused of being in collusion with the contractors in their "nefarious transactions." February third, Phillips added to his charges by informing the Secretary of the Interior that an effort was about to be made to get "friends of the *corrupt money* corporation put in as Indian agents."[199] Perry Fuller, for instance, had already come forward as a candidate for the Creek agency. By this time Phillips had incontrovertible evidence to sub-

traband has been held in abeyance, as I understand it. The order was therefore framed to meet the exigencies of the case . . . "

[197] McDonald & Fuller to Usher, January 12, 1865 [I. D. Files, Bundle, no. 53 (January to May, 1865)]; *ibid.*, (*Register of Letters Received*) "Indians," no. 4, p. 376).

[198] Phillips to Usher, January 17, 1865; same to same, February 4, 1865 (I. D. Files, Bundle, no. 53; *Register of Letters Received*, "Indians," no. 4. Phillips' letter of January 17th bears the Indian Office file-mark, *Southern Superintendency*, P. 309.

[199] Phillips to Usher, February 3, 1865 (I. D. Files, Bundle, no. 53; *Register of Letters Received*, "Indians," no. 4, p. 427). With this letter is filed Lieutenant Houston Benge's report to Phillips, dated February 4, 1865. On February 6th, McDonald and Fuller filed their reply to the charges contained in Phillips's letter of January 17th. The firm name is now given as, McDonald, Fuller, McKee & Co. On the 20th Usher had interrogated them regarding the quantity of goods shipped by them under permits from the Treasury and War departments. They had replied the following day. On the 7th of February, A. B. Eaton, Commissary General of Subsistence, inquired of Usher regarding their contracts (O.I.A., *Southern Superintendency*, E 63; I. D. Files, Bundle, no. 53). February 21, 1865, Dana, Assistant-secretary of war, communicated to Usher the information that General Herron's report relative to their transactions had been transmitted to Congress. On the 23rd, the firm preferred charges against Phillips and requested that a Court of Inquiry be instituted before which they might plead their case. They demanded that Phillips' charges should be ignored entirely unless supported by competent evidence (*ibid.*).

stantiate his every indictment; for Lieutenant Houston Benge, Provost Marshal, especially authorized under General Order, No. 4, had made some investigations with astonishing results.

The accused Indian agents rallied to their own defense and to defence of their superior officer, Superintendent Coffin;[200] but his had been conduct not so easy of exoneration.[201] Beef and corn contracts [202] were

[200] Cutler to Usher, February 9, 1865 (O.I.A., General Files, *Southern Superintendency*, 1865, C 1233; I.D., *Register of Letters Received*, "Indians," no. 4, p. 206) ; Coffin to Dole, May 17, 1865, enclosing reports of Agent Harlan and others (O.I.A., General Files, *Southern Superintendency*). May 27, 1865, Dole reported to Secretary Harlan (*ibid., Report Book*, no. 14, pp. 285-286) testifying to the efficiency and good conduct of Agent H. W. Martin, whom he had known personally and intimately for twenty years. Subsequently, on June 14th, (*ibid.*, p. 317) he recommended, on similar grounds, that Isaac Coleman, Justin Harlan, and Milo Gookins be continued as agents. Charges of dishonesty, involving the contractors, Carney and Stevens, were preferred, July 5, 1866, against Martin (N. P. Chipman to D. N. Cooley, July 5, 1866, *ibid.*, General Files, *Sac and Fox*, 1862-1866, C 318. See also C 361, I 667, M 407, M 409, W 455). Agent Elder seems to have thought that Curtis condoned the stealing of cattle (Elder to Chess, January 12, 1865, *Official Records*, vol. xlviii, part i, p. 872).

[201] The beginning of the next year, Coffin was called upon to render an account of what he had done with hides and tallow of beef cattle, slaughtered for the refugees (Cooley to Coffin, January 8, 1866, O.I.A., *Letter Book*, no. 79, p. 101; Cooley to Harlan, January 17, 1866, *ibid., Report Book*, no. 15, p. 45). Concerning the permits that he had granted, see Coffin to Hamilton, September 22, 1864, *Official Records*, vol. xlviii, part i, pp. 872-873; Phillips to Pope, February 16, 1865, *ibid.*, pp. 873-874; Joel Moody to Phillips, August 22, 1864, *ibid.*, p. 873. Additional material in the case against Coffin can be found in the following letters: Harlan to Cooley, January 29, 1866, O.I.A., *Southern Superintendency*, I 59 of 1866; Dole to Coffin, February 2, 1866, *ibid.*, C 45 of 1866; D. R. Anthony to Harlan, February 5, 1866 and Sidney Clarke to Harlan, February 5, 1866, *ibid.*, C 64 of 1866; Henry Smith to Harlan, February 10, 1866, *ibid.*, S 122 of 1866; Coffin to Cooley, February 6, 1866, *ibid.*, C 55 of 1866. In the letter last cited and in an affidavit of February 2, 1866, Coffin endeavored to explain his conduct. He claimed that he had, indeed, disposed of the hides and tallow; but had used the proceeds, over five thousand dollars, in purchasing supplies for refugees [*ibid.*, C 44 of 1866].

[202] Phillips to Herron, January 16, 1865, *op. cit.* Cutler to Coffin, April 16, 1865, Commissioner of Indian Affairs, *Report*, 1865, pp. 274-275.

coupled with the cattle stealing in the list of Phillips'
accusations and Usher intimated a wish for a thorough
overhauling.[203]   It was well he did for other forces
were already at work with a similar end in view.

Beginning with the spring of the last year of the war,
the State of Kansas undertook, on a large scale, to invite immigrants within her borders.[204]   Somewhat in
the fashion of William Penn in old colonial days she
advertised her resources far and wide.   The law and
order party strove for ascendancy.   Governor Crawford took office January ninth and just one week later
legislators from the southwestern part of the state approached him on the matter of the Indian cattle stealing, which must be put a stop to or the settlers already
there would depart.[205]   The legislators solicited Crawford's good offices in making proper representations to
the Federal government regarding the wide range of
the traffic.   Almost coincidently Senator Pomeroy,
February twenty-fifth, introduced a resolution calling
for copies of all licenses that had been issued relative to
trade in the Indian country.[206]   The report on the same
was forthcoming from the Interior Department, March
first,[207] and, on March third, a provision making cattle-

[203] Usher to Dole, February 10, 1865 (O.I.A., General Files, *Southern
Superintendency*).   See also Dole to Coffin, February 14, 1865, Commissioner
of Indian Affairs, *Report*, p. 270.

[204] *Kansas in the Sixties*, pp. 215, 227.

[205] R. H. Abraham and others to Crawford, January 16, 1865 (A.G.O.,
Fort Gibson File Box, 1864-1868; *Official Records*, vol. xlviii, part i, pp.
1133-1134).   For Crawford's account of the cattle-stealing, see *Kansas in
the Sixties*, pp. 204, 208.   There were other disorders that called for prompt
action.   See W. G. Brewer to Curtis, dated Mapleton, January 24, 1865,
regarding "property smuggled out of Missouri and run up the Osage River."
(*Fort Gibson File Box*, 1864-1868).

[206] *Cong. Globe*, 38th cong., 2nd sess., p. 1088.

[207] Dole to Usher, February 28, 1865, I. D. Files, Bundle, no. 53; *Cong.
Globe*, 38th cong., 2nd sess., p. 1219.

stealing a felony punishable by heavy fine or imprisonment or both became law.[208]   A loophole for further abuses was, however, embodied in the selfsame measure since each agent was invested with discretionary power, under regulations of the Interior Department, to sell Indian stock for Indian benefit and was forbidden to interfere with the execution of orders lawfully issued for supplying army needs from the same Indian product.

All this time, although under grave suspicion himself, Coffin had prosecuted his inquiries into the source and extent of the illicit traffic.   He had secured the preceding year the very efficient services of George A. Reynolds and, upon the basis of reports that Reynolds as secret agent made, he offered, in April, new evidence in the case against the army officers.[209]   The Indians meanwhile were growing more and more resentful; for the refugees were, if anything, in a more distressful state than ever, on the very verge of starvation.[210]

Indian Territory had now been included once again in Blunt's command,[211] a circumstance which, in the light of past events, was a bad augury for the cleaning of the Augean stables. In May, Coffin was superseded by Sells, who, having been an employee of the Treasury Department previously,[212] probably had some inside

[208] It was embodied in the concluding sections of the Indian Appropriation bill (13 *United States Statutes at Large*, p. 563).

[209] Coffin to Dole, April 14, 1865 (O.I.A., General Files, *Southern Superintendency*, 1865, C 1328). Reynolds' report was dated Fort Scott, March 20, 1865.

[210] *Official Records*, vol. xlviii, part 2, pp. 117, 136, 177, 295.

[211] Pope notified Blunt, April 7th that he was to include Indian Territory in his command (*ibid.*, p. 46).

[212] Sells had been Third Auditor of the Treasury under Chase (Davis, *Elijah Sells, Annals of Iowa*, 3rd series, vol. ii, p. 522).

knowledge of the corrupt practices obtaining in the southern superintendency. He retained the services of Secret Agent Reynolds [213] and added to them the military furnished by Generals Mitchell and Dodge,[214] who were both untiring in their efforts to destroy the cattle-stealing traffic. Meanwhile Phillips did his best to relieve the necessities of the refugees. He induced them to plant sufficient corn to secure them against starvation [215] and he protected them, to the limits of his ability in the possession of what little remained to them of their live-stock.

With the surrender of Kirby Smith and the Trans-Mississippi Department, the indigent Indians within the late Confederate lines became an additional charge upon the southern superintendency and it taxed the energies of both civil and military authorities, co-operating with each other at last, to prevent further spoliation.[216] Even Blunt,[217] contrary to expectations, set to

[213] Sells to Reynolds, May 30, 1865, O.I.A., General Files, *Southern Superintendency*, 1865, S 681; Sells to Dole, June 7, 1865, *ibid*. Before long Reynolds became agent for the Seminoles.

[214] It was discouraging work and there were times when Dodge at least despaired of accomplishing the great end sought. On one occasion, August 12, 1865, he wrote to Pope that it seemed to him as if "all the rascals in the West are combined to swindle Government." (*Official Records*, vol. xlviii, part ii, p. 1179).

[215] Phillips to General J. J. Reynolds, April 19, 1865, I. D. Files, Bundle, no. 53. On conditions among the refugees in and around Fort Gibson, see Captain J. S. McClintock's report of issues made to them for the month of May (O.I.A., *Southern Superintendency*, M 725); Office letter to McClintock, August 22, 1865; J. J. Reynolds to Harlan, July 15, 1865 (I. D. Files, Bundle, no. 54). Opoethleyoholo's family was among the refugees.

[216] The want of harmony had been very demoralizing and had created conditions perplexing in the extreme. On the relations between the two departments, see *Official Records*, vol. xlviii, part ii, pp. 742, 933-935, 986, 1153, etc. Better things were hoped for when Harlan became Secretary of the Interior. July 27th the new commissioner, D. N. Cooley, sent out a circular letter bespeaking co-operation [O.I.A., *Letter Book*, no. 77, p. 519].

[217] There is much evidence of Blunt's activities. The following indicate

with a will to restrain the lawless who, for so long, had
had things almost entirely their own way. Some special agents were appointed by the Indian Office and
some very necessary changes made in the regular force;
but the work of all was more than supplemented by that
of the provost-marshals,[218] who patrolled the country in

their nature: Blunt to Herman H. Heath, Provost-Marshall, March 9, 1865,
Official Records, vol. xlviii, part i, pp. 1132-1133; Heath to Blunt, March 16,
1865, A.G.O., *Fort Gibson File Box*, 1864-1868. Heath testified that "gangs
of men have banded together on the southwest border (of Kansas) for
illicit trade and perhaps plunder . . . " A lot of cattle had been seized
by one of Blunt's scouts. May 16, 1866, Blunt suggested to Harlan [I. D.
Files, Bundle, no. 56] that a commission should be appointed to investigate
the Indian cattle stealing that had been going on since the Spring of 1862
and notoriously so.

[218] Among the most energetic of the provost-marshals were two deserving
of special mention; viz., Leroy J. Beam, lieutenant, 15th Kansas and assistant
provost-marshal for the District of South Kansas, and Lieutenant George
Williams, provost-marshal for the District of North Kansas. An order
had been issued revoking all passes and permits and apparently the thieves
tried to get away with their ill-gotten gains before it could be executed.
Beam found one man, Samuel Hartsel, in possession of four hundred and
seventy cattle that some Indians had driven out of the Territory (Beam to
Wm. H. Hewett, dated Camp Blair, Eureka, Kansas, March 20, 1865, A.G.O.,
Fort Gibson File Box, 1864-1868). Lieutenant Williams was detailed by
the War Department at the request of the Indian Office to proceed to Kansas
especially "to investigate certain alleged frauds" in the Interior Department.
He employed B. B. Mitchell as a detective (Taylor to Browning, February
6, 1869, O.I.A., *Report Book*, no. 18, p. 151) Mitchell started out the very
day he received Williams' telegram of instructions and according to his
own story he proceeded "to Council Grove, Kansas, for the purpose of
observing the movements of persons engaged in stealing and receiving
Indian cattle. With the same object I subsequently visited the counties
of Shawnee, Morris, Chase, Lyon and Butler.

"After the most careful and thorough investigation I am convinced
that for the present no more cattle are being brought from the Indian
Country to this part of the state. Those who have been engaged in
this business are deterred by the vigor which the Department is showing in putting it down from continuing their operations. From the
same reason many persons who have had contraband and stolen Indian stock in their possession have turned it loose, while others though
still exercising supervision over such animals are unwilling to acknowledge the ownership. I ascertained that there were many small herds
of this character, numbering from ten head to four or five each, on

the interests of law and order.   It was no easy matter to apprehend the offenders, especially when the failure of the Fort Smith Council widened, as it was inevitably bound to do, the breach between the tribal factions.

In October, Superintendent Sells prepared his first annual report [219] and had much to say regarding the cattle-stealing, a regular system as he had found it to be.   It was a system that had two kinds of operators, those who seized the cattle on the original range and those who received them at the border and had charge of their final disposition.   Cattle brokers, Sells called the latter, and it was they who constituted the strength of the system; for their number, social standing and influence [220] were such, " that it was almost fatal to inter-

the Neosho and Cottonwood Rivers . . . " (O.I.A., General Files, *Central Superintendency,* 1863-1868).

Williams also employed Lieutenant James H. Clark as a detective under himself. Clark reported, August 1, 1865, on the way cattle were still being driven from the Indian Territory. Citizens in the vicinity of Humboldt had tried to get him to fail in his duty in following up the stolen herds (*ibid., Southern Superintendency,* 1865, W 1218). In the autumn, under date of October 10, 1865, Williams sent in to Cooley a full report on the result of his investigations (*ibid.*).

H. E. McKee, who, April 20, 1865, had replied to Phillips' charges about the fraudulent corn contracts (McKee to Coffin, April 20, 1865) and again, in August, when Lieutenant-colonel St. Clair was detailed to look into the matter (McKee to St. Clair, August 18, 1865) professed to be highly indignant when stolen herds grazing in the Neosho Valley were assigned to his ownership. He could hardly believe he said "that anybody would dare to drive cattle from Indian Territory on his credit; "for he was a licensed trader. He swore that he had never had any interest whatsoever in cattle (McKee to Sells, dated Fort Gibson, October 16, 1865).

Sells, July 19, 1865, in a report to Cooley, testified also to the herds, unaccounted for, that were held in southern Kansas and he emphasized "the importance of procuring from the Hon. Sec^y of War an order directing Genl Mitchell, Com^dg the Dist. of Kansas, to seize and hold for investigation of title all cattle and ponies, supposed to be Indian stock, and especially a lot of from 300 to 400 head in the possession of Coffin . . . " On this matter, see Report to the Secretary of the Interior, July 20, 1865.

[219] Commissioner of Indian Affairs, *Report,* 1865, pp. 252-ff.

[220] Lane's name was among those connected with the contract frauds.

pose obstacles in the way of their success." It was reckoned that, in the course of the war, fully three hundred thousand head of Indian cattle had been stolen. The vigorous measures that Sells and his coadjutors instituted accomplished much in the discrediting of the traffic and the limiting of its operations; but it was years notwithstanding before it finally disappeared and [221] with it the " Knights of the Brush."

The insinuation against him appeared in the *Chicago Tribune* and he held Phillips responsible for it. George W. Deitzler, one of the contractors with Perry Fuller, was the authority upon which Phillips based his accusation (Speer, *Life of Gen. James H. Lane*, 313-314). McDonald and likewise Fuller testified to Lane's innocence (*Johnson Papers*, vol. 96). The following letter is Fuller's affidavit:

" . . . It gives me pleasure to state that I am the active business partner of the firms of McDonald & Co. & Fuller & Co., principal contractors for furnishing goods and supplies for the Southern Indian Superintendency, and I aver that not only have you never been paid a dollar from either of the firms represented by me or any other person for you or for your benefit but that no proposition or suggestion was ever at any time made to secure to you or for your benefit any sum of money, any share of the profits or any other consideration for any services you have rendered us in your public or private capacity . . . " (Perry Fuller to Gen. James H. Lane, dated Washington City, D.C., May 28, 1866, *Johnson Papers*, vol. 96).

Preston B. Plumb had presumably some interest in cattle driving. It was while he was lieutenant in the Eleventh Kansas Infantry. No direct charge against him has been substantiated; but a man, who lived a few years ago and for a short time only in Elkton, Maryland, claimed that, under orders from the young lieutenant, he, personally, drove cattle up from the Indian country into Kansas.

[221] The amount of material on the subject is enormous. The following citations illustrate the various sources from which it can be obtained:

J. B. Luce to Cooley, August 11, 1865, O.I.A., General Files, *Choctaw*, 1859-1866, L 762; Letters from Major Morrow, Fort Clark, Texas, *ibid.*, *Central Superintendency*, W 525 of 1872; Enoch Hoag to J. T. Gibson, July 5, 1870. *ibid.*, *District of Nebraska Letter Book*, vol. i, pp. 254-255; Documents transmitted by Hancock, May 27, 1867, *ibid.*, *Miscellaneous Files*; Henry J. Hunt to John Levering, October 9, 1865, *ibid.*, General Files, *Southern Superintendency*, 1865, L 805; Cooley to Gen. J. M. Hedrick, June 4, 1866, *ibid.*, *Letter Book*, no. 80, p. 299; Lewis C. True to John N. Craig, October 9, 1865, A.G.O., Archives Division, *Fort Gibson Letter Book*, no. 20, p. 107; True to H. D. B. Cutler, October 19, 1865, *ibid.*, p. 109.

IV. THE MUSTER OUT OF THE INDIAN HOME GUARDS

The cattle stealing business could never have grown and flourished unchecked until it made of itself a system, regular and gigantic in its operations, had the United States government afforded to the Indians the military protection that its own domestic war had made so vitally necessary. The protection, whatever its occasion, had been guaranteed by treaties, a point to be fatally lost sight of when the final account was rendered in 1866; but one that, in the interests of historical justice, if not of legal, cannot be too strongly emphasized. Furthermore, the protection ought assuredly to have been furnished by a competent armed force, by which is implied, not men of the frontier, recruited from the locality, wild and lawless, and certainly not Indian warriors, transformed, for the time being, into a Home Guard, but the highly trained of the regular army, having the best of its traditions to guide them, disinterested men, devoted to duty. In ante-bellum days, it had been the professional soldiers who invariably constituted the frontier defense, the famous dragoons for example, and more than one commander that later distinguished himself on a Civil War battlefield, especially on the Confederate side, had won his spurs in an Indian fight. Protection against both domestic and foreign foes had been among the great inducements held out to the southern tribes for the accomplishment of their removal westward. Truly enough, a United

States civil war was not then anticipated not even though its underlying cause when it did come was the very same thing that had driven the Indians across the Mississippi. The coming, in no sense, diminished the government obligation and never was it at any time in contemplation that the exiles should themselves supply the protective force promised to them.

In eighteen sixty-three, and four and five, they were, however, supplying that force and, as was to have been expected, it was an exceedingly poor one. Colonel Phillips might make his charges against contractors and agents and might parry the thrust they made against him in their counter-charges; but, in one point, he was always indefensible. That point was his Indian Brigade, which, in the later days of the war particularly, was more often under fire of criticism than of rifle. To its incompetency was to be ascribed much of the wretchedness that had come to be the ordinary lot of the refugees. The Indian soldiers were condemned by one who knew them fairly well, Lieutenant-colonel Fred W. Schaurte [222] of the second regiment, as lazy, ignorant and irresponsible.[223] They were constantly deserting, going home to their miserable and suffering families, and then returning to the ranks, oblivious of having offended, but disgruntled and demoralized. They had their vindicators [224] as well as their harsh

---

[222] According to Special Indian Agent, John T. Cox, Schaurte was "very hostile to the Indians generally." (Cox to Coffin, December 5, 1863 O.I.A., *Cherokee,* C 633).

[223] Report to General Thomas, dated Camp Williams, C.N., August 31, 1863, A.G.O., Old Files Section, S 1963 (V.S.) 1863, Jacket 1 of 15.

[224] See a letter of General Blunt's, dated February 9, 1863, in reference to reports condemnatory of the Indian regiments. Blunt's testimony was distinctly favorable and should be cited in proof of their courage, their loyalty, their helplessness, their neglect by the U.S. Government, their service, etc. ("Extract of Letter and Endorsement Book," in *Consolidated Indian Home Guard Papers,* B 1013 (V.S.) 1863, Jacket 2 of 15).

See also, in the same collection, many letters issuing from the pen of Phillips, who was the Indian soldier's most fearless advocate. Two of the letters in particular are worthy of mention, one, of date, December 10, 1863, the other, to President Lincoln, transmitted by Congressman A. C. Wilder, of date, January 4, 1864. They were written when the mustering out of the Indian Brigade was under consideration and opinions were being called for. The letter to the president is here quoted:

"As Commanding Officer of the Brigade which includes the Indian Regiments, I desire to call to your personal attention the condition of that little understood and too much neglected Command.

"I have forwarded a report of the condition of the Indian Regiments in response to a request for evidence on the proposition of mustering them out. I send an additional copy to you through Mr. Wilder.

"The Indian Command as an 'experiment' has been entitled to more consideration than it has received. A portion of the Army Officials (honestly no doubt) have been opposed to it from its inception. No general system has been adopted. It has been to a large extent the victim of accidents. The white troops from States have officials to fight for their interests and honor. While the Indian Regiments have really done more effective service than any others I ever knew, no State has been concerned to vindicate their glory or redress their sufferings. In their behalf I appeal to your Excellency.

"Should the Government have determined or should it determine to muster them out of the service, every facility will be heartily furnished by the officers of the Command, who, I fear, would more cheerfully listen to propositions to muster them out than to reorganize them. They were once more hopeful. When I returned to them eight months ago, after a sickness of Small Pox, caught with them, I found every one discouraged. Gen¹. Blunt, who once eulogized them, did them much less than justice. He held out hopes of promotion in Negro Regiments to all who were ambitious, and the ambition and sense of duty of these young men, whom I had picked from able sergeants and privates of white regiments, was the only element of power I had to induce them to work in so arduous a task. It was said the regiments would surely be mustered out. So long as they existed such a thing must be fatal to them.

"I had expected to get a white brigade at Fort Smith, but as this Command was going to pieces they sent me back. I found not an ounce of flour in the Commissary, the Command 400 sacks in debt to the Indian Department. No forage. The mules dead or dying. The white troops that had been with the command received 8000 starving refugees in the vicinity of the camp. Hundreds of cases of Small Pox. The white officers discouraged. No cavalry even for pickets. The Rebels threatening to take Gibson and ravaging the country.

"It has been my fortune, and I do not repine at it, to assume some severe tasks since I took my share in this War, but this was the most discouraging. I have (been) able with the most meagre re-

critics and calumniators,[225] however, and their military
record, taken all in all, was not destitute of merit or of

sources to get bread enough to exist, and pay what the Command
owed the other Department, to get forage, though obtained seventy
miles off – to repulse and break up Standwatie and Quantrel, to follow
them and beat them even with Infantry, and to drive them over the
river, and I breathe a little freer and see daylight, but after all the
command is in a condition requiring your aid.

"If it is to be mustered out, 'Very Well.' If not, I respectfully
suggest,

1st. That the Indian Nation ought to be a separate District. That
while brought as close as possible to the Blue Book standard, it be
treated fairly as an experiment.

2nd. That means be furnished to fill all vacancies in some sys-
tematic way. There being no Governor in the Indian Nation, I
picked out sergeants and privates, such as I could find, from volunteer
regiments and put them in as orderly sergeants, promising them promotion to the vacancies. A man who would not go through this ordeal
was supposed here not to be good enough stock. This is the plan
I adopted in order to do the best I could by the Command. All I ask
is the means of filling vacancies as they occur, and I would urge that
if this Command had originally mustered with the commissioned
officers and orderly sergeants white men it would have been more of
a success.

3rd. When attached to other Commands, it is made the scapegoat
of all officers. The debris of Quartermasters stores and Commissary
stores is turned over to it. It has always in such a case been treated
badly. Bad wagons, bad mules, bad tents, bad arms, the flippant
remark being that 'anything is good enough for the d—d Indians.'

4th. There ought always to be white troops with the Indian troops.
I urge these considerations on your Excellency. I would be unworthy
of the Command entrusted to me if I failed to struggle for a remedy.
I make the appeal because it concerns the honor and interest of the
Government believing that you will feel profound concern [in] it
what I submit to you."

[225] Not all submitted in criticism was calumny. D. B. Sacket, Inspector
General, U.S.A., reporting February 4, 1864, said, "I have the honor to
submit the following extract from the Report of the Dept. of the Missouri
for the month of December, 1863 . . .

C Co. (9th Kansas Cavalry) is composed of Indians and is a very
poor company. Capt. John Delashnutt of this company is not (in my
opinion) an efficient officer. He was reported on the Company Books
as being sick. My opinion is that he was intoxicated, and from the
best information that I can get he must be in that condition a good
part of the time.

"The Morning Report of Nov. 29th shows an aggregate of 60

glory. In most respects, be it adventured, they lost
nothing by comparison with white troops of the border,

present. Of that number 30 were at inspection, 6 were reported sick
and the lieut. accounted for the remaining 24 as being drunk. I would
recommend that the Company officers and men be mustered out of the
service and authority granted to raise another company in their
stead . . . " (A.G.O., Old Files Section, B 1013 (V.S.), 1863,
Jacket 2 of 15).

The reports of the brigade inspector, Luke F. Parsons, were an even
more severe indictment. The following, being part of a monthly report
for 1864, is typical:

"The Brigade was all inspected between the first and fifth of June.
Commanding Officer is Colonel William Phillips, 3d Regiment of
Indians, A.A.A.G. is William Gallaher, 1st Lt. of 3d Reg. of Inds.,
who conducts his business with system and neatness. Col. Stephen H.
Wattles commands the 1st Reg., he and Lt. Col. George Dole and
Major James A. Phillips have never been mustered yet all draw their
pay. Maj. James A. Phillips and Chaplain Evan Jones are absent
without leave. 1st Lt. S. S. Prouty, R.Q.M., has his books and papers
in good order and up to date. He has 49 mules, mostly serviceable
and daily improving. Wagons, ambulances, harness, &c. &c. are
generally serviceable. Has no public funds. Many of the First Regiment are absent on various duties, such as escorting commissary trains
to and from Ft. Scott, Refugee trains to Ft. Scott & Sauk Agency,
scouting, &c. &c. (on foot). The general appearance of the Reg.
is good. The drill and instruction in military exercises is bad. Guard
and picket duty very bad. The white officers are efficient, but they
are the only ones who are ordered on duty or detached service, where
a competent officer is required, therefore they have all of the duty
to do. In most of the cases there is but one white officer in a company and in some companies there is no officer of any kind, either
competent or incompetent, white or Indian. . . None of the 1st
Reg. have made out their Muster and Pay Rolls for 5 months past.
The company quarters and entire camp is dirty. The soldiers are
dirty in person. Only a few of the officers wear uniform. The sutler
establishment is never inspected by the Col. or by Council. His goods
are not tariffed. . . None of the officers account for company fund.

3rd. Indian Regiment is now all here (12 companies). Six companies arrived here from Ft. Smith on the 30th of May. Major John
Foreman commands the regiment, he is a firm, persevering man. Lt.
Col. Lewis Downing (Indian) is absent without leave. . . Hospital
seems well supplied. This Reg. like the first has heavy details out
of camp on duty . . . The Indian officers are not capable to make
their property returns. Few speak English, none of them read or
write. . . Sunday morning inspections are generally neglected.
Company tents and camp in general is dirty. Only a few of the

who, at their very best, so Colonel Phillips had the
temerity to insinuate on an occasion when he was out of
temper or greatly exasperated, were not much to brag
about.[226]

Against the red forces, men of the regular army and
notably those higher up treasured an intense prejudice.
Halleck had never approved of their enlistment and
had scarcely ever permitted an opportunity to escape
him for reviling them when it had been accomplished.
In the autumn of 1863, Schofield recommended their
muster out[227] and Halleck endorsed the recommendation;[228] for he honestly believed them of no use whatever. Grievously ineffective and ill-conditioned troops
they undoubtedly were, judged by any standard even
the most lenient; but the fault was by no means wholly
theirs. Halleck was right and they ought never to
have been employed as a fighting force under any circumstances. Their civilization, ground for hope
though it was, was yet only a veneer. As soldiers they
were a lamentable makeshift always, a mere conveni-
ence. At any moment the savage in them was likely
to reappear. Moreover, so long as they were there, on
the frontier, to pose as a protection to their own country, the government at Washington was able to delude
itself into thinking that it was doing all that honor required of it.

Much of the blame for their ineffectiveness should

officers wear uniform. Officers do not account for company fund.
No Council of Administration has been appointed. The sutler store
is never inspected. Goods are not tariffed, but are sold at an enormous figure. . ." (Obtained from duplicate reports in the possession
of Luke F. Parsons, Salina, Kansas).

[226] Report of Phillips, December 10, 1863, *op. cit.*

[227] Schofield to Townsend, November 2, 1863, A.G.O., Old Files Section,
M 2205 (V.S.), 1863, Jacket 1 of 15.

[228] — *Ibid.*

be laid at the door of their equipment. They had been raised originally as an infantry force and as a Home Guard exclusively.[229] The service demanded of them was cavalry and, for it, they had to resort to their own poorly-shod ponies.[230] Their guns were of any and every make, the more antiquated, the better, seeming-

---

[229] An interesting attestation of this is to be found in the subjoined memorandum of a Cabinet discussion,

"In the spring of 1862, application was made by the Secretary of the Interior to the President in Cabinet to direct the raising of two or more regiments of Indians from such loyal Indians as had been driven from their homes by other Indians in rebellion against the United States Government, for the purpose of restoring their lands to the loyal Indians and affording them protection while planting their crops.

"The proposition was maturely considered by the President and Cabinet, and it was determined,

1st. That the enlistment of Indian Regiments, or of regiments of persons of African descent, did not come within the provisions of the Acts of Congress, authorizing the enlistment of Volunteer troops.

2nd. That the condition of military affairs authorized and justified a military organization of loyal Indians, for the protection of the Indian territory as a local or Home Guard.

3rd. The Secretary of War was directed to issue authority for the raising of two or more regiments in the Department under command of Major General Halleck, for the specific purpose mentioned – the organization to be in conformity to the laws relating to volunteers, and the officers designated by the Secretary of War, in concurrence with the Secretary of the Interior to be appointed by the President.

EDWIN M. STANTON, Secretary of War
"This statement is in accordance with my recollection
WILLIAM H. SEWARD
"My general recollection accords with above.
GIDEON WELLES."

(A.G.O., Old Files Section, I.H.G., B 1013 (V.S.) 1863, Jacket 5 of 15).

[230] On the point how strenuously they had to use their ponies, the Reverend Evan Jones gives information. Jones communicated to Dole, January 8, 1864 (O.I.A., General Files, *Cherokee*, 1859-1865, J 401), the substance of what the special deputation had conveyed to General McNeil.

" . . . After asserting the loyalty of their people – reciting their services in the Army, the losses they have sustained in life, health, and property, they present to Gen¹ McNeil their earnest request for the protection of their country against the inroads and raids of the brutal bands of Quantrel, Watie and others and they respectfully

ly. Some of them had no guns at all and were forced
to resume the use of weapons suggestive of a warfare,
far more primitive and, of necessity, far more savage.
Their first and best days had been given, except during
the brief existence of the Indian Expedition, to cam-
paigns outside of their own country and with some
other object immediately in view than its recovery. The
long months of waiting, of helping fight other people's
battles, while their own families were famishing in
exile on the lonely prairies, had made heavy drains
upon their fortitude. The experience had embittered
them. Quite obviously to them the United States
government was in no hurry to make a disinterested
and effective effort for the re-possession of their land.

indicate the kind of force, which to them would seem best adapted
to meet and put them down.

"The same plan of equipment, substantially, was suggested by Col.
Wm. A. Phillips, many months ago, and which he wished the delegation to urge on the attention of the government; that was, to have the
Cherokee troops equipped as *Mounted Rifles*. He says, very truly,
that the character of the service requires mounted men, and that it
would be good economy to furnish the Cherokee troops with horses.
Thus provided and equipped, with their superior horsemanship and
their thorough knowledge of the country, no forces would be more
efficient than they. Col. Phillips considers it a matter of great importance that this should be done and he must be deemed a competent
judge in the matter, having witnessed their performances from the
beginning and having commanded the Indian Brigade for more than
a year, excepting a short interval.

"The Indian Home Guards were mustered into service as Infantry;
most of them, however, have, from the first, performed the duties of
mounted men, on *their own horses*. But in their long and arduous
marches, through the wilds and prairies of Missouri, Arkansas and the
Indian Territory, and in the many battles, in which – as attested
by the commanding officers – they performed a worthy part, their horses
were killed, worn down and died. Col. Phillips states that at the
battle of Newtonia the Cherokees of the *Third Regiment alone had
fifty-five horses* killed. Many of them, in these ways, lost two or
three horses apiece. And those who could no longer supply themselves with fresh horses were reduced to their feet and the value of
their services greatly diminished . . . " [O.I.A., General Files,
Cherokee, 1859-1865, J 401].

In its own good time, perhaps, it would send an army there, suitably large and capable; but, meanwhile, for all it seemed to care, the Indian occupants might utterly disappear.

In 1863, with the premature return of the Cherokee refugees and the concentration of the Indian Home Guards at Fort Gibson, the deficiences of the whole Federal management became glaringly apparent. In some respects, they were appalling and the irreconcilable differences that sprang up almost daily between the civil and military authorities, none of whom was Indian, accentuated whatever there was of inadequacy in men and methods. To face a winter with the situation unrelieved, the Confederates active, and marauding on the increase seemed like a tempting of Providence. Influential men cast about for plans of reform and several [231] were suggested, all without exception

---

[231] The various plans are enumerated and commented upon, more or less adversely, in the subjoined letter from Cox. This letter has been cited in other connections and is reserved for quotation here because of its very explicit references to the matter under discussion. It was addressed to Coffin and is of date, December 5, 1863.

"Sir:

"The Census Roll of the Cherokees up to the present date is shown by accompanying statement. The gathering of the remainder will be tedious and difficult. I send today to Major Coleman, Sac & Fox Agency, the necessary forms of blanks (that the classification may correspond with the census already taken) with the request that he procure correct census of the Cherokees at his Agency to be incorporated in the general registration.

"I have made this enumeration under every possible disadvantage and inconvenience and almost wholly at my own expense, and will, when completed, furnish you *direct*, a more detailed synopsis, if desired, which, I think would be of important service to the Department.

"My system for registration and distribution meets the case precisely, ensuring a more general and fair distribution, and almost entirely preventing fraud and imposition.

"I have double indexed and in many cases triple indexed the names of all male adults.

"With eighteen months very close observation of the workings of the

designed to affect, in some degree, the Indian Brigade. It was at this juncture that the Cherokee deputation,

Indian Brigade, I am satisfied that no successful plan for reorganization will or can be devised. If mustered out, at present, they would prey upon each other in resentment or retaliation for real or imaginary wrongs, besides the almost uncontrollable disposition to plunder and jayhawk friend and foe, nothing but the most rigid military discipline can restrain. There is need of tightening, rather than relaxing, the cords of military restraint, at least sufficient to prevent those temporary desertions so common among them, and which is working to great injury, to themselves, to the service and to the Government.

"I have raised the question and would like your opinion, would it not as a *general rule* be better, to withhold subsistence from the families of Deserters, would it not secure greater fidelity to the service, security to the country and prevent the supplies being consumed by these military renegades.

"Several plans have been suggested for the reorganization of the Indian Regiments, each having their clamorous champions and adherents.

"First – Reorganize with *Indian Officers entirely*, to reconcile the ranks and file.

"Second – with *all white Officers* to secure discipline and the proper rendition of reports, accounts, etc. etc.

"Third – *Muster out all*, and recruit into such white Regiments as may be stationed here, and are reduced far below minimum.

"Fourth – Organize a new Cherokee Regiment, immediately, as a Home Guard Cavalry and independent of Military Control to be used exclusively in defense of the Cherokee Country.

"As to the first – It was tried effectually at the first organization of the Indian Regiments, and their early career, thus organized, is a sufficient comment.

"As to the second – It would only be the other extreme and would excite and intensify whatever jealousy or prejudice might now exist.

"The same objection would hold against the third.

"The fourth plan (which is deemed the most effectual in breaking the Indian Brigade) even should it prove in itself a failure, is the settled policy of the discontents, and it requires no foresight to read the dire consequences of such an organization during the existence of the present Regiments. It would necessarily be made up of those who *have* or *may* desert from the other two Cherokee Regiments, causing collision at once between the 'Military' and the 'Independent Cavalry Home Guards.' The organization of such a Regiment to succeed must break the others, and would in effect be a shameful abandonment of all obligations to their Brethren, the Creeks, Seminoles and Euches, who have fought, bled and suffered in common with them to wrest the Cherokee Country from the hands of a common enemy, and

authorized by action of the National Council, November seventeenth, interviewed General McNeil, the commander of the Army of the Frontier, and proposed

have toiled more arduously than they, in the building of a sure retreat, a place of refuge and safety in their own Country. Having thus given them their homes, they now propose to turn these faithful allies adrift.

"Another object of this new military movement is to have the power to enforce the new Cherokee Confiscation Laws – Only yesterday the Sheriff of Tahlequah District, under 'due process of law' proceeded to confiscate the property of one Major Liep, who has been for several months past, a soldier in the 14th Kansas, but who was said to be an officer in the Rebel Army. This *Confiscator* by the terms of the law, is Judge, Jury and Sheriff.

"There are daily inquiries as to the 'expenses of the Nation,' 'Who pays for these supplies,' 'Will it not be charged to the Nation,' etc, etc. On this question I have uniformly replied that it was a subject for future consideration and treaty."

As an illustration of this peculiar concern, I will mention an incident.

"About six miles east of this, an old Indian Widow lady, died and the body lay some three days on the floor in her cabin. I at last prevailed on several men from my old Co. (Capt. McDaniels) to assist me. I furnished conveyance for them to the place, it was found that she had died of small pox, and the men could not be induced to touch the body, so that I with three children had to carry the corpse some hundred yards to bury it. The first question propounded by some of the Head Men was, 'Is that going to be taxed to the Cherokee Nation.' I readily relieved their anxiety by informing them that we were on that occasion at least, prompted by common dictates of humanity and decency and not by any possible gain or speculation whatever which was perfectly satisfactory.

"I must, as in my former letters and reports, urge that more abundant supplies be sent, on account of the constant decrease of supplies and the inclemency of the season. On the 16th inst rations will be due and not less than three thousand will be promptly on hand to receive them, but we will not have one pound of Flour or Meal for them, nor a possible chance for any for three weeks. Nearly all must suffer and starve.

"The small pox is still carrying off this population by hundreds and no efficient means provided for their treatment or to arrest its progress. It does seem indispensably necessary that we should have a Physician here to care for and treat them. I have suggested and urged the propriety of establishing an asylum which would incure little or no expense, and at the same time afford temporary relief to the sick and extremely destitute. This, however, would require a Physician (which is greatly needed here) and the employment at more nominal com-

the formation of a new Home Guard, a real one, a regiment of Cherokee Mounted Rifles.[232]   Phillips had suggested the same thing substantially; but, as his reputation was at its ebb-tide, even Harlan having joined the ranks against him,[233] that circumstance had little weight in Washington.   A hearty endorsement of the

pensation of a few female nurses. A suitable Building can be obtained without rent.

"Another plan has been adopted to knock the Indian Brigade, is to promote what few white officers we have in new Colored Regiments now forming. Col. Schaurte, Lt. Col. of 2nd Ind. Regt. who is very hostile to the Indians generally, is leading in this move. [O.I.A., General Files, *Cherokee*, C 633 of 1864]

[232] Instead of devoting their whole attention to a presentation of existing needs, which were, indeed, serious, they recited at great length the many services that the Cherokees had rendered in the war and the many losses they had sustained on Federal account. The idea, no doubt, was to create in the mind of the auditor or reader a sense of immense obligation. The document they submitted to McNeil is labelled, 1327, *Missouri Department*, 1863 and is filed now in A.G.O., Old Files Section, B 1013 (V.S.) 1863, Jacket 2 of 15.

[233] One of Harlan's two letters of date, December 7, 1863, was most disparaging in its estimate of Phillips. It reads thus:

"In your letter of November 10th, 1863, you inform me that in March next you intend to remove the Indians now in Kansas to their homes; and ask my advice as to what seed and farming implements should be furnished them. I think it premature to form any settled opinion now. Perhaps former trial has made me too cautious. If peace is made soon, you should conform to the altered state of affairs; but if it is not before the first of March and then not likely soon to be brought about, I, as at present advised, should say, do not remove them this coming spring.

"There seems to be no system in anything, but one, in the management of the army here. And let who will be at the head of affairs, the same system continues; and that is to keep the whole Indian force, sorely against their will, cooped up, as closely as possible, in Fort Gibson – wholly idle. Jayhawk the country for cattle for use, and abuse – horses to run off to Kansas – all the corn they can use and destroy – and garden vegetables – and when they have gotten all they could find – leave Stand Waity to glean and return to Fort Gibson to rest from their arduous labors of War, and recreate in every species of debauchery, from the highest to the lowest branches in that Department, known in this fruitful country. And by the time the poor destitute women and children shall have raised more corn and potatoes, recruited what horses are left them, and gathered together their

plan for a regiment of Mounted Rifles came from the

cattle for beef and milk, these valorous warriors will be ready for another campaign equally successful and glorious.

"From the middle of July to the 25th August, while Blunt was here, the Colorado Regiment and Blunt's body guard (more particularly the body guard) were a terror to friends and enemies (but more particularly his friends). What they did not take could not be found – but the bushwhackers had to leave. Both before and since his advent, Stand Waity and his thieves and murderers have not received a check. They come as if certain of immunity, boldly when they please, stay as long as they please, steal as much as they please, rob and murder whom they please, make prisoners of whom they please, carry across the Arkansas to some hiding place prisoners and plunder, and prepare for and repeat the raid with perfect impunity. If the same management continues, and it will unless the present officers are superseded by better men, it is my firm conviction that the Indians now safely out of the country had better stay out and those now here had better be sent out. Stand Waity to all intents and purposes has, not only virtual, but actual possession of the country beyond the reach of the guns of Fort Gibson. They robbed a house and carried off a prisoner 2½ miles from here (the fort) last week and nobody pursued. A hospital, two miles off, was removed to the fort lately for safety because the surgeons were unwilling to risk their lives so near the lines between our possessions and Stand Waities.

"Col. Phillips has been in command here most of the time since last April. He may possess courage but he is wholly wanting in firmness and manly resolution. I have no word to express my opinion of him after an intimate acquaintance of ten months, but the nearest I have is, potterer, piddler, tinker. One day he plays the fool and gets it up to the dignity of an order, next he sets the order aside and substitutes another equally foolish and without the nerve to enforce either the one or the other. He would like to be Brig. General. He and I are personal friends and always have been. I have many friends who are wholly unfit for Brig. General but, looking over my list of friends, I cannot find one less qualified than he is. He has by his foolish orders and April proclamations done this nation more injury than all the rebels. By his proclamation of April, which was in violation of his agreement with me, he induced the Indians to settle almost throughout this whole territory and furnished them with the seeds and the implements you sent me. The seeds and implements were used as bait to keep them in the north and east portion of the Nation, where Stand Waity could and did jayhawk them at will. From that day to this, except Blunt's 40 days advent, the rebels have worked and amused themselves at jayhawking and are still at it. You may not fully credit my information when I say Phillips had 3500 men and six pieces of cannon in a pretty strong stockade and suffered 1000 or

Cherokee delegation, the one headed by John Ross and the Reverend Evan Jones.[234] It failed to meet the views of the War Department, however, and was quietly dropped, recourse being had, meanwhile, to the old practice of re-shaping and re-defining military districts.

Throughout 1864, the strained relations that had developed between the civil and military powers were in no wise relaxed.[235] In October, Agent Harlan had a

---

1200 men to lay within two miles of him all night and rob him of 10 or 1200 horses and mules next morning at 10 o'clock and drive them off without following or attempting to follow them but with 16 men all told.

"A man must be here and see and hear for himself to get a just idea of the management or want of management, since I came 10th of April last, with exception of the 40 days of Blunt's administration.

"Under the present management, and it is as good, I think, as the present managers can do, seeds and implements will do no good. By spring they will have but few horses or cattle or farms or houses. The Indians are bad enough. White soldiers, settlers, wagoners, army-wagoners, foragers and the refugee supply wagoners, scouring the country in every direction, on every road have left desolation in their wake throughout the Nation. There is always room enough for one more horse at the tail of every wagon and, like an omnibus, room for one more passenger inside.

"Men are excused and sometimes justified when, under uncontrollable passion caused by a great provocation, they inflict a great injury on an enemy, causing it. But when a whole nation is ruined by its friends, which has done no wrong, there is no excuse. We are taught and believe there is a just God who rules the Universe. Why the Cherokees should be wholly destroyed, tortured little by little at a time by their friends, by those sent here by the Government under treaty stipulations, for which the Government received an adequate consideration, shakes the faith of the truest believer . . . " (Harlan to Coffin, December 7, 1863, O.I.A., *Cherokee*, C 633).

234 *op. cit.*

235 The accusation of fraud and corruption was repeatedly made, first by one set of men and then by another. That Phillips made matters worse by appropriating a portion of the Indian crops to army consumption is not disputable; but that the consequent shortage, if genuine shortage there were, was solely responsible for Indian privations is unworthy of serious consideration. The great defect in Phillips' administration was his failure to render protection. At the very close of the year, Phillips being then restored to

personal interview with Secretary Stanton and advised the dignifying of the Fort Gibson command. It was his impression that a brigadier-generalship established there would help matters. The promotion of Phillips he unqualifiedly negatived. His objection was to what he designated the "political brigadier," and the Kansas variety of such.[236] By the same showing, Blunt would

---

command, Harlan thought it incumbent upon him to seek to take precautions against a renewal of evil practices. A short while previously, in October, in fact, he had asked for the issuance of a restraining order and the Secretary of War had agreed to the proposition; but had neglected to act. Harlan repeated his request when Colonel Wattles retired to make way for the return of Phillips (Harlan to Coffin, December 31, 1864, O.I.A., *Southern Superintendency*, C 1197).

[236] The "political brigadier-general" came under the censure of Agent Harlan as shown in the following:

"When I was in Washington last October, I spoke to the Secretary of War and requested him, if it met his approbation, to send us a Brig. Gen¹ to command at this post. I thought he approved the suggestion. If he has an idle Brigadier I think it would be well to send him here. Kansas Political Brig. Generals do not answer the purpose. Kansas escorts are robbing the trains they are designed to protect, and generally go unpunished. They may be voters in Kansas or have friends who are. Army officers may be candidates for civil office in Kansas. I do not know that such a motive governs any military officer here, but a military officer who could be influenced by such motive would be very likely to not punish such delinquents and to act just as these have done. The fact is notorious that generally they are not punished. The three trains this fall have each been robbed mostly by Kansas escorts. Thirty thousand dollars worth, by estimate, I hear has been taken, wagoners have to stand guard over their teams to protect the whole. The teamsters now here prefer going home without an escort; and are hurrying to get away before one can be got ready. They say they fear the escort more than the Bushwhackers.

"A Brig.-Gen'l who had no fear before his eyes of Kansas soldiers voting against him hereafter might punish and by the punishment of a few deter many from further depredations. I think it would be well to try the experiment.

"We do not care, just now, for a very fighting General, as there is not much of that to do. We want a man in command of good sense and common honesty and who has nerve enough to perform a plain duty, and with such an one we will be well satisfied. We do not want just now any more great paper battles, nor any more great commanders who fight best in such battles. We have had enough of them

have been equally unfit. It is true he was more than a

already. They have their uses and answer a purpose to fill columns
in a newspaper as well as real battles and keep the names of commanders permanently before the public, away from the scene of action.
But here where all the facts are known, they only excite ridicule. Such
things will be done, while ridicule cannot lower the braggart when
he and his actions are known and he can get eclat where he and his
actions exaggerated are not known.

"If you can in any way aid in getting somebody in command at
this place who knows his duty and will do it, you will assist in making
a wonderful change in our situation and confer advantage on the
people of this country for which they ought to be thankful and I believe
they will be." (Harlan to Coffin, January 2, 1865, *ibid.*).

Blunt was a New Englander, born in Maine, 1828. His home, in 1862,
was at Mt. Gilead, Anderson Co., Kansas. The following documents show
the interest that politicians had taken in him:

(a)   LEAVENWORTH CITY, Decr 12th, 1862.
MY DEAR LINCOLN,

Brig. Genl J. G. Blunt is a common sense fighting man, none of your
first class Military men, or I should take but little stock in him. I
think he has done enough to merit your official appreciation. We have
13 Regiments in the war and would like him to be our Major General
for his gallantry in the field should you think him worthy of promotion.   Very truly your friend
                                 M. M. DELAHAY

We concur in asking the promotion of Brig. Gen. Blunt. He is one
of our Generals who not only fights the enemy but whips him.
                         Respectfully
                              J. H. LANE
                              S. L. POMEROY.

(A.G.O., Old Files Section, 762 B (C.B.) 1863, *Blunt's Personal
Papers*).

(b)
"If Kansas can get nothing more in the way of Gen^{ls} under the
"new deal," we want our gallant soldier Brig. Genl James G. Blunt
promoted to Maj. Genl. Let all else go rather than lose him." (*ibid.*).

(c)   WASHINGTON, Feb. 24, 1863
HON. E. M. STANTON, Sec^y of War,

The undersigned would earnestly recommend that the following
promotions be made in the Volunteer forces of the United States:
Brig. Gen. Jas. G. Blunt of Kansas to be Maj. General
Col. Albert L. Lee, 7th Kansas Cavalry, to be Brig. General.

We ask the promotion of the above named officers as a recognition
of ability and efficiency and distinguished gallantry in the field of
battle.   Respectfully yours,
                                 J. H. LANE
(*ibid.*)   A. C. WILDER   M. C.

brigadier-general [237] already but he had always put his chief reliance for preferment and promotion upon political influence exerted in his behalf at Washington. Some there had been, early in 1864 – but they were his friends in Kansas – who hoped for his return to the command of the Army of the Frontier; in order that the Indian Brigade might get its deserts.[238] It was at the moment in great distress.[239] For much the same reason, strange to say, the Cherokees of the John Ross following opposed his recall.

Muster out or reorganization of the Indian regiments was the constantly reiterated demand in 1864

[237] In brief, Blunt's military record was a series of promotions, all having their inception in political influence. In the spring of 1862, he had accepted the commission of brigadier-general of volunteers (*ibid.*, 515 B, 1862). In May, 1863, he was appointed major-general of the same to rank as such from November 29, 1863 (*ibid.*, B 106, 3 (C.B.) 1863). In January, 1864, he reported himself as recruiting commissioner for the 11th Regiment U.S. Colored Troops (*ibid.*, 104, C.B. 1864). H. G. Lorring, R. J. Hinton, and J. E. Tappan were on his staff (*ibid*, B 1015). In July, 1865, the president directed that Blunt be mustered out of the service (*ibid.*, B 757). On the tenth of August, he tendered his resignation (*ibid.*, B 890). His last military efforts are thus described by himself:

"On the 3rd day of June last, the day following the receipt of the intelligence of the surrender of the rebel forces under General Kirby Smith, I telegraphed through Gen. J. J. Reynolds at Little Rock my resignation as Major General of U.S. Vols.

"At that time I was at Fort Gibson, Cherokee Nation, organizing a cavalry force to take part in the contemplated movement against the transmississippi rebel army; but believing that the surrender of that army by Kirby Smith virtually closed the war, I did not desire to remain longer in the service.

"On the 18th day of June I received an order from Gen. Reynolds relieving me of command and directing me to proceed to my place of residence and report by letter to the Adjᵗ Genˡ of the Army . . . (Blunt to Stanton, August 10, 1865, *ibid.*, B 890).

[238] *Daily Conservative*, January 29, and February 3, 1864.

[239] *Ibid.*, February 14, 1864. A special to the *St. Louis Democrat* gave the information that it "had been moved south from Fort Gibson to North Fork Town on the Canadian River" and, at last accounts was "fighting with a largely superior force" under Stand Watie. Concerning the contact of the brigade with Quantrill, see *Daily Conservative*, May 1, 1864.

and it was no less so in 1865. Towards the end of the first of these two years, there was much talk of evacuating the various military posts from Little Rock westward to Fort Gibson because of the difficulty of supplying them, it being quite impracticable by way of the Arkansas.[240] Reynolds and Canby favored evacuation; but Grant did not and, before long, the idea was abandoned, possibly because civilians coupled their protests with the military. The withdrawal of the garrisons would have forced a new disposition of the refugees, clustered about them and without a doubt their return, in a shape more pitiable than before, to Kansas. It was against such a contingency that the civilians pitted themselves.[241]

While the matter of evacuation was yet held in abeyance and also while, after the order for vacating Fort Smith had been revoked, there was a strong possibility of its being revived, Colonel Phillips,[242] Agent Harlan,

[240] *Official Records*, vol. xlviii, part i, pp. 391, 403, 428, etc.

[241] On January 5, 1865, Lane wrote to Usher from Atchison as follows:

"Our people are greatly concerned with the fear that Forts Smith and Gibson are to be evacuated. It will throw back upon us the whole number of refugees recently removed with their numbers largely augmented and more destitute than when they first came. It will expose our state to invasion from Texas.

"I trust you will call the attention of the President to this subject and if possible prevent its consummation." (I. D. Files, Bundle, no. 53 (1865).

On the outside of the letter is the memorandum, "Order revoked, Dec. 30, 1864;" but Grant thought it advisable to send an additional order to Reynolds, January 1, 1865 (*Official Records*, vol. xlviii, part i, p. 391).

On the sixteenth of January, Coffin wrote to Dole, stating that he had heard that Reynolds had ordered Fort Smith to be abandoned as a military post. If it were true and complied with, the refugees would have to be sent back to Kansas. The expense involved, past and future, worried him (O.I.A., Land Files, *Southern Superintendency*, 1855-1870, C 1179).

[242] Phillips wrote to both Usher and Stanton on the subject, January 8th. For the letter to the latter – and it was a strong one – see *Official Records*, vol. xlviii, part i, pp. 456-457; I. D. Files, Bundle, no. 53. A copy of it was sent to the Senate in answer to the resolution of February 28, 1865.

Lieutenant-colonel Downing, and Chief John Ross separately recommended the disbanding of the Indian troops.[243] Phillips thought that, unless they were going to be reorganized on a sound basis, it would be a wise policy to send them back to their agricultural pursuits. It would be the best way of relieving the outstanding necessities of their kinsfolk.[244] General Reynolds agreed with him.[245] The advice was not taken, however, and Phillips repeated it;[246] for he feared that, if

---

[243] Dana to Usher, February 15, 1865, O.I.A., General Files, *Southern Superintendency*, 1865.

[244] On the score of those necessities, see the report of the commissary at Gibson to the effect that twenty thousand people were around about there on the very verge of starvation (*Official Records*, vol. xlviii, part 2, pp. 53, 136). That was in April after Usher had ruled that, under the seventh section of the Act of March 3, 1865 (13 *United States Statutes at Large*, p. 563) both the war and interior departments were responsible for their relief, the latter department not having been released by the inclusion of the former (Usher to Dole, April 8, 1865). Military men did their part (Captain J. S. McClintock's Abstract of Issues to Refugees at Fort Gibson, May, 1865, O.I.A., *Southern Superintendency*, M 725), but they were still being charged with helping themselves to the Indian cattle (*Official Records*, vol. xlviii, part i, pp. 142-145). The refugees in Kansas were also impoverished. Those at the Indian camp near Ohio City were most importunate in their cry for help (O.I.A., *Neosho*, W 896 of 1865); but their distress continued unrelieved (Report of Agent Snow, June 14, 1865, *ibid.*, S 714 of 1865) until Agent Snow was apportioned some of the beef cattle that had been seized, under the vigorous measures adopted by Superintendent Sells, from the range thieves (Commissioner of Indian Affairs, *Report*, 1865, p. 252). The Fort Gibson refugees were no more promptly relieved (Grant to Pope, May 26, 1865, *Official Records*, vol. xlviii, part 2, p. 608; Reynolds to Harlan, July 15, 1865, I. D. Files, Bundle, no. 54, six enclosures.

[245] Dana to Harlan, February 15, 1865, *op. cit.*; Phillips to Usher, March 25, 1865, I. D. *Register of Letters Received*, "Indians," no. 4.

[246] In A.G.O., Old Files Section, B 1013, V.S. 1863, Jacket 10 of 15, *Indian Home Guards*, are several letters and extracts of letters written by Phillips in relation to the Indian Brigade in the last days of the war that prove conclusively how much he had its best interests at heart. He wanted the Indian soldiers disbanded so that they could begin their own reconstruction work, cropping their lands, and the like. They were not disbanded and so he took the responsibility upon himself of allowing individual Indian soldiers to assist the women and children in fencing and in planting corn. By this means enough corn was put in to prevent starvation (Phillips to

not disbanded, the troops would be allowed to drift into banditti, an eventuality greatly to be deprecated.[247] Banditti, the Confederate Indians had already become and they were a terror to the country.[248]

Reynolds, April 19, 1865 (*ibid.*, 4 of 15; I. D. Files, Bundle, no. 53; *Official Records*, vol. xlviii, part ii, p. 136).

One of Phillips' letters, in particular, gives a fairly complete account of his endeavors in Indian behalf. It was addressed to Secretary Harlan, March 25, 1865,

"I came to Little Rock to confer with Major Gen. Reynolds in relation to the muster from the service of the Indian regiments.

"At the commencement of the year I recommended their muster from the service not later than the 10th of March, so that they could raise a crop, *provided* the government could send other troops to protect them. What I had desired to avoid was their muster out in the middle of the summer, when they would be stripped at once of their means of support, and could raise no crop this season.

"I find, however, that owing to the fact that troops have been sent east of the Mississippi, no garrison of other troops to protect the Indian nations can be spared, and the disbandment would leave those who have done so much good service in our cause, helpless, and exposed to the rebel organisations which still exist. An effort to move them out of the Indian nation, especially at this season, is not, I presume, contemplated by you and would be as cruel to them, as I am satisfied it would be, in every respect, unhappy and disastrous. Besides these considerations a large amount of time has been consumed sending the papers through the proper channels; it is now late, and would be the 1st of May before the muster out would be completed, too late to be of any practical benefit this season.

"These Indian soldiers have, after all, been the best protectors of their own country, the white troops sent there, or going through have too often plundered them . . . " (O.I.A., General Files, *Southern Superintendency*, 1865).

[247] " . . . I unhesitatingly deprecate any encouragement being given to let them drift into guerrilla bands. We will have banditti enough at the close of the war without fostering them . . . " (Phillips to Usher, February 3, 1865, I. D. Files, Bundle, no. 53).

[248] The movements of Stand Watie were a source of deep concern, (*Official Records*, vol. xlviii, part 2, pp. 48, 58, 70, 73, 91, 100, 104), especially after Chief Joe of the Big Hills band of Osages had given reliable information (*ibid.*, p. 162). A combination against Kansas was the thing feared (*ibid.*, p. 83). The guerrillas were passing rather easily from the Indian country into Missouri (*ibid.*, p. 356). The Indians were, however, not the only evil-doers (Brewer to Curtis, January 24, 1865, A.G.O., *Fort Gibson File Box*, 1864-1868). The Interior Department requested adequate

If Phillips had no reason for apprehension when he first remonstrated against the *status quo* for the enlisted Indians, he soon did have. In the early days of April, General Pope, completing a tour of inspection through territory recently added to the Military Division of the Missouri, his command,[249] had interesting suggestions to offer. His views on reconstruction in Arkansas [250] do not concern the present narrative; but those on new uses for the Indian Brigade do and most intimately. To further a more vigorous military policy, involving a movement southward from the Arkansas, he recommended the employment of the Cherokees as part of a force that should denude the Choctaw and Chickasaw country of its cattle and sweep onward into Texas.[251] The plan, in its entirety, Reynolds, consulted,

protection for supply trains (Dole to Stanton, March 27, 1865, O.I.A., *Letter Book*, no. 76, p. 491) and voiced the opinion that the government was financially accountable for the cost of goods lost *in transitu* (Usher to Dole, April 3, 1865). Cattle thieves abounded (*Official Records*, vol. xlviii, part 2, p. 89). They plied their trade with impunity from the Creek country northward into Kansas (*ibid.*, p. 636). Texan rangers were beginning to appear and Fort Gibson was not sufficiently central to protect against them (*ibid.*, part i, p. 470).

[249] The Cherokee delegation in the East, J. Ross, Evan Jones and Daniel H. Ross, opposed March 22nd, the redistribution of military areas,

"The undersigned Delegates of the Cherokee Nation duly appointed by authority of the National Council to look after the interests of our people in the City of Washington, being informed that an effort is being made to get the Indian Territory attached to the Department of Missouri and Kansas, respectfully request the change asked for be not made. We are all entirely satisfied to remain under the command of Maj. Gen¹ Reynolds in the Department of Arkansas. When heretofore attached to Kansas our cattle & corn have been stolen, and our country ravaged under the auspices of the authorities sent to protect us – and we greatly fear that if we are again connected with that Department our people will be still further impoverished by the same kind of misrule. We further request that Major Gen¹ James G. Blunt be not again placed in command in our country." (A.G.O., Old Files Section, B 1013, V.S., 1863, *Indian Home Guard*, 4 of 15. The old file mark was, R 52, H.Q., A., 1865).

[250] *Official Records*, vol. xlviii, part 2, pp. 125-132.

[251] — *Ibid.*, p. 51.

did not approve, most likely because its geographical features were not well considered; but also because a devastated and desolate region, nearly two hundred miles in breadth, would have to be "traversed by an army carrying all supplies with it, over difficult and neglected roads." [252]   Pope readily admitted, when Reynolds' objections came to him, that the only troops that could be trusted with the undertaking would be, "Western troops accustomed to long marches and to half rations and habituated to forage for themselves upon the country." [253]   Were a better commentary needed on the Federal method of treating the Indians, none could be found.

The force to be sent on this hazardous undertaking was to consist of four or five thousand mounted men inclusive of about twenty-five hundred reorganized Cherokees.   Canadian ponies [254] were to constitute the Indian mount, two thousand of them being then held at Fort Leavenworth for the purpose.[255]   Pope stuck to his plan regardless of the many objections to it, and, in furtherance of it, issued instructions to Blunt, to Mitchell and to others.   To Blunt was given the command of the District of South Kansas, Mitchell having that of North.[256]

The reorganization of the Indian regiments as thus

[252] — *Ibid.*, pp. 94, 150.

[253] — *Ibid.*, 150.

[254] Probably the same that Dodge had passed on to him and condemned as utterly worthless, *ibid.*, p. 350.

[255] — *Ibid.*, pp. 111, 138.

[256] The District of South Kansas was to include the Indian country (Pope to Reynolds, April 22, 1865, *ibid.*, p. 158). Mitchell assumed command of the District of North Kansas, April 11th (*ibid.*, p. 75). Before long the District of South Kansas was, to all intents and purposes, consolidated with that of North (*ibid.*, 356, 357) and Blunt's jurisdiction limited to the Indian country. The change was occasion for controversy (Blunt to Pope, May 27, 1865, *ibid.*, p. 636).

contemplated by General Pope was an entirely different thing from that which Phillips had proposed.[257]

[257] It is interesting to observe that, at the selfsame moment, there were those in the Confederacy who were advising just such a reorganisation of the Southern Indian commands as Phillips was for the Northern. Captain B. W. Marston, A.I.G., April 2, 1865, reported, in this wise, to Colonel Ben Allston, inspector-general on General Kirby Smith's staff. The letter is instructive for yet other reasons.

"I have the honor to report for your information, that it is impossible to forward a tabular Inspection Report of this Corps of the Trans. Miss. Army for the month just passed. I will give you the situation of affairs here from my personal observation. The only command at present in the District is the Indian Division commanded by Brig. Gen. Stand Watie. The *Indian* part of this command, officers and men, almost without exception, are absent on a recognized general furlough. A small proportion of the *white* men of this Division are in camps and at posts supplying the places of the two Infantry Batteries, recently ordered to report to Gen. S. B. Maxey.

"This command is badly provided for in every respect and the white men, composed of as good material as there is on the globe, fare alike and, in their present Indian organizations, without sufficient arms, drill, order, regularity or system, the effect of totally incompetent officers, are no more reliable or efficient than the Indians. The difference between the effectiveness of the white and Indian soldier, in their crude, original state, can hardly be drawn; but if there is any difference the superiority is with the Indian. But under discipline there can be no comparison. The white man is infinitely the superior of the Indian, yet the improvement in the latter, with the same advantages is marked and astonishing.

"The evil of the white men and the Indians being mixed in the same companies and regiments, or even brigades, has long since been discovered by the com^dg generals and, upon the recommendation of General Cooper last winter, Gen. Smith gave Gen. Maxey instructions which could have remedied the evil forever, had the same been carried out.

"Under those instructions the white men are being allowed to volunteer in a separate white organization, which it is hoped will effect the object in course of time.

"Indian commands in their present organizations and under the existing state of things – treaty stipulations, established precedence, etc. — can never become efficient soldiers. Their efficiency can however be improved and I think the measures now being adopted will effect the same.

"The question of supplies is now the all important one. The transportation is very limited and to use a common expression nearly 'broken down.' Every thing, except beef and salt, for the subsistence

Reorganization along the old lines meant having the officers either all Indian or all white so as to eliminate friction and secure discipline. The need for deciding upon something was exigent now since the term of service for all three Indian regiments was about to ex-

and defence of the Dist. is hauled from a great distance and a most inclement and rainy winter has left the roads in an almost impassable condition.

"Every energy can now but scantily supply the Reg^{ts}. The coming of the grass will soon relieve the present embarrassment to a very great degree. But if the troops were now in camp, they could not (but) be sick, and it is policy also to allow them all the time which can possibly be given this spring, so that they may plant their crop.

"The great want of arms has been frequently represented by me while Insp^r of the Indian Division. This matter deserves the earliest attention of the Gov't.

"It is not for me to pass censure and judge as to who is responsible for the utter 'broken down' and almost (?) condition in which this Dist. is left; but aside from this there are many external causes which cripple, and remove the responsibility from the Dist. Com^{dr}. *First,* – There are upwards of (15,000) fifteen thousand of Indigents, all of whom have to be fed from the 'public crib.' It would be inhuman and a violation of the spirit of the treaties to refuse them bread, yet it is next to disaster to give it to them. The Gov't will however be greatly relieved by the coming of the next crop from this great weight, as the Dist. Com^{dr} has afforded them every facility for repairing their farming utensils, by allowing time to remain at home, as long as possible, and by furnishing them with seed-corn.

Second, – The Commissariat is almost beyond the control of the Dist. Com^{dr}, it being conducted by Com^{ys} who are not subject to his orders and are not responsible to him for any shortcomings.

"This is a rough outline of the situation of this Dist. and I trust it may prove satisfactory in lieu of the formal report required by Orders. As soon as the troops can be concentrated, giving a tangible base to operate upon, I shall endeavor to give you a formula report as required.

"With the discouraging picture before you there are yet many encouraging features which are auspicious of good results. The fidelity of the Indian allies, the . . . zeal and energy being exhibited in the small staff Depts, the confidence of the troops, and their perfect resignation to the fate of the Confederacy – if peace and independence, or dire extermination. These facts are cheering and bid fair to result in a happy recuperation from the utter destitution which has throughout the winter been staring them in the face." (A.G.O., *Confederate Archives*, chap. 2, no. 259, pp. 141-143).

pire.[258]   All had been mustered in for three years' service, the First Indian on May 22, 1862 and, consequent-

[258] The First Regiment, I.H.G., dates its history from May 22, 1862; but, in view of facts gleaned from the Indian Office files in connection with Jackson Lewis' claim "for supplies furnished by him to the soldiers of the first and second Indian regiments at the time of their enlistment into the U.S. Army, at Neosho Falls, Kansas, in the month of June, 1862, amounting to $419.45," (Coffin to Dole, March 2, 1863), I am a little hesitant about being too precise as to the time of actual organization.   Dole's memorandum on the back of Coffin's letter was as follows: "If these provisions were furnish^d to the Indians previous to their being mustered into the service & were Refugees, the Dep^t should make payment . . . "   The Indian Office reported on the case, March 12, 1863.   Robert W. Furnas, later on Agent for the Omaha and Winnebago Indians and still later Governor of Nebraska, was the first colonel of this regiment (A.G.O., Old Files Section, *Personal Papers of Robert W. Furnas*, C 533, V.S., 1867).   Furnas sent in his resignation just prior to the formation of the Second Indian Expedition. The Indians asked that Ellithorpe be his successor,

"There is, we understand, a petition in circulation asking that you recommend some person with whom we are unacquainted, for Colonel of this Regiment.   We are fully aware that said petition has been put forth by a few of the dissatisfied officers, some of them are under arrest upon charges of stealing, or swindling the soldiers & the Government.   Our present officer in command, Maj. A. C. Ellithorpe, is fast bringing to light these frauds & clearing the Regiment of these swindling tricksters.

"We hope should the resignation of Col. Furnas be accepted, that you will recommend & urge the promotion of the officer who has been with us from the first, and proved himself competent for the position, and worthy of our fullest confidence" (Letter to Blunt, dated Camp Babcock, November 23, 1862; A.G.O., E 322, V.S., 1863, *Indian Home Guards*).   J. Howard Gillpatrick, who was 1st Lieutenant and Adjutant, endorsed the request.   In February, 1863, Blunt notified department headquarters of Wattles' resignation as lieutenant-colonel and urged that if Wattles would not accept the post of colonel, it be conferred upon Ellithorpe.   It was at this stage that Coffin and his subordinates, protested against the assumptions of the military men. In transmitting a report of Agent Martin's, dated December 20, 1862, Coffin complained to Dole, "If the programme as fixed up by the military officers, and which I learn Dr. Gillpatrick is the bearer to your city and the Solicitor General to procure its adoption, is carried out, the Indian Department, superintendents and agents, may all be dispensed with . . .   (I.O.F., *Cherokee*, C1950 of 1862).

The Second Indian Regiment was organized shortly after the First.   In September, 1862, Company E, Captain Chetopa's company, composed of Osages, deserted in a body.   A new company, Captain Kendall's, was

ly, its term would expire very shortly. The War Department had resolved in February [259] upon the disbanding of the entire force and the Cherokee delegation, apprised of that fact, revived its earlier hope of
procuring a genuine Home Guard. Accordingly it
requested Stanton that, if the Indian soldiers were indeed to be mustered out, they be mustered out with
arms [260] and straightway reorganized as a protection to
the Cherokee Nation against guerrillas.[261] Whether
it was by way of rejecting this proposal or of discount-
enancing Pope's, certain it is that Halleck, who had
obviously never deviated ever so little from his original
position that the red men were unfit for civilized warfare, soon let it be known that he wholly disapproved
of their continuance in the service. A few might be

mustered in, November 11, 1862 at Camp Bowen, Arkansas by Major Van
Antwerp. It was made up of Cherokees (A.G.O., B 1013, V.S., 1863,
Indian Home Guards, Jackets 1 and 4 of 15).

The Third Indian Regiment was slightly irregular in its origin. A
question arose within the War Department as to the legitimacy of its
authorization, for which Blunt stood sponsor, he having issued instructions
to Phillips (*ibid.*, Jacket 1 of 15). In connection with the matter of the
authorization of the First and Second, the letters and telegrams from the following persons are important, Schofield, August 29 and 31, 1863; Hannibal
Hamlin, December 24, 1863 and June 17, 1864; E. D. Morgan, February 10,
1864; W. S. Rosecrans, March 17, 1864, J. H. Lane, December 12, 1864
(*ibid.*, Jacket 12 of 15).

[259] "The 1st, 2nd, and 3rd regiments of Indian Home Guards will be
mustered out of military service on the 31st day of May, instant, pursuant
to authority granted by the War Department, dated February 13th, 1865"
(Portion of Special Orders, issued by John Levering, A.A.G., by order of
Reynolds, dated Little Rock, April 29, 1865). See also War Department
letter of March 20, 1865 and its enclosures.

[260] This request was renewed at the time of the actual muster out on
the plea that they had had arms of their own when they were mustered in
(Reynolds to the Adjutant-general, June 19, 1865, *Official Records*, vol. xlviii,
part 2, p. 935).

[261] John Ross and others to Stanton, March 27, 1865 (A.G.O., Old Files
Section, B 1013, V.S., 1863, *Indian Home Guards*, Jacket 4 of 15).

employed as scouts and guides; [262] but the rest, he insisted, must go back to civil life.

In ignorance of this decision or of its determinative character, Pope went ahead with his plans for a forward movement southwestward. Towards the last of April, Reynolds, upon whose hearty co-operation he depended, ordered Blunt to re-organize the Indians [263] and Blunt, [264] nothing loath, prepared to comply; but the War Department interposed its authority and the order, almost as soon as made, was revoked. The way was then clear for demobilization. Special orders, [265] issued on the eighth of May, provided for the muster out at the end of the month. [266]

---

[262] Halleck to Reynolds, April 10, 1865, *ibid.*; *Official Records*, vol. xlviii, part 2, pp. 64, 77.

[263] *Ibid.*, p. 332. Phillips, having heard nothing definite about either reorganization or demobilization, wrote, April 19th, for information (*ibid.*, p. 136).

[264] Disappointed of an Indian force, Blunt sought to have the Fifteenth Kansas at Fort Gibson (*ibid.*, p. 356). They had a far worse reputation than had the Indian Brigade. Dodge thought they should, if possible, be kept out of Missouri (*ibid.*, p. 553). Edmund G. Ross, the same who, when United States senator from Kansas, he having succeeded Lane, cast the determining vote for acquittal in the impeachment trial of President Johnson, reported, in February, that the regiment was in grave danger of general demoralization because so many of the officers were absenting themselves from duty. (A.G.O., Archives Division, *Fort Gibson File Box*, 1864-1868). Blunt was denied his wish (*ibid.*, p. 357) and, in June, arrangements were made for retaining one company at Fort Riley and posting another at Salina (*ibid.*, 949).

[265] *Ibid.*, Old Files Section, B 1013, V.S., 1863, *Indian Home Guards*, Jacket 4 of 15; *Official Records*, vol. xlviii, part ii, p. 349.

[266] For additional material on the Indian Home Guards, their muster in and their muster out, see House *Report*, no. 96, 42nd congress, 2nd session (Serial No. 1543); *Official Army Register of the Volunteer Force of U.S.A.*, part vii, pp. 364-369, published in compliance with Joint Resolution, March 2, 1865; *Petition of William P. Ross*, Principal Chief of the Cherokee Nation, May 14, 1874 in behalf of those erroneously called "deserters" from the Indian Home Guards, House Miscellaneous Documents, no. 276, 43rd congress, 1st session; Indian Office, *Report Book*, no. 21, p. 453. The First

Regiment would appear to have been mustered out by reason of the expiration of its term of service, May 8th, the Second and Third, May 31st. (A.G.O., *Indian Home Guards*, Jacket 8 of 15). Provision had been made by act of congress, June 30, 1864 (13 *United States Statutes at Large*, 413) for the settlement of the claims of the officers of the Fourth and Fifth regiments. The regiments themselves never had an organic existence.

V. THE SURRENDER OF THE SECESSION-IST INDIANS

The muster out of the Indians in Federal employ was only remotely connected with the actual military situation. Their services, undervalued always, were being dispensed with the first opportunity, the expiration of a term being but the flimsiest sort of a pretext, the one for which, apparently, Halleck and Stanton had long waited. The Home Guard so-called was dismissed without any reference whatsoever to the approaching end of the war. The need for it was as great now as it had ever been. The southern Indians were yet unsubdued, a pacification with them not even planned. Moreover, peace within the Indian world was likely to be of indefinite deferment. Tribes of plains and of mountains were infuriated as never before in their history.[267] Why then were the loyal In-

---

[267] Major-general G. M. Dodge was inclined to be relentless in his dealings with the wild tribes. He had little faith in Leavenworth's manoeuverings for peace and argued that the Indians, having grievously sinned, should be punished (*Official Records*, vol. xlviii, part ii, p. 141). For additional information, see *ibid.*, pp. 59, 107, 114-115, 141, 338, etc. Pope whose experiences with "hostiles" had been of wide extent was of the opinion that the Indians were not doing all the marauding on the plains (*ibid.*, p. 751). They were very restive, however, and, in late May, were adjudged guilty by Dodge of attacking the Wichita camp in southern Kansas (*ibid.*, pp. 687, 698). Senator J. R. Doolittle of the Select Committee sent out by congress to investigate Indian affairs generally seems to have taken a humane view of things and to have solicited permission to negotiate a peace. His request, submitted to President Johnson, was complied with (Stanton to Doolittle, May 29, 1865, *ibid.*, p. 669); but proved to have been made prematurely. In July, the tribes of the plains seemed, to Sanborn, ready for peace (*ibid.*, p. 1115). The wary and relentless Dodge thought differently and advised pushing the armed columns into their coun-

dians demobilized? Is it conceivable that the authorities in Washington, having already resolved upon Indian spoliation, deemed it the wisest part of valor to
disarm betimes those who were to be despoiled or were
they afraid that the factional hatred, engendered and
intensified by the war, would be a thousand times more
serious if, arrayed against the southern Indians with
whom a pacification would shortly have to be negotiated, were to be found those, arms in hand, who had
done their best to preserve the integrity of the American Union?

The decision to muster out the Indian Home Guards
was a trifle disconcerting to General Blunt, who, nevertheless, went on with his plans for raiding the Indian
country intervening between Fort Gibson and the Red
River. It was his way of forcing an early peace and,
for the accomplishment of his purpose, he bent his
whole endeavor. The departure of the Indians, upon
whom he had hoped to rely, impelled him to no re-
laxation of effort, no change of intentions.

Blunt's chief antagonist in the undertaking would
of necessity be General D. H. Cooper who, the object
of his ambition at last achieved, was in full charge of
the secessionist Indians. No mean antagonist was he.

try. It would then be time enough to determine whether peace could be
safely made previous to whipping them (*ibid.*, p. 1117). Considering that
the "brutal and cowardly butchery" of the Cheyennes on Sand Creek had
occurred so short a time before (Doolittle to Harlan, May 31, 1865, *ibid.*, p.
868), it was not surprising that the aborigines were obdurate. Dodge might
think them unjustifiably so (See his views on the Sand Creek Massacre, *ibid.*,
pp. 971 ff); but not Dole who felt that all endeavors of the Indian Office
to restore peace were being continually thwarted by the military commanders
in the West (Dole to Harlan, June 12, 1865, *ibid.*, p. 870). Dodge had no
more respect for the Indian agents than he had for Colonel Leavenworth
whom he contemptuously described as standing up for the Southern Indians
and as blowing "hot or cold with singular grace. To my officers he talks
war to the knife, to Senator Doolittle and others he talks peace" (*ibid.*,
p. 973).

Alert, energetic, and resourceful, he was not long in ignorance of Blunt's plans or in doubt as to means of circumventing them.[268] To concentrate troops at Little Boggy was his first device; but already rumors were in circulation of the fatal events transpiring eastward and he discovered to his chagrin that some of the Indian leaders, chief among them P. P. Pitchlynn,[269] were not so ready as formerly to furnish him men.

As Pollard so well stated, when he wrote his *Lost Cause,* the effect that Lee's surrender of Richmond might have upon the Trans-Mississippi Department,

[268] In Cooper's *Letter Book*, there are many letters, written between the thirteenth and the fifteenth of May, that indicate his consciousness of the danger impending. Aside from those that will be here quoted because not published in the *Official Records*, there are several of equal interest in *Confederate Archives*, chap. 2, no. 258, pp. 6, 7, 8, 12, 16; *Official Records*, vol. xlviii, part 2, pp. 1301-1306.

(a) " . . . We have a report that Blunt is getting up an expedition to start from Gibson on a raid into Texas, and I wish the Governor to have the Militia and (lacuna in paper) up towards the mouth of Little River to keep a sharp lookout and notify me of anything suspicious in that direction. I will send a scout of white men towards Gibson via mouth of Little River soon. The people need not fear them. They will start from this place & go by Colbert's Mills. Since the above was written, as the scout have to go by Boggy Depot any way, they will go up the Gibson road." (Cooper to Judge Wm. H. Harrison, Tishomingo, C.N. dated May 14, 1865, *Confederate Archives*, chap. 2, no. 258, pp. 13-14).

(b) "Your communication of the 13th inst is received & in reply will say that I have stationed three companies of the Chickasaw Regiment at Cochrans and will send Major Nair up with two other companies. This arrangement will enable you to concentrate the 3d Indian Brigade on Little Boggy in conjunction with the 1st Indian Brigade. The 2d Ind. Brigade will be moved up as soon as possible – except McCurtain's Reg^t and the Chickasaw Reg^t to the camp on Little Boggy. Arrangements should be made for the supply of the three Brigades at the camp on Little Boggy." (Cooper to Lt. Col. O.H. Brewer, May 14, 1865, *ibid.*, p. 14).

[269] . . . What did Col. P. P. Pitchlynn say in his speech to the Choctaws? It is reported that he swears I shall not have the troops, but I do not believe it . . . (Cooper to Scott, May 14, 1865, *ibid.*, pp. 9-11; *Official Records*, vol. xlviii, part ii, p. 1304).

almost entirely isolated since the loss of Vicksburg, was a subject for surmise and conjecture.[270] Texas, indisputably a sovereign state at the time of her annexation and admission to the Union, might reasonably contemplate a resumption of independent existence and Kirby Smith, one of her sons, in making an appeal to his soldiers, under date of April twenty-first, boldly suggested a protraction of the struggle since the Trans-Mississippi region was in possession of "the means of long resisting invasion."[271] Magruder, another son, believed that whatever might happen east of the great Father of Waters, Kirby Smith's department had it in its power "to present a menacing and determined front to the foe."[272] And so it most certainly had provided its parts would hang together, the Indian country no less than Louisiana and Arkansas. There was hope, too, of foreign aid. Was it to come from Europe or from Mexico? To the Emperor of Mexico, General Smith sent an accredited agent, Robert Rose, who was, however, to disclaim any authority, diplomatic, from the Confederate government as such. Because of the well-known expansionist designs of the United States it was incumbent upon the Confederacy and her southern neighbor to realize their contiguity to each other and the probability of a need for mutual helpfulness.[273] It was with Kirby Smith, intrenched in his remote command, that President Davis and his cabinet expected to find refuge.[274]

---

[270] Pollard, *Lost Cause*, p. 725.

[271] *Official Records*, vol. xlviii, part ii, p. 1284.

[272] *Ibid.*, p. 1289. In addressing a public meeting in Houston, Magruder is credited with having declared that he would rather be "a Camanche Indian than bow the knees to the Yankees." (Pollard, *Southern History of the War*, pp. 523-524).

[273] Smith to Robert Rose, May 2, 1865, *Official Records*, vol, xlviii, part ii, pp. 1292-1293.

[274] Reagan, *Memoirs*, p. 212. John H. Reagan was in President Davis'

To what degree General Cooper shared and approved Kirby Smith's optimistic notions it is not easy to determine. When the surrender came, he professed surprise, as was natural, notwithstanding that the conference with the southern governors, of which he had heard and of the true significance of which he was well aware, foreshadowed it.[275] A wholesome dread of Federal revenge he had taken pains to instill into the minds of his Indian troops;[276] but against the propa-

Company at the time of his capture (*Official Records*, vol. xlviii, part ii, p. 507).

[275] "I send letters for Gen. Throckmorton and Col. Adair – which please forward by special express.

"We have no news except that the Council of the Gen's and the Governors has adjourned and Gov. Allen of La. gone to Washington to negotiate for peace. Of course as usual there are ten thousand rumors afloat, but the above is all that any one knows. We must act merely on the defensive – *preserve order and await the result*. I have suggested the call of the 'Grand Council of the Six Allied Nations' to take into consideration the present 'situation' and to receive the report of their commissioners to the Indians of the Plains when they return . . . " (Cooper to Col. R. W. Lee, Fort Arbuckle, C.N., dated Fort Washita, May 22, 1865, *Confederate Archives*, chap. 2, no. 258, p 30). See also Cooper to Throckmorton, May 16, 1865, *Official Records*, vol. xlviii, part ii, p. 1307, and same to same, May 22, 1865, *ibid.*, p. 1317.

The foregoing is given in illustration of the fact that Cooper had a true conception of the outcome of the conference. The conference of governors – Henry W. Allen of Louisiana, Pendleton Murrah of Texas, H. Flanagin of Arkansas, and Thomas C. Reynolds of Missouri – had been called at the invitation of General Smith (Letter of May 9, 1865, *Official Records*, vol. xlviii, part i, pp. 189-190). In a formal statement of May 13th, Allen and Flanagin advised surrender (*ibid.*, 190-191). The surrender, as Pope warned Blunt, June 3, 1865, (*ibid.*, part ii, p. 760) changed everything. On June 4, Grant ordered Pope to relieve Blunt from duty (*ibid.*, p. 772).

[276] For example, he liked to dwell upon the thought that, following in the train of Blunt, would come the Pins and the negroes (Cooper to Tandy Walker, May 13, 1865, *Official Records*, vol. xlviii, part ii, p. 1302). Even that reference, however, would not allow him to entertain the idea that Blunt could muster enough men to warrant an invasion. Counting in the Pins and negroes, he would not be able to get at Forts Gibson and Smith more than four hundred. With such a force he might possibly attempt a raid on Boggy Depot (Cooper to Anderson, May 16, 1865, *Confederate Archives*, chap. 2, no. 258, p. 19).

gation of adverse reports he had resolutely set himself, [277] and he had taken time by the forelock in guarding against disorder.   In anticipation of his own surrender, General Lee had issued no orders for the maintenance of discipline, a course of action "unprecedented
in all deliberate and strategic retreats;" [278] but far
otherwise Cooper. Well he knew what disorder of the
kind, inevitably associated with the movements of an
army that had abandoned hope, would entail of misery
and horror in the Indian country.   In prescribing
against such a contingency, Cooper had measured up
to the best that was in him and for that he deserves un-
stinted praise.   Whiskey he prohibited absolutely; [279]

[277] " . . . It is folly to act upon every wild rumor afloat upon the
breeze. We must wait and watch, every man doing his duty, until
such time as those in authority may determine what is proper to be
done. Above all I counsel the Indian nations and the people of each
nation to be united and firm." (Cooper to Tandy Walker, May 21,
1865, *ibid.*, pp. 28-29; *Official Records*, vol. xlviii, part ii, pp. 1315-
1316). There are many other letters of the same sort. See, in particular, Cooper to Scott, May 10, 1865, *ibid.*, p. 1297.
[278] Pollard, *Southern History of the War*, p. 507.
[279] "I am glad to learn from Capt. Anderson that you have returned
to Boggy. The Capt. has presented your views and the reasons for
not moving camp up to Little Boggy. I was not aware that your field
transportation was so short. I thought you had the greatest abundance. I would suggest the propriety of having your wagons gathered
up immediately. Notwithstanding the report reinforcements are not
large enough to justify much apprehension of invasion, the condition
of the country is such that the troops must be kept in camp ready to
act according to circumstances & free from the popular excitements
around them.
     " . . . We must preserve *order* in the country, & I rely upon
your aid & co-operation in that as well as in all other things. We
must all keep cool & quiet & wait to see what course things will take.
If the people in this Ter^y get into difficulties among themselves it will
be very disastrous. Let there be respect for private rights & forbearance one with another & all will I hope be well. Do not let your
men get any whiskey. If excited by drink they will get into difficulties
among themselves & their people . . . " (Cooper to Stand Watie,
May 18, 1865, *Confederate Archives*, chap. 2, no. 258, pp. 24-25).

for, as he himself said, *"Quem deus vult perdere prius quam dementat."* [280] His soldiers he kept active,[281] his officers he exhorted to self-control.[282] The indigents he provided for to the utmost of his ability.[283] Profiteering, speculating and thieving he rigidly pro-

[280] Cooper to Scott, May 14, 1865, *ibid.,* pp. 9-11. This quotation was omitted when the letter was published in the *Official Records,* vol. xlviii, part ii, pp. 1303-1304.

[281] "I have to acknowledge receipt of your communication of the 19th inst and say, that I approve your views relative to encamping the troops. You will remember I first directed the 1st Indian Brigade and also the Creeks and Seminoles to be moved out to Little Boggy. The best policy is to keep them all employed in front scouting and driving out beef from the Arkansas River . . . " (Cooper to Stand Watie, May 21, 1865, *Confederate Archives,* chap. 2, no. 258, pp. 27-28). See also Cooper to Scott, May 15, 1865, *ibid.,* p. 18.

[282] " . . . all officers of this Dist. are expected to do their duty and encourage the people to bear with fortitude necessary and unavoidable privation. I have no use for grumblers and croakers." (Cooper to Capt. F. R. Young, May 10, 1865, *ibid.,* p. 5). See also Cooper to Lt. Col. J. M. Bryan, May 13, 1865, ordering the arrest of seven deserters, *ibid.,* p. 5, also this from Cooper to Judge W. F. Harrison, May 18, 1865, *ibid.,* p. 24:
  " . . . There are many wild reports afloat thro the country. I advise all to keep cool & quiet & preserve order and enforce the laws against all who violate them."
  A particularly strong appeal of the sort indicated appeared in a confidential letter to Scott, May 17th (*Official Records,* vol. xlviii, part ii, pp. 1310-1312).

[283] See Cooper to Young, May 10, 1865, *Confederate Archives,* chap. 2, no. 258, p. 4; Cooper to Smith, May 15, 1865, *ibid.,* p. 18; Cooper to Young, May, 19, 1865, *ibid.,* p. 26; Cooper to Welch, May 19, 1865, *ibid.,* (These last two have reference to supplying the destitute family of Chilly McIntosh). The following indicate that the people of Texas were entreated to help relieve the distress of the Indians. There was danger of their breaking out beyond all restraint. If suffering from hunger, they could not be prevented from depredating. "It is certainly the interest of the farmers of Texas," urged Cooper upon McCulloch, "to contribute a part of their substance rather than have it wasted by depredations." (Cooper to McCulloch, May 23, 1865, *ibid.,* p. 33; Cooper to Stand Watie, May 23, 1865, *ibid.,* p. 32). Texas was chiefly responsible for the task of supplying the indigents being a doubly hard one. Purchasing agents there appropriated "the lion's share of money" and forced the driving of cattle thitherward (Cooper to Anderson, May 15, 1865, *Official Records,* vol. xlviii, part ii, p. 1305). See also letter to Scott, May 14th, *ibid.,* pp. 1303-1304.

scribed.[284] He permitted no diminution of the sense of obligation resting upon the Confederacy towards its Indian allies and debts, owing by the government to private individuals, he did his utmost to liquidate, even to the extent of disposing of all movable property.[285]

Early in April when so much was happening to presage ultimate disaster, Kirby Smith had arranged at the instance of Governor Murrah and others conversant with frontier conditions, for a mission to the wild tribes and, in the fateful days of May, Cooper advanced the project just as though, for him, the end of the war were yet afar off. The object of the mission was an alliance, offensive and defensive,[286] not a bad idea, inasmuch

---

[284] As late as May 27th, as shown by a letter of that date to Stand Watie (*ibid.*, p. 43), Cooper was taking great precautions against "property being carried off by deserters and thieves." He desired Capt. Haskins' company "to be used in piqueting the road about Boggy Depot and patrolling the neighborhood."

[285] (a) " . . . I am willing to part with anything . . . except ammunition. We shall want that if the terms proposed by the Governors are refused by the U.S. Government.

"The question would then be plainly printed, Shall we submit to be plundered of our property and then hung? If the terms (?) there will be a general pacification. If not we will have '*war to the knife, and the knife to the hilt*'." (Cooper to Scott, May 25, 1865, *Confederate Archives*, Chap. 2, no. 258, pp. 40-41).

(b) " . . . I shall trust to your judgement in managing your Dept. We must do what is right towards the creditors of the C.S. as far as public property will go, in case the final catastrophe occurs. We must also provide for the indigents and the troops. To this end I have placed all the available property of the different departments at Maj. Oliver's disposal who will barter anything for food that can be dispensed with . . . " (Cooper to Maj. J. N. Norris, May 25, 1865, *ibid.*, p. 40). See also various letters, *ibid.*, pp. 37-41.

It was this way of disposing of public property pending the negotiations for surrender that induced Sheridan to denounce Kirby Smith's surrender as in the nature of a swindle (*Official Records*, vol. xlviii, part ii, p. 1015). Sheridan, by the way, thoroughly distrusted Smith. He believed he and other southern generals were conspiring together relative to a Mexican colonization scheme (*ibid.*, p. 1192).

[286] Lynch, in his *Bench and Bar of Texas*, states that pacification was

as the Federals had succeeded in completely alienating the denizens of the plains. It being thought the height of inexpediency to give Texans, eager in their own emergency for the alliance but hated by Kiowas and Comanches, a too prominent part in it,[287] the headship was tendered to Albert Pike.[288] As it happened, however, he was unable on account of family matters to accept [289] and the whole affair devolved, after all, upon Texans, upon Brigadier-general James W. Throckmorton [290] and Colonel W. D. Reagan, then judge of the military court in the Indian country. At Cooper's suggestion,[291] representatives from the allied slaveholding tribes were included, a tripartite treaty being deemed desirable.[292] The place of meeting was to be Council Grove near the False Washita and the time, May fifteenth.[293] Some apprehension existed lest Blunt, hearing of the council, should venture himself in its direction "or send a flanking party that way." The place, therefore, was changed to Elm Springs on the Washita so that, should the enemy from Gibson arrive, the negotiators could drop back into Texas.[294] Still

likewise an object; for "the Indian tribes inhabiting the Texas border . . . had assumed a threatening attitude seriously endangering the safety of the frontier settlements . . . " This is substantiated by Smith's instructions.

[287] Smith to Throckmorton, April 8, 1865, *Official Records*, vol. xlviii, part ii, pp. 1271-1272.

[288] Smith to Pike, April 8, 1865, *ibid.*, pp. 1266-1269.

[289] West to Reagan, April 15, 1865, *ibid.*, pp. 1279-1380.

[290] Throckmorton had had quite a little to do with the Indians. He had "participated in the capture of Forts Washita and Arbuckle" at the outset of the war and he had led a company at the Battle of Chuste-nallah and in the two days' fight at Elkhorn (Lynch, p. 419).

[291] Smith to Cooper, April 8, 1865, *Official Records*, vol. xlviii, part ii, p. 1270.

[292] Smith to Cooper, same date, *ibid.*, pp. 1270-1271.

[293] West to Reagan, April 15, 1865, *op. cit.*

[294] Cooper to Throckmorton, May 13, 1865, *Confederate Archives*, chap. 2, no. 258, p. 8; *Official Records*, vol. xlviii, part ii, p. 1301.

later it was changed to North Fork and there the council was expected to meet on the day appointed. A preliminary council between the Confederate commissioners and the representatives of the allied nations had been held previously at Cooper's headquarters, Fort Washita, and the question of inducing the Indians of the Plains to make a raid into Kansas discussed, Cooper having grave doubts whether it would, under existing circumstances, be either proper or politic to turn loose the savages, known to be thirsting for revenge, upon the almost defenceless Federal settlements.[295] Cooper's views prevailed, pending a reference of the matter to General Smith,[296] and Throckmorton was instructed to confine his negotiations merely to the securing of friendly relations.[297]

Foregatherings of the storm soon to burst were beginning to cause Cooper great uneasiness. Ignore the Indian nations as Smith, McCulloch and Magruder safely might, he could not and would not if he could. They were all about him. Their mutterings he could hear when all else was silent. Steadfast in their interests he purposed to stand. Oblivious seemingly of the many evidences that the Confederacy was, in reality, already defunct, he applied himself to the work in hand, his determination being to go ahead "without deviation until the Government of the Confederate States" should speak "in some tangible and authoritative manner." [298]   He placed an injunction upon all moves for separate managements, his policy being to

---

[295] Cooper to Anderson, May 15, 1865, *Confederate Archives*, chap. 2, no. 258, pp. 15-16; *Official Records*, vol. xlviii, part ii, p. 1306.

[296] Cooper to Adair, May 16, 1865, *Confederate Archives*, chap. 2, no. 258, p. 20; *Official Records*, vol. xlviii, part ii, pp. 1307-1308.

[297] Cooper to Throckmorton, May 16, 1865, *Confederate Archives*, chap. 2, no. 258, p. 19; *Official Records*, vol. xlviii, part ii, p. 1307.

[298] Cooper to Scott, May 14, 1865, *op. cit.*

hold the command intact so long as it was humanly possible; for in no other way could he hope to avert the disaster that would inevitably threaten when the community learnt the worst and became wild with excitement.

On May 26, 1865, Lieutenant-general S. B. Buckner, chief of staff, signed at New Orleans, on behalf of General Smith, the convention for the surrender of the Trans-Mississippi Department.[299] All attempts at a prolongation of the struggle for independence had proved unavailing. Officers might have their plans and their ambitions but the rank and file were weary of war. Reports that the surrender was about to take place had reached Cooper and he had concluded that it was now high time that the Indians, whom he had restrained thus far, should be permitted to do as they desired, "provide for themselves."[300] As a matter of fact, unbeknownst to him, they were already doing it.

At that very moment, the half-breed Cherokee, E. C. Boudinot, the same who, in 1861, had taken what for him was a prominent part in the Arkansas secession convention, was in Arkansas in the company of A. H. Garland to whom he had voluntarily attached himself at the time when Garland was posing as a commissioner on the part of the "secession government" in the state and, in its interests, seeking conferences with General Reynolds and Governor Murphy. Boudinot took advantage of the opportunity to present to the same men the case of the Indian Territory; for, as he himself confessed, the interests of the nations there "are so blended with those of Arkansas that they will and must follow her fortunes. It was this fact that induced prominent

---

[299] *Official Records*, vol. xlviii, part ii, pp. 600-601.

[300] Cooper to Anderson, May 25, 1865, *Official Records*, vol. xlviii, part ii, p. 1319.

citizens of the State at Washington to invite me to deliberations which have resulted in the mission of Mr. Garland . . ."[301] Garland's mission failed in its immediate object because of his insistence upon being considered a commissioner of a government, the political status of which Reynolds refused to recognize.[302] Boudinot had only very recently returned home, apparently;[303] but he had probably returned with advanced and inside information as to what were the intentions of Kirby Smith. Political acumen was his most noticeable characteristic at all times and he now with admirable promptitude sought the rehabilitation of himself and his people, old scores forgotten. Blandly and naively he offered himself as a mediator for "restoring peace and quiet upon the frontier." If responsibility for the original disturbance were the chief qualification for the office, Boudinot was assuredly a most promising candidate.

The re-establishment of peace upon the frontier was, however, for the time being in other hands. Throckmorton's council had not been heard from as yet; but Cooper was anxious that it should have military protection until the fiery savages from the plains had returned to their ranges.[304] No contemporary evidence of a meeting at North Fork has been forthcoming; but, of a fateful one at Camp Napoleon, on the Washita,

---

[301] Boudinot to Reynolds and Murphy, May 26, 1865, *Official Records,* vol. xlviii, part ii, p. 631.

[302] Reynolds to Garland and Boudinot, May 26, 1865, *ibid.,* p. 630.

[303] I infer this from the fact that about the middle of the month, Cooper had had word from him that "the Confederate States has passed an act to pay the annuities to the Indians in cotton." (*ibid.,* p. 1308). Cooper presumably took alarm at the incident and doubtless Boudinot did also, hence the rapidity with which he sought to identify himself with the leaders in Arkansas.

[304] — *Ibid.*

May twenty-fourth and subsequently, much.[305]   If
Throckmorton and Reagan were present [306] – supposing that Reagan had joined Throckmorton as contemplated – they were minor characters in a great assemblage. The Indians had it all their own way for once.
As later events divulged, the purpose of the gathering
was to arrange for peace regardless of anything General Smith was doing or might do. The calm effront-
ery of the proceeding has its ridiculous side. Was it
possible that the southern Indians were oblivious of the
fact that their fortunes were inextricably entangled
with those of the Confederacy? Were they unapprecia-
tive of the completeness of the Confederate defeat?
Kirby Smith's dilatoriness in surrendering had made
them almost desperate and it had emboldened them to
strike out for themselves and to take their own precautions against further aggressions. They had long been
out of sympathy with the Southern Union, had known
themselves to be only its catspaw, and had repeatedly
at intervals, whenever righteous indignation out-
weighed loyalty, exerted their utmost to detach themselves from it and to form an Indian league for mutual
protection. Outraged cruelly as they had been, betrayed basely, injured beyond recovery, they doubtless
felt that they had nothing to gain and everything to
lose from a continued connection with the southerners.
A pity it was that they had not thought of it sooner.
Such a re-tracing of steps as they were now about to
deliberate upon was forever too late.

---

[305] Reynolds to Harlan, June 28, 1865, O.I.A., General Files, *Southern
Superintendency*, 1865, I 1118; Commissioner of Indian Affairs, *Report*, 1865,
p. 295; *Official Records*, vol. xlviii, part ii, p. 1018.

[306] Leavenworth heard of "a great council near Fort Cobb," at which
"a Texan officer was present" (*Official Records*, vol. xlviii, part ii, p. 1009).
See also, p. 1042. Chisholm informed H. J. Tibbits that a Mexican officer
was present (*ibid.*, p. 1021).

The conference at Camp Napoleon had its pathetic features. The Indians congregated there; reviewed the long and troubled history of the relations between the red and white people and drafted a compact, signed on the twenty-sixth, to safeguard the interests of their race for the future. Shades of Pontiac and of Tecumseh ought to have warned them of the utter futility of their undertaking. A cry that was almost that of despair was sounded in the preamble to the compact, as was also a note of defiance.

"Whereas the history of the past admonishes the red man that his once great and powerful race is rapidly passing away as snow beneath the summer sun, our people of the mighty nations of our forefathers many years ago having been as numerous as the leaves of the forest or the stars of the heavens; but now, by the vicissitudes of time and change and misfortune and evils of disunion, discord and war among themselves are but a wreck of their former greatness; their vast and lovely country and beautiful hunting grounds, abounding in all the luxuries and necessities of life and happiness, given to them by the Great Spirit, having known no limits but the shores of the great waters and the horizon of the heavens, is now on account of our weakness being reduced and hemmed into a small and precarious country that we can scarcely call our own and in which we cannot remain in safety and pursue our peaceful avocations, nor can we visit the bones and the graves of our kindred, so dear to our hearts and sacred to our memories, to pay the tribute of respect, unless we run the risk of being murdered by our more powerful enemies; and

"Whereas there still remains in the timbered countries, on the plains, and in the mountains many nations and bands of our people, which, if united, would present a body that would afford sufficient strength to command respect and assert and maintain our rights; Therefore, we . . .   do, for our peace and happiness and the preservation of our race, make and enter into the following league and compact, to wit: . . .   " [307]

[307] *Official Records*, vol. xlviii, part ii, pp. 1102-1103.

Before General Smith had actually surrendered his command and before the civilized and uncivilized Indians had formed their league, Cooper had advised with Stand Watie [308] as to the expediency of convening the Grand Council; that is, the council of the six allied nations, which had, for some time now, been meeting pretty regularly at Armstrong Academy. It would be the function of that body to receive the report of the commission to the Indians of the Plains, to take into consideration the condition of the Indian nations, and to determine their future course. To call the council in the emergency that had arisen was the only wise thing to do and Cooper so notified various of the influential Indians, [309] as likewise General Smith's assistant adjutant-general. [310] The date for the called session was put at June tenth.

The Grand Council met. The outcome of its discussions and deliberations was significant and took the form of what for want of a better name might be called an armistice. This armistice the Indians, not as a defeated party, utterly vanquished, but as a victor, insolently offered to their unionist brethren and to the United States, the real conqueror. By the terms of the armistice, however, couched in the language of formal resolutions, [311] the great and underlying motive of

[308] Cooper to Stand Watie, May 22, 1865, *Official Records*, vol. xlviii, part ii, p. 1318; *Confederate Archives*, chap. 2, no. 258, p. 31.

[309] Colonel W. P. Adair, May 22nd, Colonel Tandy Walker, May 23rd, Colonel Jock McCurtain, May 24th, *Confederate Archives*, ibid., pp. 30-31, 35, 36; *Official Records*, vol. xlviii, part ii, p. 1318.

[310] May 25, 1865, *Official Records*, vol. xlviii, part ii, p. 1319. See also Cooper to Colonel R. W. Lee, commanding at Fort Arbuckle, May 22, 1865, *Confederate Archives*, chap. 2, no 258, p. 30; Cooper to Captain T. M. Scott, A.A.G.D.I.T., May 23, 1865, ibid., pp. 34-35; and Cooper to Throckmorton, May 22, 1865, ibid., p. 29; *Official Records*, vol. xlviii, part ii, p. 1317; Cooper to Buckner, June 28, 1865, *Bussey Correspondence*, G.G.

[311] Copies of the resolutions were sent, in duplicate and in triplicate, to

their gathering at Camp Napoleon stands revealed. It was the mustering of full Indian strength for the tug of war that was inevitable. None knew better than they that their possessory rights in Indian Territory were now in jeopardy and that with forces divided they could never hope to hold out against the covetous white man. Their first concern, therefore, was to mend the breach in their own tribal ranks and for that their armistice was cleverly contrived. Never a hint of wrongdoing, of mistaken judgment, of miserable, egregious failure was suffered to appear. The integrity of Indian Territory was to be a *sine qua non* and, to maintain that integrity, all nations in alliance with the Federal Government or hostile to the contracting powers were to be invited to join the Indian confederacy conceived at Camp Napoleon. A solidarity secured, peace negotiations with the United States were to be opened up. To act independently of everything governing General Smith's surrender was their audacious purpose.[312] "As independent powers and allies of the rebels," [313] they had entered the war and, in identical guise, proposed to settle its accounts. Their right to make a separate peace they would obstinately maintain.

The secessionist Indians, half-breeds mostly, now as formerly attempted yet one other thing. They arrogantly took it upon themselves to specify where the negotiations for peace should take place and selected Washington. Beyond the reach of frontier politics and

the United States government and to each of the tribes interested. With a full list of signatories, they were printed in the Fort Smith *New Era,* July 29, 1865. The text minus some of the signatures is to be found in *Official Records,* vol. xlviii, part ii, pp. 1103-1104.

[312] Bussey to Colonel John Levering, A.A.G., Little Rock, dated Fort Smith, June 25, 1865, *Bussey Correspondence,* B.

[313] Veatch, reporting to Crosby, July 20th, stated the case very precisely (*Official Records,* vol. xlviii, part ii, p. 1095).

tribal disputes they might hope for a fair statement of their case and justice. Forgotten had they that their position with reference to the United States could never be so strategic as it had been with the Confederate. Their demeanor towards their unionist tribesmen was presumptuous in the extreme, particularly as those same tribesmen, supported by their powerful ally, had already shown a determination, grim and inexorable, to impose the hardest of possible conditions upon them, conditions that would have implied loss of citizenship and property rights. Against such, the worst of contingencies, the secessionist Indians purposed to defend themselves in advance by stipulating that no terms of peace should be binding until ratified in full national council.

The terms of the armistice resolved upon, the Grand Council at Armstrong Academy adjourned and a delegation of Choctaws, accompanied by Captain G. Wilcox, A. A. G. on General Cooper's staff, started out for Fort Smith, the headquarters of General Cyrus Bussey,[314] commanding the Frontier District. They carried with them the resolutions of the council and, by way of credentials, a letter [315] from Winchester Col-

---

[314] Cyrus Bussey, Major-general by brevet, U.S.V., was one of the men who, at Pea Ridge, reported on Indian atrocities. He testified that eight of the Third Iowa had been butchered and scalped (*Annals of Iowa*, vol. v, no. 3 (July, 1867) p. 909. See also Barron, *Lone Star Defenders*, p. 69. When General Reynolds was assigned to the Department of Arkansas and Seventh Army Corps (A.G.O., *Personal Papers of J. J. Reynolds*) relieving General Steele, a reorganization of the command was contemplated and Bussey was chosen to assist in it. "Grave charges of corruption had been made against all the officers who had served in the District. The War Department had sent several inspectors to examine the charges. One of them, Maj. Gen. Herron, recommended the removal of all the important officers of the District, which was done, and General Bussey was selected with the view of breaking up the corruption and restoring discipline . . . " (*Annals of Iowa*, vol. v, no. 3, pp. 902-913).

[315] Winchester Colbert to General Bussey, June 16, 1865, *Bussey Cor-*

bert, governor of the Chickasaw Nation. Were any doubt remaining on the score of the extreme independence of attitude assumed by the secessionist Indians, Colbert's letter would amply suffice to dispel it. After calling attention to the circumstance that no troops, hostile to the United States, were now in Indian Territory, he announced it as the wish of the confederated nations, expressed through the resolutions of their general council, that no more forces from the outside should cross the border. In somewhat similar strain Cooper had previously assured Colonel Tandy Walker, of Winchester Colbert's own tribe, that "I do not desire collision with the Federals, but they must keep out of the Choctaw country until the grand council otherwise determine." [316] Another request that Colbert made, and in terms somewhat curt, was that a passport be issued permitting the several commissioners who were to conduct the Indian side of the peace negotiations, to proceed to Washington unmolested. The said commissioners [317] were not yet on hand, but the resolu-

respondence, A. Two sets of correspondence, bearing upon the events narrated in this chapter, were forwarded to D. N. Cooley by Bussey, under date of September 12, 1865, with distinct reference, no doubt, to the Fort Smith Peace Council. One set is lettered from A to T, the other, from AA to JJ. Some of the documents are to be found in printed form in *Official Records*, vol. xlviii, part ii.

[316] May 23, 1865, *Official Records*, vol. xlviii, part ii, p. 1318.

[317] The Cherokee commissioners had evidently been appointed. They were, E. C. Boudinot, Wm. P. Adair, Clement N. Vann, Richard Fields, J. T. Davis, and Smallwood. The sixth commissioner was probably a substitute. Their credentials were not issued until August 1st, were signed then by Stand Watie, and read as follows:

"At a Grand Council convened at Armstrong Academy on the 10th day of June, 1865, you were appointed and constitutionally confirmed delegates on the part of that portion of the Cherokee Nation over whom I have the honor to preside as Chief Executive, to meet commissioners on the part of the United States, with full authority and power, to negotiate by treaty or otherwise a full and final adjustment of all questions of interest affecting our rights or property . . . " (O.I.A., Land Files, *Indian Talks, Councils*, &c., Box 4, 1865, 1866).

tions of the grand council had called for the appointment of five from each constituent member of the confederation.

On the arrival of the delegation in Fort Smith, Wilcox reported that at the time of his parting company with Cooper on the twentieth no notice had come of General Smith's approaching surrender although, about the fifteenth, unofficial information respecting it had been disseminated by means of a Fort Smith newspaper, the *New Era.* [318] Cooper had retired to his home at Fort Washita, which for some time past had been his military headquarters, and of that fact General Smith, the department commander, had been duly apprised.[319]

Concerning the contents of Governor Colbert's let-

[318] "Capt. G. Wilcox, A.A. Gen¹ on General Cooper's staff, and a Delegation of the Choctaw Indians have just arrived here with communications from Gov. Colbert of the Chickasaw Nation, which I forward for your information and such instructions as you may have to give. Capt. Wilcox informed me that General Cooper has never received any notice of the surrender of Kirby Smith's Department except a notice in the Fort Smith New Era which reached him about the 15th inst. and that Cooper had disbanded all his troops and was at his home at Washita nor had any official communication been received from Kirby Smith on the 20th when he left Cooper. He reports that the wild Indians who started on the expedition to attack trains on the Santa Fee Road were recalled about the 10th of June and that several of these wild Indians are represented in the Grand Council and are now anxious for peace. These Indians express a desire to surrender themselves to the U. S. authorities and do not wish to be governed by the surrender of Kirby Smith. This I learn from the delegation. I will telegraph you the resolutions of the Grand Council if you desire. Will it be proper for me to furnish the passport to Washington asked for by Gov. Colbert for the delegation. In the present state of affairs some definite understanding should be arrived at with these people. Capt. Wilcox and party gave their paroles and will return as soon as I can reply to their communication. They are extremely anxious for some assurance that they can return to their homes and be protected in person and property." (Bussey to Colonel Jchn Levering, A.A.G., June 25, 1865, *Bussey Correspondence*, B).

[319] Cooper to Anderson, May 25, 1865, *Official Records*, vol. xlviii, part ii, p. 1319; Cooper to Bussey, September 5, 1865, *Bussey Correspondence*, II.

ter, Bussey straightway reported to his superior officer, General J. J. Reynolds, at Little Rock and to the Interior Department; but, while he awaited advices from one or the other as to how he should proceed, a commission from Louisiana, acting under authority conferred by General F. J. Herron,[320] accomplished that with the Indians which rendered unnecessary the journey of the Choctaw delegation. The commission,[321] consisting of Lieutenant-colonel Asa C. Matthews, assisted by Adjutant William H. Vance, both of them from the United States Volunteers, had been empowered by Herron to journey to the Indian country and effect a truce with the various warring tribes.[322]

In organising such a commission, General Herron, stationed, as he was, in command of the Northern District of Louisiana with newly assigned headquarters in its western part at a distance not very remote from the Choctaw domain and in a position to know what was going on there, was unquestionably animated by the best of intentions.[323] Canby had confided to him "the management of matters in the Red River country dur-

---

[320] For an account of the prominent position taken by Herron in the surrender of the Trans-Mississippi Department, see a biographical sketch of him in *Annals of Iowa*, vol. v, no. 1, pp. 801-807.

[321] Herron's reasons for sending the commission are to be found recited at length in a letter from him to Banks, dated Shreveport, June 8, 1865 (*Official Records*, vol. xlviii, part ii, p. 818). He had heard from Buckner of Throckmorton's mission also of the meeting of the council called for June 10th. He inferred that the latter was for the purpose of carrying out the former. The place of meeting, so he supposed, was Fort Towson and thither he sent his messengers. It seemed to him "a fine opportunity to meet the chief men of the different tribes, and to have at the same time the cooperation of the Confederate commissioners."

[322] F. J. Herron to Col. A. C. Matthews, June 9, 1865, *Bussey Correspondence*, JJ; *Official Records*, vol. xlviii, part ii, pp. 830-831.

[323] No better evidence of this need be produced than Herron's own letter to Forsyth, Chief of Staff, June 27, 1865. He felt he had reason to congratulate himself on the good results of his mission (*ibid.*, pp. 1005-1006).

ing the important period required for paroling Kirby Smith's army and receiving the surrendered public property." [324] That affairs concerned with the capitulation of the Indians came rightfully within his jurisdiction constitutes a debatable theme. [325] Canby's instructions to him were not explicit and the broadest possible interpretation of them would not comprehend the conveyance of treaty-making power. Obviously there was grave danger of his trespassing not only upon the preserves of the Interior Department but upon those of the military commanders in Arkansas. On the score of the latter, the commander at Fort Smith in due time complained; but as yet he rested in blissful ignorance.

Meanwhile, Herron's commission, ignoring General Bussey and General Reynolds, too, for that matter, crossed the boundary into the Indian Territory and forthwith began its work, fair play and great magnanimity, its watchwords. Its main object was soon accomplished, notwithstanding that it met, at the outset, with a serious disappointment, the Grand Council, which Herron had heard of and which his commission had expected to deal with, being adjourned. Formal truces had therefore to be made with individual tribes through their principal chiefs. On the nineteenth [326] of June, at Doaksville, Matthews negotiated with

---

[324] C. T. Christensen to Herron, May 30, 1865, *ibid.*, p. 681.

[325] It would appear that Herron had a reputation for liking to do things his own way. For Dana's opinion of him, see *Recollections of the Civil War*, pp. 70, 87-88. Before the full effects of his mission were known, he was relieved. James C. Veatch was ordered, June 21st, to relieve him (*Official Records*, vol. xlviii, part ii, p. 956).

[326] Most references to the truce made with Pitchlynn give its date as the nineteenth; but Pitchlynn's own proclamation would indicate an earlier date. The proclamation is among the *Bussey Correspondence* and, with some slight verbal modifications, was published in *Official Records*, vol. xlviii, part ii, p. 1105.

Governor P. P. Pitchlynn, acting for the Choctaws,[327] and, on the twenty-third, near Doaksville, with Brigadier-general Stand Watie, acting for the secessionist Cherokees.[328] A correspondence looking to the same end was opened up with Governor Colbert;[329] but not until Bastile Day, the fourteenth of July, did it meet with fruition.[330]

The discord conceivably always imminent where one officer or department of a government encroaches upon the rights of another soon arose and itself gave rise to a disputatious letter-writing and report-making touching the details of Cooper's surrender, the domestic infelicities of the tribes, and the time and place of peace-making. What Herron had done needed to be done and that right promptly. A consciousness of that fact was, perhaps, the reason why his action was never wholly and publicly repudiated; but was allowed to stand in so far as it served the purposes of the powers that were, to be cavilled against occasionally, its irregularity the subject of reproach eventually, and its resulting amnesty provisions most enjoyed by those who least deserved them.

News of Colonel Matthews' success in the making of

---

[327] *Bussey Correspondence*; I. D. Files, Bundle, no. 54; *Official Records,* vol. xlviii, part ii, p. 1006; Harlan to Stanton, August 7, 1865, O.I.A., Land Files, *Indian Talks, Councils, &c.,* Box 4, 1865, 1866.

328 The truce with Stand Watie was, except for the substitution of other names, the exact counterpart of that with Pitchlynn. A printed copy of it is in *Official Records,* vol. xlviii, part ii, pp. 1100-1101.

[329] Matthews to Colbert, June 23, 1865, *ibid.,* pp. 1105-1106; *Bussey Correspondence.*

[330] *Official Records,* vol. xlviii, part ii, p. 1097. On July 16, 1865, General Veatch, who had succeeded Herron in command in the Northern Division of Louisiana, acknowledged the receipt of the text of the truce and registered his approval of the whole proceeding. (*Ibid.,* pp. 1106-1107). On July 24th, Stanton notified Doolittle that Grant had reported an informal treaty made with the secessionists under authority from Herron (*ibid.,* pp. 1117-1118).

truces reached General Bussey through a communication from Governor Colbert, who, writing on the twelfth of July, announced that the passports for an Indian delegation to proceed to Washington would no longer be required since arrangements had been made "by commissioners sent out by Maj. Genl. Herron for another call of the Grand Council at Armstrong Academy with the understanding that commissioners would be sent out by the United States Government with full power to conclude all necessary treaties with the Indian Nations represented in the late Grand Council." [331] Bussey, meanwhile, had obtained permission to issue the passports and was perplexed by the new developments in the case; for Secretary Harlan,[332] surmising that peace commissioners had been appointed by the Grand Council and were, therefore, of more than ordinary status, was preparing to receive them as negotiators, fully accredited, in Washington.[333]

[331] Colbert to Bussey, July 12, 1865, *Bussey Correspondence*, E.

[332] James Harlan, secretary of the interior in the stead of Usher resigned, had been a personal and political friend of President Lincoln and it was Lincoln who first offered him the portfolio which, when accepted, made him the chief determining factor in Indian pacification. The history of his life by Johnson Brigham, which is largely based upon the *Autobiographical Manuscript and Papers* "in the care and custody of his daughter, Mrs. Robert T. Lincoln of Chicago," throws little light upon the Indian affairs aspect of his career as Secretary of the Interior. As will be seen from this narrative, the loyal Indians suffered outrageous injustice at his hands. To the present investigator it is still a mystery why Lincoln, who held out hopes of justice and reparation to John Ross, selected for the post that commanded the entire situation the one person who, in the Senate, had been most assiduous in devising means of further despoiling the red loyalists.

"On March 9th James Harlan was appointed secretary of the Interior by President Lincoln," affirms Clark in his life of *Kirkwood* (p. 303). The Senate unhesitatingly confirmed the appointment; but Harlan himself seems not to have been over-eager for the place. He made himself believe, however, that he could purge the department of the corruption that had disgraced it under his predecessors (Brigham's *James Harlan*, pp. 195-196).

[333] Bussey to Colbert, July 6, 1865, *Bussey Correspondence*, C; Bussey

The cancelling of passports was, however, by no manner of means, the full extent of the difficulty. Upon leaving Shreveport, Matthews had been entrusted with yet another commission. He had been made the bearer of dispatches, of dispatches to Throckmorton and Reagan, and, above all, to Cooper. The dispatches to Cooper were orders, forwarded by Buckner, providing for the formal surrender of the District of Indian Territory, Cooper's entire command.[334] Obviously, the one commission had little in common with the other. As executed it might even be considered its contradiction. The expectation seems to have been that Matthews would fall in with Cooper at Fort Towson and, having delivered the orders governing the surrender, would proceed to Armstrong Academy and confer with the Indians, supposedly in council there. The well-laid plan miscarried. Cooper was at Washita, the Grand Council was adjourned, the Indians were dispersed. There was nothing for Matthews to do, apparently, but to reverse the order of proceedings and, as the pacification of the Indians seemed urgent and two, at least of the Indian governors near at hand, at Doaksville or in its vicinity, he made his truces and then, when opportunity offered, forwarded Buckner's dispatches to Washita.[335]

Astutely circumspect as ever and thoroughly alive to the main chance, Cooper prepared to stand upon his dignity. He knew of the truces and at once determined to profit by them, if he could. He professed himself

to Reynolds, July 24, 1865, *ibid.*, F; O.I.A., General Files, *Southern Superintendency*, 1865; Commissioner of Indian Affairs, *Report*, 1865, p. 296.

[334] See Special Orders, issued by General Smith, June 2, 1865 (*Official Records*, vol. xlviii, part ii, pp. 727, 728; Buckner to Cooper, June 6, 1865, *ibid.*, pp. 1322-1323, June 8, 1865, pp. 818-819).

[335] Cooper to Buckner, June 28, 1865, *Bussey Correspondence*, GG.

a citizen of the Chickasaw Nation and, as such, protected personally by the agreement, the truce, the amnesty, in point of fact, that Matthews had by this time
made with Governor Colbert.[336] By Cooper's understanding of the matter there was, in reality, no command to surrender.[337] The Indian forces were all ben-

---

[336] The most explicit statement of this claim is to be found in one of
Cooper's later letters, one addressed to General Bussey from Armstrong
Academy, September 5, 1865, *Bussey Correspondence*, II.

"I have to acknowledge your two communications of the 26th ulto.
and to say that it has been no fault of mine that the terms of surrender agreed upon between Gen. Canby of the United States Army
and Lt. Gen. E. K. Smith, late of the Confederate States Army, were
not carried fully into effect within the District of the Indian Territory.

"In the first place, Gen. Smith was duly notified some time previous
to the surrender that Head Quarters of the District of Indian Territory
had been removed to Fort Washita. No notice ever reached me that
it was expected or required that the surrender should take place at
Fort Towson, so far from it. I received orders from Lt. Gen. S. B.
Buckner, Chief of Staff, Trans-Miss. Dept., that directed me to apply
to the nearest U.S. Military Post and complete the surrender of troops
and public property within the District of the Indian Territory. Lt.
Col. Mathews, Commissioner in behalf of the United States, sent by
Maj. Gen. Herron brot these orders & forwarded them to me after he
had entered into a "Truce" with Gov. Pitchlynn, Gen. Stand Watie
& others, the terms of which covered all the Indian troops & citizens.
Maj. White came, as I learn, to Dockrodla, but left the Territory
without communicating with me in any manner. I have been ready and
willing, although myself a citizen of the Chickasaw Nation & therefore embraced within the amnesty contained in the "Truce" entered
into by Lt. Col. Mathews with Gov. Winchester Colbert, to do all that
honor and good faith require in compliance with the terms of surrender, entered into between Gen^ls Canby & Smith, so far as practicable under the circumstances, and shall avail myself of the earliest
opportunity to give my parole & obtain the necessary certificate of the
same, also to turn over such public property as I can preserve."

[337] It is admissible that, even had no truce been made, a surrender
of the Indian forces would have been utterly impracticable. As Cooper
informed Buckner, in the letter of June 28th, it would have endangered his
life to have attempted it. Veatch acquiesced in the idea of impracticability
(Veatch to Crosby, July 20, 1865, *Official Records*, vol. xlviii, part ii, pp.
1095-1097). That uncertainty existed in the minds of the Indians themselves as to their status under usages of the war is to be inferred from the
letter which Colonel W. P. Adair and Colonel J. M. Bell addressed to

eficiaries under Matthews' commission and the white forces had practically disappeared. Cooper, therefore, asked for further instructions.[338] He also communicated with General Bussey and requested that a properly-authorised officer be detailed to receive his parole.[339] Bussey's rejoinder was, that such an officer

Veatch, July 19, 1865 (*Official Records*, vol. xlviii, part ii, pp. 1099-1100). Veatch's reply drew a sharp distinction between red and white troops (*ibid.,* pp. 1101-1102, see also p. 1107). The matter that caused the Indians most concern was, however, not the cessation of war or its technical complications, but the destitution of their numbers cast adrift, about nine thousand people (Veatch to Crosby, July 20, 1865). The Indians put the estimate at fifteen thousand (Adair and Bell to Veatch, July 20, 1865, *Official Records*, vol. xlviii, part ii, p. 1102). See also Veatch to Crosby, July 21, 1865, *ibid.,* 1110-1111.

[338] Cooper to Buckner, June 28, 1865, *ibid.,* pp. 1097-1099; *Bussey Correspondence*, GG.

[339] "I have to enclose copies of instructions from Lieut. Genl S. B. Bucknor, dated June 6th, 1865, my reply, dated June 28th, asking further instructions in consequence of Truce entered into between Lieut. Col. A. C. Mathews, Col. P. P. Pitchlynn, Principal Chief of the Choctaw Nation, Brig. Genl Stand Watie, Chief of the Cherokees and Comdg Indian Division, and Brig. Genl Veatch's letter, dated July 15th, 1865, enclosing Order no. 6 and informing me that my communication had been forwarded to Genl Bucknor at New Orleans and that his answer would be sent to me when received.

"Not hearing anything further from Genl Veatch and being desirous to complete the surrender of troops and public property in the Dist. of Indian Territory as far as practicable without further delay, I have to request that you will designate some staff or other officer to act in conjunction with Capt. T. M. Scott, late A. A. General of said District for that purpose.

"The order no. 6 of Brig. Genl Veatch will provide for most of the whites, not citizens of any of the Indian tribes, if carried out by yourself, but there are some few scattered about among the Indians who ought to be paroled and required to go to their proper homes. To this end I would suggest that the officers designated to act with Capt. Scott be stationed here and authorized to parole such officers and men belonging to the Dist. of the Indian Territory as have not yet reported at some U.S. Military Post.

"There is some little property which belonged to the late Confederate States in my possession and also some in the hands of Gov. Colbert, Col. Pitchlynn, and other Indian authorities, which was taken charge

had already been sent by Reynolds to Fort Towson and, finding nobody there in authority, had returned to Little Rock, his mission unaccomplished.[340]

of for safe keeping at the time of the dispersion of the troops who took most of the public property.

"I have done all in my power to preserve order and protect public property and have here among other things six brass cannons, dismounted (the carriages and caissons having been taken away by some unknown persons) which I should be glad to turn over to any properly authorized officer of the United States.

"As you probably have been informed by Genl Colbert, Fort Washita was burned on the night of the 1st inst. I have not been able to trace the perpetrators of this outrage but am satisfied it was the work of incendiaries.

"By Mr. Jno. B. Yumer, late an A.D.C. on my staff, at the request of Gov. Colbert, I send you a communication from him relative to the proposed negotiation between the U.S. and the confederated Indian Nations. Gov. Colbert and nearly all the commissioners were desirous to meet the commissioners on behalf of the U. S. at Fort Smith in accordance with the request of the Secretary of the Interior on the 1st of September next; but it seems the Choctaws had not appointed and could not appoint their commissioners until the meeting of their council, 1st of Sept. The regular annual meeting of the Grand Council also takes place at Armstrong Academy on the 1st Monday of Sept. next and cannot be held elsewhere, so for that reason as well as the non-appointment of Choctaw commissioners, it appears to be necessary that the commissioners should meet at Armstrong Academy, the place designated by Col. Mathews and Col. Pitchlynn and, if necessary, proceed thence to Fort Smith to meet the U. States commissioners.

"It is with reluctance I learn that the Indians, especially the Choctaws, will proceed to Fort Smith being poorly provided for such a trip, and they would be highly gratified if the U.S. commissioners would come out to Armstrong Academy; but if this cannot be done they will proceed to Fort Smith. Please return answer without delay by Mr. Yumer who will convey it to the Grand Council at Armstrong Academy by 1st Monday in Sept.

"With a renewal of the tender of my services made through Genl Veatch . . . " (Cooper to Bussey, August 20, 1865, *Bussey Correspondence*, DD).

[340] Bussey to Cooper, August 26, 1865, *ibid.*, HH; *Official Records*, vol. xlviii, part ii, pp. 1214-1215. On June 16th, Reynolds notified Pope that he was sending "a commissioner to Fort Towson to parole the Indians, if any of them can be found embodied, and to receive the C.S. property in the Indian Territory." (*ibid.*, p. 905). The very next day, interestingly enough, Pope wrote to him expressing a desire that he would "send a mounted

Discrepancies between the Smith-Canby convention and the Matthews' agreements were not long in revealing themselves. By the former, all arms were to be delivered up, by the latter, no disarmament was required, but simply a cessation of hostilities and peaceable retirement to former homes. Divided or overlapping jurisdiction, here again, threatened to make for serious trouble. General Bussey's ire was at length aroused, particularly since the retention of arms seemed likely to increase the domestic infelicities of the tribes.

The tribal cleavage caused by the war was no light matter; but the grand council of June, in the spirit of complete self-sufficiency, had taken the first step towards its repair. In this connection let it be remembered that, ostensibly, the primary object of the special session of the Grand Council had been, not to arrange for the surrender that recent events called for, but to form and to consolidate an Indian confederation, preliminary and preparatory to peace negotiations with the United States. It was not intended that the confederation should be limited in membership to those tribes or parts of tribes that had, under the emergency of war, united for concerted action and later come to institute, as a legislative organ, the grand, or Armstrong Academy, council; but it was to embrace, if the same were feasible, the unionist and the secessionist Indians as well as some, at least, of the wild tribes of the great southwestern prairies. If the clever half-breeds could prevent it, it should certainly not be possible for unscrupulous white men to steal a march on the red and, in the interests of advancing civilization so-called, play off one Indian faction or one Indian tribe against

expedition of not less than 600 men from Fort Gibson or Fort Smith to Fort Cobb . . . " (*ibid.*, p. 911).

another.   The performances that had led years before
to the disgraceful and burglarizing *Treaty of New
Echota* must not be repeated.

The provision in the resolutions of the Grand Council for the re-union of warring elements was not permitted, so far as the Cherokees were concerned, to become a dead letter.   Towards the last of June, the
twenty-eighth in fact, Stand Watie, Chief and General,
took action and appointed six delegates, John Spears,
J. A. Scales, J. T. Davis, Joseph Vann, William P.
Chambers, and Too-noh-volah Foster, whom he instructed to go to Fort Gibson or to any other place
where unionist Indians were congregated and open up
negotiations for the re-establishment of tribal harmony.[341]   On the subject of an ulterior motive, the recovery of this world's goods, the general was discreetly
silent.

Provided with an escort of about fifty armed men,
the delegates set forth and, as they neared Fort Gibson,
sent forward an advance guard under a flag of truce to
announce their approach.   Their coming was unex-
pected and Colonel John A. Garrett of the Fortieth Iowa
Infantry, who commanded at Fort Gibson, demurred at
receiving them.   Their appearance struck him as most
peculiar.   To him it was inexplicable how, under the
conditions of Kirby Smith's surrender, they could be
going around the country in martial array.   He seriously questioned the advisability of admitting them to
conferences with other Indians for any purpose whatsoever until he had disarmed the escort and taken the
parole of all.[342]   The loyal Indians were dubious like-

---

[341] *Bussey Correspondence*, BB.

[342] Garrett to Captain H. D. B. Cutler, July 8, 1865, A.G.O., Archives
Division, *Fort Gibson Letter Book*, no. 20.

wise, particularly as it soon became all too evident that the chief anxiety of the individual secessionists was to return to their homes and to recover their lost or abandoned property. Bad feelings had been engendered through four weary years because of the terrible losses and still more terrible sufferings that the war had entailed; resentment was very keen and very bitter; and, in view of past misconduct and betrayal, suspicion of motives and of intentions was not to be easily allayed. The precautionary spirit that was spurring forward the secessionists was quite unknown to the mass of the unionists. They little dreamed that their tribal rights and privileges might be interfered with as a punishment for what a portion of the Nation, the half-breed at that, had done. Surely their guardian, their Great Father, the powerful and victorious United States government would never harm those who, against fearful odds, had remained loyal. Such a course would be contrary to one of the most fundamental of Anglo-Saxon principles of justice, the one, forsooth, that emanates from the idea that it is better by far to let the guilty escape than to run the risk of punishing an innocent man.

It was about the eighth of July when the delegates from the Cherokees, under sanction of the Grand Council, first put in an appearance at Gibson. Their mood was not conciliatory as it should have been. It was Indian-like and arrogant. At times it became defiant. They roamed the streets, armed, and they used language that was likely to exasperate. Such was Garrett's complaint. He grew more and more uneasy and finally insisted that the secessionists cross to the hither side of the Arkansas River and stay there. Only a few, and those unarmed, would he allow on the Fort Gibson side each day.[343] The unionist Indians he made responsible for the maintenance of peace. To add to his perplexity, seemingly, the delegates produced the papers that testified to the inception of Matthews' mission and to its accomplishment. They submitted them in evidence of their own right to bear arms; but Garrett was not to be convinced or mollified. The papers described an occurrence so unprecedented that he doubted their genuineness and appealed to headquarters for confirmation one way or the other.[344]

Meanwhile, Lewis Downing, in the absence of John Ross, called his followers together in council at Tahle-

[343] L. A. Duncan, A.A.A.G., to Major Scales, dated Fort Gibson, July 10, 1865, *ibid.*

[344] (a) "Captain, I have the honor to state that a delegation of Cherokees of the late Rebel Army has reported to me, for the purpose of securing aid in efforts to effect a meeting of a council between the two parties of Cherokees, the Loyal and those who have been in the Rebel service.

"They have submitted a number of papers, a part of them purporting to be from the United States authorities and from Maj. General Herron, another from officers in the service of our Government, acting under General Herron's authority.

"Notice of these papers, if genuine, should certainly have reached these Head Quarters officially; but not a word or an intimation of their existence has come to this office.

"I want information on the subject. The Brig. General Comdg Division, having telegraphic communication with the Department Head Quarters at Little Rock and with Washington, D.C., is respectfully asked for information in regard to these papers and for any instructions he may see proper to give. Are the papers, the copies of which I send you, genuine? If so and the parties agree to meet in council, shall I have them deliver up their arms? Shall I permit them (the Rebel party) to go back to their friends in the south with their arms without being paroled? Or should I take their arms and parole the men?

"There is some bad feeling between the parties but I hope no disturbance will result from it. I shall use every effort to prevent anything of this kind and, should any occur, will be prompt to restore quiet and order.

"I will state, should the party return to the South, I think they should be permitted to take a part of their arms with which to protect

quah to deliberate as to whether or no the delegation should be given an audience. July thirteenth, amnesty was resolved upon and, on the fourteenth, elaborately proclaimed.[345] At the same time, Scales, who seems to

themselves and to supply themselves with something to eat." (Garrett to Captain H. D. B. Cutler, A.A.G., 3rd Division, 7th Army Corps. July 9, 1865, *Bussey Correspondence*, AA; A.G.O., Archives Division, *Fort Gibson, Letter Book*, no. 20).

(b) "Col. Garrett, commanding at Fort Gibson, reports that about fifty armed Indians have reported there for the purpose of counciling with the loyal Indians about returning to their homes. He also sends me a copy of General Herron's letter to Lieut. Col. Mathews appointing him a commissioner on the part of the United States to negotiate a temporary treaty of peace and inviting the Indians to appoint a Grand Council some time in August at which time Commissioners from the United States Government at Washington will meet them for the purpose of negotiating permanent peace.

"General Herron does not demand the surrender of these Indians or their arms; but Col. Mathews formed a temporary treaty with them, leaving arms in their hands.

"I have also received a copy of the treaty entered into between Stand Watie, Chief of the Cherokees, and Lieut. Col. Mathews in which Mathews assumed to treat for the return of all the Rebel Indians to their homes without demanding their paroles or their arms which were clearly surrendered by Kirby Smith. Col. Garrett has disarmed the Rebel Indians at Fort Gibson. I desire to know if they will be permitted to take their arms when they return or will they be paroled and their arms retained? Much bad feeling exists between the Loyal Cherokees, Creeks and Seminoles and the Rebels of those tribes and it is feared there will be trouble between them.

"I am not advised by what authority Genl Herron assumes to direct officers in your department. It seems that we are likely to get into trouble in consequence as I have been acting under the impression that the Rebel Indians were all surrendered by Kirby Smith and that they should be disarmed. I have not been notified by Lieut. Col. Mathews of any negotiations entered into by him except the letter telegraphed you some time since. Copies of the treaties, letters, &c. came through the Indians at Fort Gibson. The loyal Indians are now in council at Tahlequah and it is hoped they can agree with their rebel brothers. Please advise me what to do in the present situation of affairs." (Bussey to Reynolds, July 10, 1865, *Bussey Correspondence*, CC).

[345] "Whereas, The National Council did adopt an act, dated and approved July 13th, 1865, which said act is in the following language, to wit:

have been the leader and spokesman of the delegation, was informed of a willingness to confer and of the

"Whereas, Certain citizens of the Cherokee Nation became involved in the war in the United States on the side of the Rebellion and,

"Whereas, The success of the Union arms has closed the war, and now offers a suitable opportunity for the return to the Cherokee Nation of such citizens as became enemies to the Government of the Cherokee Nation, by joining and adhering to said rebellion, and,

"Whereas, The National Council are sincerely desirous of restoring peace and harmony, and of reuniting, as far as practicable, all the Cherokee people in the support of the Constitution and Laws of the Cherokee Nation, regardless of past differences; therefore,

"*Be it enacted by the National Council*, That the Principal Chief be and he is hereby authorized and directed to offer amnesty and pardon to all citizens of the Cherokee Nation, who have directly or indirectly participated in the rebellion in the United States, and against the existing Government of the Cherokee Nation, except as hereinafter excepted, on condition that every such person shall subscribe, on his return to the Cherokee Nation, to the following oath, which shall be registered and preserved in the office of the clerk of the Supreme Court of the Cherokee Nation, to wit:

"I do solemnly swear or affirm, in the presence of Almighty God, that I will hereafter faithfully abide by, support and defend the Constitution and Laws of the Cherokee Nation.

"And all such persons so subscribing to said oath are allowed to be thereby readmitted to citizenship in the Cherokee Nation, and restored to all rights and privileges enjoyed by other citizens, except the right to possess or recover any improvements, or other property, that has or may be sold under provisions of any act confiscating the effects of persons declared to be disloyal to the Cherokee Nation.

"*Be it further enacted*, That the following persons are excepted from the benefits of this act:

"1st. All who have been military officers in the rebel service above the rank of captain since the first day of March, 1865.

"2d. All persons who held the pretended offices of Principal Chief and Assistant Principal Chief, Treasurer, and members of the National Council, in opposition to the existing Government of the Cherokee Nation.

"3d. All those citizens of the Cherokee Nation who may have violated their parole as prisoners of war, or deserted to the enemy from the 2d and 3d Regiments, I.H. Guards, or killed or otherwise maltreated loyal citizens or soldiers, while prisoners of war, and all white men, citizens of the Cherokee Nation by intermarriage, who may have joined and adhered to the rebellion.

"*Be it further enacted*, That persons who may wish to return to the Cherokee Nation, under the provisions of this act, shall do so on or

basis upon which the truant members of the tribe, with
certain exceptions, would be taken back.[346]   They were

before the 1st of January, 1866, or be thereafter debarred the benefits
of the same.

"*Be it further enacted*, That special application may be made by
any person excepted from the benefits of this act to the National Council for pardon and readmittance to citizenship in the Cherokee Nation.

"Now, therefore, be it known, that I, Lewis Downing, Assistant and
Acting Principal Chief of the Cherokee Nation, do hereby offer amnesty and pardon to all citizens of the Cherokee Nation who participated in the Rebellion in the United States, and against the existing
Government of the Cherokee Nation, upon the conditions set forth in
the foregoing act, and earnestly invite all such citizens to return to the
Cherokee Nation, comply with the requirements of said act, and henceforth lend their support to law and order in the Cherokee Nation.

"Lewis Downing,
"Ass't and Acting Principal Chief, C.N.

Executive Department, July 14, 1865."

(The foregoing is a copy of the "Official Copy," signed by Geo. W.
Ross as secretary and sent, on application, to Garrett, July 19, 1865. It
was forwarded to headquarters by L. A. Duncan, A.A.A.G.).

[346] "Whereas, A communication, dated Ft. Gibson, July 7th, 1865, has
been presented to the National Council from J. A. Scales, 'Delegate of
the Grand Council &c.', addressed to Lewis Downing, Ass't and Act'g
Principal Chief of the Cherokee Nation, submitting the communications
therein referred to and requesting a conference in behalf of himself
and associates, *delegates*, with the authorities of the Cherokee Nation:

"*Therefore*, Be it enacted by the National Council, That the Principal
Chief and William P. Ross, Smith Christie, Budd Gritts, Thos. Pegg,
Jones C. C. Daniel, White Catcher, James Vann, and Houston Binge
be and they are hereby directed to grant and hold said conference
with Messrs. John Spears, J. A. Scales, J. T. Davis, Joseph Vann,
Wm. P. Chambers, and Too-noh-volah Foster, as Cherokees and late
citizens of this Nation, to assure them of the amicable feelings of the
people and authorities of the Cherokee Nation towards those Cherokees
who have been involved in the late war on the side of the Rebellion;
of their desire for peace and of their willingness to receive and re-
admit to citizenship all such Cherokee individuals, in the manner, and
upon the condition, embodied in an act of the National Council, approved July 13th, 1865, with a copy of which they will be furnished;
but the Cherokee Nation is not to be understood by their present action
as recognising the said Cherokees in any other capacity than private
persons, nor as representing any Government, association or political
community of Cherokees, independent of or in opposition to the Government of the Cherokee Nation; nor as committing them in any manner to the terms of any agreement entered into by said Cherokees

to subscribe to an oath of allegiance and surrender all claims to individual property rights. Reconciliation seemed farther off than ever. Colonel Garrett was nonplussed and tried to persuade Scales that the best thing for him and his people to do was to go quietly and peaceably to their homes and there abide until such time in September as the Grand Council should re-convene. The disconsolate reply was, "We can't do it – our homes are occupied by the loyal Indians, who have bought our improvements." [347] A sale of some of the improvements was at the moment being advertised. Garrett's first thought was, that such sales "were intended to be in pursuance of the confiscation acts" of the United States government and that it would be wise for him, under the circumstances, to order their suspension; [348] but an examination of the Cherokee enactments, of which he had asked for and obtained official copies, [349] caused him to change his mind. It was only too apparent that the unionist Cherokees were

and other parties without the knowledge or sanction of the authorities of the Cherokee Nation; nor of their willingness to submit the adjudication of any question pertaining to their domestic affairs to any council, tribunal or authority than that presented by the Constitution and laws of the Cherokee Nation.

TAHLEQUAH, C.N. July 14, 1865.

SMITH CHRISTIE, Pres't National Committee
BENJ. SNELL, Speaker *Pro Tem.* of Council

H. D. REESE, Clk, Committee ⎱ Concurred.
ALLEN ROSS, Clk, Council *pro tem.* ⎰

Approved: LEWIS DOWNING, Ass't and Actg Principal Chief of Cherokee Nation."

[347] Garrett to Cutler, July 15, 1865, Interior Department Files, Bundle, no. 54; A.G.O., Archives Division, *Fort Gibson Letter Book*, no. 20.

[348] Garrett to Cutler, July 20, 1865, *Bussey Correspondence*; A.G.O., Archives Division, *Fort Gibson Letter Book*, no. 20. In this Fort Gibson Letter Book, the date is given as July 25th; but internal evidence proves it to be an error.

[349] Garrett to Downing, July 19, 1865, A.G.O., Archives Division, *Fort Gibson Letter Book*, no. 20.

claiming "the right to settle the matter, without the aid or assistance of any outside parties." [350]

And why should they not? Their domestic affairs were entirely their own concern, recognized so to be under treaty stipulations with the United States government. Participation in the war had cost them dearly. It had reacted altogether against the tribe as such. The nation had paid the price for defection many times over in the ruin that war had wrought. Ruin was everywhere. The injury that Indian adherence to the Confederacy had done to the United States was slight in comparison. It had been more in the nature of an embarrassment than anything else or, at most, an injury to national pride that had no right to be too sensitive and it had been amply justified by the original negligence of the guardian. The United States had abandoned its wards, the dependent people that it was bound in honor and in law to protect, at the very moment when its protection was most needed and when self-interest could have been served by the opposite course of action. The protection it had sworn over and over again to give was to be protection against both domestic insurrection and foreign foes.

The promised conference with the Scales delegation took place on the eighteenth [351] and ended in general disappointment. To say the least, the attitude of the unionists was uncompromising. The conditions they proposed to exact were undeniably harsh; but who dare assert that they were unjust? Were they not commensurate with the offense? Were they not the exact counterpart of those embodied in President Johnson's

---

[350] Garrett to Cutler, July 20, 1865, *op. cit.*

[351] — *Ibid.*

amnesty proclamation of May 29th,[352] in all essentials the same? Such variations as there were may easily be accounted for. The United States made an exception of all above the rank of colonel, the Cherokee Nation of all above that of captain. There were few Indian officers of the higher ranks in the Confederate service and none at all in the Union. In the former, Stand Watie had attained to a brigadier-generalship; but his case was most exceptional. The United States made clemency an executive privilege, a part of the president's general pardoning power, the Cherokees left it with their National Council. They thus would seem to have removed it beyond the realm of personal prejudice or caprice. At all events their arrangement had decidedly the advantage in one respect. It indicated a more democratic distribution of justice.

The difference between the Cherokee confiscation, outright, of improvements and the United States legal procedure under authority of confiscation acts was more apparent than real. In the working out, the element of time and of numbers would count to the credit of the United States; but would leave to the Cherokees a balance on the side of mercy. The land belonged to the tribe as a whole; for the Cherokees had not yet introduced holdings in severalty. In effect, the men, who had occasioned so vast a diminution of tribal wealth, had mortgaged all tribal prosperity for years to come, and had put the very national existence itself in jeopardy, were to get off rather easily. They were to lose only their movable possessions, their chattels, so to speak, while their tribal, their community rights, their

---

[352] Richardson, *Messages and Papers of the Presidents*, vol. vi., pp. 310-312.

civil and political rights and privileges, were to be left
absolutely intact. The people, rightly enough, who
were to be the most severely chastised were the adopted
white men, adopted through intermarriage with
squaws, and the half-breeds. These were the folk who
had done practically all the mischief and it was only
just that they should suffer proportionately. The brunt
of tribal expiation ought justifiably to be theirs. Yet
even to them the door of clemency was open. In the
states of the American union, be it remarked, it would
never have been possible to fix so exactly the responsibility and to make crime and punishment both an affair of the individual man.

While the Cherokees were attempting systematical-
ly but so unavailingly an adjustment of their national
difficulties, other divided and estranged southern tribes
followed their example although in a more haphazard
way and with, in the long run, an even smaller measure
of success. Their conduct in the matter can be outlined
no better than in the somewhat terse report of Colonel
Garrett. "The Creeks," said he, "seemed undecided
where to meet to talk over their matters. When the
loyal Chief called on me for advice, I gave him my
opinion that the rebel party should come to the loyal
party, but if he wished to waive the question [of pre-
cedence] it would be right for him to meet the other
party wherever they might desire. I understand that
Mr. Sands sent the rebel delegates word to meet the
loyal Creeks here, but, instead of doing so, they have
gone back to the south.

"A delegation from the Seminoles was on the way
here, but I hear from some cause unknown to me,
turned back. A few men came on, but the loyal party
refused to confer with them .   .   .

"The Chickasaw country is distant a hundred miles or more. The greater number who joined the loyal regiments here died leaving but a small number here now. A party from the south, some of whom were in the rebel army, came up a few days since and, with a few loyal ones here, called on me yesterday. There seems to be a good feeling between these men, those who were in our army, representing that these friends were pressed into the service and vouching for their loyalty. The men in from the south represent that the disloyal party want and intend to control affairs in their country and they want some understanding with the Government about what is to be done.

"Both parties of the various tribes so far as I have ascertained from conversation with them express a desire for reconciliation . . ."[353]

Nothing really constructive resulted from any of the midsummer conferences, wherever held. All attempts to reconcile interests so diametrically opposed to each other proved abortive. Local conditions had much to do with this and Garrett's observation, in consequence, was, that the contemplated general council for the final consummation of peace ought by all means to be held in Washington,[354] away from the scene of desolation that so harrowed their souls, the constant and painful reminder of what had been.

Washington had had the honor of being the original choice of the secessionist Indians and the Interior Department had acquiesced. An early settlement[355] with

---

[353] Garrett to Cutler, July 15, 1865, *op. cit.*

[354] — *Ibid.*

[355] There is some reason to think that Secretary Harlan expected that the council would be held in July. July 8th, Reynolds telegraphed, "Indian delegates have not yet arrived at Fort Smith. Will notify Department of Interior when they arrive." (Interior Department Files, Bundle, no. 54).

the civilized tribes would suit its purposes exactly and the more amicably affairs started off the better. It could well afford to be compliant at the beginning since it would have most unwelcome propositions to make and to insist upon before the close. It acquiesced also when the secessionists, at the suggestion of General Herron abandoned their choice of Washington and resolved upon a place of meeting in the West. Up to that point it took no umbrage at their assumption of the role of initiator and it must have been perfectly well aware of the fact that never yet had the secessionist Indians condescended or been compelled to make a surrender in actual form. The limit of forbearance for the one and of audacious venturing for the other was, however, soon reached, and it was then seen that the United States government had lost none of its consciousness of its own real position. It could be firm when occasion called for firmness.

The test came when, in making their choice of a place in the West, the secessionists decided upon Armstrong Academy. There was something very fitting in the choice, since Armstrong Academy was the capital of the Choctaw Nation, the leading secessionist tribe, and it had always been the site of the meetings of the Grand Council. It represented the union of the tribes in a common cause. Unfortunately, also it represented the dominance of one Indian faction over another. Worse still, it was far distant from the homes of many of the tribes that were expected to participate in the great settlement that was coming. Much turned on the choice of place. Indian councils have always meant a rare gathering of all sorts and conditions of men and a rare picking for others than Indians. Harpies and vultures come from all directions to get what they can for nothing or at somebody else's expense.[356] And there would be a special political significance attaching to this forthcoming council.

For a brief period, Fort Gibson,[357] through some misunderstanding on the part of Secretary Harlan,[358] but with the approval of President Johnson,[359] seemed destined for the place of meeting; but Fort Smith, ample in accommodations,[360] although in that respect

---

[356] A good illustration of this, in the case under discussion, is seen from the following letter, written to the Hon. Sidney Clarke, presumably, by Wm. Weir from Wyandotte, Kansas, July 26, 1865:

"I suppose you are aware that the Southern Indians are to have a grand gathering upon the 1st Sept. in the Choctaw country at which it is expected Com'rs from Washington will be present. If you are not posted, please hunt up the St. Louis Republican of 20th inst.

"The Wyandots are preparing to send a delegation. White men from here and Kansas City will go along. Treaties will be made – railroad grants fixed up and things done generally. Will a delegation go from Lawrence? If so would like to join. Please inform me if you are posted – and let me beg you to write to Washington in order to ascertain if the Council will be held at the date mentioned or when & where. The paper states that 50,000 Indians are looked for. At all events the meeting is an important one to our railroad interests & we should have a hand in it. Please answer . . . " (O.I.A., General Files, *Southern Superintendency*, 1865, C 1496). The required information was given by the Indian Office, August 16, 1865.

[357] Note the following telegrams:

(a) "Commissioners will be sent from Washington to treat with Indians, at or near Fort Gibson, about the 1st of September next." (Harlan to Reynolds, July 29, 1865, *ibid.*).

(b) "Your telegram of seventh instant received. The council will meet at Fort Gibson. Messengers have been sent throughout the Indian country to give notice to that effect. Too late to change." (Harlan to Reynolds, August 8, 1865, *ibid.*).

(c) "Do you wish the Delaware chiefs to attend the council Fort Gibson?" (Agent Jno. G. Pratt to Cooley, August 19, 1865, *ibid.*, *Delaware*, 1862-1866). See also Levering to Bussey, June 10, 1865, *Official Records*, vol. xlviii, part ii, p. 844 and Grant to Sherman, August 21, 1865, *ibid.*, 1199.

[358] Cooley to Reynolds, August 8, 1865.

[359] Stanton to Doolittle, July 25, 1865, *Official Records*, vol. xlviii, part ii, p. 1122.

[360] "I am directed by the Secretary of the Interior to inform you that

Armstrong Academy might rival it,[361] and swarming
with politicians, was finaly resolved upon, despite the
manifold objections that the secessionist Indians saw
fit to raise.   With all the arguments [362] of propriety and
expediency at their disposal, they were insistent for
Armstrong Academy and their shrewd ex-agent added

commissioners from Washington will meet the Delegates of all the
Indian Tribes in Grand Council at Fort Smith, Arkansas on the 1st
of September next.   At this place the Government has supplies of subsistence and barracks for the accomodation of the Council and telegraphic communication with Washington, which is important.

"Please notify all the Indian Tribes in the Territory as it will be
impossible for me to communicate with them.   An early reply is
requested.

"My General Order, no. 30 is not construed to prohibit the Indians
selling their cattle but was designed to protect them from cattle
thieves from Arkansas and elsewhere."   (Bussey to Colbert, to Pitchlynn, to Downing, and to Levering, August 2, 1865, *Bussey Correspondence*, G).

[361] Pitchlynn to Bussey, August 9, 1865, *Bussey Correspondence*, I.

[362] The arguments are all set forth in the Pitchlynn letters;

(a) "A copy of your letter of July 6th, 1865 to his Excellency
Winchester Colbert, Governor of the Chickasaw Nation, in reply to his
of June 15th, I have just received.

"I learn from it that arrangements have been made through you with
the Secretary of the Interior at Washington for Delegates from each
of the tribes that were convened in Grand Council at Armstrong
Academy, Choctaw Nation, to proceed to Washington City to negotiate
a permanent peace.

"This is something I did not expect to hear.   Gov. Colbert was
writing on the 15th of June and four days previous to the date of the
treaty of peace made with Lieut. Col. Mathews and Capt. Vance in
which there is an express provision for a Grand Peace Council to be
held on the 1st of September at Armstrong Academy, C.N.   There is
an apparent conflict in these two arrangements.   I think Gov. Colbert,
of necessity when he wrote you, was ignorant of the provision made in
Col. Mathews treaty.   Besides I wish to call your attention to the section of the Treaty of 1855 between the United States and the Choctaw
and Chickasaw Indians to show you that the Choctaws and Chickasaws
are bound to act only in concert about their common interests.

"I trust that such a course will be adopted by the United States
government as will save us from all the dangers of conflicting arrangements, and, more than this, I trust that the United States government will favor the meeting of the one Grand Council of the

his protests to theirs. Armstrong Academy, declared they, had been agreed upon with Colonel Matthews,

Indian Tribes determined upon in the Treaty of June 19th, 1865. I have made all my arrangements and issued my proclamations, accordingly.

"Hoping that the Treaty of Peace of June 19th and its provisions may lead to permanent and just relations of peace and amity with the United States government, that our tribes may prosper and have the constant blessing of our Father in Heaven and live in peace with each other as well as with your Government . . . " (Pitchlynn to Bussey, dated Eagle Town, C.N., July 31st, 1865, *Bussey Correspondence*, J).

(b) "I have the honor to acknowledge the receipt of your communication of the 2nd inst stating that you had been directed by the Secretary of the Interior to inform me that Commissioners from Washington will meet the Delegates of all the Indian Tribes in Grand Council at Fort Smith, Ark. on the 1st proximo.

"I have to state that for several reasons of importance I regret that any change of place for the meeting of the Grand Council should be made from the one agreed upon between myself and the military commissioners sent out here in June last.

"I issued my proclamation several weeks ago calling an extra session of the General Council to be held at Armstrong Academy on the 1st of September next and, as the time has nearly arrived for that body to meet, I cannot well make any other arrangement for the reason that at that council we will appoint delegates on the part of the Choctaws to meet the commissioners of the United States.

"Immediately after concluding the temporary treaty with the military commissioners and agreeably to arrangements made with them, I issued a proclamation calling upon all the tribes of the Indian confederation to send delegates to meet the commissioners of the United States at Armstrong Academy on the 1st of September next for the purpose of entering into permanent treaties of peace and friendship, which proclamation they are all acquainted with and will accordingly meet at the time and place appointed by me. The time is now so short that I find it impracticable to communicate to them the change proposed by the Secretary of the Interior for holding the Grand Council at Fort Smith, Ark.

"I have no doubt but there will be at Armstrong Academy on the 1st of September next the greatest assemblage of Indian Chiefs and Warriors that ever met together in Council on this continent and it is highly important that the Commissioners should be there. If, however, the government of the United States require that the Delegates from all the Indian tribes shall meet in Grand Council at Fort Smith, I shall use my utmost exertion to prevail on the Prairie Tribes to accompany me to that place at as early a day as practicable. As it doubtless will

a United States commissioner, and had been publicly proclaimed. It was too late in the day to make a change. The wild tribes [363] had been invited and they would probably refuse to venture so far as Fort Smith. Besides, the Grand Council would, under any circumstances, be holding its regular session at the regular place, in September, and attendance upon that would be an insuperable obstacle to a meeting at Fort Smith, the beginning of the month. It seemed an unanswerable argument; but the United States authorities were not to be worsted in debate. They, too, had sent out notices that could not, at so late a date, be recalled and they steadfastly adhered to their decision. One by one

be a great disappointment to the Prairie Tribes, who may come to the Grand Council at Armstrong Academy not to meet the commissioners of the United States then I would respectfully request that some suitable person be sent to represent the wishes of the Government of the United States to meet the commissioners at Fort Smith.

"In conclusion I would state that as soon as I shall have appointed, in conjunction with the General Council, the Choctaw Delegates and which can only be done constitutionally at the capitol of the Choctaw Nation (Armstrong Academy) I shall proceed at once with them to Fort Smith but I cannot but express the wish that the United States Government will direct the Commissioners to meet us at Armstrong Academy, where provisions can be procured in abundance and the place is far more suitable and healthful for an Indian Council than Fort Smith and where the United States commissioners can be accommodated with several pleasant commodious rooms in the capitol and see much of our people and the wild tribes of the confederation."
(Pitchlynn to Bussey, August 9, 1865, *Bussey Correspondence*, I).

[363] The Reserve Indians were probably included among these and they were then camping "near the Old Cherokee Village on the Washita River." Colbert undertook to invite them (Colbert to Bussey, August 8, 1865, *Bussey Correspondence*, H). Downing forwarded an invitation to the Creeks and Seminoles; but said that with the other tribes expected to appear there was no communication from Fort Gibson. The Cherokees would send delegates to the peace conference, not because they had any business with the tribes south of them, but out of regard for Bussey. For the settlement of "large claims" that they had against the United States, they would send commissioners to Washington in the autumn (Downing to Bussey, August 7, 1865, *Bussey Correspondence*, K).

the Indian chiefs and governors yielded the point. Colbert was the most gracious of all and used his influence with the others. He consulted, August 15th, with commissioners from his own and the Cherokee and Creek tribes and got them all to agree that commissioners from all the tribes would meet at Boggy Depot the evening of August twenty-fourth and go from there together to Fort Smith.[364] So far so good; but Colbert had reckoned without the Choctaws, who, whenever it suited their purpose, liked to remind the Chickasaws that, under the Treaty of 1855, the political affairs of the two tribes were so closely interwoven that one tribe dare not presume to act without the other. They now contended that the arrangement about Boggy Depot would not suit them at all; for they had not yet appointed commissioners to treat for peace and could not until the meeting of their national council in September. In the dilemma thus created, Governor Colbert again urged that Armstrong Academy be the place for conducting the negotiations with the United States;[365] but General Bussey, to whom he appealed, refused to entertain the suggestion. The United States commissioners were already *en route* for Fort Smith and everything there was in readiness for the assemblage. He, therefore, extended an invitation to all the tribes east of the Rockies to come; a large delegation was hoped for; much important business was to be transacted; and he suggested that the grand council convene, as arranged, at Armstrong Academy and then adjourn to Fort Smith.[366]

[364] Colbert to Bussey, August 17, 1865, *Bussey Correspondence*, L.

[365] Colbert to Bussey, August 19, 1865, *Bussey Correspondence*, M.

[366] This idea had suggested itself to Bussey before he heard from Colbert and he had made arrangements to send Major S. Hunter, U.S. Vols., as a special messenger to the Grand Council (Bussey to Pitchlynn, August 25,

1865, *Bussey Correspondence*, O) ; but Hunter was taken ill and he had
no other suitable officer of his own to send. He finally entrusted despatches
to Lieutenant Yumer, Cooper's late aide, who was going direct to Armstrong Academy (Bussey to Pitchlynn, August 27, 1865, *Bussey Correspondence*, R; Bussey to Colbert, August 27, 1865, *Bussey Correspondence*, P).
His communication to the Grand Council was as follows:

"Head Quarters Frontier Division,
FORT SMITH, Ark.,
Aug. 26, 1865.

TO THE HONORABLE
    Grand Council of the Confederate Indian Nations:

"I have the honor to inform you that Commissioners from the Government at Washington will arrive here on the 1st of September next
for the purpose of meeting the Delegates of the various Indian tribes
to negotiate a permanent Treaty of Peace and to invite you to adjourn
your council to Fort Smith or to send delegates to meet the Commissioners of the United States at this place.

I am directed to inform you that it will not be possible for the
United States Commissioners to attend the Council at Armstrong
Academy as at Fort Smith they have appointed to meet various other
parties having business with them . . . " (*Bussey Correspondence*, Q).

VI. THE PEACE COUNCIL AT FORT SMITH, SEPTEMBER, 1865

General Bussey [367] had said in his despatch to the Grand Council that one reason why it would be impossible for the United States commissioners to journey to Armstrong Academy was because they had invited various persons having business with them to meet them at Fort Smith, a clear intimation that the consummation of peace with the southern tribes was not the only occasion for their trip westward. Subsequent events were to prove that that was only too truly the case. Had the recipients of Bussey's communication studied his words carefully, they would surely have had a foreboding. The words in themselves were ominous; but who were the people who were to have business dealings with an ostensibly Indian peace commission, business of such importance that it received more consideration beforehand than

[367] With this act, Bussey virtually retired from the scene. His military record, from the Battle of Pea Ridge on, seems not to have been an enviable one. He was accused of avarice, of dishonesty, and of being connected with corrupt army contracts (A.G.O., Old Files Section, *Cyrus Bussey's Personal Papers*, B 1432, V.S., 1863); but nothing of all that was revealed while he was with the Third Division of the Seventh Army Corps and stationed at Fort Smith. As far as his dealings with the Indians were concerned, he would appear to have been above reproach. John A. Garrett was his admiring friend to the last (–*ibid.*, G 294, C.B., 1865; 5721 A.C.P., 1889). He was mustered out of the service (Townsend to Cooley, September 20, 1865, O.I.A., Land Files, *Indian Talks, Councils, &c.*, Box 4, 1865-1866) before the Peace Commission concluded its work at Fort Smith, although he was there up to the twentieth at least, when the Commission voted him resolutions of thanks for the facilities he had rendered (Commissioner of Indian Affairs, *Report*, 1865, pp. 348-349). His place was taken by Brevet Major-general Henry J. Hunt, U.S. Vols. (*ibid.*, p. 312).

did the people whose fortunes hung in the balance?
Were they land speculators or would-be railroad mag-
nates? Were they politicians from Kansas, eager to
relieve, by hook or by crook, their sunny state of an
obnoxious aboriginal encumbrance? Who were they?
Assurance may be doubly sure that whoever they were
they were not disinterested friends of the red men.

It had been thought well to have the Peace Commission consist of several persons. In numbers there
is a certain kind of strength imparted and not necessarily a contrariety of disposition. Were it to become
incumbent upon the commission to bring any undue
pressure to bear upon the Indians, who were not only
brave fighters, but also educated and keenly intellectual men, as all their public documents attest, it might
not be amiss to have a variety of skill, subtlety, and some
sternness to pit against excessive obstinacy. Was it for
that reason that the men selected were all, with a single
exception and that an afterthought, taken from the official and military[368] classes? Those originally approached with an offer of appointment by President
Johnson[369] were, Dennis N. Cooley,[370] Commissioner
of Indian Affairs, the choice of whom was most deplorable from the standpoint of the Indians but un-

[368] There were undoubtedly other reasons why military men were
placed upon the commission. The War and Interior departments had
recently come to an understanding on the conduct of Indian affairs into
which Congress, not long before, had authorized a searching investigation.
On July 11, 1865, Harlan had informed Cooley (O.I.A., *Miscellaneous Files,*
1864-1867) that, where hostile Indians were under consideration, the Interior
Department would subordinate its policy to that of the War and, where the
peaceful were, co-operate with it.

[369] Johnson to Cooley, July 31, 1865, *ibid.*, General Files, *Southern Su-*
perintendency, 1865; I. D. Files, Bundle, no. 24 (1852-1868).

[370] Cooley was born in New Hampshire, 1825, and emigrated to Iowa
about 1854. "In 1864 he was appointed by President Lincoln, Commissioner to South Carolina and acted then as Special Commissioner

avoidable, James M. Edmunds, Commissioner of the General Land Office, Elijah Sells,[371] Southern Superintendent, Major-general Francis J. Herron,[372] Brigadier-general William S. Harney,[373] and Colonel Ely S. Parker.[374] In consideration of what the commission was going to do, the selection of Edmunds was significant and the disappointment of Secretary Harlan must have been considerable when, the duties of his own bureau being such as to keep him at his desk in Washington, Edmunds was compelled to decline the appointment.[375] General Herron [376] likewise declined,

to settle titles to cotton and rights to possession of land. He served as Secretary of the National Republican Congressional Committee during the campaign which resulted in the triumphant reëlection of President Lincoln.

"In 1865 he was appointed by President Johnson, Commissioner of Indian Affairs, which position he resigned in September, 1866 . . ." (Oldt, Franklin T., *History of Dubuque County, Iowa*, p. 761).

[371] Sells to Harlan, August 5, 1865, I. D. Files, Bundle, no. 54; Elijah Sells "had been active in his efforts to secure Senator Harlan's appointment as Secretary of the Interior and the Senator insisted that he should take a position in his Department. Their relations had been so close and friendly that he felt obliged to acquiesce . . . " (Davis, Elijah Sells in *Annals of Iowa*, 3rd series, vol. ii, pp. 518-530). He was appointed in April (Whiting, Chief Clerk, to Commissioner of Indian Affairs, April 28, 1865). He relieved Coffin in May (O.I.A., *Letter Book*, no. 77, p. 127).

[372] Herron resigned his commission in the army, July 16, 1865 (*Annals of Iowa*, vol. v, no. i, pp. 806-807).

[373] Harney was one of the few military men that appreciated the strategic importance of Indian Territory; but at the outset of the war he was somewhat discredited at Washington. McNeil said of him, "If he could have armed, organized and commanded the Indians of the Indian Territory, such was the power of his name in Arkansas and the Southwest, that Missouri would, I am convinced, have been saved from pillage and devastation and a wedge inserted between the Confederacy and her best source of supplies, that would have materially shortened the war." (John McNeil to L. U. Reavis, February 27, 1878, quoted in Reavis, *Life and Military Services of Harney*, pp. 385-386).

[374] Harlan to Parker, August 4, 1865, I. D., *Record of Letters Sent*, "Indian Affairs," no. 5, p. 312; Parker to Harlan, August 12, 1865, *ibid.*, Files, Bundle, no. 54.

[375] Edmunds to Harlan, August 14, 1865, *ibid.*; Harlan to Edmunds,

which was a pity; for he had already shown an inclination to be pacificatory towards the Indians. Sells
was an Iowa man, like the Secretary of the Interior,
and the Commissioner of Indian Affairs and, that said,
more need scarcely be; since Iowa to a greater extent,
perhaps, than any other middle-western state or territory had had no conscience whatsoever where Indian
rights were concerned. Of Parker, little can be said,
though much was then expected. He was a Seneca
and might be thought to have possessed some inherent
sympathy for his own race. Frankly-speaking, however, it must be admitted he gave little evidence of it.
Was his appointment somewhat of a blind? Harney [377]
seems to have been the only commissioner towards
whom there was public antipathy on grounds of personal unfitness. As one man said, who sought a post
himself, he was "noted for his want of humane qualities and especially for his barbarity to the Indians
. . . ",[378] but it is exceedingly doubtful if a past
record for inhumanity would have disqualified anyone
for the Fort Smith commission. To the number of
commissioners that accepted was shortly added Thomas
Wistar, a Quaker.[379] As secretaries to the commission,

August 16, 1865, *ibid., Record of Letters Sent,* "Indian Affairs," no. 5, p 329.

[376] Herron to Harlan, August 13, 1865, *ibid.,* Files, Bundle, no. 54.

[377] Harney to Harlan, August 14, 1865, *ibid.* On the outside of this
letter, it is of some interest to observe, appears an office memorandum,
"There ought to be a special file for all these papers about that Commission
so that should Congress or the Senate call for them they can be readily
got at.   WILLIAMSON,
                    18 Aug. 1865"

[378] W. H. Goode of Richmond, Indiana, to Harlan, August 8, 1865 (I. D.
Files, Bundle, no. 54). Harlan's reply, August 12, 1865, conveys the in-
formation that Harney was "put on the Commission at the request of the
Chairman of the Senate Committee on Military Affairs." (I.D., *Record of
Letters Sent,* "Indian Affairs," no. 5, 325).

[379] Wistar was recommended by his cousin, Thomas Evans of Phil-

went Charles E. Mix from the Indian Office force, George L. Cook, W. R. Irwin, John B. Garrett, a friend of Wistar's,[380] and J. L. Harvey.[381]

By August seventeenth, all of the appointees, who had been resident in or near Washington had left that place and were journeying by rail towards the trans-Missouri region. They carried with them the blessing of Secretary Harlan who had written on the day of their departure to Cooley thus: "Wishing you and the Gentlemen associated with you health and, under the guidance of an overruling providence, success in the great enterprise submitted to you by the President." In yet another communication, Harlan had given them what, for their purpose, was of more practical concern instructions, but instructions altogether too elaborate and too important for merely general mention here. They were themselves based upon a bill for the organization of Indian Territory that had passed the senate at the last session of congress, Bill No. 459, commonly known as the *Harlan Bill.* Self-elucidative, the instructions will be given full quotation in the next chapter, when the principle of cause and effect can be brought into play. They alone explain the temper of the tribes that was so very different after the Fort Smith council meetings from what it had been before,

adelphia (Evans to Harlan, August 11, 1865, I. D. Files, Bundle, no. 54). The order of President Johnson for his appointment was dated the day following (*ibid.*, Bundle, no. 24). Harlan communicated with him immediately (*ibid., Record of Letters Sent,* "Indian Affairs," no. 5, pp. 323-324). Cooley was authorized by Harlan to employ "on the ground" such other clerical force as he should find necessary (Harlan to Cooley, August 15, 1865).

[380] Evans to Harlan, August 14, 1865, *ibid.*, Files, Bundle, no. 54.

[381] An accident befell Harvey on the way out, which soon necessitated his separating himself from the commission and, finally, terminated fatally (O.I.A., "Rough Draft of Fort Smith Negotiations, 1865").

yet no contemporary sources [382] of the council proceedings so much as refer to them. Senate Bill, No. 459, was, however, in private, brought to the attention of certain prominent secessionists. That the commissioners endeavored to comply with Harlan's instructions yet had not the courage or the honesty to make a full report thereon is abundantly and conclusively certified to in all subsequent transactions. They told only what, in case of emergency, would bear the scrutiny of public opinion.

With the exception of General Harney, Cooley's party reached Fort Leavenworth, August 22nd, was received by the commandant there with all courtesy [383]

[382] The contemporary journalistic sources, thus far discovered, are four in number; viz.,

1. *General Report of Proceedings*, made by Commissioner Cooley and published in his annual report for 1865, pp. 295-312.

2. *Detailed Report of Proceedings*, made by Secretary Charles E. Mix, published daily while the council was in progress, two hundred copies being distributed, and later in Commissioner of Indian Affairs, *Report*, 1865, pp. 312-353. Several sets of the two hundred copy issue are on file in the Indian Office.

3. "Rough Draft of Fort Smith Negotiations, 1865," MS. (O.I.A., Drawer, labelled, *Treaties, &c., 1864-1868*). Filed with this document and possibly originally a part of it is a document entitled, "Report of — Wilson of the *New York Herald*." It is valuable because it contains detail about the degradation of John Ross not found elsewhere. Wilson is the only newspaper correspondent mentioned by name as having been present at the Fort Smith Council. The commissioners, in their private meetings, considered the advisability of employing him to make a stenographic report of the proceedings of the council. An examination of New York newspapers, *Tribune, Times, World*, and *Herald* has proved most disappointing. Their accounts of what took place at Fort Smith in September, 1865 all seem to have emanated from the same source and are meagre in the extreme.

4. "Minutes of the Private Meetings of the Commissioners at Fort Smith." MS. (O.I.A., Land Files, *Indian Talks, Councils, &c.*, Box 4, 1865-1866).

Duplicate and, in some instances, additional documents touching the Fort Smith Council are to be found in O.I.A., *Special Files*, no. 153.

[383] "Rough Draft of Fort Smith Negotiations, 1865."

and, on resuming the journey on the morning of the twenty-fourth,[384] was, in obedience to instructions from the War Department,[385] provided by him with an escort of cavalry – 100 strong, officers and men – and "with a train of horse wagons and horse ambulances." According to Cooley, "the train, although none too great, proved amply sufficient for the wants of the Commissioners and their attaches."[386] They reached Fort Scott, the evening of August twenty-seventh,[387] and Fort Smith, via Fort Gibson, the evening of September fifth.[388] At their destination, they found Harney awaiting them. He had travelled in a pleasant and leisurely fashion by water from St. Louis, while they had traversed, for the entire period of the last thirteen days, a "plain, wholly uninhabited by white men" except for a comparatively short distance south of Leavenworth. Along most of the route of about four hundred miles they had found it "difficult, owing in part to the lateness and dryness of the season, to obtain a supply of water for the animals of the expedition and no timber had been seen except in thin belts along the streams."[389]

In preparation for its work with the Indians, the commission met at nine o'clock the second day after its arrival and organized its own body, Cooley first as chairman and then as president presiding. Mix was

---

[384] Telegram, Cooley to Harlan, August 24, 1865, O.I.A., General Files, *Southern Superintendency*, 1865.

[385] Sherman to Reynolds, August 22nd, *Official Records*, vol. xlviii, part ii, p. 1202.

[386] "Rough Draft of Fort Smith Negotiations, 1865."

[387] Telegram, Cooley to Harlan, August 28, 1865, O.I.A., General Files, *Southern Superintendency*, 1865.

[388] Telegram, Cooley to Harlan, September 7, 1865, *ibid.*, I 1249; I. D. Files, Bundle, no. 55.

[389] "Rough Draft of Fort Smith Negotiations, 1865."

made chief secretary and, on motion of Superintendent
Sells, requested "to take part in the deliberations of
the Commission, . . .   and to furnish information." Such information as Mix possessed in virtue of
his connection with the Indian Office was likely to be
in great demand, sooner or later. It is to be hoped Mix
proved reliable; but misgivings will arise and obtrude
themselves; for, though he may have had the knowledge of an expert, he was not always, in the course of
his clerical career, reputed to have had integrity of
character. Various duties were to devolve upon Sells,
such as giving proper notice to the Indians of meetings,
arranging matters with press-agents, and the like. At
first it was decided that the press-agents should be allowed freely to attend meetings but not to publish reports of proceedings except under strict censorship,
the censorship of Cooley himself. Before long, however, that vote was reversed, the restriction removed
and the newspaper men simply put upon their honor
"not to publish anything pertaining to unfinished business that might tend to embarrass the action of the
Commission in any way." At the organization meeting, Cooley submitted the draft of an address, which
he intended to deliver "in opening Council with the
Indians." It was discussed by "Sells, Parker, Wistar
and Harney, amended and adopted." "On motion,
President Cooley was appointed spokesman for the
Commission." At an adjourned meeting in the afternoon, "On motion, Secretarys Cook and Garrett were
authorized to procure a dozen chairs for the Council
room.   Comm^r. Wistar submitted a resolution in favor
of reading selections from the Scriptures at the opening of the Councils – after consultation, the resolution
was withdrawn and, on motion, Comm^{rs}. Sells and

Parker were appointed a committee to make arrangements for opening the Council with prayer." Early the next morning, the commission held another private meeting and resolved upon three things; viz., that it would be inexpedient to circumscribe its own actions by parliamentary rules, that the first meeting of the council should be open to visitors, and that General Bussey should be so informed.[390]

The first meeting of the Fort Smith Council was necessarily to be but preliminary in character. It began at ten o'clock the morning of the eighth. A goodly number of Indians were assembled but only from the unionist party. They included representatives from all of the Indian Territory tribes except those belonging to the Leased District, the so-called Reserve Indians, Wichitas and their associates, and representatives from three [391] Kansas tribes, one indigenous, the Osage, and two emigrant, the Shawnee [392] and Wyan-

---

[390] *Minutes of the Private Meetings of the Commissioners at Fort Smith, 1865.*

[391] Agent Colton asked permission of Cooley, August 17, 1865 for a "male delegation" to go to Fort Smith from the Osage River agency (O.I.A., General Files, *Osage River, 1863-1867*). The Sacs and Foxes wanted to go but had doubts of their being able to "get ready in time." (H. W. Martin to Cooley, August 28, 1865, O.I.A., Land Files, *Indian Talks, Councils, &c.,* Box 4, 1865-1866). It is a little strange that the Delawares were not on hand at the opening meeting. Their agent, Jno. G. Pratt, apparently not quite up to date in his information, had telegraphed to Cooley from Leavenworth, August 19, 1865, "Do you wish the Delaware chiefs to attend the council, Fort Gibson?" The office memorandum for reply had been, "Respecty ref'd to the Act'g Com. of Indian Affrs with instructions to telegraph him if Delawares desire it, a delegation of not over *five* may go to Fort Smith with Com. who leave Ft. Leavenworth on the 21st or 22nd inst. Whiting" (O.I.A., General Files, *Delaware, 1862-1866*).

[392] At a meeting of the Shawnee Council, called by Agent Abbott for that purpose and held at the Council room on the 10th day of August, 1865, the following persons, members of the Shawnee Tribe of Indians, were appointed to attend the Grand Council to be held at Fort Smith, on the 1st day of September, 1865, and there to represent their tribe

dot.[393]   Agents Justin Harlan, *Cherokee,* Isaac Coleman, *Choctaw and Chickasaw,* J. W. Dunn, *Creek,*
George A. Reynolds, *Seminole,* G. C. Snow, *Neosho,*
Milo Gookins, *Wichita,* and J. B. Abbott, *Shawnee,*
were also present.   The invocation that had been
agreed upon in private meeting of the commissioners
was delivered by the Reverend Lewis Downing, Cherokee chief, in the Cherokee tongue.[394]

On the way out, Cooley had wired Harlan from
Leavenworth, "Train just starting.   All well.   Shall

and to transact such business as may in their judgment be for the best
interest of their Tribe:

Delegates { CHARLES BLUEJACKET, 1st Chief
GRAHAM ROGERS, 2nd Chief
MOSES SILVERHEELS
ELLIS BLACKHOOF
SOLOMON MADDEN

We, the two Chiefs of the Shawnee tribe of Indians, do certify that
the foregoing is a true statement of the proceedings of the Shawnee
Council at a meeting held at the Council room on the 10th day of
August, 1865.

CHARLES BLUEJACKET, 1st Chief
GRAHAM ROGERS, 2nd Chief

I hereby certify the Council mentioned in the foregoing certificate
of the chiefs was duly elicited in accordance with the laws and customs of the Shawnee tribe of Indians.

JAS. B. ABBOTT,
U.S. Agent for same Tribe.

FORT SMITH, Sept. 8, 1865.

(O.I.A., Land Files, *Indian Talks, Councils &c.,* Box 4, 1865-1866).

[393]   WYANDOTT, KANSAS, Aug. 17, '65.

This is to certify that on Tuesday, the 15th instant (the regular
election day) the Wyandott people assembled and proceeded to elect
a Board of Chiefs to serve for the ensuing year.

The election being through, the Board met and organized; then
proceeded to elect out of their body, delegates to attend and represent
the Wyandott people at a proposed convocation of various Indian
tribes at some point south of Fort Scott.   Whereupon, Silas Armstrong,
principal chief, and Mathew Mudeater, counsellor, were appointed.

WM. WALKER, Clerk of the Council, *pro tem.*

(*Ibid.*)

[394] Commissioner of Indian Affairs, *Report,* 1865, pp. 297, 312-313.

we, as a matter of policy, make opening propositions, or say we are there to hear what they want? Answer at Fort Smith."[395] The secretary had replied, "You will be controlled by circumstances. You may commence by saying the President is willing to grant them peace; but wants land for other Indians, and a civil government for the whole Territory."[396] Harlan had evidently anticipated that the secessionists would be at Fort Smith in time for the opening of the council and could not refrain from taking an additional opportunity of airing his pet notion. The secessionists were not there, however, and, as Cooley well knew, were not to be looked for for several days.[397] None the less, he prepared an address that would have been appropriate for their ears alone. Such as it was, it savoured a little too much, in its insistence upon the fact of the rebellion, of being almost an insult to the present audience, an audience composed, in so far as it was Indian, exclusively of men, who, in a war that had been none of their seeking, had sacrificed and lost everything, victims of circumstances most tragic. The address[398] had the usual amount of cant and hypocrisy in its exordium, of appeal to a beneficent Great Spirit; but it had also sentences that were a forecast of intimidation to come with only the barest suggestion of gratitude, of appreciation and recognition of loyalty.

The Indians were somewhat taken aback as well they might be. Not one of them, so their delegates

---

[395] Cooley to Harlan, August 24, 1865, *op. cit.*

[396] Harlan to Cooley, August 24, 1865, O.I.A., General Files, *Southern Superintendency*, 1865.

[397] He had wired Harlan only the day before, September 7th, "Arrived safely – thirteen days out. Indians coming in slowly. Creeks well disposed. Cherokees and Choctaws in council at Armstrong Academy not well disposed. This best place for Council . . . " (*op. cit.*).

[398] Commissioner of Indian Affairs, *Report*, 1865, pp. 297-298, 314.

said, had until then known the object of the council. They would have to have time to reflect, to consult together, and to be further instructed. Cooley then adjourned the council until four-thirty in the afternoon, having first informed the Indians that their several delegates must be prepared, at the next meeting to present their credentials and five from each tribe or nation must be selected and authorized to speak and to sign treaties. A rather strange injunction, was it not, considering that he had just been notified that they were delegates only in a very general way and that treaty-making was not to be one of their functions? The Cherokees, besides being bound by immemorial tribal custom as the others were, had the way of making treaties prescribed for them by a provision in a regular constitution, modelled upon that of the United States and adopted at an earlier and very similar crisis in their tribal and national history.

The commissioners had a conference among themselves immediately after the adjournment of the council and again, following a brief recess, in the early afternoon. Their minutes give scarcely any indication of what they deliberated about. One thing of importance they decided. It was to postpone making their wishes known to the Indians until the morning. At the afternoon session, therefore, the Indians had the floor and good use they made of it. Their protestations were largely a reiteration of those of the day before. They were not empowered to make treaties; they had never, when summoned to the council, been told its business but supposed it would be to make peace with the secessionists and to restore harmony within the various tribes. The Wyandots were the only ones that admitted having had beforehand an inkling of the ul-

terior purposes of the government.[399]   Lane had told
them "that the Commissioners would probably put in
force the Act of Congress obliging all Kansas Indians
to leave the State."   They had seen the armistice resolutions in a St. Louis newspaper and had supposed an
Indian confederation was in process of formation.
Believing that their possessory rights in their Kansas
homes were doomed, they favored concentration within the Indian Territory.

The Wyandot first chief, Silas Armstrong, who spoke
on this occasion, introduced his remarks by the comment that the council was taking a different course from
what he expected.   Did he have in mind the stern emphasis that the commissioners were placing upon what
they chose to call "the great *crime*" of the secessionists
and upon the consequent rightful forfeiture of "all
annuities and interests in the lands in the Indian Territory?"   There had been no reference in Cooley's
address to the initial defection of the United States, its
desertion of its wards.

From the "talks" made, it was very noticeable that
the Indians were astonished to have the work of the
council go forward, as seemed to be the case and the
intention of the commissioners, prior to the arrival of
the secessionists, who, from an announcement that
Cooley made at the conclusion of the meeting, were

---

[399] The men who were to be most arbitrary in forcing the southern tribes
to receive other Indians within the sacred precincts of Indian Territory
seem to have been, as yet, not very sure of their own ground.   It is quite
likely that, when at Fort Smith, they realised the extent of bad feeling
existing between the loyal and secessionist groups, they gained courage and
made up their minds to take advantage of tribal disruptions instead of
doing what they could to mend them.   A letter written by Harlan to Pope,
July 6, 1865 (*Official Records*, vol. xlviii, part ii, p. 1057) shows that at
that time persuasion was to be his method of approach; but it was not so
later.

expected to arrive the following Monday, September eleventh. They were then on their way from Armstrong Academy. The Grand Council had opened as arranged for, had transacted some business, and had then adjourned to re-convene at Fort Smith, the fifteenth instant. Minor arrangements provided that the delegates, *en route* for Fort Smith, should gather together either at Middle Boggy on the ninth or at Skullyville on the fourteenth and proceed eastward in a body.⁴⁰⁰ It is difficult to see how Cooley had any right to expect their attendance on the eleventh; but whether he did or not is immaterial since he had no idea of letting his business wait upon their coming. On Saturday, he gave the Indians assembled, an exclusively

⁴⁰⁰ "Your communication of the date of August 26th, 1865, to the Grand Council of the United Indian Nations has been duly received. In reply, I am directed by the Grand Council to inform you and, through you, the commissioners of the United States Gov't that the Grand Council has adjourned from this place to convene at Fort Smith on the 15th inst, at which time and place, commissioners from the several United Tribes expect to meet the commissioners of the U.S. Gov't for the purpose of entering into negociations with them, all of which will be in accordance with Resolutions of the Council this day appointed. Copies of which are herewith transmitted for your information."

(Israel Folsom, President of the Grand Council of the United Indian Nations, to Bussey, September 6, 1865, *Bussey Correspondence*, T).

(Enclosure)

"*Resolved*, by the Grand Council of the United Indian Nations, That this Council adjourn at this place to convene at Fort Smith, Arkansas on the 15th inst, in order that the several tribes comprising this confederation may be enabled to enter into negociations with the United States Government.

"*Resolved*, That the several delegations of the different tribes to treat with the United States Government meet at Middle Boggy at Mrs. Plaxes place on Saturday, the 9th inst, and that they all proceed thence together to Fort Smith.

"*Resolved*, That should any of the delegates fail to meet at Middle Boggy as required then such delegates thus failing shall meet the delegations at Skullyville, C.N. on the 14th inst.

"*Resolved*, That the President of the Grand Council as soon as pos-

loyal body yet, his own rendering of Harlan's instructions. The lapse of time had given harshness and positiveness to what had been, if anything, too harsh and too positive before. The terms now offered had the manner and spirit of an ultimatum and Cooley was determined that even the loyal Indians should think them, a *sine qua non*.

They had been discussed in commissioners' meeting that same morning and the address embodying them read to the different agents, who were expected, subsequently, to expound it to the respective tribes. As delivered in council the address [401] ran,

> "*Brothers*: — After considering your speeches, made yesterday, the Commissioners have decided to make the following reply and statement, of the policy of the Government:
>
> "*Brothers*: — We are instructed by the President, to negotiate a treaty, or treaties, with any or all of the nations, tribes or bands of Indians, in the Indian Territory, Kansas, or of the plains, west of the Indian Territory and Kansas.
>
> "The following named Nations and tribes have by their own acts, by making treaties with the enemies of the United States, at the dates hereafter named, forfeited all right to annuities, lands and protection by the United States:

---

sible notify by special courier the commanding officer at Fort Smith that this Council with the several delegations expect to meet at that place on the 15th inst for the purpose of negotiating with the United States Government.

"ARMSTRONG ACADEMY, C.N., Sept. 6th, 1865, Approved,

> CLERMONT, Chief Osages
> CO-NOT-SA-SONNE, Comanche Chief
> GEORGE WASHINGTON, Chief Caddoes
> LUCK-A-O-TSE, Chief Arrapahoes
> JOHN JUMPER, Chief Seminoles
> WINCHESTER COLBERT, Gov. Chickasaw Nation
> STAND WATIE, Prin. Chief Cherokee Nation
> SAMUEL CHECOTE, Prin. Chief Creek Nation
> P. P. PITCHLYNN, Prin. Chief Choctaw Nation

Official Copy, J. A. SCALES, Secretary Grand Council."

[401] Commissioner of Indian Affairs, *Report*, 1865, pp. 298-299, 318-319.

"The different Nations and tribes having made treaties with the rebel Government are as follows, viz:

The Creek nation, July 10, 1861.

Choctaws and Chickasaws, July 12, 1861.

Seminoles, August 1, 1861.

Shawnees, Delawares, Wichitas and affiliated tribes residing in the leased territory, August 12, 1861.

The Comanches of the prairie, August 12, 1861.

The Great Osages, October 2, 1861.

The Senecas, Senecas and Shawnees (Neosho agency) October 4, 1861.

The Quapaws, October 4, 1861.

The Cherokees, October 7, 1861.

"By these nations having entered into treaties with the so-called Confederate States, and the rebellion being now ended, they are left without any treaty whatever, or treaty obligation for protection by the United States.

"Under the terms of the treaties with the United States, and the law of Congress of July 5, 1862, all these nations and tribes forfeited and lost all their rights to annuities and lands. The President, however, does not desire to take advantage of or enforce the penalties for the unwise actions of these nations.

"The President is anxious to renew the relations which existed at the breaking out of the rebellion.

"We, as representatives of the President, are empowered to enter into new treaties with the proper delegates of the tribes located within the so-called Indian territory, and others above named, living west and north of the Indian territory.

"Such treaties must contain, substantially, the following stipulations:[402]

1. Each tribe must enter into a treaty for permanent peace and amity with themselves, each nation and tribe, and with the United States.

2. Those settled in the Indian territory must bind themselves, when called upon by the government, to aid in com-

---

[402] The stipulations embodied terms far harsher than anything yet offered the South. President Johnson's suggestions for Mississippi (Garner, *Reconstruction in Mississippi*, p. 84) may be taken as the high water mark of what he would, up to August of 1865, have wished done for the negro within the limits of the old slave states.

pelling the Indians of the plains to maintain peaceful relations with each other, with the Indians in the territory, and with the United States.[403]

3. The institution of slavery which has existed among several of the tribes must be forthwith abolished, and measures taken for the unconditional emancipation of all persons held in bondage, and for their incorporation in the tribes on an equal footing with the original members, or suitably provided for.

4. A stipulation in the treaties that slavery, or involuntary servitude, shall never exist in the tribe or nation, except in punishment of crime.

5. A portion of the lands hitherto owned and occupied by you must be set apart for the friendly tribes now in Kansas, and elsewhere, on such terms as may be agreed upon by the parties, and approved by the government, or such as may be fixed by the government.

6. It is the policy of the government, unless other arrangements be made, that all the nations and tribes in the Indian territory be formed into one consolidated government, after the plan proposed by the Senate of the United States, in a bill for organizing the Indian territory.

7. No white person, except officers, agents, and employés of the government, or of any internal improvement authorized by the government, will be permitted to reside in the territory, unless formally incorporated with some tribe, according to the usages of the band.

"*Brothers*: — You have now heard and understand what are the views and wishes of the President, and the commissioners, as they told you yesterday, will expect definite answers from each of you upon the questions submitted.

"As we said yesterday, we say again, that in any event those who have always been loyal, although their nations may have

---

[403] The alliance between the secessionist Indians and the wild tribes of the plains may perhaps explain the insertion of this provision. In June, 1864, when Senator B. Gratz Brown of Missouri urged that the annuity-receiving Indian be obliged to contribute a quota of troops or pay for substitutes, a portion of their money being withheld for the purpose, Doolittle moved as a substitute plan that the enrollment of peaceful Indians to oppose hostile be authorised (McPherson, *Political History of the United States During the Great Rebellion*, p. 264).

gone over to the enemy, will be liberally provided for and dealt with."

The consideration of the seven propositions submitted by the commissioners constituted the order of the day at the next meeting of the peace council, Monday, the eleventh.   Definite word had then come from Pitchlynn and Colbert that the secessionists would not appear before Friday.[404]   The loyal delegates declared themselves no more authorized to make treaties than they had been formerly, therefore, all they could do now with respect to the seven propositions was to express opinions, favorable or unfavorable, and even for that the Creeks and Seminoles were unready.   They must have more time to think about them.   The fullest approval came from a direction unlooked-for, from Agent Gookins, who took upon himself the responsibility of saying in behalf of the still absent Reserve Indians that they would surely approve all proposals applicable to their situation.   Had the assurance come from the Indians themselves it would not have been much of a concession since the tribes belonging to the Leased District were only tenants of the Red River nations.   Any approval on the part of loyal Choctaws, miserably few in number as they were, could scarcely be of even equal consequence.   They did, however, approve all the propositions except the seventh and of that they suggested the following modification, which indicated a certain reservation regarding the third:

"No white person, except officers, agents, and employés of the government, or of any internal improvement authorized by the government of the United States; also, no person of African descent except our former slaves, or free persons of color who are now, or have been, residents of the territory, will be per-

[404] Pitchlynn and Colbert to Bussey, Sept. 5, 1865, *Bussey Corres.* S.

mitted to reside in the territory, unless formally incorporated with some tribe, according to the usages of the band." [405]

The Chickasaws offered the same modification, the idea of opening their territory indiscriminately to the negroes being evidently repugnant to them. Suitable provision for their own blacks, something short of actual incorporation into the body politic of the tribe, they were willing to concede. They approved the first and second propositions; but refused to give an opinion, they being unauthorized, of the fourth, fifth, and sixth.

Some of the delegates put in a plea of *not guilty*. They resented the imputation, contained in Cooley's addresses and in his seven propositions, that the Indians were solely responsible for what had occurred. To them it appeared most flagrantly unjust that whole nations and all the nations should be punished alike and so severely, quite regardless of the fact that some large minorities had never yielded at all and some nations only under compulsion. They denied that they had forfeited their annuities and their lands. The Senecas outlined their own case, which was likewise the case of their neighbours, the Quapaws and the affiliated Senecas and Shawnees. Agent Dorn and Commissioner Pike had intimidated them; they had signed a treaty under duress and had escaped from their Confederate persecutors the very first opportunity that offered. [406] The Cherokees had a longer and even more pathetic tale to tell, a tale of broken faith, of misplaced trust, of submission to the inevitable. They, too, had returned to the earlier allegiance, and whole-heartedly, the moment that the Confederate menace was removed and the Federal protection once more a possibility. [407]

[405] Commissioner of Indian Affairs, *Report*, 1865, pp. 320-321.
[406] — *Ibid.*, pp. 321-322.
[407] — *Ibid.*, pp. 322-323.

The argument of the Cherokees was historically true
and irrefutable; but it was couched in language that
bespoke the white man's civilization.   It was no more
logical and far less quaintly simple than was the Osage
reply, which followed it,

> " . . . In one of the propositions you told us red chil-
> dren that we had made treaties with the south.   It is true that
> some of our headmen were at that council, and that they were
> deceived and misled.   They had their allegiance to their
> Grand Father in their hearts, but were deceived and enticed
> away . . .
>
> "Of course they had an understanding with the south, but
> as soon as they could get away they went to their Great Father,
> expecting that he would protect them in their rights and prop-
> erty.   Again, in your propositions you stated that the President
> of the United States wished to make an Indian territory.   That
> we understood.   Now it is your places, commissioners, to talk
> with the Indians in the territory, and see if you can agree with
> them and form a territory.   And if so, we that are outside will
> have to come in.
>
> "You told them also that no white men, except officers, should
> be allowed in the Indian country.   Now you have prohibited
> the white man, and why do you say that the negro may come in?
> That is all that I have to say." [408]

The repugnance to the negro colonization idea was
shared by the Seminoles, who were ready with their
expressions of opinion at the next day's meeting.   Their
suggestion was, "that article 3 should be so changed as
to admit only colored persons lately held in bondage
by the Seminole people and free persons of color
residing in the nation previous to the rebellion to a
residence among" them "and adoption in the Seminole
tribes, upon some plan to be agreed upon by" them
"and approved by the government."   They were "willing to provide for the colored people of" their "own

[408] — *Ibid.*, p. 324.

nation," but did not desire their "lands to become colonization grounds for the negroes of other States and Territories." [409]

Some anxiety lest, judging from the determined tone of the Cherokee protest, they may have gone a little too far in expressing the wishes of the government and in interpreting the law of congress led the commissioners, on this the fourth day of the council, to attempt an explanation of Cooley's remarks regarding forfeiture of annuities, lands and protection. The Cherokees had wrongly inferred that he spoke of forfeiture as a fact accomplished. The idea he had intended to convey was, that, rightfully, forfeiture might take place and had been authorized by congress but that the president wished to be merciful and not "to enforce the *penalties* for the *unwise* action" of the nations. The word, *unwise*, is scarcely a synonym of *criminal* or *treasonable,* nevertheless, Cooley went on,

> "The commissioners only stated what was the legitimate legal consequence of the great crime of treason on the part of those who had so solemnly abjured their allegiance to the United States, and we expressed the hope, as coming from the President, that each nation would place itself in such a position as to enable the President to waive the forfeiture and reinstate the nation."

How Cooley dared to make such a statement when he knew positively what Harlan's design was it is impossible to surmise!

However, he next reviewed with strong bias and avoidance of all reference to extenuating circumstances the course of Cherokee defection. He made out a good case. Half-truths that are usually more mischievous than downright falsehoods figured in his recital; but so also did the falsehood and the deliberate shifting of

---

[409] — *Ibid.,* p. 325.

emphasis. Cooley affected not to know that the Cherokees had long since repudiated their treaty of October
7, 1861 and he pointed out with unnecessary directness;
unnecessary, that is, if his object were other than mali-
cious, everything that the Cherokee Principal Chief
had ever done or said that could be construed as inimical to the United States and friendly to the Confederate. Facts of contrary purport that had been
stressed by the delegation to palliate or to vindicate
individual or national conduct were scornfully rejected
by him or held to go only in mitigation. The Principal Chief, the Nation, he would not excuse; but in-
sultingly said that men who had fought for the Union,
the president having "been advised of their chivalric
valor," would be "honored, respected, and protected
in every right and interest individually." [410]

The attack upon the Principal Chief, who was none
other than the aged and stalwart John Ross, was pre-
meditated. Here was another case of history repeat-
ing itself. John Ross, now grown very old in the service of his people, was the same man that in the days
of his prime had resisted President Jackson and others
of less exalted station when they were intriguing for
the Cherokee lands in Georgia. The Cherokees and,
in particular, John Ross, were in a position to be the
great stumbling-block in the way of the accomplishment of Harlan's purpose. It was in full realization
of that uncomfortable fact that Harlan and his friends,
in the course of the Senate debate on bill, no. 459, had
so contemptuously underrated Ross' loyalty and dubbed
him, in derision, a pensioner of the United States government, although they knew perfectly well that all

---

[410] — *Ibid.*, pp. 325-327.

monies appropriated for Indian relief had been drawn from tribal funds.

The Indian Office [411] had been long in possession of all the evidence against John Ross that by any sort of manipulation could be called incriminating. In Dole's time, it had been honestly handled, never separated from its context; for Dole knew, as Mix and Cooley and Harlan should have known, exactly under what conditions the Cherokees had allied themselves with the Confederacy. Early in August of the present year, Superintendent Sells had obtained from the Creeks copies, or maybe the originals, of Ross' correspondence with Opoeth-le-yohola whom, in order that the Indians might not be divided wherever they stood, he had tried to persuade to join the South. These letters and also a copy of the speech that Ross had addressed to Colonel Drew's deserting companies, Sells transmitted to Washington.[412] He had the zeal of a swaddling-clothes official. Harlan and Cooley might have found,

---

[411] So also had the War Department. See A.G.O., Old Files Section, B 1376, July, 1862; 280 K, 1862. The following letter indicates how Cooley, besides having what the Indian Office could furnish, tried to procure other material from the War Department:

"In order that the Commission about to visit the Southern tribes, may be as fully as possible advised of the conduct of those tribes during the late rebellion, I have the honor to request that you will ask the War Department to furnish this Office at the earliest moment possible with the original, or a copy, of a letter forwarded to General Halleck, sometime between 18th February and the last of March, 1862, by either General Curtis or Mr. H. Z. Curtis, containing a newspaper printed at Fayetteville, Arkansas, about 15th January, 1862 showing the relations of John Ross to the so-called Confederate States. Also with any other official reports of General Curtis in regard to the conduct of the Southern Indians and their connection with the rebellion." (Cooley to Harlan, August 15, 1865).

[412] Sells to Harlan, August 10, 1865, I. D. Files, Bundle, no. 54; *Register of Letters Received*, "Indians," no. 4, p. 485. For copies of the letters, see Commissioner of Indian Affairs, *Report*, 1865, pp. 353-354, and for a copy of the address, *ibid.*, pp. 355-357.

had they searched, the same documents in their own files along with others of a far different tenor; but these suited their present purpose and Cooley, at Harlan's suggestion,[413] had carried them west with him, to use if political need should arise. That need had now arisen and Cooley read extracts from them to the confusion, as he surmised, of his audience.

The incident fitted in, as it happened, with the Creek "talk," [414] which was delivered towards the close of the meeting. The Creek delegates recounted the deeds of Cooley's "pure patriot," Opoeth-le-yohola. There could be no doubt that fully half of the Creeks had been staunchly loyal throughout, that intimidation had been tried upon them, and had failed. Commissioner Pike, indeed, had not scrupled to permit the forged signatures of absent chiefs to be attached to the treaty he negotiated; but the absentees, Ok-ta-hassee Harjo, Tullisse Fixico, and Mikko Hut-kee, impressed it upon Cooley that they could easily prove an alibi.

The fifth day of the council was momentous. It saw the arrival of Governor Colbert,[415] E. C. Boudinot, and J. W. Washbourne,[416] the first of the secessionists to put

---

[413] Harlan to Cooley, August 15, 1865, O.I.A., General Files, *Cherokee,* 1859-1865, I 1188.

[414] O.I.A., Land Files, *Indian Talks, Councils, &c.,* Box 4, 1865-1866; Commissioner of Indian Affairs, *Report,* 1865, pp. 328-330.

[415] "I am requested by Hon. D. N. Cooley, Com^r. to say that Govr. Colbert of the Chickasaws has just come in from Armstrong Academy & reports a delegation of 70, representing that & the Choctaw Nations, as on the way thither. The work progresses fairly. They will all be here tomorrow." (John B. Garrett to Harlan, September 13, 1865, I. D. Files, Bundle, no. 55).

[416] Boudinot and Washbourne, Cherokees, to Cooley, September 13, 1865, urging him to delay proceedings until all the southern delegates are present (O.I.A., Land Files, *Indian Talks, Councils, &c.,* Box 4, 1865-1866). On the last day of the council, Boudinot made a statement in which he claimed to have been in Fort Smith since the commencement of the sessions (Commissioner of Indian Affairs, *Report,* 1865, p. 312).

in an appearance at Fort Smith, and it saw also the reading of the *treaty of peace*.[417] This Cooley and his colleagues had prepared and now presented, notwithstanding that the audience was almost exclusively unionist as it had been from the very beginning. The provisions of the treaty were peculiar. They gave large attention to the alliance with the Confederacy and to the liabilities which it involved and they recorded, although untruthfully, the maintenance of federal military supremacy in the Indian country and the generous and magnanimous intentions of a paternalistic government; but, in their minutiae, they bore little resemblance to the seven propositions that Cooley had so boldly announced. In effect, the so-called treaty of peace was a mere recognition of the allegiance due to the United States. It possessed no reconstruction features so that with it to the fore Harlan's great purpose had been thrust to one side, at all events, seemingly and for the time being.

The formal signing of the treaty of peace and amity began at the next meeting, the United States commissioners leading the way, followed by the more insignificant, numerically speaking, of the unionists, the Chickasaws, the Seminoles, and the various tribes of the Neosho Agency, some of whom were jubilant at the return of peace and some, the Osages, hopeful that their Great Father would now protect them against their enemies, the white men of Kansas. The absurdity of unionists being asked to sign such a treaty and the implication involved in their acceding could

---

[417] Kappler's statement in *Indian Laws and Treaties*, vol. ii, p. 1051, *note* 1, that the text of this agreement is not on file in the Indian Office, is inaccurate. It is to be found in Land Files, *Treaties*, Box 3, 1864-1866. For the printed document, see Commissioner of Indian Affairs, *Report*, 1865, pp. 330-331.

not have been lost upon the Creeks; for they refused
to sign unless a statement [418] exonerating them from all
complicity in the making of the alliance with the Confederacy were accepted for filing by the commissioners.
At first, Cooley objected and, in objecting, impeached
their sincerity,[419] forgetful of the fact that he deemed
it unnecessary for the Shawnees of Kansas to sign;
inasmuch as they had "never been a party to any treaty
with the enemies of the government." [420]   Sign they did,
notwithstanding, in testimony of their good-will.   It
was a renewal of their allegiance to the United States.

Reservations seemed now to become the fashion and
were registered by one group after another through the
succeeding days.   On the fifteenth, the Leased District
Indians came forward to sign but they vowed that they
had never been "otherwise than strictly true and loyal
during the war." [421]   The three Wichita chiefs, who
had signed Pike's treaty of August 12, 1861, had signed
while prisoners and under compulsion.   Another
Wichita chief, for refusing to sign, had been killed.
Cherokees of the loyalist element went one step farther

---

[418] "We, the loyal Creek Indians, represented by the delegation now
present, solemnly declare that the Treaty of July 10, 1861, was alone
made by the rebel portion of the Creek Indians and never was executed
or assented to by the Union portion of the Nation, and is, not now,
and never has been, obligatory upon them and the signing names to
said treaty of the loyal party was a forgery." (O.I.A., Land Files,
Indian Talks, Councils, &c., Box 4, 1865-1866).

[419] "We are surprised to know that any nation or tribe which
assumes to be loyal should object to the signing of the treaty, inasmuch as there is nothing in it to which any truly loyal person may
take exception." (Commissioner of Indian Affairs, *Report,* 1865, pp.
303, 333).

[420] — *Ibid.,* 303, 334.

[421] — *Ibid.,* pp. 304, 334.   Additional material evidential of constant loyalty is to be found in O.I.A., Land Files, *Indian Talks, Councils &c.,* Box
4, 1865-1866.   Note particularly a penciled affidavit signed September 15,
1865.

in the making of reservations and would sign only upon the understanding that they did not acknowledge that they had forfeited their rights and privileges to annuities and lands, for they were not guilty. They asked that the following statement be spread upon the record,

"We, the loyal Cherokee delegation, acknowledge the execution of the treaty of October 7, 1861; but we solemnly declare that the execution of the treaty was procured by the coercion of the rebel army." [422]

It was useless for Cooley to interpose his objections; for Reese, the Cherokee spokesman, was more obstinate and determined than perhaps Cooley, with all his arrogance, dared be. The commissioners yielded the point and the Cherokees signed.[423]

The afternoon session of the fifteenth witnessed a renewal of the attack upon the aged Ross, whom, in a statement,[424] inconceivably unjust, false, and villainous, the commissioners, upon the recommendation of Agent

---

[422] — *Ibid.*, pp. 304, 335-336.

[423] Not all the loyal Cherokee signatures were obtained on this occasion. See, *ibid.*, p. 341.

[424] "Whereas, John Ross, an educated Cherokee, formerly chief of the nation, became the emissary of the States in rebellion and, by means of his superior education and ability as such emissary, induced many of his people to abjure their allegiance to the United States and to join the States in rebellion, inducing those who were warmly attached to the Government to aid the enemies thereof; and

"Whereas, he now sets up claim to the office of principal chief, and by his subtle influence is at work poisoning the minds of those who are truly loyal; and

"Whereas, he is endeavoring by his influence as pretended first chief to dissuade the loyal delegation of Cherokees, now at this council, from a free and open expression of their sentiments of loyalty to the United States; and

"Whereas, he has been for two days in the vicinity of our council-room (without coming into the same) at this place, disaffecting the Cherokees and persuading the Creeks not to enter into treaty stipula-

Harlan and Superintendent Sells [425] and with the approval of Cooley, acting in his capacity as Commissioner of Indian Affairs,[426] refused to acknowledge [427]

tions which were arranged for the benefit of the loyal Creeks and of the United States; and

"Whereas, he is by virtue of his position as pretended first chief of the Cherokees, exercising an influence in his nation and at this council adverse to the wishes and interest of all loyal and true Indians and of the United States; and

"Whereas, we believe him still at heart an enemy of the United States and disposed to breed discord among his people, and that he does not represent the will and wishes of the loyal Cherokees, and is not the choice of any considerable portion of the Cherokee nation for the office which he claims, but which by their law we believe he does not in fact hold; and

"Whereas, the Agent and Superintendent have recommended that the said Ross be deposed and not recognized by the Government as the principal chief of the Cherokee nation, and the Commissioner of Indian Affairs having approved the same and he refusing to recognize the said Ross as the representative of the Cherokee nation,

"Now, therefore, we the undersigned Commissioners sent by the President of the United States to negotiate treaties with the Indians of the Indian territory and southwest, having knowledge of the facts above recited do approve the above recommendation and decision and refuse as Commissioners in any way or manner to recognize said Ross as chief of the Cherokee nation.

"Witness our hands at Ft. Smith, Ark., this fifteenth day of September, 1865.

> D. N. COOLEY, President.
> WM. S. HARNEY, Brig. Gen. U.S. Army, Commissioner
> ELIJAH SELLS, Com'r.
> ELY S. PARKER, Commissioner.
> THOMAS WISTER."

(The foregoing document was found among the *Fort Smith Council Papers* in the Indian Office. It was sent, marked, "Private," by wire to Secretary Harlan, September 16, 1865. See General Files, *Cherokee*, 1859-1865, C 1577. It is also on file in the Interior Department, Bundle, no. 55. With certain important omissions, it was included in Cooley's report. See Commissioner of Indian Affairs, *Report*, 1865, pp. 304-305).

[425] Cooley to Sells, September 15, 1865, O.I.A., Land Files, *Indian Talks, Councils, &c.*, Box 4, 1865-1866.

[426]   "FORT SMITH, Sept. 15, 1865.

"I am satisfied from facts which have come to my knowledge that John Ross, who claims to be the 1st Chief of the Cherokee Nation, should not be recognized as Chief of said Nation. I do therefore here-

as the Principal Chief of the Cherokee Nation.[428]   The
incident in its ulterior design was not without precedent [429] in the history of the political relations between the United States government and the Indian
tribes although that history may well blush to record
it; but, in the existing circumstances, it was peculiarly
unjust, arbitrary and offensive, degrading to all con-

by declare & make known that the said John Ross will not hereafter
in any manner be recognized as such officer by the Indian Department
of the Government of the United States.

"D. N. COOLEY,

"Com^r. of Indian Affairs."

(*Minutes of the Private Meetings of the Commissioners*)

[427] From a memorandum found in the Indian Office among the papers
bearing upon the negotiations of the next year, I judge that there was some
indecision as to whether the commissioners should *depose* or *refuse to
recognize*. The former procedure might be interpreted as unwarrantable
interference in tribal affairs and might give rise to complications, embar-
rassing at some future time to the government. Agent Harlan, undoubtedly,
had deposition in mind.

  (a) Discretion that will not *"recognise"*

     Pres^t. issues Proclamation not to recognise

     "Consuls," &c. – We do not depose – only

     refuse to *recognise.*

     Halseman – Webster

     Gennett — in 179 — who appealed to people &c

 – Washington – was sent out of the *country* –

  (b)

"I am satisfied in view of the facts and circumstances in the case
that it would be for the benefit of the great Cherokee Nation that
their present Chief John Ross be deposed from his said office of principal Chief of the Cherokee Nation" (Harlan to Superintendent Sells,
September 15, 1865).

[428] "Parker and Irwin, with escort, leave for Colorado today. Four
or five hundred Southern Indians came in yesterday. We are succeeding. We unanimously refuse to recognize John Ross as Chief of Loyal
Cherokees. He has been in our way. We have documents to back us.
Get Cook's leave extended 30 days. We leave here, I trust, about first
of October." (Telegram, Cooley to Harlan, September 16, 1865, O.I.A.,
General Files, *Southern Superintendency*, 1865; I. D. Files, Bundle,
no. 55).

[429] The arrest of Ross himself, in 1835, might almost be considered a case
in point. Consult, Royce, *The Cherokee Nation of Indians*, p. 281; Abel,
Indian Consolidation, p. 404.

cerned and entirely without justification. It was the
project of government officials exclusively, although
Ross' opponents within the tribe were not slow to take
advantage of it.   E. C. Boudinot, wily schemer that he
was, saw in his enemy's discomfiture and disgrace, an
opportunity for ingratiating himself with Cooley, for
settling old scores, for frustrating the plans of the
unionists in the matter of confiscations, and for rein-
stating the secessionists in their ante-bellum rights and
privileges.   The action of the commissioners received
Secretary Harlan's endorsement and, likewise, President Johnson's.[430]   Without so much as the pretense of
a trial, one of the noblest of red men had been condemned, his only crime too keen a comprehension of
a new plot against his race.[431]   Ross had his friends,
however, and they were soon to be heard from.

Thus far the secessionists had not presented them-

[430] "Your telegram of 16th in relation to *John Ross* has been submitted
to the President. He authorizes and directs me to say that on your
understanding of the facts as stated, your action is approved.

"Should he persist you are authorized to recognize such other party
or parties as representative of the Cherokee Nation, as may appear
to you to be the true representatives of their sentiments and wishes.
And should those who have been in rebellion against the Government
of the United States refuse to harmonize with the loyal portion of the
Nation, you will recognize as the organ of each party such persons as
seem to you to be the true representatives of their sentiments &
wishes . . .

"P.S. Send telegram through the War Department

"By order of the President . . . "

(Secretary Harlan to Cooley & Harvey, Comm^rs., September 17, 1865,
O.I.A., General Files, *Cherokee*, 1859-1865, I 1271; *ibid., Fort Smith Council
Papers*; I. D. Files, Bundle, no. 55. The letter ought to appear in I. D.
Letter Book, no. 5; but is not there).

[431] At this point specific reference to the report of Wilson of the *New
York Herald* is in order; for he alone gives a full account of what actually
occurred and was said at the afternoon session of September fifteenth. It
is designated in the records a *verbatim* report and is given here *verbatim*.

The Council was called to order at three o'clock & forty minutes.

The Chairman (Comm^r. Cooley) – The Council is now in session.

selves officially to the council; but, on the sixteenth, they did appear after the room had been sufficiently

Before proceeding with the business of the afternoon, I will read a paper prepared this morning by the Commissioners.

The Chairman then read as follows, viz.:

(Here insert the address of the Commissioners deposing Jno. Ross.)

The Chairman – The business of the afternoon is to receive the delegates from Armstrong's Academy & listen to anything they might have to offer.

Jno. Ross – May I make a few remarks?

The Chairman – Yes Sir.

Jno. Ross – Sir I deny the charges asserted against me. I deny having used any influence, either with the Cherokees, Creeks, or any other persons to resist the interests of the Indians, or of the Gov^t. of the U.S. I came to this place, Sir, at the special invitation & urgent request that I should do so. I came to Ft. Gibson on Sunday afternoon. I had no opportunity of getting away from there. I went to see my sister, my children & my relatives at Park Hill. I defy any person to come forward & prove these charges against me, who will state truth. I know prejudices have existed against me for years past, but, sir, I have maintained a peaceful course throughout my whole life. I claim to be as loyal a man as any other citizen of the U.S. There are certain documents which have found their way upon your table & which I signed. I have testimony which I hope I may be permitted to lay before you on that subject. I have been forty odd years Chief of the Cherokees, elected time after time. They reëlected me in my absence & I came on at my advanced age, after burying my wife & burying my son. I had three sons in your army, also three grandsons & three nephews. If I had been disloyal I would not have shrunk from going in the direction where the enemies of the U.S. were. I came on with the hope that I might be useful to my people, to those of my people who had separated from the Nation, to the Government of the U.S. I came here not for the purpose of resisting the policy of the U.S. If we have rights, we ought to be permitted to express them. I never recommended any other course than that which could be sustained consistent with the laws of the U.S. I have been three years residing in Washington. I have been in communication with the Department, Sir, with the President. With Mr. Lincoln I was constantly in communication, & up to the last moment I communicated with the present President U.S.

I have never been charged with being an enemy of the U.S. I hope I may be permitted to make a respectful statement in reply to what has been preferred against me. I have some testimony too. This I will lay before the Hon. Commissioners. Far from a desire to use influence to prejudice any against the interests of the U.S., I resisted to the last moment the policy of disunion that was set out by a portion

cleared of miscellaneous visitors, officers of the gar-

of the border states of Arkansas & Texas. I hope I may be permitted to enter a reply to the charges just made.

THE CHAIRMAN – You shall have every opportunity afforded you to lay any reply you may desire to submit before the Comm^r. We have been here about 8 days. We were engaged during most of that time in attempting to negotiate with the loyal Cherokees a treaty of peace & amity. Evidence has been laid before the Commissioners which shows that you, sir, have been playing the part which this address shows. This address was prepared, not knowing that it was your intention to visit the Council. You were on the other side of the river, & yet you did not visit us. We learned that you were in consultation with the loyal Cherokees. Previous to that they were prepared to sign the treaty we had drawn up. . . Anything you may have to say at any time in explanation of this, you will be afforded an opportunity to say.

JNO. ROSS – As to my being here for several days I have this to say. It was suggested that as I was Principal Chief of the Nation it would be best & proper to consult me before signing the treaty. I did no more than express my own opinion upon the subject. . . I consulted nobody. I did it openly & honorably. I have a character which is more sacred to me than my life. I have borne a reputation that I have maintained up to the present time, sir, which is worth more to me than is my life. I have done nothing that was wrong. I was consulted, as other men are often consulted, for my opinion. I remarked that this preliminary treaty, as I understood it, goes to show that the Cherokees admit that they did forfeit all right to lands & annuities in consequence of having entered into a treaty with Genl. Pike. Well, sir, I said that we could show that we did not do that thing willingly. It is true I signed it, but I did it upon the resolutions, & upon the whole voice of the people of the Nation. I did not do it within myself. My course goes to show that I repudiated the idea that the southern states would bring about a successful rebellion against the U.S. Gov^t. I always counselled that we as a weak people ought not to do anything to violate the laws of the U.S. I counselled obedience to the Gov^t. Well, sir, could I do more than that? When the very first federal soldiers came into the Country, a regiment of Cherokees went & joined them. Another regiment was raised & went out to join them. . . As a weak people I recommended no other course than that which could be supported by our treaties. I thank you for the privilege you have given me to respond to these charges.

THE CHAIRMAN – (To Mr. Ross). At any time & at length. (To the Council). If any of the delegates have any thing to say, we will be pleased to listen to them now.

E. C. BOUDINOT, a Cherokee said, . . . Many of our delegates have already gone into camp . . . They do not desire to enter into

rison and ladies, to make way for them.[432]   The treaty

any business today nor until the whole delegation is present. I have
been informed that the delegates from Armstrong's Academy will be
required to sign the preliminary treaty of peace prepared by the Commissioners before proceeding to other business. Perhaps it is not
known to the Commissioners that these Indians have already signed
such a paper. We have a good deal to say & we want to lay this
before the Commissioners & before all our people who are here & can
hear us. I wish to make a statement of facts in regard to the last
four years, of material interest to ourselves & to those of our own
nation who have differed from us. The Gentleman (Jno. Ross) who
has addressed the Commissioners respecting a paper read by the Pres[t].
desires to know who the person or persons are who have charged him
with duplicity & bad faith. So far as those particular charges are
concerned, I do not suppose that any member of the delegation from
the South has had anything to do with it. But, Sir, there are serious
charges which I will make against him, & I here announce my willingness & intention to make such charges, to state such facts & to prove
them too, as will prove his duplicity. The fact is the Cherokee Nation
has been long rent in twain by dissensions & I here charge these upon
this same John Ross. I charge him with it here today & I will do it
tomorrow. I will show that the treaty made with the Confederate
States was made at his instigation. I will show the deep duplicity &
falsity that have followed him from his childhood to the present day,
when the winters of 65 or 70 years have silvered his head with sin;
what can you expect of him now . . .

THE CHAIRMAN – The object of this Council is not to stir up old
feelings. The paper you have heard read was drawn up out of a
sense of duty, by the Commissioners, to the interests of the U.S. & as
an act which was due to the loyal portion of the Cherokee Nation.
I trust that no one may come into this Council and attempt to stir up
bad feelings which ought to have been buried years ago. . . I wish
it to be understood that the document read here today will not give
any license to different portions of your nation to bring up matters that
long ago ought to have been buried in oblivion. We trust that Jno.
Ross will be able to exculpate himself from the very serious charges
which have been made against him. We hope he will be able to fully
explain his actions so that we can shake hands too with him in peace
& amity.

E. C. BOUDINOT – It was not my intention to stir up bad blood
between our brothers, or between any other section or sections of the
Indian Country, but to let you know I propose to give a view of our
feelings & actions for the last four years. It will be impossible to do
so without referring to the acts of prominent men, John Ross among
the number. . .

ADJOURNED.

[432] Commissioner of Indian Affairs, *Report*, 1865, p. 305.

being interpreted, they asked time for its consideration, all of them except the Seminoles that is, and were given until Monday. The Seminoles [433] signed forthwith and, as it proved, prematurely;[434] for they had not yet acquainted themselves with all that the Articles of Agreement signified and they apparently knew nothing about the seven propositions.[435]   On this occasion, Com-

[433] The credentials of the Southern Seminole delegation had been issued at Armstrong Academy. The text of them may be found, as also the text of the Northern Seminole credentials, issued at Fort Gibson, in Land Files, *Indian Talks, Councils, &c.*, Box 4.

[434] Perhaps, they signed early because they were in a desperate hurry to get away. Their people were destitute, their country denuded of provisions. Moreover, they had not a full delegation at Fort Smith. Some of their headmen were absent. They got J. L. Morrow to ask permission of Sells for them to depart and for Chief Jumper to be accorded an interview with Sells before leaving (*ibid.*).

[435] On the 20th, they asked to be allowed to reconsider and their request granted, they registered their approval of all the terms the commissioners had proffered except the third and sixth (Commissioner of Indian Affairs, *Report*, 1865, pp. 350-351). Their address, embodying their views, bears date, September 18, 1865, and runs as follows:

"The Southern Seminoles have considered the ultimate propositions so far laid down by you and cordially assent to all but the 3rd and 6th.

"We know the abolition of slavery to be a fact throughout the United States. We are willing to recognize that fact by the proper acts of our Council. But the proposition to 'incorporate' the freed negro with us on an 'equal footing with the original members' of the Seminole tribe is presented to us so suddenly that it shocks the lesson we have learned for long years from the white man as to the negro's inferiority. We honestly think that both the welfare of the Seminole and the freed negro would be injured if not destroyed by such 'incorporation.' The emancipated black man must, of necessity, be 'suitably provided for.' Such provision requires time and consultation as to how it shall best be done, and we, consequently, beg the indulgence of further time before we decide. We, however, bind ourselves to agree in good faith to any wise plan which shall be deemed just and equitable to all parties.

"The proposition touching the consolidation of all the tribes and fragments of tribes into one government is one of so great moment and interest to us that we must request time for its due consideration. The plan proposed by the United States Senate may be a good one. We have not seen it, but would like to do so and lay it before our Council so as to enable our people to determine thereupon. We will, how-

missioner Wistar addressed the council, emphasizing the pacific objects of himself and his colleagues. It was well he did for those objects had recently become somewhat obscure. The southern Cherokees followed, filing an expression of opinion [400] on Cooley's proposals, to five of which they gave ready assent. Tribal incorporation of negroes, the general colonization of negroes, and the organization of Indian Territory they could not and would not approve. The reasons given were incontrovertible; but not such as would have made any impression upon politicians and it was with politicians that the unfortunate Indians had to deal. In the course of the discussion, Boudinot attempted to introduce the subject of Cherokee dissensions, doubtless with the idea of insinuating that, if some Cherokees did really oppose the alliance of the nation with the Confederacy, they did so, not because they had any love for the United

---

ever, cheerfully agree to any plan which may be adopted by the other nations of the Indian Territory and sanctioned by the President of the United States.

"Our country is a small one and remote. It will neither bear a location within its borders of a numerous or an unruly tribe.

"Our course during the past four years has been what we considered an honest one. We were in earnest in pursuing it. We shall be equally in earnest in fulfilling all relations which we may enter into in this Convention, or hereafter in others, with the United States. And we here announce to you and the Government that you may discover that a once earnest enemy can become a better citizen, a more faithful liege than those who make pretense to fealty on account of interest.

"We beg to assure you that we desire nothing more ardently than peace with the United States, peace with our brother Indians, peace among ourselves.

"James Factor,
Foohatchee Cochucme,
George Cloud,
Paencah Yohola,
John Brown."

(O.I.A., Land Files, *Indian Talks, Councils, &c.*, Box 4, 1865-1866).
[436] Commissioner of Indian Affairs, *Report*, 1865, pp. 306-307, 339.

States, any true sense of loyalty, but because they hated
their rival compatriots more.   The Creeks, by the bye,
were to use the same sort of disparagement of Opoeth-
le-yohola's endeavors.   Boudinot intimated that a division of territory was the only road to tribal harmony.
He began a denunciation of some of his chief adver-
saries but there he went a trifle too far and Cooley
silenced him;[437] for the time was not yet ripe for their
general downfall.   Moreover, Cooley had no desire yet
awhile to tackle the subject of factional disputes.   It
would be preferable to leave the earlier stages of their
consideration to a joint conference committee and the
appointment of such he was shortly to propose.

The concluding business of the eighth day, just narrated, had been preceded by a circumstance that indicated that the commissioners felt their labors at Fort
Smith had passed the crisis.   The Indians to the west
and northwest had yet to be treated with; for the great
pacification, as planned in Washington, was to include
them.   In private meeting on the thirteenth, the commissioners had resolved [438] to send Parker and Irwin to
a council on Bluff Creek that General John Sanborn
had arranged for long since;[439] but the measure failed
to meet with the approval of the Indians at Fort Smith.

[437] — *Ibid.*, p. 307.

[438] "On the recommendation of the President, Com^r. Parker and
Assistant-Secretary Irwin were detailed to attend Council to treat
with Indians at Bluff Creek, Oct. 4, 1865 – Com^r. Parker as a member
of the Commission and Sec^y Irwin to be Secretary of the Commission –
and the President was authorized to furnish them with proper instruction." (*Minutes of the Private Meetings of the Commissioners at
Fort Smith, 1865*).

[439] (a) "Arrived here last evening.   Roads bad and train slow.   We
leave tomorrow.   Party all well.   We shall not arrive at Smith before
fifth.   General Sanborn has called a council at mouth Little Arkansas,
October fourth.   I telegraph him to change the place to Council Grove
and, if Indians will assent, then at Seorah, known as Walnut Creek,

Not that it was any concern of theirs; but they had counted so much upon Parker's interceding for them, of his saving them from the worst consequences of their folly that they took the liberty of petitioning that his

and to telegraph me at Smith. Will then inform you whether I can attend." (O.I.A., General Files, *Southern Superintendency*, 1865).

(b) " . . . General Sanborn has appointed a council for October the fourth, at Bluff Creek, ten days forced march from Leavenworth. I asked change of place to Council Grove, but Genls Pope and Dodge say impracticable. 'Tis too early and far off for any of my party. Either send a commission from Washington or get Pope to order delay of ten days and I will send some of our party. If not, authorise me to appoint a commission from the west, and I will send Irwin, clerk. Answer." (*ibid.*, I 1249).

The Bluff Creek council had really been arranged for, in the original instance, by Agent J. H. Leavenworth (Leavenworth to Sanborn, August 1, 1865, *Official Records*, vol. xlviii, part ii, pp. 1162-1163). As already stated in this text, the select congressional committee, with Senator Doolittle at its head, had been authorised to negotiate a peace with the tribes of the Upper Arkansas. Leavenworth hoped the negotiations would begin not later than the tenth of September (*ibid.*, p. 1176). In June, Harlan had instructed Dole to undertake the pacification of the tribes of Dakota, Iowa, Montana, and Colorado (Letter of June 22, 1865, O.I.A., *Miscellaneous Files*, 1864-1867) and, July fifth, he had occasion to inquire why nothing had as yet been done (*ibid.*). The Select Committee to which reference is made had been authorised under a joint resolution of congress, passed at the recent session and approved, March third (13 United States Statutes at Large, pp. 572-573). The committee prepared its itinerary and Dole instructed, March 13, 1865, (O.I.A., *Letter Book*, no. 76, p. 393) all the superintendents and agents along the route to co-operate in fullest measure. The committee apportioned itself and its work into three parts, Doolittle, Lafayette S. Foster, vice-president *ex officio*, and Representative Lewis W. Ross taking the southern section. Samuel Bowles, editor of the *Springfield Republican*, who had accompanied Schuyler Colfax on a trip west that same summer, overtook them as they were about to start for New Mexico (Bowles, *Across the Continent*, pp. 7-8). General A. McD. McCook had been relieved at Helena and detailed to accompany them with a military escort (*Official Records*, vol. xlviii, part ii, pp. 284, 485, 708).

On the ninth of September, Doolittle was still in Wisconsin and, on that date, wrote, from Racine, a "private" letter which was in due course transmitted to President Johnson, and which, for the present narrative, has an especially large significance because of its bearing upon Indian policy relating to the freedmen. Doolittle had as yet not travelled quite so far on the road of injustice as his erstwhile colleague on the Senate Indian Affairs committee had. The letter is quoted at length in chapter viii.

departure be deferred until after their council had ended its sessions. The result of their action was, the substitution of Harney on the Bluff Creek mission.[440]

Over Sunday some reconciliations were effected. Creek and Seminole factions buried the hatchet and announced their re-united state when the council resumed its functions on the eighteenth, a day, as it developed, of multifarious business. The Seminoles, in more compliant mood since their reunion, expressed a general willingness to consider favorably the terms offered by the commissioners. If the government so desired, they would receive their friendly brothers from Kansas; but all such matters could not be decided immediately. They must be left for future negotiations.[441] The Creeks continued to express their views separately. Indeed, they were radically at variance on many matters. How they could ever have professed themselves reconciled to each other is an enigma. The loyal were magnanimous enough to accept, in prospect, even the incorporation of the negro. To them as full-bloods the idea was not nearly so repellant as was that of territorial organization; for that, they feared, would eventually mean the end of their tribal existence.[442] The disloyal, on the other hand, were so lacking in magnanimity, that they discredited, as has been already remarked upon, the whole refugee movement. In their estimation, Opoethle-yohola was no patriot, no loyalist of fine instinct, but a factionist serving his own and party ends, nothing more. As for negro incorporation, why the very idea to them was preposterous. How

---

[440] Commissioner of Indian Affairs, *Report*, 1865, p. 338.

[441] Commissioner of Indian Affairs, *Report*, 1865, p. 342.

[442] —*Ibid.*, p. 341.

could the United States ask the Indian to do what it had not yet done itself? [443]

Additional signatures to the Articles of Agreement were secured. Southern Creeks, southern Osages, southern Comanches, and southern Cherokees [444] were now in the group with the unionists and the southern Seminoles. The secessionist Choctaws and Chickasaws alone remained outside and on this ninth day of the council they, too, were heard from. No weak suppliants were these Indians. Of the allies of the late Confederacy, they were among the most proud-spirited and, unlike the New Hope conventionists, [445] they shouldered the whole blame for their own defection. They spurned the thought of having been overpersuaded by Cooper or by Pike. Not by the machinations of hired emissaries but by their own free-will had they revolted. They had honestly believed in the doc-

[443] The southern Creeks handed in two statements, one, incriminating Opoeth-le-yohola, the other, dealing with Cooley's propositions, accepting them in part and rejecting them in part. Their rejoinder to the third proposition was significant; e.g.,

" . . . we agree to the emancipation of the negroes in our nation but cannot agree to incorporate them upon principles of equality as citizens thereof – and we cannot believe the Government desires us to do more than it has seen fit thus far to do, and trust that at some future day our immense losses in liberating our slaves at the instance of the United States may be in some manner and degree repaired . . . " (O.I.A. Land Files, *Indian Talks, Councils, etc.* Box 4, 1865-1866.)

[444] Stand Watie signed on the 18th.

[445] Perkins, representing the New Hope Conventionists, had, in a rather cowardly way, thrown the entire blame upon Cooper. On one occasion he wrote of the Choctaws that they "misled by the counsel of Douglas H. Cooper . . . and overawed by the rebel troops surrounding us were swept into the vortex of the present rebellion. The same causes which forced the U.S. Government to withdraw its protection from our border forced us to take the position which for the past three years we have occupied . . ." (Perkins to Dole, April 18, 1864, O.I.A., General Files, *Choctaw*, 1859-1866, P 166).

trine of secession and had supposed "the right of self-government" to be "the great cardinal principle of republican liberty." [446]   Upon the more delicate phases of the negro question, they ventured at this time no opinion.   Had they done so, it can be imagined what they would have said.   They would have told the North, not to ease its own conscience by forcing the Indian to bear the whole expense of compensation to the negro.   The Choctaw would never submit to being made chargeable for indemnity to the white man's slave.   He would do rightly by his own but he would not be dictated to.   Nor would he allow his tribe to be put into the position of a suppressed nationality, without protest.   Manifest injustice he had had to submit to many times before.   He had yielded to a force stronger than himself; but he had never allowed his oppressor to delude himself into thinking that the Indian was oblivious of the wrong done.   His indignation had echoed and re-echoed until the all too self-righteous white man had been put to shame by the ruthless exposure of his own hypocrisies.

The indomitable spirit that fired the Choctaw fired also the Cherokee.   The two opposing factions had been advised to submit their cases to a joint conference committee; but the unionists had something on their minds that demanded attention first.   The indignity and obloquy that had been visited upon their venerable and greatly revered chief they could not endure in silence, so they prepared a declaration of dissent and addressed it to the council with a request for a re-hearing.   It merits quotation here because of the sincerity, repression, and loftiness of its tone, notwithstanding

[446] O.I.A., Land Files, *Indian Talks, Councils, &c.*, Box 4, 1865-1866; Commissioner of Indian Affairs, *Report*, 1865, pp. 310-311, 345-346, 349-350.

that it failed utterly of producing the effect hoped for. The commissioners were adamant and refused to rescind their action [447]

"The delegation of the Cherokee nation beg leave to file their respectful but solemn protest against the action of the honorable United States commissioners, on the 15th instant, in regard to John Ross, principal chief of the Cherokee nation; that it was based upon erroneous information, and because it destroys at once the right of the people of the Cherokee nation to choose their own rulers, a right which has never been withheld from them in the whole history of the government. John Ross has never, as far as our knowledge extends, been an emissary of the States in rebellion, nor used his influence to seduce our allegiance to the United States. On the contrary, long after all the tribes and States in our immediate vicinity had abjured their allegiance, when there was not one faithful left among the Indians, and all troops in the service of the United States had been driven off by the enemies of the government, and all protection was withdrawn, he adhered to his allegiance, and only yielded when further resistance promised the entire destruction of his people. For three years past he has been our authorized delegate at Washington city, and the recognized head of the Cherokee nation, and we are advised of no action on his part during this time that in any way impugns his loyalty to the United States or his fidelity to the Cherokee nation. He only arrived at our place of stopping, on the other bank of the river, on the 14th, after we had left to attend the council. The day after he crossed the river, he attended the council-room in the afternoon. We affirm that he used no influence to dissuade us from the free expression of our views in the exercise of our own actions.

We are authorized also to state that he had no conference, or communicated, directly or indirectly, with any Creek Indians, either at this place or since his return to the Cherokee nation. We also beg leave to assure the honorable commission that Mr. John Ross is not the pretended chief of the Cherokee nation, but that he is principal chief in law and fact, having been

---

[447] Commissioner of Indian Affairs, *Report*, 1865, pp. 347, 350.

elected to that position without opposition, on the first Monday in August, for the term of four years, by the qualified voters, in accordance with the provisions (of the constitution) of the Cherokee nation. We further request that the honorable commissioners rescind their action in the premises.

Lewis Downing, Assistant Principal Chief,
Smith Christie,
Thomas Pegg,
Nathaniel Fish,
H. B. Downing,
Whitecatcher,
Mink Downing,
Jesse Baldridge,
Chee Chee,
Samuel Smith,
H. D. Reed.[448]

Just what impelled the commissioners, in the face of such a strong and dignified protest, to persist in their obstinacy it is impossible to say. That John Ross would be antagonistic to any scheme of theirs for the despoiling of the Indians was to be expected. The documentary evidence against him was colorable and was to be added to the very next day in the form of a "talk," [449]

---

[448] —*Ibid.*, pp. 344-345.

[449] After some of his colleagues had held a conference with the Osages, Cooley notified the Cherokees that the commissioners, instead of finding a reason why they should recede from the position they had taken in the case of John Ross, "were being" confirmed in the opinion of the justice "of their action by accumulating evidence." (*ibid.*, p. 350). The following is the record of Black Dog's "talk:"

"Fort Smith, Arkansas, September 19th, 1865

"In a talk held at the rooms of the Commission, with Commissioners Sells and Parker, the following statement was this day voluntarily made by Shon-tah-sob-ba ('Black Dog') the Chief of the Black Dog band of the Osage Indians, relating to a treaty with the so-called Confederate States. In answer to a question by Commissioner Sells, 'How did you happen to be in this southern country?,' Shon-tah-sob-ba (Black Dog) replied, 'I am glad you have asked that question, for I wish to make some statements in explanation. We came down here upon the invitation of John Ross, Principal Chief of the Cherokee

delivered by Chief Black Dog of the Osages; but all such evidence, in the interests of justice, should have been considered only in connection with the time and circumstances of its production. It was all prejudicial, yet, given another setting, would have redounded only to the credit of the accused, if the fortune of war had been but different or the present judges more impartial.

Nation, who sent us a letter asking us to attend a Council for the purpose of making a treaty with Albert Pike.'

"COMMR. SELLS – 'Have you that letter now in your possession?'

"ANSWER – 'We don't know where the letter is. It was sent to Clermont, whose son had it in his possession when he died & we suppose it was buried with him. But I have it here in my head & will never forget it. John Ross, the Cherokee Chief, said in that letter, "My Bros., the Osages, there is a distinguished gentleman sent by the Confederate States who is here to make treaties with us. He will soon be ready to treat, and I want you to come here in order that we may all treat together with him. My Brothers, there is a great black cloud coming from the North, about to cover us all, and I want you to come here so that we can counsel each other & drive away the black cloud." This is all that he said & signed his name. All the Osages went. We were all there together, Pike, John Ross, and I, sitting as you are. Pike told us he was glad that we had come to make peace & a treaty. "All your other brothers have made treaties & shook hands &, if *you* want to, you can do so too." I will tell you what John Ross said at the time. John Ross told us, "My Red Bros., you have come here as I asked you & I am glad to see you & hope you will do what the Commissioner wants you to do. The talk the Commissioner has made is a good talk & I want you to listen to it & make friends with the Confederate States. You can make a treaty or not but I advise you, as your older brother, to make a treaty with them. It is for your interest & your good." After he had finished talking, John Ross told us we could consult among ourselves on the talk over there (pointing to our camp near his residence) & decide among ourselves. We consulted on the matter &, on the request of John Ross, we signed the treaty. He asked us to do it. He was the man that made us make that treaty and that's how we came to be away from our country.'

"The above statement was endorsed by Wah-tah-in-gah, Chief Counselor of the Black Dog & Clermont bands of the Osage Indians.

"The above is a correct statement as interpreted.

"E. S. PARKER, Comr.
"ELIJAH SELLS, Comr.
"GEO. L. COOK, Asst. Secy."

With this new grievance, this new cause for irritation, to express it very mildly, is it to be wondered at
that the tribal differences proved incapable of adjustment? The conference committee accomplished nothing at all. The unionists rejected all concessions, all
suggestions of compromise. Their confiscation laws
they positively would not repeal. Greater than any
wrong done to the United States was the wrong that the
secessionists had done to the Cherokee Nation. It was
a wrong that could never be remedied. It had placed
not the Cherokees alone, but the Five Civilized tribes
and the whole of the Indian Territory within the power
of the white men for all time.

The Fort Smith council transacted no new business
of importance on the twentieth, for one reason because
President Cooley was physically indisposed. On the
twenty-first, it had its last meeting, a morning and
afternoon session, at the former of which, the commissioners presented to the Choctaws and Chickasaws
the draft of a treaty other than that of peace and amity.[450] Similar treaties had presumably been earlier
submitted [451] to the southern Osages and to the united
Creeks with the result that the promise of a huge cession of land had, in each instance, been secured, the
Creeks alone having agreed to surrender all their territory north of the Arkansas River.[452] Silently and in
ways unknown to their public record, the commis-

[450] Commissioner of Indian Affairs, *Report*, 1865, p. 353.

[451] —*Ibid.*, p. 312.

[452] On the fifteenth, the Creeks had most emphatically said that they
were not prepared to make a treaty at Fort Smith; but they would go to
Washington at an early day for the purpose (O.I.A, Land Files, *Indian
Talks, Councils, &c.*, Box 4, 1865-1866). On the thirteenth, they had been
more amiably inclined. They had then asked for a conference with a committee; in order to effect changes in their unratified treaty of 1863 (Commissioner of Indian Affairs, *Report*, 1865, p. 330).

sioners had thus been accomplishing some of the larger objects of their mission. With the politic Boudinot, they must have had many private audiences and, on this last day, he revealed himself as ready to betray his country to the United States politician as he had, some months before, been ready to betray it to the Confederate.[453] On inquiry, the Cherokees had been informed that the Matthews truces were of no binding force since in the Interior Department exclusively resided the power of Indian treaty-making.[454] All hope of clemency vanished and Boudinot craftily made a complete surrender. His almost servile remarks, so greatly in contrast to those of the Choctaws, were the last received at the great council. In his opinion, the organization of Indian Territory was "one of the grandest and noblest schemes ever devised for the red men, and entitles the author to (mark the flattery) . . . the lasting gratitude of every Indian."[455]

Comments in resumé have here a place; for, strange to think upon, matters had been so conducted by the United States commissioners that the late secessionists were the only Indians that left Fort Smith satisfied. Rage and indignation unspeakable surged in the breasts of the erstwhile unionists. Instead of ending the discord, within the larger tribes, Cooley's procedure had but augmented it and Pitchlynn and Colbert, who had, like Boudinot, assumed an attitude of complacent and even congratulatory friendliness towards the commissioners, were obliged to solicit the intervention of the United States for the maintenance of "domestic tran-

[453] Abel, *The Indian as a Participant in the Civil War*, pp. 279-281.
[454] Commissioner of Indian Affairs, *Report*, 1865, p. 343. Harlan had informed Stanton, August 7th, that they could be deemed but temporary in character (Land Files, *Indian Talks, Councils, &c.*, Box 4, 1865-1866).
[455] Commissioner of Indian Affairs, *Report*, 1865, p. 312.

quility," pending "the adoption and ratification" of definitive treaties.[456]   Such definitive treaties were to be made, for reasons easily imagined, in Washington City.   Cooley, therefore, adjourned the Fort Smith council, *sine die*.   If it met again, it would be at the call of Secretary Harlan.

---

[456] P. P. Pitchlynn and Colbert to Cooley, September 21, 1865, O.I.A., Land Files, *Indian Talks, Councils, &c.,* Box 4, 1865-1866; General Files, *Southern Superintendency,* 1865. No doubt it was to the prominent secessionists that Cooley made such a point of introducing Bussey's successor, Brevet Major Henry J. Hunt (Commissioner of Indian Affairs, *Report,* 1865, p. 312). Hunt had been assigned to Reynolds in July (Bowers to Sherman, July 21, 1865, *Official Records,* vol. xlviii, part ii, p. 1111).

VII. THE HARLAN BILL

The seven propositions that the peace commissioners had submitted to the Indians at Fort Smith were deduced from Secretary Harlan's instructions,[457] prepared August sixteenth and handed to Cooley on the eve of his departure from Washington. The importance of the instructions can scarcely admit of exaggeration; for they were to prove, in the sequel, to have been the groundwork of the whole reconstruction policy of the United States government towards the tribes of the Indian Territory.

DEPARTMENT OF THE INTERIOR
WASHINGTON, August 16, 1865

GENTLEMEN:

The President having designated you as a board of commissioners in behalf of the United States, "to negotiate, under the instructions of the Secretary of the Interior, a treaty or treaties with all or any of the nations, tribes, or bands of Indians now located in the Indian territory, or in the State of Kansas, and also with the Indians of the plains west of Kansas and the said Indian country," it becomes my duty to indicate to you the general policy which should be observed in discharging the important trust thus committed to you.

You are doubtless familiar with the general condition of affairs in the "Indian territory," since the breaking out of the rebellion, and with the legislation of Congress in reference thereto. Many of the tribes were induced, by the machinations of the emissaries of the so-called Confederate States, to throw off their allegiance to the general government, and to enter into treaty stipulations with them, thereby subjecting themselves to

---

[457] I.D., *Record of Letters Sent*, "Indian Affairs," no. 5, 1864-1865, July 1 to December 12, pp. 335-344.

the forfeitures specially provided for in the act of Congress of 5th of July, 1862. – (Statutes xii, 528.) With the return of peace, however, it is the desire of the government to re-establish order and legitimate authority among the tribes, encourage them in peaceful and industrial pursuits, and secure to them the blessings of Christian civilization, as the only means of attaining permanent prosperity and well-being. While the claim of any tribe to the benefit of the provisions of a former treaty may be justly forfeited, if such tribe, or a majority of its members, has been in rebellion against the general government, such disloyal Indians are not, by their own bad faith, released from the obligation to perform their treaty stipulations, if insisted on by the United States.

You will enter into a convention with the various nations, tribes, and bands, with whom you may negotiate, for permanent peace and amity with the United States and with each other. The more civilized Indians, located within the Indian territory, should be induced, if practicable, to bind themselves, when called upon by the government, to aid in compelling the Indians of the plains to maintain peaceful relations with each other, with the Indians of the said territory, and with the people of the United States.

The Indians of the plains should be required, whenever difficulties may arise between them involving the question of peace or war, to submit the same for the arbitrament of the President of the United States, or such person or persons as he may designate, and to abide by and faithfully observe the award that may be made in the premises.

The nations and tribes located within the Indian territory should agree to the orgnization of civil governments, containing guarantees for the rights of person and property, providing for the due enforcement of the local laws and usages of each tribe within its proper territorial limits, if consistent with the laws and Constitution of the United States, and ordaining the trial of civil and criminal causes by a judge to be appointed by the President, and with the advice and consent of the Senate. A common or central government should be established, with jurisdiction and authority coextensive with said territory, and limited to general purposes. The executive should be appointed in the same manner as the judges. A general council, composed of members elected by the tribes residing in said territory, in proportion to their numbers, should be clothed with general legislative powers, and with authority to appoint a delegate to the Congress of the United States.

As an intimation of what the Senate would approve in this regard, you are referred to the accompanying copy of Senate bill No. 459, which passed the Senate at its last session. You will consider it as a part of these instructions, and adopt such of its provisions as are consistent with the actual condition of the tribes, and acceptable to them, and reject whatever may be repugnant to them and not material to the general object sought to be accomplished.

The institution of slavery, which has existed among several of the tribes, should be forthwith abolished, and adequate measures taken for the immediate and unconditional emancipation of the persons held in bondage, and for their incorporation into the tribes on an equal footing in all respects with the original members. The same just and wise policy attests the propriety of conferring civil and political rights upon persons who have escaped from a state of slavery elsewhere and taken refuge among them.

The tribes would act in harmony with the spirit of the age, and the prevailing sentiment of the American people, by declaring by treaty, and in the organic law which has been or may be adopted for their government, that slavery, or involuntary servitude, shall never exist among them, otherwise than in the punishment of crime, whereof the party shall have been duly convicted.

Strife and dissension may, in some instances, have prevailed to such extent in a particular nation, or tribe, as to result in the formation of contending parties. If it is impracticable to reconcile them to each other, and re-establish their former harmonious relations as members of the same organization, you may recognize them as distinct communities. In that event you will authorize a division, on equitable terms, of its funds and annuities, and the settlement of each party on separate portions of their reservation, to be clearly marked by metes and bounds. Such parties will thereafter be treated as independent tribes.

You will, however, assure them of the anxious desire of the President that all past differences should be buried in oblivion, and that they should live together as brothers. Your consent to the arrangement above suggested will not be given until all efforts to restore harmony and union shall have proved utterly unavailing.

Some of the Indians with whom you will negotiate have tribal funds invested in State bonds, held in trust by the Secretary of the Interior. The interest thereon up to the outbreak of the rebellion was received and paid to them annually, or expended for their benefit. Those issued by the southern States are now of merely nominal value, and pay no interest. It is desirable that the Indians should consent to the sale of these bonds and the investment of the proceeds in United States registered bonds, or the deposit thereof to their credit on the books of the treasury. Payment will be made to them annually of the interest accruing thereon. You will explain to the Indians that the depreciation of these securities is the result of the rebellion in which they have participated, and urge the plan herein proposed, as the best means of guarding against the possibility of further loss.

Several of the tribes of civilized Indians in Kansas, and possibly from other sections of the country, will, I am informed be represented in this council. They propose to obtain the required consent to their permanent settlement within the limits of the Indian territory. Should such consent be obtained, you will encourage them and the resident Indians to unite their funds for the common benefit, and to live together as one people. If, however, separate tribal organizations be insisted upon, you will negotiate with the resident Indians for the sale or cession by them to the United States of suitable lands for the Indians whom it may be found desirable to remove to that territory; and, in either aspect of the case, you are authorized to enter into such further stipulations as may be necessary to carry into effect such intended emigration and settlement. Treaties have been negotiated with several of the tribes in Kansas in reference to that object. These treaties have not yet been ratified by the Senate, but I transmit herewith copies of them for your information. They are communicated to you in confidence, and you will therefore not disclose their contents.

In your conferences with them, in relation to the securities and the cession of lands, you will state that Congress has authorized the President to suspend the payment of all appropriations to carry into effect treaty stipulations, or otherwise, in behalf of Indians in a state of hostility to this government, and to abrogate all treaties with them. The President, however, is disposed to treat his red children with forbearance and liberality. He is willing that they should have the benefit of the securities, and that they should receive the value of all lands that may be ceded to the government.

Some of the appropriations heretofore made have been expended by the President in providing for the relief of such individual members of tribes as were driven from their homes and reduced to want on account of their friendship to this government. You will inform the tribes explicitly that no part of the sums so expended will be refunded to them.

You will make known the President's high appreciation of the conduct of those Indians who have kept faith with the government and adhered with unalterable loyalty to the national flag. You are authorized to recognize, in some appropriate manner, the services of all who, during the recent arduous struggle, have deserved well of the country.

Should a treaty be made with any Indian tribe not in your judgment capable of making a judicious and economical use of money, you will be careful to provide that any and all annuities and amounts payable to them by the United States may, at the discretion of the Secretary of the Interior, be paid in stock, goods, provisions, implements of husbandry, and other articles suitable to their condition and wants.

To secure to the tribes the absolute and undisturbed possession of the Indian territory, a clause should be inserted in the treaty, prohibiting any white person, except officers, agents and employes of the government, from going to or settling in said territory, unless formally admitted and incorporated into some one of the tribes lawfully residing there, according to its laws and usages.

Your attention is specially invited to the establishment of schools for the instruction of the children in industrial pursuits and the elementary branches, including the English language. Benevolent societies, with means furnished by voluntary contributions, have been formed to elevate the intelligence and moral character of the Indian population. Their disinterested efforts have, in many instances, been crowned with signal success. Should any such society be disposed to labor among the Indians, its wishes should be respected and its interests protected. Its opinions and views should, however, be in harmony with those of the tribes. No attempted coercion of the religious faith of the latter will be tolerated, nor should any denomination of Christians be suffered to have the exclusive control of their educational interests.

Ascertain the population of each nation and tribe within the Indian territory, and insist upon a cession by it of all lands not needed for its uses, to be appropriated as the home of other Indians. The terms you offer must unavoidably be left to your own discretion. They should be just and fair; but I can give no specific instructions on the subject. You may agree that no part of such ceded lands shall be appropriated to Indians not on friendly relations with the party making the cession. You will impress upon them, in the most forcible terms, that the advancing tide of immigration is rapidly spreading over the country, and that the government has not the power or inclination to check it. Our hills and valleys are filling up with an adventurous and rapidly increasing people, that will encroach upon and occupy the ancient abodes of the red man. Such seems to be an inevitable law of population and settlement on this continent. It leads to collisions, always followed by lamentable results, and sometimes by bloody and devastating wars. It is for the interest of both races, and chiefly for the welfare of the Indian, that he should abandon his wandering life and settle upon lands reserved to his exclusive use, where he will be protected in his rights and surrounded with every kindly and elevating influence by a paternal government. The prosperity of the inhabitants of the Indian territory affords a striking proof and illustration of the wisdom of this policy. The President desires to extend its blessings to the Indians now scattered in Kansas and other localities. The propriety of settling them within that territory is obvious and undoubted. You will inform the resident Indians that they will consult their own interest and given evidence of good will to this government, as well as a becoming sympathy for their brethren, by giving their cheerful and efficient co-operation in carrying this policy into effect.

You will assign to each tribe of Indians with whom you may treat, and who may continue to reside west of the Indian territory, a district of country as remote as practicable from any of the leading routes across the plains, or the usual thoroughfares of the people of the different Territories. Such districts should be designated by definite boundaries, and include such territory, if possible, as will afford the Indians means of support by industry in their ordinary avocations. A sudden transition from a savage and nomadic life to the more quiet and confining pursuits of civilization is not to be expected; but in such assignment reference should be had to their ultimate adoption of pastoral and agricultural pursuits. As their withdrawal from the country adjacent to the great routes of travel will necessarily diminish their means of support, you may promise them an equivalent in food, clothing, implements of husbandry, live stock, &c., which will be furnished them annually, provided they observe in good faith the terms of their agreement. The extent of the aid to be thus rendered should not be so large as to appear prodigal, nor so meagre as to amount to a mockery of justice. It is the purpose of the government to encourage the Indians to gain a livelihood, advance in the pursuits and arts of civilized life, and improve their moral, intellectual, and physical condition. The nation cannot adopt the policy of exterminating them. Our self-respect, our Christian faith, and a common dependence on an all-wise Creator and benefactor, forbid it. Other nations will judge of our character by our treatment of the feeble tribes to whom we sustain the relation of guardian. Morally and legally there is no distinction between directly destroying them and rendering it impossible for them to escape annihilation by withholding from them adequate means of support. You must habitually bear in mind the purpose to which I have referred, and you will endeavor to make it available.

The President is in possession of information rendering it probable that the Indians on the Upper Arkansas, hitherto hostile, desire to make peace with the United States. Should you become satisfied that this information is correct, you are instructed, as soon as you terminate these negotiations, to proceed to some common rendezvous, and to make the necessary treaties with them, so as to secure future peace and amity. Or, if you deem it wiser, you may detail a part of your number at an earlier period for this purpose. The commissioners thus detailed will associate with them the Indian superintendent having control of said Indians, and likewise the agents of the respective tribes, and proceed at once to the discharge of their duties, regarding the foregoing as their general instructions as far as applicable. In that case they will put themselves in communication with the proper military commander for the necessary assistance, and with this department for any additional instructions they may require.

In every treaty which you may negotiate, the Indian parties thereto should expressly agree that any amendment thereof which the Senate of the United States may make shall be taken and held to be a part of the same, and as binding in every respect as if it had, after being made, been formally submitted to and ratified by such parties.

It is probable that some of the members of the joint committee of the two houses of Congress appointed to examine into the condition of the Indian tribes may be present at your council. If so, you will consult freely with them, and respect their suggestions and advice.

You may possibly find it necessary to treat separately with one or more of the tribes you may meet in council, as well as to make a general treaty or compact with them all. If so, you will consider yourselves authorized to do so.

The department will receive with pleasure such information as you may be enabled to obtain, during your negotiations, in regard to the condition of the Indians, or any suggestions from you on that and kindred subjects, and will communicate any additional instructions which you may desire.

I have the honor to be, very respectfully, your obedient servant,   JAS. HARLAN, Secretary.

The prominence accorded Senate bill,[458] no. 459, in

---

[458] The text of the bill as it passed the Senate is a little difficult of location. The copy, examined by the author, was found filed in the

Harlan's instructions warrants an extended treatment of the same here. It was a bill for the organization of Indian Territory, a presumably innocent and altogether desirable measure. So those ignorant of the less advertised facts of United States history might well think it; but, in reality, it was pernicious in the extreme, designedly deceptive. Its real object was nothing more and nothing less than capitalistic exploitation of southern Indian preserves. Under the pretext of bringing the red man more nearly within the range of his white brothers's wholly materialistic civilization, its framers intended to nullify the important treaty pledges upon which the successful execution of the Removal Act of 1830 had depended.[459] Although differing in detail from the Douglas measure of 1854, the Harlan bill, had it been enacted, would have had identically the same effect upon Indian property rights.

The idea of territorial organization for the Indian country was not at all new. When the eastern tribes were first placed as immigrants there, it was occasionally bruited.[460] By the Indian country was then meant both present Kansas and present Oklahoma [461] and, in those earlier days, the government undoubtedly intended, whether organization took place or not, to retain and to maintain the isolation, the territorial

Indian Office along with Albert Pike's letter to Harlan of date, December 6, 1865 (O.I.A., General Files, *Southern Superintendency*, 1865, P 499). The text of the bill as it was reported back from the Committee on Indian Affairs can be seen in *Cong. Globe*, 38th cong., 2nd sess., pp. 1021-1022.

[459] For the initiatory circumstances of general Indian removal, see Abel, *History of Events Resulting in Indian Consolidation West of the Mississippi*, American Historical Association, *Report*, 1907, pp. 233-450; *Indian Reservations in Kansas and the Extinguishment of Their Title*, Kansas Historical Society, *Collections*, vol. viii, pp. 72-109.

[460] Abel, *Proposals for an Indian State in the Union, 1778-1878*, American Historical Association, *Report*, 1907, p. 95.

[461] For varying content of the term, see Gittenger, *Formation of the State of Oklahoma*.

separateness, the political integrity of its more advanced wards.[462] A slight departure from this well-established policy came with the Mexican War and was consequent upon its successful issue. Failure on the part of slavocracy to realize to the full its expansionist expectations diverted attention, for a time, from the southwest and the ways thither; but, during the agitation over the Kansas-Nebraska bill and subsequent to its passage, southern men, inhabitants of Arkansas chiefly, began to bestir themselves for the economic development of the lower part of the mid-continental region. Their interest involved railway construction and the establishment of new routes of travel. A matter of intimate knowledge to them was the fact that the cattle-raising industry of Indian Territory was second only to that of Texas. The plantations of the Red River tribes were the exact counterpart of those of the slave belt farther east and across the river.

It was primarily the interest of an Arkansas man that Johnson displayed when he introduced into the United States senate, February 23, 1854, a bill for the establishment of three territories within the limits of the Indian country, lying north of the Red River and immediately west of his own state.[463] The dissemination of the idea among the Indians he left with Elias Rector, personal friend and party coadjutor, who no sooner took office

---

[462] A. R. McIlvaine of Pennsylvania, reporting from the House Committee on Indian Affairs, June 27, 1848, on the expediency of organizing Indian Territory, went fully into the history of the United States policy relative thereto. He reviewed Indian removals and drew the conclusion that everything tended to show that the main object of the government from first to last had been to secure the control of their own affairs to the tribes and plan for "ultimate admission to political equality with the citizens of the United States."

[463] *Cong. Globe*, 33rd Cong., 1st. sess., p. 449. The territories were to be named, Chahlahkee, Muscogee, and Chahta.

as the successor of Charles W. Dean in the southern superintendency than he gave it public indorsement.[464] In one annual report after another he urged it upon the Indian Office.[465] The extent of his whole political plan may be gauged by the fact that he favored conceding to each of the big groups, Cherokees, Choctaws and Chickasaws, Creeks and Seminoles, a congressional delegate.[466] Justice to them, highly-civilized as they were and well set up economically, demanded it. Judicially, their present status left much to be desired. The trade restrictions to which they were subjected were an absurdity, a travesty upon fair-play. The monopoly rights of the post trader and the sutler implied profiteering of the worst description under the protection of government license. All such were well-grounded arguments, regardless of the motives, disinterested or otherwise, humanitarian or sectional, that lay behind their presentation.

The interest of Kansas in the same or a similar project had its beginnings with the appointment of Robert J. Walker as territorial governor. A Democrat, born in Pennsylvania and bred in Mississippi, a particular friend, through long years, of Buchanan,[467] Walker affected a tremendous respect for law and order, for the deference due to higher authority, to the central government, yet his very first official utterance implied either a negation of all he was presuming to stand for or as appears more likely an overweening economic ambition beside which treaty guarantees to the southern Indians paled into insignificance. His political conscience was but a garment, loosely-woven. Like

[464] Commissioner of Indian Affairs, *Report*, 1857, p. 201.

[465] — *Ibid.*, 1858, pp. 127-128; *ibid.*, 1859, pp. 163-165.

[466] — *Ibid.*, 1857, p. 197.

[467] Moore, *Works of Buchanan*, vol. ix, p. 14.

many another American he took pride in the territorial immensity of his country, her boundless
possibilities. In his computations, Indian rights,
natural or acquired, had not the shadow of a place.
He had not been many days in Kansas, where
thousands upon thousands of acres were yet to be developed, where the white population was relatively as yet
but a handful, before he cast covetous eyes upon the
Indian country to the southward. To him it was only
too obvious that the red man could just as easily be
ousted from that region as he was then being ousted
from Kansas. The diminished reserve policy might be
as effectively introduced into the one place as the other
and in both places it would presuppose the diminution
of Indian territorial rights to the vanishing point.

It was in his inaugural address, May 27, 1857, that
Walker made bold to express his views, although the
occasion scarcely justified so great and unreserved a
display of sectional interest since his audience was most
vitally concerned with the elimination of his particular
brand. Moreover, what they were eager to discover
was the prospect, under a new administration, for the
triumph of the squatter-sovereignty idea. Not until
Indian Territory presented itself as a desirable home
for expelled Kansas tribes did the Kansas settler have
any designs against it. The capitalist may have had
and the politician, frequently one and the same person,
but not the settler.

In expressing his expansionist views, Governor
Walker spoke in this wise:

> Upon the south Kansas is bounded by the great southwest-
> ern Indian territory. This is one of the most salubrious and
> fertile portions of this continent. It is a great cotton growing
> region, admirably adapted, by soil and climate, for the products

of the south, embracing the valleys of the Arkansas and Red rivers, adjoining Texas on the south and west and Arkansas on the east; and it ought speedily to become a State of the American Union.[468]   The Indian treaties will constitute no obstacle any more than precisely similar treaties did in Kansas; for their lands, valueless to them, now for sale, but which, sold with their consent and for their benefit, like the Indian lands of Kansas, would make a most wealthy and prosperous people, and their consent on these terms would be most cheerfully given.   This Territory contains double the area of the State of Indiana, and, if necessary, an adequate portion of the western and more elevated part could be set apart exclusively for these tribes, and the eastern and larger portion be formed into a State, and its land sold for the benefit of these tribes (like the Indian lands of Kansas) thus greatly promoting all their interests.   To the eastern boundary of this region [bordering] on the State of Arkansas, run the railroads of that State, to the southern limits come the great railroads from Louisiana and Texas, from New Orleans and Galveston, which will ultimately be joined by railroads from Kansas, leading through this Indian territory, connecting Kansas with New Orleans, the Gulf of Mexico, and with the southern Pacific railroad, leading through Texas to San Francisco.   It is essential to the true interests, not only of Kansas, but of Louisiana, Texas, and Arkansas, Iowa and Missouri, and the whole region west of the Mississippi, that this coterminous southwestern Indian territory should speedily become a State, not only to supply us with cotton and receive our products in return, but as occupying the area over which that portion of our railroads should run which connect us with New Orleans and Galveston; and by the southern route with the Pacific from her central position, through or connected with Kansas, must run the central, northern, and southern routes to the Pacific, and with the latter, as well as with the Gulf, the connexion can only be secured by the southwestern territory becoming a State, and to this Kansas should direct her earnest attention as essential to her prosperity.[469]

---

[468] Buchanan in his First Annual Message advocated much the same thing (Richardson, *Messages and Papers of the Presidents*, vol. v, p. 460).
[469] Quoted by John Ross in a Message to the Cherokee National Council,

So brazen an avowal of cupidity bespoke a certain confidence in the answering sentiments of the audience; but an immediate response was neither expected nor required. Rather was it the case that Walker threw out his remarks tentatively, suggestively, and more to allay suspicion, to ward off objections, and to prepare the public mind for some contingency of the future than to call for instant action. The action that he wanted would come not from directions politically uncertain or avowedly hostile but from those most friendly and most anxious to see the old balance in the senate restored. His insistence upon the statehood idea was made with a very definite purpose in mind. Years afterwards when Kansans made response to his suggestions, after their own fashion and in their own interest, they ignored his main contention. Fortuitous events, happening in the interval, had rendered it quite unnecessary to grant so large a boon to red men.

Walker's inaugural was given wide circulation. It reached Indian Territory and there met with the denouncement its injustice and misrepresentation so richly warranted. The Indians took alarm; for it was not true as he had intimated that, provided large gains were in prospect for themselves, they would not be averse to receiving proposals for the sale of their lands. John Ross, alert as always where plans and policies of white men for red men were under consideration, exposed the real purport of Walker's address. Of its sentiments, he had this to say, "Coming from the distinguished source they do, they can but admonish us that the renewal may be at hand of those measures of agitation which but so recently forced us from the

October 5, 1857. See Commissioner of Indian Affairs, *Report*, 1857, pp. 218-223.

homes of our fathers." [470]   His recollection was that Walker was in the United States senate [471] at the time when the removal policy was being adopted and therefore fully conversant with the promises made the prospective exiles that the country to which they were being consigned should be a home for them and their descendants "forever and never be embraced within the limits of any State or Territory without" their consent.   The baseness of the Walker sentiments Ross left to inference; but he warned his people of their ominous character.   In his opinion, they were "important" as indicating the principles of the source whence they "emanated" and the pleas of necessity that might "imperil" the Indian's "most precious interests.   The 'Indian territory' spoken of," said he, "is the only country in the United States occupied by Indians, not within State or territorial limits, and is the only spot where the Indian can rest under his own laws and customs; and if we would avert the fate of the Indians in Kansas and Nebraska [472] from ourselves, and the precipitation of events that would bring strife, injury, and political destruction, it behooves us to stand united, to watch with a jealous eye every aggression, to strengthen our government, and to cling to the protection often and solemnly pledged by the United States." [473]   In declaiming thus against language and sentiment, the spirit of which he held to be "at war with the stipulations of solemn treaties and" an encouragement to aggression,

[470] — *Ibid.*, p. 221.

[471] Walker was in the Senate from February 22, 1836 to March 5, 1845, *Cong. Biog. Dict.*

[472] The agitation for the opening up of Kansas and Nebraska had originated in similar suggestions for the organization of civil governments.   See the recommendation of G. W. Manypenny, Commissioner of Indian Affairs, *Report*, 1853.

[473] Commissioner of Indian Affairs, *Report*, 1857, p. 222.

Ross would fain believe the president of the United States deserving of exoneration from all responsibility in the premises; but what would he have said had he known that Buchanan had not only perused Walker's inaugural address but had given it his approval? [474]

It was not only Democrats who, by indiscreet utterances, gave to the southern Indians occasion for apprehension. The Republican campaign of 1860 took W. H. Seward westward and it was he who most offended; for, in a speech [475] delivered in Chicago, he hinted at, not Indian statehood, Indian citizenship or anything else that held at least a measure of belated justice for the government wards, but the seizure and occupation of their lands. His suggestions were as seed sown in fertile soil. They quickly sprouted and bore fruit. They were taken up by agents of the Confederacy to induce the five great tribes to revolt and by the more radical citizens of Kansas to effect the removal of the red men from the country north of the thirty-seventh parallel. The accomplishment of their purpose by the one group furnished arguments galore for the other and the confiscation of land in Indian Territory as a punishment for disloyalty became the most convenient means to the end sought for by the Kansans. Commissioner Dole resisted the pressure brought to bear upon the Indian Office to the best of his ability; [476] but so many and so varied were the projects introduced into congress for one and the same purpose that he was forced to exercise

---

[474] Brown, Geo. W., *Reminiscences of Gov. R. J. Walker*, pp. 19-20.

[475] Baker, *Works of W. H. Seward*, vol. iv, p. 363.

[476] One of the earliest and best of Dole's rejoinders in illustration of his position is the following:

"My attention has been called to the letter of the Hon. J. M. Ashley, referred by (you) to this office during my absence, in which he requests that he may be furnished with the number of Indian tribes supposed to be in rebellion against the Government, and asking your

great ingenuity in order to hold his own. The extension of the southern boundary of Kansas down to

views as to the expediency of placing a territorial government over
them.

" . . . I have to state that the number of Indians in the Southern Superintendency, according to our most reliable data, is 68,417,
classified as follows:

Creeks		13,500
Seminoles		2,267
Osages, Senecas, Shawnees, &c.		5,000
Cherokees		22,000
Choctaws		18,000
Chickasaws		5,000
Wichitas, Caddoes, Comanches, &c.		2,600

68,417

"Of the above mentioned tribes the majority of the first three are
loyal. The others are disloyal, with the exception of the Wichitas,
Caddoes, Comanches, &c. who are neutral but are well disposed
towards the Government, and were the former States restored would
yield ready obedience to the constituted authorities.

"I doubt very much the propriety of establishing a Territorial Government over the country occupied by these Indians, and am unable
to perceive any advantage to be derived from the adoption of such a
measure, since the same military power that would be required to
enforce the authority of Territorial officers is all sufficient to protect
and enforce the authority of such officers as are required in the management of our present system of Indian relations. By such a measure
we should consequently gain nothing in the ability of government to
enforce its authority and a compliance on the part of the Indians to
their treaty stipulations and should introduce a system at variance with
our long established Indian policy from which I apprehend great confusion and embarrassment in the execution of its details.

"It seems to me that the measure proposed presupposes that at no
distant day the country mentioned will be opened for the settlement
of the White Man, than which in my judgment nothing could be more
detrimental and disastrous to the Indians . . . Whatever opinion
may be held as to the binding effect of the legislative and treaty
stipulations mentioned, in releasing the obligations of government
towards that portion of the Indians who have rebelled against its
authority, there can be no question that those obligations remain
intact as to those who have remained loyal, so that to violate the same
would constitute a gross breach of national faith . . .

" . . . I look forward hopefully, and as I think not without reason, to the day, when these children of the wilderness once more
under the benign sway of our benificent laws and institutions will be

Texas,[477] the territorial organization of the Indian country west of Arkansas, the establishment of the Territory of Lanniwa,[478] and the concentration of all Indian tribes, especially those of Kansas, within a limited area outside and beyond any and all state limits were among the measures presented.

Engineered by Senators J.H. Lane and S. M. Pomeroy [479] with a constant impetus from their state legis-

so far reclaimed and civilized that of their own volition they will seek to add another star to the flag of our country, acceptable and not discreditable to our nation, and until that time shall feel it my duty to oppose officially and otherwise, with all my energies, any steps that may have a tendency to open the way for the settlement of their country by a white population." (Dole to Smith, March 17, 1862, O.I.A., *Report Book*, no. 12, pp. 335-337).

[477] This was the burden of a resolution introduced by Lane, March 17, 1862 (*Senate Journal*, 37th cong., 2nd sess., p. 310). Dole's opinion, expressed in a letter to Secretary Smith, April 2, 1862 (O.I.A., *Report Book*, no. 12, p. 353) was decidedly against its acceptance; for he was convinced that any such project, absurd though it might be while failure confronted northern arms, would eventuate in the occupancy of Indian Territory by white people. The Senate Committee on Indian Affairs was excused, June 25, 1862, from a further inquiry into its expediency (*Senate Journal*, 37th cong., 2nd sess., p. 707, Serial Number, 116).

[478] H. R. 492, *House Journal*, 37th cong., 3rd sess., p. 56, Serial Number, 1155.

[479] As evidence of their activities in this direction, the following may be noted as being, not exhaustive, but typical:

March 24, 1862, Pomeroy obtained leave to bring in a bill (S 245) for the removal and consolidation of certain Indian tribes (*Senate Journal*, 37th cong., 2nd sess., p. 332, Serial Number, 1116).

June 25, 1862, On motion of Doolittle, Chairman, the Senate Committee on Indian Affairs, was discharged from further consideration of various subjects. Among them were, S 245 and certain resolutions of the Kansas Legislature in favor of extinguishing the title of Indian lands (*ibid.*, p. 707).

November 22, 1862, Dole reported to Secretary Smith, in customary wise, on a memorial that had been presented by Pomeroy upon the subject of concentrating the Indians of Kansas in the country south of Kansas (O.I.A., *Report Book*, no. 12, pp. 505-506; I.D., *Register of Letters Received*, "D").

December 15, 1862. Agreeably to notice, Mr. Lane of Kansas asked and obtained leave to bring in a bill (S 413) providing for the extinc-

lature, the removal of the Indians from Kansas became more and more a subject for urgent consideration by the United States congress. Agents in the field reported several of the tribes exceedingly anxious to go [480] and

tion of Indian titles in Kansas and the removal of the Indians from said State . . . (*Senate Journal*, 37th cong., 3rd sess., p. 48, Serial Number, 1148). This bill, with an amendment, was reported from committee, January 21, 1863 (*ibid.*, p. 128) and passed by the Senate, six days later (*ibid.*, p. 154). On motion of Doolittle, January 25, 1863, it was added to the Indian Appropriation bill then pending (*ibid.*, p. 335).

February 26, 1864. Lane presented resolutions from the Legislature of Kansas "in favor of making only such treaties with the Indian tribes within that state as will provide for their removal therefrom, and secure to said State the right to tax . . . " (*Senate Journal*, 38th cong., 1st sess., p. 191, Serial Number, 1175).

May 25, 1864. Lane of Kansas submitted a resolution to the effect that the Committee on Indian Affairs be requested to consider the question of confiscating the reserves of all Indian tribes who are or have been in arms against the government and providing homes for the loyal (*ibid.*, p. 474).

May 26, 1864. Lane submitted a resolution calling upon the Secretary of the Interior to furnish information on the subject of the loyalty of the Indians, their reserves, the nature of their tenure, the money furnished them by the Confederacy, &c. (*ibid.*, p. 480).

[480] Special Agent Augustus Wattles reported upon the matter. He had been associated with Geo. W. Brown on the *Herald of Freedom* and had probably heard Governor R. J. Walker's inaugural address. In 1861, he conducted a special investigation for the Indian Office (O.I.A., *Special Files*, no. 201; *Sac and Fox*, W 220 of 1861; *Central Superintendency*, W 222 of 1861, W 474 of 1861) and the following year served as accredited attorney for the Sac and Fox Indians (*Sac and Fox*, K 127 of 1862; *Central Superintendency*, W 528 of 1862; *Southern Superintendency*, D 576 of 1862, C 1912 of 1862). He made a point of inquiring into the Indian disposition toward consolidatiion.

(a) "After making my official report to you concerning the improvements of the Sac & Fox Indians & also of the Kaw, or Kansas, tribe of Indians and also of some incidental matters which came under my notice, I received a private communication from you, asking my opinion of a plan for confederating the various Indian tribes in Kansas and Nebraska into one and giving them a Territory & a Territorial Government with political privileges.

"I gave you an immediate answer promising to investigate further & report accordingly.

"I immediately started on a tour of observation & inquiry amongst

undoubtedly such was the case since no means were left
untried to impress the fact upon them that their pro-

the Indians and sent you from time to time reports. I visited &
reported to you of the tribes which I examined personally, the Miamies, the Peorias, the Weas, Kaskaskias, & Piankashaws, Chippewas,
Muncies & Ottawas. I procured information from reliable sources of
the other tribes which I mention. The Indians, I find, with small
exceptions, are willing & anxious to exchange their present reserves
& improvements for land & improvements in the southern Indian
Territory.

"A number of tribes have already made arrangements with the
Cherokees & Creeks, for land, and requested me to act as their agent
with the Government to complete & legalize the transaction.

"So well satisfied were the Indians of my sincerity to serve them,
they followed me several miles after I had left them and induced me
to return. I went with them to the Agent, not knowing what their
purpose was, when they requested the Agent to draw up a paper,
making me their Agent, with a salary of $200 per mo., which I shall
present to you. They said to me repeatedly, 'Take no more white
man's money, take Indian money, &c.' I told the Agent that, if you
continued to pay my salary, I should take nothing from the Indians.
If not, with the consent of the Government, I should act as their Agent.

"You will see that this movement ought to be kept entirely away
from speculators & jobbers. The Indians as well as other races need
vastly more property in civilization than in barbarism, consequently
they must husband their resources and see that nothing is spent in vain.

"In the midst of my labors I was severely injured by a fall one
night when out on a scout. I came to New York as soon as I was
able to travel and, while under treatment, I consulted with our political
friends in New York concerning this movement and they not only
gave it their approbation, but were anxious that this administration
should have the credit of originating & carrying out so wise & so
noble a scheme for civilizing & perpetuating the Indian race.

"In consultation with them I have prepared a bill which will be
laid before Congress after having been critically examined by yourself & the Secretary of the Interior. All the facts & arguments which
go to sustain it I have already laid before you and with others furnished from different departments I hope you will be able to perfect
a bill which will practically meet the necessities of the case." Wattles to Dole, dated Washington, January 10, 1862, O.I.A., Special
Files, no. 201, *Central Superintendency*, W 528 of 1862).

(b) "Permit me to solicit your favorable consideration to a plan
originating either in your department or with the western Indians
for uniting them into one people & admitting them into the United
States as an organized Territory with political privileges, a plan for
treating them as friends rather than enemies, as human rather than

longed residence in Kansas was out of the question.
The longer it continued, the more uncomfortable it

wild beasts, as men capable of improvement & self support rather than imbeciles & idiots.

"The plan is one for treating with the remnants of thirty Indian tribes who once owned & occupied this continent for the privilege of a home of safety & for their future existence as a race.

"These little remnants of nations, in order to save themselves from utter extinction, petition that they be confederated into one people & allowed to give their allegiance to the United States, adopt our language & laws and, so far as practicable, our civilization.

"I give below the tribes south & west of the Missouri River & the amount of their population & annuities in 1860 and the number of acres of land held by each tribe in 1839.

POPULATION		ANNUITIES	ACRES
22,000	Cherokees	$43,562	13,800,000
18,000	Choctaws	68,647	15,000,000
13,500	Creeks	60,824	13,140,000
5,000	Chickasaws	3,322	
2,264	Seminoles		
300	Senecas & Shawnees	5,360	100,000
250	Quapaws	2,660	9,600
Already in the Indian Territory			
217	Weas, Piankeshaws, Peorias & Kaskaskias	19,260	259,840
287	Ottawas	2,600	74,000
810	Shawnees	5,000	1,700,000
1,034	Delawares	58,977	2,208,000
397	Kickapoos	14,000	768,000
4,000	Osages	2,910	7,564,000
803	Kaws	11,503	2,510,000
708	Otoes & Missourias	16,940	1,536,000
950	Omahas	33,940	4,990,000
400	Iowas	11,615	156,000
488	Sac & Foxes of the Missouri	7,870	100,000
1,280	Sac & Fox of the Mississippi	73,880	435,200
3,413	Pawnees	40,000	16,000,000
2,143	Pottawatomies	75,496	576,000
300	Wyandotts	5,345	
250	Miamies	11,540	276,480
78,889		$575,251	81,203,120

Total population of thirty tribes 78,889
Total annuities, the price of a continent $575,251
Total number of acres held in 1839 81,203,120

"The absurdity of the present system of governing the Indians is

would become.   Finally, in 1863, Lane's persistency [481]
had its reward and a law was passed providing for

apparent, when you consider that each one of these tribes is a *foreign
nation*, with which we have treaties, and support a minister, or agent,
with attaches, &c. at an expense of probably $25,000 per annum, with
corresponding expenses in the Department in Washington.

"1st.   The expense of this item may be reduced from $50,000 nearly,
to about $20,000, perhaps less.

"2nd.   All the land in Kansas & Nebraska held by Indians, nearly
30,000,000 acres, will be given up for white settlement by concentrating them in one Territory, which is already set apart exclusively
for their use.

"3rd.   By far the larger part of the Indians desire to move south
and some tribes (the Delawares, Kickapoos & Shawnees) have selected
localities & commenced settlements, by agreement with the Cherokees
& other tribes, who are equally desirous they should come there as
permanent residents.

"4th.   I was specially authorised & solicited by the Indians to bring
this measure before the Government and urge its adoption.

"On a recent visit to the Delawares I attended a council and was
shown a memorial soliciting the Government to take their lands &
improvements and legalize their arrangements made with the Cherokees signed by those representing 500 of the tribe. This memorial
was two years old, the agents having steadily refused to transmit it
to the department for them. The same condition I found in other
places.

"The Indians gave as reasons for desiring to consolidate that their
little reserves are like islands, that the emigration sweeps over them
like a flood carrying off all their property & means of living, and
that they are entirely powerless in their present position in competing
with the whites, as they do not understand their language, customs
nor laws, that many of the tribes are diminishing at the rate of more
than a hundred a year over & above the births, that by certain arrangements which the agents & traders are able to make they are often
reduced to starvation & death, and that diseases superinduced by
exposures, privations & vice, largely fostered by their contact with
the whites, are rapidly & fearfully destroying their name & race.

"I send this to you because it is nearly a copy of what I sent to Mr.
Dole and I wish you to know what I am doing."

(Wattles to Smith, March 4, 1862, I.D., *Register of Letters Received,*
"Indians," no. 4, p. 517; O.I.A., *Central Superintendency,* W 528).

[481] The measure was known to the Indians as *Lane's bill.* See Baptiste
Peoria to Dole, February 9, 1863, O.I.A., General Files, *Osage River,*
1863-1867.

removal.[482] Not immediately, however, could it be completely executed; for as Dole adroitly remarked, Indian Territory was not yet in Federal possession.[483]

So far so good. One group of envious, covetous white men had apparently reached the goal towards which all its endeavour for years past had pointed; but negotiations for removal were not actual removal and removal was not territorial organization, without which the necessary control over Indian Territory and its tribes, necessary both for the completion of the removal scheme and for the economic enterprises of another group of promoters, would be absolutely wanting. In realisation of this fact, the project for tribal consolidation and political reorganization, of which the territorial idea was compounded, came again to the fore and at first with Senator Lane as the usual chief sponsor. The intervening time had not been squandered. Several treaties for final cession and ultimate removal had been bargained for and a few negotiated; but of greater consequence even than they, as far as the outlook for relief from the aboriginal encumbrance was concerned, was the fact that success had at last come to the Federal armies. The Confederacy was tottering to its fall. Indian Territory would soon be completely at the mercy of the conqueror.

On Candlemas Day, 1865, Connelley's "grim chieftain of Kansas" took up the cudgels once more and offered for consideration in the United States senate a resolution under which the Committee on Territories was to "be instructed to inquire as to the policy of organizing a territorial government for the country

---

[482] (Indian Appropriation Act, March 3, 1863, 12 *U.S. Stat. at L.*, p. 793).

[483] Dole to Usher, July 29, 1863, O.I.A., *Report Book*, no. 13, p. 211.

lying between Kansas and Texas, known as the Indian country, and to report by bill or otherwise." [484] Two days subsequently the same individual submitted another resolution [485] of purpose identical but bearing two significant modifications. The Committee on Indian Affairs, of which Lane was himself a member, had been substituted, although somewhat inappropriately, were all things right and regular, for the Committee on Territories and the word, *policy*, had been changed to *expediency*. To the second resolution the senate gave its "unanimous consent."

The Committee on Indian Affairs was not long in making its inquiry. On the twentieth, James Harlan of Iowa, another of its members, came forward with a bill [486] for the organization of Indian Territory upon the model of that initiated by the Ordinance of 1787. It was referred to his own committee and, after an interval of two days only, reported back by Chairman Doolittle of Wisconsin with amendments. [487] On the docket, the bill stood, henceforth, as S 459. As Harlan's bill, it had been hurriedly drafted; but its subject matter was old to most of the committee and was to become venerable in congressional history long before enactment was to be in any way possible. The evident intention of the Harlan Bill supporters was to get it "railroaded" through the Senate and they practically succeeded. It was never debated in the House of Representatives, because of early dissolution, [488] this

---

[484] *Senate Journal*, 38th cong., 2nd sess (1208) p. 124.

[485] — *Ibid.*, p. 133.

[486] — *Ibid.*, p. 915. The bill was read twice by title and ordered printed.

[487] February 22, 1865, *ibid.*, p. 981.

[488] It came from the Senate, March 3rd (*Cong. Globe*, 38th cong., 2nd sess., p. 1401). Ashley of Ohio moved its consideration but Holman of Indiana objected (*ibid.*, 1420).

being the short session; but lack of action by the lower branch was a circumstance of trifling moment, since what was really needed was an expression of opinion from the more permanent legislative body, from the men, in short, who might later on have Indian treaties of peace to ratify.

The provisions of the Harlan Bill, as originally drafted, may be briefly summarised. They comprised the erection of a regular *territory* with definite boundaries, the boundaries of the existing Indian country and the introduction of governmental machinery somewhat similar to that found in other organized territories of the United States. There were to be a governor and a secretary, appointed by the president, each with a four year tenure. The governor was to be *ex-officio* superintendent of Indian affairs and was to have an absolute veto over the proceedings of a legislative assembly, or council. The council was to be composed of men, selected, according to population, by the qualified, or enfranchised, members of such tribes as might agree to the arrangement. Should an election fail to take place, it was to be composed of tribal chiefs. The legislative power, vested in the governor and legislative council was to be extensive. It was to cover all matters of a domestic character; but a supervisory control over certain fiscal affairs was to reside permanently in the United States congress. The Indian Territory thus constituted was to be represented in Washington by a delegate.[489]

An understanding of the deeper meanings of the Harlan Bill can be obtained most easily and most fairly from the senatorial probings and comments in debate. Artfully contrived though it was and so timed as to be

[489] — *Ibid.*, pp. 1021-1022.

able to claim but scant attention, it yet did not escape censure. Its perfidy was exposed by Lafayette S. Foster, a senator with universal training and wide legal knowledge, from Norwich, Connecticut, in politics, a conservative Republican. The course of the debate will here be traced by its main points only. It began on the twenty-third of February, was continued for a short time on the twenty-fourth, and was concluded on the second of March.[490] The ulterior purposes of politicians, as likewise the lowering of the status of the Indian country that would be incident to its statutory organization, and the advantage that might so legitimately be taken of any such condition, were revealed in Pomeroy's preliminary observation that, should it be desirable at some future time to change the boundaries, the change should take place without previous consultation with the Indians. Their consent to a change should not be requisite. To a discrimination so manifest, Doolittle retorted and the debate was well on.

SENATE, February 23, 1865.

DOOLITTLE: "In relation to that I will say to my friend from Kansas that we specially reserve that the consent of the Indians shall be necessary. We are under treaty obligations with those Indians in relation to this matter which we ought not to depart from, and which we cannot depart from without violating the faith of the United States."

HENDRICKS of Indiana: "I do not want to interpose any objection to this measure if it be the pleasure of the Senate to adopt it, but it is very new in its character, and it seems to me the attention of the Senate to some little extent ought to be given to it. This is a proposition coming from the Committee on Indian Affairs,[491] not having been considered, I believe, by

[490] *Cong. Globe*, 38th cong., 2nd sess., pp. 1021-1024, 1058, 1303-1306, 1308-1310.

[491] J. R. Doolittle of Wisconsin, M. S. Wilkinson of Minnesota, James

the Committee on Territories,[492] to organize a new Territory, with all the machinery applicable to a territorial government, with two peculiarities not found, I believe, in any other territorial organization: first, that there shall be a Legislature to be selected from among the Indians themselves to legislate upon all questions of a domestic character; and in the second place, that there shall be a delegate to Congress [493] selected by the Indians. I merely desire to call the attention of the Senate to the bill. I hardly know whether I am in favor of it or against it. I am not prepared to vote for it without some consideration. It is a bill that was introduced by the Senator from Iowa (Mr. Harlan) I observe, three days ago, on the 20th of this month, and referred to the Committee on Indian Affairs, and reported by that committee yesterday, and laid upon our desks to-day."

RAMSEY of Minnesota: "I should like to learn from the chairman of the Committee on Indian Affairs what tribes it is contemplated to collect upon this reservation." [494]

DOOLITTLE: "This Indian Territory is very peculiar from all the other Territories of the United States. It belongs in fee simple as it stands, by patent from the United States, to the Cherokees, the Creeks, the Seminoles, the Choctaws, and the Chickasaws . . .[495] The rebellion, it is true, involved some

H. Lane of Kansas, James Harlan of Iowa, James W. Nesmith of Oregon, B. Gratz Brown of Missouri, Chas. R. Buckalew of Pennsylvania.

[492] B. F. Wade of Ohio, M. S. Wilkinson of Minnesota, John P. Hale of New Hampshire, J. H. Lane of Kansas, John S. Carlile of Virginia, Garrett Davis of Kentucky, W. A. Richardson of Illinois.

[493] On earlier propositions of the sort, see Abel, *An Indian State in the Union*, and, on Indian representation in the Confederate Congress, Abel, *Slaveholding Indians*, vols. i and ii.

[494] The Sioux outbreak in Minnesota might well elicit an inquiry such as this from Alexander Ramsey. Dr. Lucy E. Textor's thesis, *Official Relations between the United States and the Sioux Indians*, gives a general account of the causes of the outbreak; Helen Hunt Jackson's *Century of Dishonor*, one less dispassionate, more particular, and no less accurate.

[495] The Indian title rested primarily upon a provision in the Removal Act of 1830-.

"Sec. 3. *And be it further enacted*, That in the making of any such exchanges, it shall and may be lawful for the President solemnly to assure the tribe or nation with which the exchange is made, that the United States will forever secure and guaranty to them, and their heirs

of those tribes in the rebellion against the United States, and in
this Territory there have been terrible conflicts, and wars, and

or successors, the country so exchanged with them; and if they prefer it,
that the United States will cause a patent or grant to be made and
executed to them for the same: *Provided always*, That such lands shall
revert to the United States, if the Indians become extinct, or abandon
the same." (4 *U.S. Stat. at L.*, p. 412).

The following extracts disclose the nature of the Indian title. The
northern emigrants, as a general thing, took no advantage of the privilege
held out to them in the enactment just quoted; but their rights were solemnly
guaranteed none the less. The southern emigrants were more politically
astute, more wary, and they preferred to fortify their claim by every legal
means open to them. Titles in perpetuity were granted to some of them
before 1830; but the patents were all of later issue than that date.

(Preamble) " . . . *a permanent home*, and which shall, under
the most solemn guarantee of the United States, be, and remain, theirs
forever – a home that shall never, in all future time, be embarrassed by
having extended around it the lines, or placed over it the jurisdiction
of a Territory or State, nor be pressed upon by the extension, in any
way, of the limits of any existing Territory or State . . . "
(Treaty with the Western Cherokees, 1828, Kappler, vol. ii, p. 288).

"Article 2. The United States agree to possess the Cherokees, and
to guarantee it to them forever, and that guarantee is hereby solemnly
pledged, of seven millions of acres of land, . . . In addition to the
seven millions of acres . . . , the United States further guarantee
to the Cherokee Nation a perpetual outlet, West, . . . " (*ibid.*,
pp. 288-289).

The guarantee was renewed, in 1833, with this additional proviso:
" . . . and letters patent shall be issued by the United States as soon
as practicable for the land hereby guaranteed." (*ibid.*, p. 387). In the
Treaty of New Echota, 1835, the guarantee was again renewed and was
extended to cover the new grant of the so-called Cherokee *Neutral Lands*
(*ibid.*, p. 441). The principle of territorial integrity was likewise re-
asserted:

"Article 5. The United States hereby covenant and agree that the
lands ceded to the Cherokee nation . . . shall, in no future time
without their consent, be included within the territorial limits or
jurisdiction of any State or Territory . . . " (*ibid.*, p. 442).

In attempting to adjust, by the treaty of 1846, the Cherokee domestic
difficulties that had grown out of its own questionable negotiations with the
tribe, the United States government reiterated the earlier promises (*ibid.*,
p. 561).

In the fourteenth article of the Creek treaty of 1832, the principle of
territorial integrity was laid down by implication and protection and a
patent were promised,

"The Creek country west of the Mississippi shall be solemnly guar-

anarchy, and confusion. The committee, after full consideration, have deemed that the best form in which to get at this
Territory, and get it into some shape, and bring some kind of

antied to the Creek Indians, nor shall any State or Territory ever have
a right to pass laws for the government of such Indians, but they shall
be allowed to govern themselves, so far as may be compatible with
the general jurisdiction which Congress may think proper to exercise
over them. And the United States will also defend them from the
unjust hostilities of other Indians, and will also . . . cause a
patent or grant to be executed . . . (*ibid.*, p. 343).

By a treaty with the Seminoles in that same year, 1832, the Creek privileges were extended to them (*ibid.*, p. 344) and, in the following year,
both tribes were specifically promised a patent in fee simple, the Seminoles
sharing the rights and privileges of the Creeks as a constituent part of the
Creek Nation (*ibid.*, pp. 390, 394).

The incorporation of the Seminoles with the Creeks was productive of
"unhappy and injurious dissensions and controversies" and, in 1856, the
United States government had again to intervene. The opening up of
negotiations proved an occasion for the renewal of former pledges. Both
tribes were reassured as to their land tenure and the following was said
as to their territorial integrity:

"ARTICLE 4. The United States do hereby, solemnly agree and bind
themselves, that no State or Territory shall ever pass laws for the
government of the Creek or Seminole tribes of Indians, and that no
portion of either of the tracts of country defined in the first and second
articles of this agreement shall ever be embraced or included within,
or annexed to, any Territory or State, nor shall either, or any part of
either, ever be erected into a Territory without the full and free
consent of the legislative authority of the tribe owning the same."
(*ibid.*, p. 758).

The date of the treaty in which the foregoing was embodied is most
significant, 1856, two years after the passage of the Kansas-Nebraska Act,
a piece of Federal law-making that filled the Indians with alarm.

The Chickasaws were slower in finding a western home than were the
Creeks and Cherokees; but, in 1834, the United States government stipulated
that when they should find a new home it would "agree to keep them without
the limits of any State or Territory." (*ibid.*, p. 418). It was the boast
of this tribe that it had "never raised the tomahawk to shed the blood of
an American" and because of that and because it had surrendered to the
white people extensive and valuable lands at a price wholly inconsiderable
and inadequate (*ibid.*, p. 424) it felt that it had a peculiar claim upon the
generosity and fairmindedness of its *Great Father*.

The Chickasaws eventually came to be co-beneficiaries (*ibid.*, Treaty of
1855, pp. 707-708) under government protection with the Choctaws, a tribe
that by the Treaty of Dancing Rabbit Creek, negotiated in 1830, was guaranteed, not only a title in fee and territorial integrity, but the fullest possible

order out of this chaos and anarchy, was to provide by some
law of Congress for some mode by which these Indians them-

protection, even such as might be legally demanded of the United States
by its own citizens.

"ARTICLE II. The United States under a grant specially to be made
by the President of the U.S. shall cause to be conveyed to the Choctaw
Nation a tract of country west of the Mississippi River, in fee simple
to them and their descendants, to inure to them while they shall exist
as a nation and live on it . . .

"ARTICLE III. In consideration of the provisions contained in the
several articles of this Treaty, the Choctaw nation of Indians consent
and cede . . .

"ARTICLE IV. The Government and people of the United States are
hereby obliged to secure to the said Choctaw Nation of Red People
the jurisdiction and government of all the persons and property that
may be within their limits west, so that no Territory or State shall
ever have a right to pass laws for the government of the Choctaw
Nation of Red People and their descendants; and that no part of
the land granted to them shall ever be embraced in any Territory or
State; but the U.S. shall forever secure said Choctaw Nation from, and
against, all laws except such as from time to time may be enacted in
their own National Councils, not inconsistent with the Constitution,
Treaties, and Laws of the United States; and except such as may, and
which have been enacted by Congress, to the extent that Congress under
the Constitution are required to exercise a legislation over Indian
Affairs. But the Choctaws, should this treaty be ratified, express a
wish that Congress may grant to the Choctaws the right of punishing
by their own laws, any white man who shall come into their nation,
and infringe any of their national regulations.

"ARTICLE V. The United States are obliged to protect the Choctaws
from domestic strife and from foreign enemies on the same principles
that the citizens of the United States are protected, so that whatever
would be a legal demand upon the U.S. for defence or for wrongs
committed by an enemy, on a citizen of the U.S. shall be equally binding in favor of the Choctaws, and in all cases where the Choctaws
shall be called upon by a legally authorized officer of the U.S. to fight
an enemy, such Choctaw shall receive the pay and other emoluments,
which citizens of the U.S. receive in such cases, provided, no war shall
be undertaken or prosecuted by said Choctaw Nation but by declaration made in full Council, and to be approved by the U.S. unless it be
in self defense against an open rebellion or against an enemy marching into their country, in which cases they shall defend, until the
U.S. are advised thereof.

"ARTICLE XXIII. The Chiefs of the Choctaws who have suggested
that their people are in a state of rapid advancement in education and
refinement, and have expressed a solicitude that they might have the

selves could be brought, with their consent (because the bill contemplates the consent of these tribes that are at peace with the United States) into a measure of this kind, which would authorize them to choose their own legislators or counselors, and by which the United States would be authorized to appoint a Governor . . . "

RAMSEY: "This is somewhat a question of geography, and I should like to understand . . . whether it is calculated to bring the northern tribes down into the country south of the southern line of Kansas."

DOOLITTLE: "There is nothing in this bill on that subject, but I will state frankly to the honorable Senator from Minnesota that there has been a hope entertained by the Committee . . . and I believe by the Department, that the more civilized portions of our Indian tribes might be induced, not forced, but by some treaty arrangements made, to go and join their fortunes with the Indians in this Territory, and better their condition and advance in civilization . . . "

HENDRICKS: "The fourth section of the bill provides for the selection of the Legislative Council. It does not require that the members of the Legislative Council shall be Indians, but that they shall be selected for the Indians; that is, there shall be 'one member for each one thousand Indians or a fraction of a thousand greater than five hundred.' The person selected may be an Indian, or he may be a white man. He is to be selected by the Indians, or the members of the tribe (and I believe that white persons may become members of the tribe) by the persons who are defined as voters in this section. If there is no election, then the head of the tribe is to be the legislator for that tribe. When that mixed Legislature, then, part Indian and part white, meet, they will have jurisdiction by the sixth section to legislate upon –

All rightful subjects and matters pertaining to the intercourse of the Indian tribes in said Territory, and the administration of internal justice –

privilege of a Delegate on the floor of the House of Representatives extended to them. The Commissioners do not feel that they can under a treaty stipulation accede to the request, but at their desire, present it in the Treaty, that Congress may consider of, and decide the application." (*ibid.*, pp. 311, 312, 315).

This is very comprehensive language –

I desire Senators to observe that all legislative power in respect to the Indians and in respect to all other persons in this Territory is conferred upon this Legislative Council, selected in the manner in which I have suggested; but no laws upon certain subjects, that is, for the 'sale, taxation, or incumbrance of real estate' or the compulsory collection of debts shall be in force until approved by Congress. I take it that all other laws upon all other subjects that can affect the Indians are to be in force without the approval of Congress; so that by the passage of this bill Congress surrenders to this Legislative Council the right to legislate for the Indians."

DOOLITTLE: "In relation to that, perhaps there is some force in the objection of the Senator from Indiana. I do not know that I have any objection to make the approval of Congress essential to the validity of all laws passed by the Council. That was the form of the early territorial governments. . . . "

HENDRICKS: "I believe that in the acts passed recently for the organization of territorial governments, the right of Congress to say whether the territorial laws shall be in force or not is not found except in respect to Utah . . . But I would not consider that of much importance. I have never known the laws of any Territorial Legislature to receive the careful consideration of Congress . . . "

DOOLITTLE: " . . . we have already by treaty surrendered to the Indian tribes in that Territory the soil and the jurisdiction, and the whole power of legislation over all persons coming within the jurisdiction of the tribes . . . By an express provision and by a patent we have given them the land in fee simple; and prior to the rebellion they had regularly-organized governments . . . "

LANE of Kansas: "Mr. President, when this war commenced there were sixty-five thousand Indians in this Indian Territory . . . By the war we have had thrown upon our hands about eighteen thousand . . . The balance have gone over to the traitors. There are eighteen thousand refugees who are left in the Territory entirely unprotected, and who are being maintained by the Government at an expense of a million and a half a year, perhaps two million a year.[496]   There is no subject that can come before the Senate in which the people I represent feel more interest than this . . .   I presume three fourths of the entire body of these Indians are three fourths white blood, as intelligent as any people that we have, and as well educated.   The Indian regiments now in our service are commanded to a considerable extent by Indian officers, as intelligent as our own officers; and the people there are far advanced in civilization beyond any other Indians on the continent."

HENDRICKS: "I take it . . .   before we can take away from any one tribe the power to legislate exclusively for itself and to confer it upon a council . . .   we must obtain the consent of each particular tribe."

HARLAN: "That is contemplated by this bill.   It provides distinctly that their rights shall not be interfered with until they consent to it."

HENDRICKS: "Can a treaty be modified by a mere assent of the tribes?   How is that assent to be given?   What evidence are we to have of the fact? . . .   I am not going to discuss this other provision which gives to the Indians the right to be represented in the House of Representatives . . .   I might be in favor of it; but it is a very important modification of the policy of the Government . . . ; and I think that to introduce a bill on the 20th . . . "

RAMSEY: "I should like to learn . . .   what tribes it is contemplated to bring within this reservation."

DOOLITTLE: " . . .   It has sometimes been expected that the Delawares might go there, and the civilized tribes of Kansas, Nebraska, and perhaps as far north as Michigan, Wisconsin, and Minnesota . . .

"I do not understand that there is to be any attempt to force

---

[496] In 1862, Congress authorized the suspension of the payment of their annuities to "any tribe or tribes of Indians, all or any portion of whom shall be in a state of actual hostility to the government of the United States . . . " (12 *U.S. Stat. at L.*, p. 528) and repeated the enactment each succeeding year.   The relief furnished to the refugees was paid for out of the suspended annuities (*ibid.*).   It was scarcely fair for Lane to imply that the generosity of the government had been taxed for the purpose.

these Indians to go there, . . . But it is a very fine Territory; it is as fine a section of country as there is in the United States. . . . It is a very productive Territory. It is the country that the Government long, long ago, under the policy of General Jackson, solemnly set apart for the Indians, and it belongs to them. The only thing involved in this bill is this: we could by strict right forfeit [497] the title of those Indians who have rebelled against the United States if we chose to do so; but when the war is over the Indians will still be upon our hands, as they must be provided for somehow, and perhaps it is better that we should begin an organization over this Territory, get the consent of the Indians to it, and perhaps this may be used as one of the instrumentalities to induce the Choctaws and Chickasaws who have been in rebellion against us to come into this arrangement when they find that they can take part in the legislation of this very Territory if they lay down their arms against the Government. But these are rather speculations than otherwise."

HENDRICKS: "I will ask the Senator if he does not in this provide that before they can do that they have got to swear that they will have nothing to do with the rebellion."

HARLAN: "No; that provision is in relation to office holders in the Territory only."

POMEROY of Kansas: "I would not like to put any obstacle in the way of the passage of this bill. Still, it is a new measure, and there are some features of it that do not seem to

---

[497] By the law just referred to, Congress further provided, "That in cases where the tribal organization of any Indian tribe shall be in actual hostility to the United States, the President is hereby authorized, by proclamation, to declare all treaties with such tribe to be abrogated by such tribe, if, in his opinion, the same can be done consistently with good faith and legal and national obligations" (*ibid.*). No such proclamation was ever issued and Lincoln withheld judgment in the matter as far as the Cherokees, at least, were concerned. (See his letter to John Ross, September 25; 1862, Nicolay and Hay, *Works of Lincoln*, vol. viii, p. 45; *Letters and State Papers*, vol. ii, p. 240). It is doubtful if any court in the land would have sustained Doolittle in his contention that "by strict right," the Indians could have been held to have forfeited their title since the government had been the first to violate treaty pledges when it withdrew its protection from Indian Territory and from the several tribes dwelling therein (See Abel, *Slaveholding Indians*, vol. I).

me altogether proper . . . There are three things that I think somewhat essential which are not provided for. In the first place, this sets out to be a temporary government; yet it is provided that it shall be permanent for all time to come. Secondly, it sets out to be an Indian Territory, and yet no provision is made against white people going in and actually being adopted as members of the tribes and absorbing the Government of the country; and as if to offer an inducement for that, there is a direct provision made that there shall be no forcible legal collection of debts inside this Territory . . . "

DOOLITTLE: " . . . That is one of the distinguishing features of the laws of these Indian tribes . . . , because a state of society not fully civilized it would be a dangerous power to be exercised if Indians could be permitted to contract debts and have those debts enforced against them; and we provide that there shall be no sale of lands."

POMEROY: "I do not object to a law that would prevent the enforcement of the collection of debts as against Indians; but this bill is so drawn and the existing usage is such that the Indians are to be absorbed. My colleague very well says they are bleaching out now; they are becoming white men."

LANE: "On a point suggested by my colleague I should like to ask him a question. Does he not know that a large number of black persons have intermarried with Indians of these tribes and become members of the tribes? Does he object to the provision of the bill which permits black people to continue to go in and become members of the tribes?" [498]

POMEROY: "I understand that negroes and Indians have intermarried. I do not object to it . . . " [499]

LANE: " . . . The finest specimens of manhood I have ever gazed upon in my life are half-breed Indians crossed with negroes. It is a fact . . . that while amalgamation with the white man deteriorates both races, the amalgamation of the Indian and the black man advances both races; and so far as

[498] This was a gross exaggeration. The Creeks were the only southern Indians that ever mixed freely with the negroes. On the subject of intermarriage, see Senate Document, no. 257, 59th cong., 2nd sess.

[499] Pomeroy was supposed to be more than usually interested in negro colonisation (Oberholtzer, vol. I, p. 77).

I am concerned I should like to see these eighty thousand square miles, almost in the geographical center of the United States, opened up to the Indian and to the black man, and let them amalgamate and build up a race that will be an improvement upon both.[500] I say to anti-slavery men here, if you desire to furnish a home for the black man, pass this territorial bill and let him go there. The climate is genial. He understands how to cultivate the products. They are those of the South, cotton and tobacco. In my opinion nothing can be better calculated to clear the political arena of the question of what shall be done with the black man than to pass this territorial bill, open up this country for him, and he will flock in there and become a useful member of society."

LANE of Kansas: "The bill now before the Senate is of more importance to my constitutents than any bill which will come before this body. We have now no protection from the South; this disorganized Territory of eighty-four thousand square miles lies on our border, subjecting us to raids;[501] and I move that this bill be postponed until to-morrow evening at seven o'clock, and made the special order for that hour."

(The motion was agreed to.)

SENATE, February 24, 1865.

DOOLITTLE: " . . . Two or three amendments have

---

[500] Again the Kansas senator overstated the case. The range of his observation could not have been extensive. It is conceded by all ethnologists that a mongrel race is inferior to the races contributing to the mixture or equal only to the more primitive of the two. There is always a tendency towards reversion to type. As Madison Grant so pertinently puts it, "Whether we like to admit it or no, the result of the mixture of two races, in the long run, gives us a race reverting to the more ancient, generalized and lower type. The cross between a white man and an Indian is an Indian; the cross between white man and a negro is a negro; the cross between a white man and a Hindu is a Hindu; and a cross between any of the three European races and a Jew is a Jew." (*The Passing of the Great Race*, pp. 15-16). There is something almost diabolical in Lane's suggestion and encouragement of the idea of race amalgamation. Plainly he had no regard at all for the further upward development of the southern Indian, who was recognized, even by his enemies, to be already a highly civilized being.

[501] The raids were a circumstance of the war. They had never occurred in time of peace. The southern Indians were as peace-loving and had as high a respect for other people's property as the best of the Kansans.

been suggested to me to the bill, and I have consulted with Senators on the subject, and I think it can be disposed of before recess."

POMEROY: "think there will be no difficulty in disposing of it."

FOSTER of Connecticut: "The Indian bill to which reference is made is a very important bill, and can hardly be disposed of in fifteen minutes. It is a bill which changes our whole Indian policy. It violates the plighted faith of the United States in various particulars. It is a bill which, in regard to the Indian tribes within the country that it proposes to organize as a new Territory, will do great injustice, and, it seems to me, will cast great dishonor on the United States if we pass it. It certainly ought not to be hurried through in ten or fifteen minutes. . . . "

(LANE withdrew his motion and further debate was postponed.)

SENATE, March 2, 1865.

(HARLAN insisted upon the resumption of debate.)

DOOLITTLE: "There is a verbal amendment that I desire to make to the bill. It is to insert after the words 'tribes,' . . . the words 'by a treaty stipulation duly negotiated for that purpose.' . . . The tribes there are in amity and peace with us. Our treaty stipulations forbid the extension of territorial government over these Cherokees and Creeks without their consent . . . "

(The amendment was agreed to.)

FOSTER: "Mr. President, this bill was before the Senate four or five days ago . . . It has been introduced into the Senate since the 20th of February, and printed since that time . . . It is a long bill; . . . It changes, I believe, very materially and radically our whole Indian policy. It violates our treaties. It will be very injurious to some of the Indian tribes; and worse than all, it will be a stain upon the national honor, a breach of the national faith. These are a portion of its evils.

"One of the tribes that this bill contemplates to bring within territorial jurisdiction is the Cherokee tribe of Indians. I am old enough to remember the time when the people of the United

States were very considerably exercised, and I may say agitated, on account of what seemed to be a most cruel and unjustifiable course pursued by our Government toward that tribe. This tribe had its home in what I believe made a portion of the States of Georgia, Tennessee, and North Carolina; and the section occupied by them was among the very finest portions of those States. A portion of that Cherokee country was as attractive and beautiful as any within the limits of the United States. It was looked upon with desire, it was coveted by the surrounding whites, especially in the State of Georgia. They determined that these people should be expelled from those lands, and they carried that determination into effect. The United States for a time struggled against that effort on the part of Georgia, and seemed disposed to protect the tribe in their rights; but very soon our Government yielded, and the State of Georgia triumphantly drove those Indians beyond the Mississippi, took their lands, disposed of them by lottery, and hanged some of our citizens within the Territory, on the charge that they were attempting to impede or thwart the laws of Georgia and the purposes of that State against the Cherokees. In the case of one of those men, after a decision by the Supreme Court of the United States that the conviction was erroneous, and after a writ of error had been issued to bring up the record to the Supreme Court for revision, the State of Georgia, by her authorities, proceeded to execute the man, notwithstanding the pendency of the writ of error, thus flinging defiance in the face of the Government of the United States in the most odious and offensive, and, I will add, in the most savage manner.[502]

"These Indians were driven off, under these circumstances, west of the Mississippi. The United States made a treaty with them within a few years after this; I believe in the year 1835. These events occurred in the years 1829 and 1830, and so on up to 1835 . . . We had previously made treaties with this same tribe. In this treaty of 1835 we entered into very solemn stipulations as to their rights to the country west of the

---

[502] Foster's statements are a little awry here. For the case referred to, see Phillips, *Georgia and State Rights*, p. 75 *et. seq.* and, for a fuller account of the conditions resulting in Cherokee removal, that work and also Abel, *Indian Consolidation.*

Mississippi river, over which we now propose to extend our jurisdiction and create a Territory. One of the stipulations in that treaty is short, and I will read it, in order that we may see whether or not it is consistent with good faith for us now to incorporate a Territory taking in this tract of country which we then covenanted in the most solemn manner should remain to this Cherokee tribe. The fifth article of that treaty is as follows:

'The United States hereby covenant and agree that the lands ceded to the Cherokee nation in the foregoing article shall in no future time without their consent be included within the territorial limits or jurisdiction of any State or Territory. But they shall secure to the Cherokee nation the right by their national councils to make and carry into effect all such laws as they may deem necessary for the government and protection of the persons and property within their own country belonging to their people or such persons as have connected themselves with them . . . ' [503]

BROWN of Missouri: "I will state to the Senator that the bill which is pending provides that this territorial government shall not extend over that tribe except their assent be first obtained through treaty stipulation."

FOSTER: " . . . and therefore what is the necessity or propriety of passing this territorial bill until we first obtain that consent?"

DOOLITTLE: " . . . this country held by the Cherokees is larger than the State of Massachusetts. Immediately below the Arkansas lies the country of the Creeks, which probably is larger than New Jersey. Then below that, south of the Canadian river, is the country of the Choctaws and the Chickasaws and the affiliated Indians that were put in there from Texas, which is larger than both the others put together. Those Indians, by their hostilities against the United States, have forfeited all treaty stipulations with the United States, and we are therefore not bound to regard the treaties which we entered into with the Chickasaws or the Choctaws on that subject, they having broken them by open, flagrant war for three or four years against the United States."

[503] Article 5. Kappler, vol. ii, p. 442.

FOSTER: " . . . In reply to the suggestion of the Senator from Wisconsin, as to the Creeks, Seminoles, and Chickasaws, who are at war with the United States, I will remark that I have said nothing whatever about them. I speak of the Cherokee tribe, which, as a tribe, has remained true and faithful to the Government of the United States. No doubt a portion of the tribe have joined the rebels; but they were a small portion comparatively, and they did so under duress and compulsion – "

LANE: "The Cherokee tribe of Indians, as a tribe, received annuities from the confederate government for two years."

FOSTER: "That may be. If they have received annuities from the confederate government they have not been paid for a tithe of the property which the confederate government have stolen from them . . . "

FOSTER: " . . . when the Senator from Missouri suggested that this bill provides that we shall first obtain the consent of the tribe before we extend this territorial government over them, does not every Senator know what that means, and what the passage of this territorial bill creating these officers to go there means? Is there any doubt that these tribes will consent? Does not everybody know that their consent under these circumstances is a mere farce? How would it be if we had a treaty like this with any foreign Power that had sufficient strength to avenge an insult of this sort? If we had made this treaty with such a nation, and then undertook to extend jurisdiction over it, provided we could get their consent after we had thus exerted our authority and created a Territory, what would be the result?"

" . . . If this treaty was with any nation in the world which had any power to resent an insult would we not understand that the passage of this bill was a declaration of war, and would it not be war, certainly and speedily? I know it will not be war with these poor Cherokees, because they are a powerless tribe; that is, powerless as against the United States. They have sent two regiments into your Army, a greater number of men in proportion to the number of fighting men belonging to the tribe than has gone from any State in this Union; and those men are now fighting as gallantly and as bravely in the

ranks of the Union Army as any other men in it, as I am informed. Now, we propose, in violation of these treaty stipulations, to extend our government over this Indian Territory,
putting in, by way of parenthesis, 'provided they consent.' If
that parenthesis means anything, we should not pass this bill,
because we should first get their consent; . . . "

CLARK of New Hampshire: "I move that the further consideration of the bill . . . be postponed . . . "

HARLAN: "I hope this may be done . . . The design
of the bill is to protect these Indians from utter annihilation –
not to establish a government there for white men, to introduce
white men, but to prevent them from entering the Territory or
becoming inhabitants of the Territory . . .

"But is it fair to keep all the other Indian tribes, many of
whom are very feeble, in a condition little short of anarchy,
because a chief of the Cherokees, now a pensioner of the Federal
Government in the city of Philadelphia, remonstrates against
the passage of such a bill? The chief of that tribe, from whom
these objections originally enmanated, is now a pensioner on the
Federal Government to the tune of $10,000 a year;[504] and of
course he objects to any organization that might in the end take
from him any of the despotic power that he now attempts to
wield over these helpless people. A majority of the Cherokee
nation have been in rebellion against the Government of the
United States; they have forfeited all their rights;[505] but this
bill does not propose to confiscate [506] their property or to deprive

---

[504] Ross was in no sense a pensioner of the United States government.
The funds supplied him by the Indian Office were regular Indian funds
and chargeable to the Indian account.

[505] In a legal sense, forfeiture and liability to forfeiture are two entirely
different things. By their insistence upon the use of the former, the members
of the Indian committee, particularly Doolittle and Harlan, purposed to
prejudice the case of the Cherokees, to poison the mind of the public, and
to convey the idea of positive guilt before anything had been proved and
before the case had been so much as heard.

[506] Even if the president, under the discretionary power vested in him
by the act of July 5, 1862 (12 *U.S. Stat. at L.*, p. 528) had, by proclamation,
declared the Indian treaties abrogated, it is exceedingly doubtful if confiscation would have resulted. The landed property rights of the Indians
rested, not upon government favor, but upon territorial cessions, the tender
of value received. On the confiscatory processes of the Federal govern-

them of any rights until, by express treaty stipulation, they shall have agreed to the provisions contained in this bill; and even then, with the adoption of the bill, it is intended to protect the Cherokees, and every other tribe within the limits of the Indian country, from aggression from the white man, those from whom the Senator himself fears encroachment.

"We were told a day or two ago by the Senator from Ohio (Mr. Sherman) that he was opposed to making any more treaties with the Indian tribes . . . "

FOSTER: " . . . What is the purpose of the bill? Is it honest? I ask again, do we mean to send these officers there to organize this government, and are these officers, after they get there with commissions in their pockets, to negotiate with the Indians first whether they may stay and organize the government?"

BROWN: "I will explain to the Senator. There is abundance of territory outside of the Cherokee nation which will require this organization. Their territory will not be included in it in any sense; it will not be part of it until they give their assent any more than it is now included in the Government of the United States."

FOSTER: "Mr. President, the bill which is reported from the Committee on Indian Affairs, by lines and limits takes in this very Territory. It extends north to the south line of the State of Kansas; it extends west to our other territorial possessions; it extends east to our recognized possessions, and south to our recognized possessions; and it takes in the whole Territory."

LANE: "Have we organized a territorial government since the passage of the Kansas-Nebraska bill, including that bill, that does not contain that same provision, and does not include Indian reserves? When the Kansas-Nebraska bill was passed there was more territory in Indian reserves provided for by a similar stipulation than there was soil belonging to the United States Government.[507] We could not extend our jurisdiction over

ment as they affected the property of white people, see Randall, *Captured and Abandoned Property During the Civil War*, American Historical Review, vol. xix, pp. 65-79.

[507] The Kansas-Nebraska Act, which provided for the organization of the territories of Kansas and Nebraska (May 30, 1854, *10 U.S. Stat. at L.*,

those Indian reserves, and have not to this day; and yet we exercise power over all other portions of the Territory." [508]

FOSTER: "If we have learned by experience, as the honor-

pp. 277-290) expressly exempted the lands belonging to the Indians from all except Federal and tribal jurisdiction. See *ibid.*, pp. 277, 284.

[508] The Act for the Admission of Kansas into the Union, January 29, 1861, contained stipulations, borrowed and adapted from the Organic Act of 1854 just quoted, which continued to safeguard the rights, personal and territorial, of the Indians (*12 U.S. Stat. at L.*, p. 127). The boundaries of Kansas, as defined by the selfsame law, included the *Cherokee Neutral Lands*, the *Cherokee Strip*, and some Quapaw lands, every bit of which had had its integrity incontestably guaranteed. Moreover, the Cherokee territory had been conveyed by patent in fee simple. Despite all this, Kansas districted the Indian lands, expressly excluded from her jurisdiction by one federal enactment after another, exactly as if they were her own. And that was not the limit of her aggression; for she taxed the diminished reserve and trust lands of the northern immigrants, the law of the United States to the contrary notwithstanding. On this point the following are referred to as furnishing irrefragable evidence: Abbott to Dole, October 1, 1864, Commissioner of Indian Affairs, *Report*, 1864, p. 380; Colton to Dole, November 1, 1864, *ibid.*, p. 392.

They are typical of the dealings that Kansas meted out to the Indians and what a reflection upon frontier justice, they consitute! Bad as they are they do but epitomize the experience and the inevitable fate of the American Indian everywhere within the present limits of the United States. Kansas imitated Georgia. She adopted the very same tactics to dispose of the Indian and, in the long run, she was equally successful, notwithstanding that every precaution had been taken by the United States government to prevent a recurrence of the outrageous injustice of Jackson's time. Kansas held neither law nor treaty sacred and she brought such heavy pressure to bear upon the defenceless Indian owners that, finally in sheer desperation and utter weariness, they yielded to her insistence and agreed "to move on." It was the white man's greed, tenacity, hypocrisy, duplicity, subterfuge, against Indian helplessness. The initial wrong-doing should, however, be charged against the United States government; for it ought never to have allowed lands for which it had given a title in perpetuity to be included within the metes and bounds of an organized Territory. The farmers and the advocates of the Kansas-Nebraska Bill dealt with treaty guarantees as with *scraps of paper*. Their specious talk about safeguarding the rights of the aborigines was all humbug; for well they knew that once within the defined boundaries of Territory or State, the Indian lands would be at the mercy of the settlers or the capitalist. There would be no force in the entire country strong enough to keep them intact. Injustice of the kind that has been constantly meted out to the Indian is one of the prices paid for democracy. *Consent* under circumstances of irritation and oppression has always proved in Indian history synonymous

able Senator says we have, that when we undertake to violate our plighted faith we cannot really carry out the violation, I think it is time we stop the attempt. The honorable Senator appeals to certain things done in the State of Kansas when it was a Territory. He is much more familiar with all that than I am. I presume there were a great many things done there that were disgraceful. We have heard enough of matters disgraceful in regard to legislation about Kansas – Lecompton constitutions and all. I do not suppose the honorable Senator wishes to quote those as a precedent for legislation like this. They may be like it; but they had better be quoted by way of admonition than by way of example."

FOSTER: " . . . If the honorable Senator from Missouri is right, and we do not mean under this bill to meddle with this Cherokee country, alter the lines in this bill; except this Cherokee country from the operation of the bill. It is pretty easy to point out that portion which belongs to the Cherokee nation. Let the boundaries of this new Territory that is to be organized be amended, and let the boundaries be of a Territory that we intend to take possession of and govern, and not extend it over that which it is avowed we have no right to govern, and do not intend even to attempt to govern. Then why do it?

"Mr. President, it certainly is not for me to interpret the judgments of Providence; but in my opinion, the people who seized and occupied the territory of this Cherokee nation in the State of Georgia and the adjacent regions have been visited within the past six months in a retributive manner for the wrongs done these Cherokees thirty years ago. We have heard of the passage of an army over that country from Chattanooga down to the city of Savannah . . . It passed over this Cherokee country – a beautiful country, containing some of the fairest land on the face of the earth. The Cherokees were driven from it by the cupidity of Georgia; their lands were disposed of . . . , and the Cherokees compelled to migrate beyond the Mississippi, almost at the point of the bayonet.

---

with *coercion* and it is futile for any apologist for the pioneer, from 1607 to the present day, to attempt to argue that it has ever been otherwise. The facts are as they are and nothing can explain them away.

Bayonets have visited that section of country since . . . and I have thought – it may be fancy – that there was something of retribution upon these people who were occupying the lands of these Cherokees so unjustly, so wickedly obtained . . . Let us pause before we drive these Cherokees from their last earthly resting-place – for they have now reached it – to gratify the insatiable desire for land, which, like an evil spirit, seems to possess the minds of our people. You may pass this bill – you may exterminate these Indians and obtain the lands which you solemnly covenanted should be theirs forever – but a day of reckoning will come. It came in fire and in blood upon those who drove them from Georgia. Beware lest it come upon us . . . "

DOOLITTLE: "Since the discussion the other evening, . . . Rev. Mr. Jones, who has been for forty years a missionary among the Cherokees, called on me in the committee-room and I had a conversation with him. I called his attention to the provision of the bill that it should have no effect over the Cherokees without their consent, and I showed him the amendment which I intended to offer to the bill . . . that that consent was to be obtained by treaty stipulation. He said that gave altogether a different aspect to the question . . . I mentioned to him the fact that by this bill no one in the Territory could have any vote in the choice of members of the Council but the Indians and members of the tribe. He said that the rule of the tribe was that no white man could be admitted unless he was married into the tribe. After these facts were called to his attention he expressed to me a very different state of opinion from what my honorable friend understood him to express in the first instance."

FOSTER: " . . . I have seen him, however, since the honorable Senator has, and he gave no intimation to me of a change of opinion. The great danger he apprehended was that the organization of this territorial government would bring in the whites and surround the Indians there with what are called the 'blessings of civilization,' which are the curse and the bane of the Indians."

HARLAN: "The purpose of the bill is to prevent that very thing; to avoid it."

FOSTER: "If the intention and object of the organization of a territorial government on the part of the United States is to prevent our people from going into such a Territory and settling upon it, it certainly is a novel idea in a territorial bill."

HARLAN: "It is not called a territorial bill. The title of the bill is, 'A bill to provide for the consolidation of the Indian tribes, and to establish civil government in the Indian Territory.' "

FOSTER: "Exactly; 'to establish civil government in the Indian Territory;' and it goes on to ascertain that Territory by boundaries; and it organizes that Territory by the appointment of a Governor and other officers just like our other Territories; and if it is to exclude citizens of the United States from it, I repeat again, that it is a novel organization; it is one that will never work out its purpose. The moment the Territory is organized our people will go upon the Territory, and there will be no power to stop them. Who will have the right to stop them? Who will have the jurisdiction there, the Indians or the United States? I say the United States. And what right have the United States to keep citizens of the United States out of the territory of the United States? Where will the power be?"

HARLAN: "They have agreed to do so in the treaties to which the Senator himself has referred, and this bill is intended to carry out faithfully the stipulations of those treaties."

FOSTER: "The honorable Senator from Kansas tells us, and I think the honorable Senator, the chairman of the committee, tells us, that the Indians have broken their faith with the United States; that these treaties are all abrogated."

HARLAN: "No; but some of the Indian tribes that reside in the Territory have forfeited their rights. This bill does not confiscate their property or take away any of their rights."

HOWARD of Michigan: " . . . This bill proposes a complete revolution in the principles which lie at the bottom of our Indian policy. Hitherto the United States have not assumed to possess political power over the Indian tribes; hitherto we have regarded the Indian tribes in most respects as independent nations . . . And the principle of the tribal independence of the Indian nations is consecrated by a clause in the Constitution of the United States . . . a plain recognition of the nationality, if you please, of each one of those Indian tribes; a nationality which is as distinct and independent of us as is the nationality of any foreign country, subject to this limitation and qualification, that as to the lands owned and occupied by the Indian tribes the United States claim and enforce the right of becoming the first purchasers . . .

"Now, sir, what does this bill propose? It proposes to institute over the Indian tribes, or certain of them, a government established by authority of Congress, enforced within certain geographical limits by the power of Congress, and enforced over the Indians individually and over their tribes as tribes . . .

" . . . I think we have no authority to intermeddle with their affairs in this way . . . "

FOSTER: " . . . I agree entirely with what the honorable Senator from Michigan has said in regard to the power of Congress to legislate over these Indians. We have no power whatever . . . and there is a kind of meanness in undertaking to exercise power over those who cannot resist which the United States ought not to be guilty of . . . Does the bill intimate the manner that they shall give their consent?"

LANE: "Expressly by treaty stipulations."

FOSTER: "With whom shall that treaty be made?"

LANE: "With the tribe."

FOSTER: "With the tribe. Who is the chief of that tribe?"

LANE: "Colonel Browning is the acting chief."

FOSTER: "As I understand, he is not the chief of the tribe, but another man is chief."

LANE: "Let me correct the Senator. The Cherokees elect a first chief and a second chief, and require them to take an oath. The election has taken place since John Ross has been in Philadelphia. He must be there to take oath. Browning is there and has taken the oath. Ross has not been there, and will not go there in my opinion; and the Senator is speaking in behalf of a man who is rejected by his people."

FOSTER: "It happens very much as I anticipated. The man who will give his consent to this legislation will be the organ of the tribe, and the man who refuses his consent will be the cast-off man of the tribe, and that will be the way the consent will be obtained.

"I repeat it, the men who refuse consent will be the men without authority. They have not taken the oath, they are not in communion with the tribe! The men who do give the consent will be the men of authority, and when they give their consent, the authority and jurisdiction under this territorial bill is complete and may be exercised; and, Mr. President, I will agree, with a barrel of whisky, to procure the consent of that tribe . . . As it will be managed, it seems to me that this whole matter of consent is an outrage; it will be obtained to a certainty, and there will be no power on earth for these Cherokees to say 'no' to this treaty. Those who say no will be disloyal, will be unfaithful, and any chief who attempts to stand in the way of this legislation will be a rebel! It is said that a portion of the tribe is disloyal. It will be easy to make this charge against any man who does not admit the propriety of this legislation! Make a charge of disloyalty against him and that he does not represent the tribe because he has not complied with their requirements, and there will be no difficulty in getting consent . . . " [509]

LANE: " . . . My anxiety for the passage of this bill this session grows out of the fact that this Territory, which is utterly disorganized, bounds upon our State, and our State feels deep interest in the passage of the bill and the organization of the Territory immediately."

McDOUGALL of California: "Mr. President, I look upon this legislation, as asked for by the Senator from Kansas now, as being an outrage on one of the best bodies of Indian tribes there is or has been in our country. It is true they are now disorganized, destroyed; but we have no right to compel them or compress them as is proposed, and that kind of outrage, although it may be not important to us as a Government, is an outrage on humanity."

The Senate debate on the Harlan Bill ended with McDougall's condemnatory remark and the yeas and nays having been ordered, the vote was taken. There

---

[509] It need scarcely be said that this is precisely what happened. Foster made a correct surmise and forecast. In the light of what he charged and Lane confessed, the treatment of John Ross at the Council of Fort Smith and subsequently can be easily understood.

were only twenty-six senators out of the fifty [510] belonging present.   The bill was passed by a vote of seven-
teen [511] to nine [512] and there its present history ended
since there was no time for its consideration in the
House of Representatives.

---

[510] The number should have been fifty-two; but the representation from
two states, Virginia and Maryland, was not complete. Lemuel J. Bowden
had died January, 1864 and the Senate had not yet accepted the credentials
of his successor (McCarthy, *Lincoln's Plan of Reconstruction*, p. 138).
Senator Thomas H. Hicks of Maryland died February 13, 1865.

[511] John Conness of California (Republican), Henry S. Lane of Indiana
(Republican), James Harlan of Iowa (Republican), James H. Lane and
Samuel C. Pomeroy of Kansas (Republican), Nathan A. Farwell of Maine
(Republican), Charles Sumner of Massachusetts (elected by Democrats and
Free-soilers), Alexander Ramsey of Minnesota (Republican), B. Gratz
Brown of Missouri (Republican and son of John Brown), James W. Nye
and Wm. M. Stewart of Nevada (Republicans who had taken their seats
only in February), James W. Nesmith of Oregon (Democrat), C. R. Buck-
alew (Democrat) and Edgar Cowan (Republican) of Pennsylvania, Wm.
Sprague of Rhode Island (Republican), Peter G. Van Winkle of West
Virginia (Republican), and J. R. Doolittle of Wisconsin (Democrat).

[512] James A. McDougall of California (Democrat), L. S. Foster of Connecticut (Republican), Lazarus W. Powell of Kentucky (Democrat), Henry
Wilson of Massachusetts (Republican), Jacob M. Howard of Michigan
(Republican), John B. Henderson of Missouri (Republican), Edwin D. Morgan of New York (Republican), Henry B. Anthony of Rhode Island (Republican), Waitman T. Willey of West Virginia (Republican).

VIII. THE FREEDMEN OF INDIAN
TERRITORY

The proposition which, at the Fort Smith Council had most truly produced consternation among the Indians was that regarding their freedmen. Adoption into the tribe had been its purport and, against such a proposal, the tribes, one and all, were prepared to be inflexibly obdurate. Enfranchisement of the negro they accepted as a foregone conclusion, inevitable sooner or later; for the phrase, "within the United States, or any place subject to their jurisdiction," could most certainly be interpreted so as to make the Thirteenth Amendment cover Indian Territory. The Emancipation Proclamation had not covered it, since being a purely military measure, it had to limit its application to the places it specifically mentioned. Nevertheless, the Cherokees had not hesitated to act in accordance with its spirit and had, in 1863, when severing their unfortunate connection with the Confederacy, passed a measure abolishing slavery. It was to be expected that other tribes would follow suit in due season. Economic provision [513] for the manumitted

---

[513] While the Fort Smith Council was in session, Pomeroy addressed the following letter to Harlan. It is cited here because, in its economic provision for the freedmen of the richer white men, it offers such a strong contrast to that proposed by Harlan for the freedom of the red.

"I have thought much since leaving Washington of the *Pardoning* I saw going on there –

"I find fault with nothing – but have a suggestion to make –

"I am for having one rule, and I could advise the President (in whom I have every confidence) to amend his Proclamation and say to the South & the country, that a Pardon of all persons who come

was, however, a far more difficult matter, either to advise or to determine. Incorporation within the tribe was one way of settling it, the easiest, no doubt, but not necessarily the best; colonization within a segregated district of Indian Territory was another; and colonization outside yet another.[514] The last-mentioned was likely to find especial favor among those who felt as

within the $20,000 Restriction, will be granted – so soon as they will show to the President or some officer appointed by him, that they have executed a Deed in Fee Simple to all the late Slaves who were in their employment at the date of Mr. Lincoln's first Proclamation of Emancipation, of Ten Acres of Land to each head of a family or able-bodied single person – the title to be inalienable during the lifetime of the first owner – but to descend to his family as does property to white persons.

"Upon that one condition (with the usual oaths) I would pardon all the 20,000 $ men and women and no others.

"I need not argue to you the advantages of a *Homestead*, to the family and to the laborer.

"And Suffrage will then ere long be given safely to all the Land-holders – to persons who have served in the Army & Navy – and then the way will be prepared for all the others.

"If you will not feel that I am presuming too much, I would ask to have this subject presented to the President."

(Pomeroy to Harlan, dated Hoffman House, N. Y., September 16, 1865, *Johnson Papers*, vol 77).

[514] The best statement of the case for colonization outside is to be found in the subjoined letter from Doolittle to Johnson, elsewhere cited:

"Enclosed I send you the resolutions of our Union Convention. On my return from Washington I found here a good head of 'steam on,' and, with those who are carried away with the crazy idea which the fertile brain of Wendell Phillips has engendered upon the brains of Sumner and Greeley, viz., that the States are out of the 'Union' no longer *States* under the Constitution – but mere conquered *territories,* and that therefore the government has the right to impose negro suffrage or any other terms upon them, as a condition precedent to their being recognized as States, there was a most determined effort to be made to force it upon the convention. Unwelcome, as it always is, to me, to engage in controversies with those who profess to be our friends, even where the *Animus* which inspires them is *War* upon the Administration, I still determined to go and take the bull by the horns, and did so. The majority report submitted by me was carried triumphantly. The minority report made by Gen[l] Paine (not our member of Congress but an old leader of Abolitionists of 25 years

did some white people before the war that, if the
United States government took upon itself the responsibility of forcibly freeing the negro, it should provide
economically for him and likewise compensate the for-

standing) after a pretty warm discussion was laid on the table . . .

"The platform, in every resolution, speaks of the Union unbroken,
maintains that the States could not either *forceably* or *peaceably* be
carried out of the Union, & reaffirms this as the only ground on which
we stood in the beginning, and have stood through the War . . .

(Here follows a discussion of the proposed trial of President Davis,
omitted because irrelevant to the purpose in hand).

"There is another suggestion of great importance. Would it not be
well for Congress to authorize the President to submit to the Legislature of Texas a proposition to cede to the U.S. as *Territory* all south
and west of a given line, reserving enough for a State adjoining Louisiana. What lies west of the Indian Territory could be added to that,
and given to the Indians. The remainder could be organized into a
Freedman's Territory for the colored soldiers to enter their bounty
lands in, where they now are in large force. They could be settled
by companies upon the lands in townships; transportation could be
given to their wives and children, to join them there, and we could thus
found such a kind of armed colony as Rome in her conquering progress,
in the days of the Republic always established upon her boundaries.
For all other colored men heads of families, at the South, there could
be ample room in this territory to receive the full benefits of the Homestead Systems, of which you are the author. This Freedmans Territory could be organized with a Governor, Secretary of State, three
judges, and Attorney General, and a Commissioner of Freedmen's
Affairs. These could constitute the Legislative Council for the Territory, making all rules and regulations for its government, which should
be submitted from time to time to Congress, and if not repealed by
Congress have full force and effect.

"This might last say 3 or 5 years. After the expiration of that time
provide also for a Legislative Assembly, to be chosen by Qualified
electors, in addition to the Council which is appointed by the President.
And provide that the voters in such territory shall include all the
colored men who shall have lived on these homesteads and maintained
themselves and families say for one year; and all other male persons
21 years of age and upwards who can write their names legibly, and
read the Constitution of the United States, and all who have borne arms
in, and been honorably discharged from the service of the U.S. Perhaps we could do the same with a portion of Florida. The first territory points towards the mixed population of Mexico, the other, towards
Hayti and Cuba, which latter cannot hold slavery very long. In these
parts is a Paradise, "the land of Canaan," opened not beyond the Rio

mer master for his loss, the master having acquired property rights in human kind under protection of well-established law.   The Indians had been innocent purchasers of Africans to a much greater extent than the southern planters could ever claim to have been.[515]

The situation in which the freedmen of Indian Territory were placed by the war was identically that of their brethren everywhere else in the south.   It was a situation alarming in its preplexities.   The ex-slaves were socially and economically stranded.   The privations that the Indians endured they endured.   In February of 1864 there were five hundred of them utterly destitute at Fort Gibson alone.[516]   Farther west blacks, free [517] or unfree, were compelled by their very necessities to become desperadoes.   Cattle-driving served for them more than one purpose.

Grande and the Gulf Stream, for this people, to which I think they will gladly go, and which will save them from being trodden under foot by the advancing tide of Caucasian immigration from Europe, and from all the North.

"I have thought much upon this question.   I would like a word from you . . . " (Doolittle to Johnson, September 9, 1865, *Johnson Papers,* vol. 77).

For congressional discussion of negro colonization in Texas, see *Congressional Globe,* 38th cong., 1st sess., pp. 145, 238, 480, 586, 672.

[515] For an idea of how the Southerners shifted responsibility from their own shoulders upon those of the Northerners and the British, see Lowrey, *Northern Opinion of Approaching Secession,* p. 252.

[516] *Daily Conservative,* February 2, and 5, 1864.   Consult *Missionary Herald,* vol. lx, p. 102, for reference to a Freedmen's Relief Association.

[517] Even before the war, there were a number of free blacks in the Indian country.   In 1861, the Chickasaw Legislature passed resolutions, which were communicated by Secretary Smith to Secretary Cameron, April thirteenth, relative to the military reservations within the limits of the Choctaw and Chickasaw domain.   One of the resolutions stated that the Fort Arbuckle reservation alone was larger than the District of Columbia. It was a convenient harbor for free negroes.   Questions of their status, of exclusive jurisdiction, and of the right to cut timber were in consequence raised.   The Indians requested that all military reservations be reduced to one mile square (A.G.O., Old Files Section, 31 I, 1861).

Mistreatment of the colored people was not of usual occurrence in those days; but, as the war drew to its close and the full effects of peace were realized, it made its appearance. To the Choctaws and the Chickasaws, allies of the South to the end, the blacks became personally obnoxious, the more so as the Federals scrupled not to impress it upon them that they were now their own masters and in a position to make the most of opportunities theretofore denied them. The Indians, in a state of misery bordering upon despair, blamed the blacks for the war reverses and grew vindictive. A reign of terror is reported to have set in.[518]

[518] " . . . Reports have frequently reached me that the Choctaws and Chickasaws (nearly the entire people of both nations being, as you are aware, disloyal) are mistreating colored people attempting to travel through their territories.

"Three colored men have just made a statement to me on this subject.

"One of them was one of a party of several that attempted to come to this country some weeks ago. They were followed and fired upon — when they scattered in every direction. This man succeeded in making his escape, but reports at least two of the party killed. He came in with three other men, who went from here a short time ago to bring some friends, who are in that country, back with them – but failed, because of the hostility of those people.

"These colored men state that five colored men were in one place piled together, killed by the Indians. One told me he was in the yard of Gov. Chester (Winchester Colbert?) of the Chickasaws, and saw about two wagon loads of ammunition which had been captured from our army.

"They state that these tribes have the bitterest feeling toward the blacks, and are determined that they shall not pass through their country; nor leave it, and that they hold on to their slaves with the greatest tenacity, swearing in their enmity to the blacks that if it had not been for them (the blacks) the federals could never have whipped the south – that they (the Indians) are not whipped and that they are going to manage and control things in their country to suit themselves.

"I am satisfied that many of them are as disloyal as ever; and that the blacks are suffering a reign of terror.

"I feel confident that our Gov't will look into the matter."

(John A. Garrett to Captain H. D. B. Cutler, A.A.G., 3rd Division, 7th A. C., dated Head Quarters, District South Kansas, Fort Gibson, C.N.,

The Fort Smith Peace Council did nothing to mend matters. It made them worse if anything. Ringing the changes upon the theme of guilt and retribution left Indian misery unassuaged and accelerated the development of ill-feeling, not alone between tribal factions, implacably hostile, but between the reds and the blacks. In Indian Territory, as in the seceded states, a necessity arose for some sort of Federal interference and the conviction that it only could compel the several parties to be amenable to reason finally resulted in General Sanborn's being "assigned to such duty in regulating the relations between the Freedmen in the Indian Territory and their former masters as the Secretary of the Interior may indicate." [519]   Sanborn at the moment was in St. Louis [520] and telegraphed Harlan, November eighth, expressing his desire for a

July 22nd, 1865, A.G.O., Archives Division, *Fort Gibson Letter Book*, no. 20). The original of this communication was found by the author on the topmost floor of the Patent Office Building, Interior Department, among a lot of papers, several of which have been used in the making of this volume, that had been condemned by the congressional examining committee as valueless and consigned to destruction.

It is well to note that, although Garrett saw fit to complain thus of the Choctaws and Chickasaws, Bussey reported, June 26th, that they were using their influence for peace (*Official Records*, vol. xlviii, part ii, p. 1021) and, after the Fort Smith Council, they were most certainly desirous of adjusting themselves as soon as might be to the new conditions.

[519] Townsend to Cooley, October 20, 1865, O.I.A., General Files, *Southern Superintendency*, 1865, W 1182. Sanborn's commission was officially described as one for "regulating relations between freedmen in the Indian Territory and their former masters."

[520] He had negotiated, October 14, 1865, a treaty with the Cheyennes and Arapahoes and, October 18, 1865, one with the Kiowas and Comanches. Among Sanborn's *Personal Papers* in A.G.O. is a memorial biography of him issued by the Military Order of the Loyal Legion of the United States, Minnesota Commandery which records that, "Following this service he was assigned by the President to the duty of adjusting proper relations between the slaveholding tribes of Indians and their former slaves, which he did to the satisfaction of all concerned."

personal interview.[521]   It was accorded him on the six-teenth in Washington.

No matter what may have developed at the inter-view, Harlan's wishes were soon known.   On the twentieth he issued formal instructions, extracts of which are here given:[522]

"You will proceed as soon as practicable to the Indian Ter-ritory and establish your Head Quarters at such point as may be most convenient for the purpose herein indicated, and, as soon as possible thereafter, visit the various tribes heretofore holding slaves and make yourself acquainted with the present condition of the Freedmen and with the state of feeling, rela-tions, prejudices or difficulties existing between them and their former masters.

"In cases where the feeling existing between the parties is amicable and the relations satisfactory to both, and the rights of the Freedmen are fully acknowledged, you will not inter-fere or disturb those relations, but, in all cases where the rights of the Freedmen, as such, are denied by the Indians, or where abuses exist or wrongs are perpetrated upon the Freedmen, you will at once interfere and afford such relief as may be within your power.

"While acting thus, as the protector of the rights of the Freedmen you will be careful to impress upon them the fact that they will not be supported or encouraged in idle habits but must labor for their own support, and, to this end, you will encourage them in making contracts with such persons as may be willing to hire them as laborers, either for wages in money or receiving a share of the crops to be raised, such contracts should be made in writing and filed for reference and in no case extend for a longer period than one year, and where differences arise between the Freedmen and the Indians as to

[521] O.I.A., General Files, *Southern Superintendency*, 1865.

[522] The instructions are here given as they were published by direction of Sanborn, January 1, 1866, in *Circular no. 1*, (O.I.A., *Freedmen Files*). November 17th, Harlan, in a communication to Cooley, had concurred in his opinion that Cherokee freedmen should receive the same annuities, lands, and educational advantages as the Indians themselves.

the payment of wages, division of crops, right to property or other matters which cannot be adjusted by the parties themselves, you will act as arbitrator and make such award as equity and good conscience may appear to demand.

*   *   *   *   *   *   *   *

"It is deemed the best policy in the interest of both the Freedmen and their former masters, that the former should be provided with lands set apart for their especial and exclusive use, upon which they may reside and by their own labor, provide subsistence for themselves and their families.

*   *   *   *   *   *   *   *

"The several Indian Agents in the Territory are instructed to co-operate with you and act as your assistants . . .

*   *   *   *   *   *   *   *

"You will impress upon the Indians the justice of admitting the Freedmen to the enjoyment of all the rights of persons and property without reference to their former condition, and to an equal enjoyment of the bounty that may hereafter be bestowed by the National Government, and that it would be especially gratifying to the Government, if these Freedmen should be admitted to an equal enjoyment of civil rights. With this in view, you will explain to them that in this manner the Indians will rapidly augment their numbers and power – that they would thus be following the example of the white people of the United States who have, from the beginning, admitted to the rights of citizenship white people of all countries in the world, where there has appeared to exist no natural antagonism; that as a result of this policy the whites have grown so numerous and strong as to render it difficult for the President to prevent them crushing out the Indian race and that many of the States, including the richest and wisest, make no distinction in this respect on account of color.

*   *   *   *   *   *   *   *"

About a month after receiving his instructions from Harlan, Sanborn arrived in Fort Smith, at which place, that Mecca of all who had to do with the southern Indians, he intended, for the time being, to establish his headquarters. The opinions he had already formed regarding the status of the negroes, pre-war and post-war, can best be outlined in his own words; for he lost no time in imparting them to the government and in propagating them generally. The wide divergence of his opinions from those of General Hunt was significant.

"I arrived here on the 24th inst as previously communicated to you and had a long interview with General Hunt yesterday. His views differ widely from mine as to the status of the negroes in the Indian Territory both before and after the Emancipation Proclamation, as well as at the present time. He thinks that they were legally slaves before the war while my view is that they were only slaves in fact, as voluntary slaves, and hence always had a legal right to leave their masters and go anywhere, and that if any of them had escaped before the war to a free state they would have been free and could not have been returned by any proceeding or process of a court and only by brute force. To adopt any other view is, as it seems to me, admitting that slavery is the creature of the Common instead of the Municipal law and hence can exist anywhere in the will of any person or community. For the Government has never admitted the sovereignty of any Indian Tribe although it has recognized the tribal organization and permitted their customs to go on without interference and there was no law of Congress establishing it even by implication after the repeal of the Missouri Compromise. This question may have become impracticable and unimportant as the Constitutional Amendment has been or is about to be adopted. But I do not wish to convey incorrect ideas and impressions to the ignorant Indians and negroes and if in your judgment the above views are incorrect, I respectfully request you to

advise me at an early day.   I have no books or authorities to consult here but my recollection is that even the
"Dred Scott" decision although it went far towards it,
did not go to the length of establishing and legalizing
slavery in the Territory of the United States.   Under
Gen'l Hunt's view you will observe as this Territory
was not included in the Emancipation Proclamation
that the negroes are still slaves.   This is the one that
now obtains both with the Indians and negroes and all
are acting upon it.   General Hunt fears that if information is given to the negroes that they are free, they
will all abandon their old homes and haunts and rush
to the military posts and become solely dependent upon
the Government. [523]   I think however that such ideas
may be communicated to them of the rights and advantages they will have with the Indian tribes with
which they are connected that they will be disposed to
remain with them, and if such should be the result now,
it would probably be the same at any other time and the
sooner the trial is had the better.   Hence it is my intention to inform them all and at once that they are free
and that the Government will protect them in their
freedom where they are.[524]

"From the best information I have thus far obtained
there has been some bad treatment of the negroes by

[523] His own experience and the experience of Texas (Ramsdell, *Reconstruction in Texas*, p. 71) fully warranted the opinion.

[524] In instructing the Indian agents as to their duties in the premises,
Sanborn made it perfectly plain what he meant by this.

"Indian Agents of the respective tribes above referred to will at
once use every means in their power to impress upon the minds of
each individual of the tribes and nations, a clear and correct idea
of the new relation existing between them and their former slaves,
and these former slaves are now vested with the rights of freemen,
and that the whole power of the Federal Government is pledged to
the maintenance of their rights and the protection of their persons,
in their proper exercise; and that a wrong or outrage committed upon

the Indians; but nothing near as much as by the whites in Texas along the south side of Red River. I am already satisfied that the true course for the Government to pursue is to treat these negroes as part and parcel of the tribes to which they belong, giving them all the rights, interests, and annuities that are given to the Indians of the respective tribes, and leave it optional with the negroes to remain with the tribes or not.

"It seems to me to be of the utmost importance to confer at once upon the negroes of the Indian Territory as well as upon all the Freedmen of the country, the right to acquire title to hold and alienate real estate. Then they will soon acquire property, and will feel that they are responsible for their contracts and are liable to lose their property for a breach of them, and may be relied upon for a fulfillment of them which cannot be the case while they have no property, and can suffer no loss for their nonfulfillment.

"I met Boudinot and had a brief conversation with him. He said that he thought the incorporation of the negroes with the tribes would be satisfactory to all the tribes but the Choctaws, and that they would prefer that they should be colonized upon some portion of the Reservation but that the Indians would submit to whatever the Government thought best for them.

"These people have been born and raised together and there is no reason why they should be separated by any legal enactment. They should be granted the same rights and privileges and live together or separate as their own instincts or choice should dictate. The labor of all the negroes will be required by the Indians. The

one of them, is now looked upon, and will be treated by the United States, as a wrong or outrage committed upon a white citizen of the United States, and sooner or later to be punished accordingly." (*Circular*, no. I, *op. cit.*).

Commissary is very well supplied here and if a few supplies of that kind should be needed to prevent great suffering, they can be obtained here.

"After visiting the tribes I will make another and fuller report.[525]

"Since my arrival complaints have come to me from parties deemed responsible relative to the management of the Indian affairs here which I deem proper to communicate to you although not within the scope of my legitimate duties. These complaints are to the effect that the old house of McDonald & Co. which has been ordered out of the Indian Territory by the Sec'ty of War with its servants and agents now figures under the firm name of H. E. McKee & Co. at this place, Gray & Swift at Boggy Depot with a house also at Gibson, Washita & Arbuckle have entire control of all Indian business and that Superintendent Sells and Maj. Coleman collude with them to such an extent that all competition is excluded and contracts let to these men in the name of others at their own figures.

"As evidence of the correctness of those things the parties refer to advertisements for contracts for supplies, containing terms that no parties can possibly comply with except a "House" that has all the goods on or close to the place where they are to be delivered, and other conditions which seem to be put in for this very house.

"Of course I have not and shall not make any investi-

---

[525] Sanborn completed his tour of investigation very shortly and made his fuller report upon the basis of it in January. The report is embraced in two communications, one of date, the fifth (Commissioner of Indian Affairs, *Report*, 1866, pp. 283-285), and the other of date, the twenty-seventh (*ibid.*, pp. 285-286). Another communication in which Sanborn discussed a correspondence he had carried on with Hunt is equally important (Sanborn to Cooley, February 12, 1866, O.I.A., *Southern Superintendency*, S 119 of 1866).

gation into this matter, but it would seem at first glance that there is proper cause for complaint, and investigation and I simply communicate these complaints to you as they came to me. It is also positively asserted that the same parties are purchasing from the Indians, and constantly driving out large numbers of cattle in violation of the acts of Congress and the regulations of your Department.[526] This I think susceptible of positive proof, unless extraordinary privileges have been granted this house.

[526] The following have a bearing, direct or indirect, upon the matter:

(a) John W. Wright, Attorney for the Cherokees, to Harlan, September 22, 1865 (*ibid., Southern Superintendency,* 1865) asking that Agent Reynolds be required to render an account of money received for cattle.

(b) Henry J. Hunt to John Levering dated Fort Smith, October 9, 1865 to this effect:

"I have the honor to transmit herewith a letter from Governor Colbert, Chickasaw Nation, dated Tishomingo, C.N., September 27th, 1865, representing that robberies and horse stealing are common occurrences in the southern part of the Indian Territory, and asking that a company or two of cavalry be sent under a competent officer to afford some protection to the inhabitants.

"I have similar complaints of horse stealing from movers, coming through that country. Complaint on this subject was made by Governor Colbert and Governor Pitchlynn of the Choctaw Nation to Hon. Mr. Cooley, Commissioner of Indian Affairs, at the close of the Grand Council recently held at this place. Mr. Cooley spoke to me on the subject and stated that he would take their application to Little Rock and have it referred to me from that place.

"I had heard nothing further on the subject, when Governor Colbert's letter was received. Governor Colbert also desires that the Refugee Indians should be removed, if practicable. There is reason to fear, that some of these Indians may have been driven by their necessities, to commit depredations, but I think it will be found, that white men are the principal robbers.

"I do not know that anything can be done with the Refugee Indians, nor indeed with respect to horse thieves, until the treaty questions now pending, are settled . . . " (*ibid.,* L 805).

(c) Lewis C. True to Colonel John N. Craig, October 9, 1865. " . . . There are a great many cattle being driven through the Territory, purporting to come from Texas. Please inform me if the responsibility rests on me in the event of their having been sto-

"I see no way of raising any funds here to defray expences, and you must not be surprised if I draw upon you for a few hundred dollars at no very distant day."[527]
The high-handed way[528] in which Sanborn con-

len . . . " (A.G.O., Archives Division, *Fort Gibson Letter Book*, no. 20, p. 107).

(d) True to Captain H. D. B. Cutler, October 19, 1865, in reply to Cutler's of October 13th. True advises co-operation of the civil and military authorities and says, "Strict compliance with these suggestions . . . will most effectually prohibit cattle stealing in the future." (*ibid.*, p. 109).

(e) Cooley to Levering, October 25, 1865, acknowledging the receipt of communications relative to robberies in the southern part of Indian Territory as complained of by Governor Colbert and General Hunt (O.I.A., *Letter Book*, no. 78, p. 350. See also p. 353).

(f) Jesse Bushyhead to J. A. Coffy, May 5, 1866 complaining that he had purchased two hundred head of cattle and was driving them northward when he was stopped by the Indian agents (*ibid.*, General Files, *Cherokee*, 1859-1865, B 137).

(g) Captain Charles E. Howe to Major P. Lugenbeel, 19th U.S. Infantry, Commanding Post of Fort Gibson, dated Little Rock, June 15, 1866,

"Referring to your communication of April 28th, 1866, stating that numbers of persons are engaged in buying and stealing mules, horses, cattle &c in and through the Choctaw and Chickasaw nations of Indians, and that from the scarcity of such stock in the country, in your opinion, the continuance of such practices will have an injurious tendency, produce want, and lead to reprisals and bloodshed, I am instructed by the Major General Commanding to say that you are authorized to issue such orders as the nature of the case may, in your judgment, demand for the preventing of such injurious and illegitimate practices in future." (I. D. Files. This document, when found, bore no file-mark and had been set aside for destruction).

(h) Pinkney Lugenbeel to Howe, April 29, 1866 (A.G.O., Archives Division, *Fort Gibson Letter Book*, no. 20).

[527] Sanborn to Cooley, December 26, 1865, O.I.A., General Files, *Southern Superintendency*, 1865, S 101.

[528] Note the grandiloquent phrasing of this sixth section of his first circular,

"Every effort will be made to remove all prejudices on the part of the Indians against the Freedmen remaining in their country. That they are free is not the result of any action of their own, but that of the United States Government, and the Government having triumphed over all its enemies insists that this action shall be acknowledged and accepted by all people coming under its jurisdiction. All

ducted himself in his solicitude for the blacks, while
entirely comparable to that of other northerners elsewhere in the South and authorized by parallel principles and practices of his superiors, Harlan and
Cooley, was only to a very small degree justified. The
Cherokees, whose slaves had been free for the two years
just past, were resentful of interference in their domestic concerns.[529] They were doing their level best to
make their own re-adjustments and ought to have been
trusted to do the square thing. The re-adjustments
would never have been an easy matter under the most
favorable of conditions. Had the community been
white and fully under the jurisdiction of the United
States in normal times, certain of Sanborn's regulations
might have been conceded to have their foundation in
reason; but, as it was, they were of doubtful validity
and predestined to do no more than provoke tribal opposition. Among the loyal Indians, as in a border
state, snatched from secession, as was Maryland, self-
reconstruction might well have been given a trial.
Nothing had as yet been done to extend legally United
States laws over the Indian country and yet Sanborn
made them, by his own fiat, operative in all matters
affecting freedmen. He was himself a New Hamp-

will be made to understand that the policy of the Government as
contained in the instructions herein published, is fixed and determined
and that its whole power and energy will be devoted to carrying it
into effect, and a race famous for its prowess and shrewdness will at
once see that they have no interests that can be subserved by placing
themselves in a position of antagonism or hostility to the mightiest
power of Earth at a period of its proudest achievements and greatest
glory." (*op. cit.*).

529 Hunt to Cooley, November 28, 1865, enclosing report of Lieutenant
Holmes of conditions in the Choctaw and Chickasaw country and of
Lieutenant John H. Kellenberger of those in the Cherokee (O.I.A., General Files, *Southern Superintendency*, 1865, H 1323); Cooley to Hunt, December 15, 1865 (*ibid., Letter Book*, no. 79, p. 23).

shire man by blood and birth and breeding and found
it impossible to reconcile polygamy and promiscuous
intercourse with his Puritan self-righteousness and
highly-developed moral sense.   He therefore ordered
the discontinuance of all such practices among the Indians, they being contrary to the laws of his own government.[530]

Much less compliant than the Cherokees were the
Choctaws and Chickasaws.   Stand upon their rights
they would regardless of United States officials whatever their rank and yet they too endeavored to adapt
themselves betimes to the new order of things.   Immediately after the adjournment of the Fort Smith
Council, Chief Pitchlynn subtly took occasion, when
urging that the United States afford "protection and
domestic tranquility pending the adoption and ratifica-

[530] "The system of polygamy, or plurality of wives which has always
existed to some extent among the Indian tribes, has been adopted to a
greater or less extent by the Freedmen of the Indian Nation. This
system, being in violation of the laws of the United States, will be
abandoned at the earliest practicable day, and no Freedman will be
allowed hereafter to take to himself more than one wife and will be
bound to live with her as long as both live, unless separated by proper
authority for good cause shown. In all cases where a Freedman is
now living or cohabiting with one woman only, the parties will be
considered as legally united in the bonds of matrimony and all the
rights incident to that relation will be granted to, and enforced by
the Government against all parties interested. Marriages which have
been or may be solemnized after the custom of the Indian Nation, in
which the parties reside for the time being, will be considered binding
and valid in law where the parties are competent to marry, not having
a husband or wife living. Until other provision is made any Indian
Agent may, upon any Freedman and woman coming before him and
signifying their desire to be united as man and wife, if he be satisfied
that the man has no wife and that the woman has no husband living,
take their mutual promises to live together as man and wife, and give
them a certificate accordingly. He shall also keep a record of the
marriage, showing the names of the parties and date of marriage,
and at the end of his term, send the same or a copy thereof to the
office of the Commissioner of Indian Affairs." *Circular*, no. I, *op. cit.*).

tion of treaties," to let the pliancy and breadth of his views be known. Speaking for the Choctaws, he said, in a letter to Cooley, dated Fort Smith, September 21, 1865,

> "In concluding an abandonment of our rights of property in our slaves, we do not wish to be considered as abandoning all interest in their present and future welfare. If they are secured their freedom by the United States Government, we desire that it should be on such terms as will make that freedom as valuable to them as can be consistent with the rights of their late owners, and the peace and well-being of the community.
>
> "To this end we respectfully ask that a discreet and competent agent of the Bureau of Freedmen, &c be sent to each Nation . . . "

Between the second and seventh of October, the Chickasaws held the first session of their legislature that had been possible since the beginning of the war. In convening the body, Governor Colbert delivered himself of a message that, in loftiness of tone and obvious honesty of intention, challenges comparison with the best. Its most essential portions are as follows:

> "The annual meeting of the Legislature of the Chickasaw Nation under the providence of God being again permitted, it becomes us as a nation to acknowledge our dependence on his will and lift our hands in thankfulness for the preservation of our people amid the dangers and vicissitudes through which our country has passed.
>
> "Since my last message to the Legislature, we have experienced the effects of war in its worst form. So rapid has been the change by the late revolution, which has terminated in the submission of all the States of the United States to the authority of the General Government and so stupendous its results, present and prospective, that the mind becomes bewildered in contemplating them.
>
> "It is consolatory however to reflect that under all the trying circumstances, under which the Chickasaws have labored, they

have been true to themselves and their plighted national faith. Their course is a matter of history and we refer to the record, confidently relying upon a favorable verdict, not only from an impartial world, but from the Government of the United States itself, which is too powerful and magnanimous to take advantage of a weak people, who were compelled by the force of circumstances and the current of events, in order to preserve their existence, to assume a hostile attitude towards that Government, to whom, previously, our people had always looked for parental protection and guidance.

"It becomes my duty to inform your honorable body that by special request of the authorities of the United States the commissioners on the part of the Choctaw and Chickasaw Nations, together with those of other nations embraced in the Indian Confederation, with their respective Executives, met commissioners on the part of the United States in council at Fort Smith on the 15th of September last. The result of which was a general treaty of peace and friendship between the United States and all the Indian nations represented in said council and the submission of a *Project*, or outline of a Treaty, which the Gov't of the United States wishes to make with the various Indian nations; for which purpose and to arrange and settle all matters with the Government of the United States growing out of their connection with the so-called Confederate States, which may tend to interrupt or interfere with the resumption of their former relations with the Government of the United States, it is proposed that Commissioners be sent to Washington City by the several Indian nations . . .

"Among the subjects presented by the Gov't of the United States for your consideration the slave question stands prominently forth. It is now plain that emancipation is inevitable and it is the part of wisdom to meet the question fairly and that means be devised to bring about the manumission of slaves at the earliest practicable period, and, in the meantime, to secure the peace and quiet of that unfortunate class of persons and render them by suitable provisions and arrangements useful to the community.

"There is at present great diversity of opinion among the people as to the *status* of the negro among us. In my opinion the good of the community requires that the Legislature shall lay down a uniform rule of action for all in reference to slaves, so that there may be no confusion growing out of this subject among the people or among the slaves themselves. Their emancipation is now a mere question of time and the sooner in accordance with the constitution the better for all parties . . . " [531]

Following the receipt of Colbert's message, the Chickasaw Legislature adopted a resolution empowering the governor to issue a proclamation calling upon the people to make what arrangements they could with their slaves. It was, as Colbert adroitly remarked, in a letter to Hunt, October 11, 1865, the precise method by which Pennsylvania and other northern states had all got rid of slavery. For two reasons, legislative emancipation was not enacted. There was a clause in the Chickasaw constitution that forbade manumission without compensation to owners and the Chickasaws had no means wherewith to compensate. Moreover, since, under the recent amity, the United States had arrogated to itself the entire control over slavery, it

---

[531] D. H. Cooper submitted to Cooley, October 18, 1865, a statement of the proceedings of the Chickasaw Legislature, also a copy of the governor's message of October 4th, convening that body, and of his proclamation of October 11th, complying with its enactment. Incidentally, also, Cooper requested leave to proceed to Washington to settle his ante-war accounts and to apply for a pardon. With reference to the institution of slavery, Cooper reported,

"The people are in advance of the action of the legislature which was trammeled by the constitution as it stands.

"Nearly all in the Chickasaw Nation have set their slaves at liberty – and in most cases I believe the negroes will remain with their former owners.

"I called up mine & gave them choice to go elsewhere or remain & work, promising the able-bodied & middle aged either fair wages or a reasonable share in the crops.

"At present the latter is the only way to remunerate them – there is little or no money in the country & no sale for produce . . . "
(O.I.A., General Files, *Choctaw*, 1859-1866, C 1629).

seemed worse than useless for the Indians to act in anything like a national way.[532]

Governor Colbert's proclamation, issued at Tishomingo, October 11, 1865, outlined a policy that, in practice, could not fail to work disastrously against the negroes. It belied the fair promise of his message. The interests of the planters had decidedly first place.

PROCLAMATION

Whereas the Legislature of the Chickasaw Nation at its late session, in view of the unsettled state of affairs within said Nation and more especially in reference to the slaves, did by Resolution direct that the Governor issue his proclamation informing the people of the present position of the Nation in relation to the United States Government, and authorizing all slaveholders to make suitable arrangements with their negroes, such as may be most conducive to the interest and welfare of both owners and slaves.

Now, therefore, I, Winchester Colbert, Governor of the Chickasaw Nation, do issue this my proclamation informing the people of said nation that a treaty of peace and friendship, repudiating all treaties with any other foreign nation or power, was concluded between the Commissioners on the part of the United States and the Commissioners on the part of the Chickasaw Nation, at Fort Smith, Arks., on the 18th day of Sept., A.D. 1865, and I do hereby require all persons subject to the jurisdiction of the Chickasaw Nation to observe and conform to the same until other treaties securing the rights and interests of the Chickasaw people can be negotiated by the commissioners appointed by the Legislature to visit Washington City for that purpose.

In view of the fact that under the treaty of peace lately concluded at Fort Smith, the United States reserved jurisdiction over the question of slavery within the Indian Territory and in

---

[532] Winchester Colbert to Hunt, October 11, 1865, *ibid.* General Hunt telegraphed Colbert's letter to him to Cooley, October 24, 1865, and forwarded Colbert's message and proclamation by mail. For references to these documents, see Commissioner of Indian Affairs, *Report*, 1865, pp. 357-358.

conformity with the authority given me by the Legislature, I hereby advise all slaveholders within the Chickasaw Nation to make suitable arrangements with their negroes – such as will be most conducive to the interest and welfare of both owners and slaves.

While the owners, under the Resolution of the Legislature, are authorized to make any arrangements which may be agreed upon with their negroes, I would respectfully suggest, for their consideration, the following plan, which appears to meet the requirements and it is hoped would receive the approval of the President of the U. S., to wit,

1st. That all negroes under 21 years of age be apprenticed, under indentures in due form, to their former owners until of age, it being stipulated in addition to food and clothing for said young negroes, out of their labor the aged and infirm, over fifty years, shall be provided for.

2nd. All middle aged negroes to be employed at such wages as may be agreed upon between them and their former owners.

It is believed such an arrangement will meet the approval of the President and People of the North, it being the self-same plan upon which several, if not all, the original Northern States got rid of slavery.

Not all that General Sanborn had stigmatised as prejudice against the blacks was such. No less in Indian Territory than in Mississippi did a too generous treatment produce demoralization.[533] The negro had little disposition to labor and the contract system [534] that Sanborn devised was not conducive to the best

---

[533] Garner, *Reconstruction in Mississippi*, p. 118.

[534] "As the Freedmen of the Indian Territory seem competent to make their own contracts, it is deemed better, that the price of labor should be regulated by the demand for, and supply of the same, but every effort will be made and means used to encourage habits of industry, on the part of the Freedmen, and Agents will see that fair compensation is paid for all labor, and will furnish every facility to Freedmen to reduce or have their contracts for labor reduced to writing. Where the contract is for a longer term than one month, and no contract for a longer term will be enforced by the Government, unless the same shall be reduced to writing and signed in triplicate by the respective parties thereto and a copy sent to the Head Quarters of this Commission to

economic results. Moreover, much that the government stipulated should be done, tended to create a prejudice since it was very patently based upon the idea of giving the negro so-called justice regardless of how much injustice might thereby be meted out to the Indian. The most glaring instance of the kind is to be found in a ruling of the Commissioner of Indian Affairs, November sixteenth, "that no distinction be made between members of the Cherokee tribe who were held in bondage and those who were free. That in all cases they should receive the same annuities, lands and educational advantages . . . " In this requirement, Secretary Harlan concurred [535] notwithstanding that, by no treaty arrangement yet made, had it been endorsed either by the United States government or by the Indian nation.

The setting apart of the negroes as objects of consideration,[536] especially worthy, at a time, too, when

be filed, and one retained by each party. This contract shall be in the following form . . . (Circular, No. 1, *op. cit.*).

[535] Harlan to Cooley, November 17, 1865, O.I.A., General Files, *Cherokee, 1859-1865.*

[536] That Sanborn did make them objects of special consideration the regulations embodied in his Circular, no. 4 amply bear witness. They are published here entire.

HEAD QUARTERS, COMMISSION FOR REGULATING RELATIONS BETWEEN FREEDMEN OF THE INDIAN TERRITORY, AND THEIR FORMER MASTERS.

Fort Smith, Ark., January 27th, 1866

CIRCULAR No. 4.

I...That all may have a full and clear understanding of the rights of the Freedmen of the Indian Territory, and the liabilities of such persons as retain and employ them without any specific contract, the following principles or rules are published:

1st. Every Freedman, woman and child, retained by, or for any person without a definite contract, is entitled to receive from the party so retaining them, or for whom he or she works, so much as his or her labor and time, is reasonably worth, at any time within six years, before any competent tribunal.

2d. The father, if living, and if not, the mother or guardian, is

the Indians themselves were in misery from economic dislocation, was most inexpedient. Not so badly off

entitled to the pay and compensation for the services and labor of the child.

3rd. The husband is entitled to the compensation for the labor and services of his wife, when the parties are living and co-habiting together.

4th. Any person who refuses to deliver a child, to his or her parent or guardians, upon demand or request made by such parent, or guardian, becomes liable to a suit in the U.S. District Court, at the instance of the party entitled to the custody of the child, for damages for false imprisonment, and to have such child taken from them, by a writ of Habeas Corpus.

5th. Contracts for work and labor of minor children, will in all cases, when possible, be made with their parents, or guardians, and will, in all cases, provide for the subsistence, clothing, and if possible, for a certain amount of schooling for the child, each year.

6th. Contracts for the labor of the wife, must, in all cases, when possible, be made with the husband.

The slave code, or laws relating to the Negroes of the respective Indian tribes, who have held slaves, are no longer in force, and will not be executed. The United States Government having abolished slavery throughout its domains, the laws relating to slaves, are no longer of any force or validity, and any officer of any of the nations who executes the same, will be liable to be arrested and punished in the United States Court in the same manner as if his action was without color of legal proceedings.

II...In those nations and tribes that have incorporated the Freedmen into their tribes, and granted them tribal rights and privileges, the Freedmen will be subject to their laws and customs in the same manner, and to the same extent as an Indian of such tribes. But in those nations that have not thus incorporated them or recognized them as a part and parcel of their nation, or tribe, the Freedmen are not, and will not, be subject to their laws, or customs, but stand upon the same footing as to legal rights, as all other citizens of the United States, except that they are in the Indian Territory, by proper authority, and will in no case be interfered with, unless guilty of some criminal offence.

III...While all are requested to recognize the legal rights of the Freedmen, they will not forget that their comfortable subsistence, clothing and education, are the paramount objects sought to be attained at present, and as the season has so far advanced that it will be impracticable for the Freedmen to secure and open farms for themselves in time to raise a crop the coming summer, they are all advised and recommended to remain with their present employers, in all cases where comfortable clothing and subsistence for themselves and their families for one year will be secured thereby, unless they are certain

were the negroes but that they could have waited, until after the crying needs of refugees and of indigents had been attended to, to have their exact political status determined. Some of the refugees were not yet restored and the indigents were widely scattered. At the time of the Fort Smith Council there were reported to be six thousand Cherokees on Red River,[537] needy and friendless, far distant from their own desolate homes, and there were Seminoles in the lowlands of the Washita.[538] Of the refugees, there were some yet in Kansas and there were some freedmen there also. The latter had been ordered out of Indian Territory and away from danger by the United States military authorities when the country north of the Arkansas had been first regained in 1862.[539] They had gone across the border;

they can do much better before, they make an attempt to change their condition.

In some instances, children will be better off, living with their former masters than with their parents, until their parents secure a home, and more means of supporting them; and it may be better that parental affection in such cases, should for the time being, yield to policy.

At a time like the present, all, of all classes, should exercise the greatest prudence, soundest judgment and longest forbearance, and make the greatest efforts to harmonize what seems conflicting; to bring system and order out of confusion; to elevate and enlighten the laboring masses; to repair the great waste of war by constant industry, and to secure protection, competency, and happiness to all classes of men.

IV...The copy of contract designed for this Commission as required in Circular No. 1, may in all cases, be filed with the Indian Agent for the tribe, to which the parties or any of them belong.

JOHN B. SANBORN,
Brevet Maj. Gen'l. & Commissioner.

Fort Smith New Era, Print.

[537] Boudinot and others to Cooley, September 19, 1865, Commissioner of Indian Affairs, *Report*, 1865, p. 347.

[538] John Jumper to Cooley, September 19, 1865, *ibid.*, p. 351.

[539] See O.I.A., *Cherokee Freedmen, Claim*, no. 68 (1892), being the case of Isabell Vann, who was the property of Washington Adair "until some time in July, 1862 when all the Freedmen in the Cherokee Nation were ordered by the U. S. officers to go to Kansas . . . " There are many

but the Kansans, once so solicitous about the negro's welfare, were now importuning for the removal of all Indian freedmen still lingering there.[540]

At the Fort Smith Council, Cooley, appealed to by prominent Indian secessionists like Boudinot and John Jumper, had been convinced of the urgent necessity of relieving Indian distress south of the Canadian and, upon his return to Washington, had made arrangements whereby a corps of special agents[541] were employed to administer relief to the southern indigents, the additional expence, since there was no special congressional appropriation to cover it, to be borne by the regular Indian funds.[542] Under a budgetary system, a proceeding of the sort would have been legally impos-

other cases of the same sort on record in the Indian Office. Claim, no. 27, was the case of Emily Walker who, a negress, was employed as an interpreter and scout by Colonel Phillips.

[540] Sells to Cooley, November 14, 1865, enclosing a communication from Sidney Clarke, member of congress, and Dr. W. S. G. Miller, applying for aid to remove Cherokee colored persons to their former homes in the Cherokee country (O.I.A., General Files, *Cherokee*, 1859-1865, S 829).

[541] "During the late rebellion, a large number of the Indians inhabiting the Indian Territory, espoused the cause of the enemies of the Government and joined with them in open hostilities against our laws and people. The result of this was, that the desolation of war was carried into the Indian country and, at its close, these deluded people find themselves impoverished and houseless. But they, in common with our other enemies, have submitted to the supremacy of the constitution and laws and are now at peace with the Government; and although it is not a matter of duty on the part of the Government to take care of them, the common dictates of humanity indicate that they should not be allowed to suffer and perish.

"You have therefore . . . been appointed a Special Agent . . .

"The tribes . . . are those south of the Canadian River and near the Red River and include part of the Cherokees, Creeks, Seminoles, possibly a few Choctaws and Chickasaws, and the Wichitas . . . "
(Cooley to Smith, November 10, 1865, O.I.A., *Letter Book*, no. 78, pp. 416-418).

[542] " . . . The employment of Special Agents in your superintendency, being rendered necessary by the peculiar condition of affairs there, and not being provided for by any treaty nor expressly author-

sible; but it was no new thing to divert tribal money
from its legitimate purposes and, as usual in the case
of such emergencies in the Indian service, the whole
affair proved but another opportunity for graft and
speculation.[543]   A new set of "harpies" had been let
loose.   The most prominent of the special agents was
Egbert T. Smith, whose services as Acting Assistant
Commissioner of Freedmen General Sanborn early
secured.[544]   Smith's relief was distributed from Boggy
Depot; but relief failed to reach the Indians and, in
February, Cooley was compelled to subject Smith,[545]
likewise John Field,[546] who had charge of the Wichitas
and had been similarly remiss, to a severe reprimand.
Not even Sells escaped censure and admonishment.
He had far exceeded the authorized amount of expenditure and with nothing appreciable of the results
intended.[547]   With maize purchasable at a dollar a
bushel in the Choctaw country[548] and Indian funds

ized by law, their salaries must be paid out of the appropriations for
the various tribes . . . " (Cooley to Sells, November 14, 1865,
ibid., p. 428).

[543] There is a great deal of material in the Indian Office records and
files to substantiate this statement; but note especially *Letter Book*, no. 79,
pp. 186-187, 227, 234, 541-542, 559; no. 80, p. 108. Smith's corn and blanket
contracts were held to be fraudulent. Perry Fuller and his associates were
involved in the nefarious transactions.

[544] See Circular, no. 3, dated January 17, 1866. In Circular, no. 2, of
date January 2, 1866, Sanborn had shown to how great an extent he had
acted upon the authority given him to requisition the services of Indian
agents.

[545] Cooley to Smith, February 3, 1866, O.I.A., *Letter Book*, no. 79, p. 249.
[546] For the criticism of Field, *ibid.*, p. 255.
[547] Cooley to Sells, April 6, 1866, *ibid.*, p. 559.
[548] "Col. Levering who is with Mr. Smith at Boggy Depot says corn
can be procured in that region for one dollar per bushel. It is
doubtful if the condition of the freedmen can be much improved till
military posts are established and garrisoned in the country . . . "
(Telegram, Sanborn to Cooley, December 28, 1865, O.I.A., General
Files, *Southern Superintendency*, 1865).

dwindling at a deplorable rate, the indigents remained indigents.[549]   All through the spring and the summer of 1866 there was never any report but that of absolute destitution.[550]

The freedmen were fellow-sufferers with the indigent Indians; but Sanborn had long since discovered that the reports of their ill-treatment by their ex-masters had been grossly exaggerated.[551]   Only in very rare instances had they been genuinely discriminated against.   Such measures as the odious black laws of Mississippi [552] had small chance of enactment where full-blooded Indians had a voice.   Almost might it be contended that the United States authorities themselves created the negro problem in Indian Territory and it was largely because of the half-breeds, the same who had betrayed the tribes to secession that they did so. Rough was the road of transition from slavery to free-

---

[549] In June General J. M. Hedrick was authorized to begin an investigation into the "irregularities and frauds committed by persons supplying the destitute Indians at and near Boggy Depot . . . " (Cooley to Hedrick, June 4, 1866, *ibid., Letter Book*, no. 80, p. 299).

[550] For example, see Cooley to Harlan, May 10, 1866, O.I.A., *Report Book*, no. 15, p. 268; Cooley to Harlan, August 22, 1866, *ibid.*, p. 433.

[551] In illustration, note the single instance of something derogatory reported to Sanborn about Governor Colbert.   The informant was a chief, Lewis Johnson.   His story was "that Governor Colbert stated to many people, and publicly, before leaving for Washington, that they should hold the slaves until they could determine at Washington whether or not they could get pay for them, and if they could not then they would strip them naked and drive them south to Texas, or north to Fort Gibson.   So bitter is the feeling against the return of the negroes that have been in the federal army, that Major Coleman and myself have concluded that it is not safe or advisable for Lewis Johnson and party to return until troops are stationed at Arbuckle . . . " Sanborn reported the foregoing the fifth of January (Commissioner of Indian Affairs, *Report*, 1866, p. 284) and, on the thirty-first, when his knowledge was broader, he telegraphed to Cooley, " . . . things look better . . . Choctaw and Chickasaw people accept the policy of the Government . . . Accusation against Governor Colbert not correct . . . " (O.I.A., General Files, *Choctaw*, 1859-1866).

[552] Chadsey, *President Johnson and Reconstruction*, p. 44.

dom; but far rougher was that that the once opulent Indian had to tread in order to get back to political security and economic ease. In Alabama and Georgia [553] forsooth, the ex-slaves manifested a disposition to migrate, to wander away from their old haunts with nothing but memory to remind them of previous bondage; but not so those of Indian Territory. There existence had never been irksome. Indian and negro had, fundamentally, a great deal in common. They were both naturally slothful and incompetent. The rebuilding of the country under their auspices had all of the character of a forlorn hope. The possibility of it could scarcely be envisaged. Had it not been for the half-breeds, sheer chaos would have come and stayed. Nevertheless, it was the half-breeds that semi-philanthropists like Sanborn distrusted and it was on their account that the mistake was made of thinking that whatever was done for the freedmen in the states ought, in the same or larger measure, to be done for the freedmen of Indian Territory. There were those who would have insisted that Trumbull's civil rights bill comprehended the Indian freedmen; but such a contention would have been absurd. Indians not taxed were excluded from its operation and its benefits. Indian tribal law held sway in Indian Territory. Assuredly then the negroes there could not claim to be a privileged class.

In January, General Sanborn, after having made himself acquainted by actual examination with the conditions prevailing among the Indian freedmen, was able to correct some of his own earlier notions. He made a preliminary report [554] on the fifth, valuable only

[553] Thompson, *Reconstruction in Georgia*, p. 44.

[554] Commissioner of Indian Affairs, *Report*, 1866, pp. 283-285.

as it concerned itself with the Cherokees, Seminoles and Creeks, whose countries were the ones he had then visited. A canvass of opinions had convinced him that the Muscogee, Creeks and Seminoles, would not be found averse to an actual incorporation of the freedmen into the tribes; but that the Cherokees would prefer and would probably insist upon the removal of the freedmen either to another place altogether or to a tract of Cherokee land, which the tribe would set apart for their exclusive use. "Colonel Downing," so Sanborn reported, "says that this policy will obtain in the nation, and that civil rights will be accorded to the freedmen before a great while."

To ameliorate the condition of the Choctaw and Chickasaw freedmen, Sanborn vigorously recommended the establishment of a strong military force at Boggy Depot, and at Forts Lawson, Washita and Arbuckle. He had not, when he prepared his report of the fifth, made any investigation of his own; but he hesitated not to discuss conditions as hearsay evidence represented them. Before the twenty-seventh, he had visited the Red River country and had then occasion to modify and even to repudiate much of what he had earlier believed.[555] The prejudice against the negroes he found to be "rapidly passing away." The treatment of them had "not been so bad and cruel as might be inferred" and such cruelty and injustice as did exist could legitimately be attributed to the existence of a slave code, which was considered by the Indians to be "still in force" and was being "executed upon all blacks accordingly." The situation of the freedwomen made a peculiar appeal to Sanborn and, for them, he asked particular attention. In individual cases, they had a

[555] Sanborn to Harlan, January 27, 1866, *ibid.*, pp. 285-286.

numerous progeny and yet "have not and never have had any husbands." "The large number of children of this class of females is a bar to their receiving good husbands, and unless some provision is made for them their case and that of their children is most hopeless." Sanborn's prognostication, in this regard, was only too true; for the Choctaws, most stubbornly of all the Indians, have ever insisted that legally the offspring of Indian men and negro women are negroes, unalterably and forever. Their status is different from that of the offspring of Indian women and negro men. The squaw belongs to her tribe always. Her children, legitimate or illegitimate, are its care.[556]

Sanborn's latest solution of the freedman problem was a treaty arrangement and, for that, he had many suggestions to make, a consideration of which will find its proper place in the next chapter. His investigation made, he felt that his work was done. What remained was the province of the Indian agents. He, therefore, asked for his discharge; but was told that he must first be relieved of the task as set by the Department of the Interior.[557] The entire country was then agitated over increasing signs of controversy between congress and

---

[556] *Senate Documents*, nos. 257, 298, 59th congress, 2nd session.

[557] Your muster-out of service as directed in General Orders, no. 168, from this office of Dec. 28, 1865 will not take effect until you are relieved from the duty to which you were assigned by Special Orders, no. 559, from this office, dated Oct. 20, 1865, under the direction of the Interior Department (Townsend to Sanborn, January 11, 1866, A.G.O., Old Files Section, 26 S.C.B., 1866). Sanborn reapplied for discharge in April (Commissioner of Indian Affairs, *Report*, 1866, p. 287) and was mustered out, May 31, 1866 (*Memorial Biography*, A.G.O., *Personal Papers of John B. Sanborn*). The Minnesota delegation, in July, and again, in August, requested his appointment to the post of sutler at Fort Wadsworth, Dakota Territory (Wm. Windom, Ignatius Donnelly, and Alexander Ramsey to Stanton, July 24, 1866; Ignatius Donnelly to Stanton, August 24, 1866, *ibid.*, 1019, S.C.B., 1866).

the president. Johnson had vetoed the Freedmen's Bureau Bill and, although his papers [558] reveal that he had much popular support for his action, nevertheless the times were growing politically critical. The treatment of the negro anywhere and everywhere was become a sensitized theme. In March, Pinkney Lugenbeel assumed command at Fort Gibson and, before very long, he saw reason to report that hostile feelings towards the freedmen were on the increase. The reverse of what Sanborn had prophesied was happening. Cherokee purchasers of confiscated property were ordering the former slaves of the original owners to vacate their little cabins. The tribe was opposed to their leasing property. It was opposed to the idea of their acquiring citizenship and was increasingly anxious for their final departure from the country. Lugenbeel found the negro inordinately lazy; but, nevertheless, he aimed, and rightly, to secure to him a measure of justice. [559]

[558] Examine particularly volumes 87-91.

[559] The following are selected from Lugenbeel's numerous reports to prove these various points:

Lugenbeel to Craig, March 7, 1866, A.G.O., Archives Division, *Fort Gibson Letter Book*, no. 20; Lugenbeel to General Commissary of Subsistence, June 16, 1866, *ibid.*; Lugenbeel to Ord, September 12, 1866, *ibid.*; Lugenbeel to Assistant Adjutant-general, Department of Arkansas, October 20, 1866, *ibid.*; Lugenbeel to Major O. D. Greene, December 27, 1866, *ibid.*

Supplementing Lugenbeel's reports, although in cases antedating them, are the following from the Indian Office files:

Telegram, Sanborn to Cooley, February 13, 1866 expressing a wish that President Johnson's disapproval of the Choctaw and Chickasaw laws relative to their former slaves might be telegraphed to the agents (*Southern Superintendency*, S 120 of 1866) ; J. J. Reynolds to Harlan, February 12, 1866 with various enclosures (*ibid.*, I 127) ; Sanborn to Cooley, March 28, 1866, transmitting his Circular, no. 6 (*ibid.*, S 203) ; Sanborn to Cooley, April 10, 1866, transmitting copies of a correspondence between him and Lugenbeel, touching conditions in the Cherokee country (*ibid.*, S 216) ; J. Harlan to Sells, April 30, 1866 on same subject (*ibid.*, S 237).

IX. THE EARLIER OF THE RECONSTRUC-
TION TREATIES OF 1866

The Fort Smith Council had resulted in nothing more than the establishment of formal peace between the government at Washington and the several nations of Indian Territory; but it would have been all-sufficient for the resumption of the old-time relations between guardian and ward had the United States authorities been disposed to act magnanimously or even justly in the premises and to take their due share of responsibility for the original Indian defection, since Federal troops had, under orders, abandoned the region at the first threat of war and white agents, holding office by Federal appointment, had directed Indian thought towards secession and, repudiating allegiance to the Union themselves, had lured the red men on. Unfortunately for the national honor, however, the Indian land was coveted. So good an opportunity for revoking the agreements of earlier years, made when the Indians were stronger than now, more unquestionably in the right, was not to be lost. The Homestead measure was law.[560] Settlers were already proving its efficacy in the acquirement of homes and farms easily and surely. The country was bound to fill up rapidly. Then too the era of gigantic railway enterprises and of equally gigantic government land grants to would-be capitalists was just beginning. The future location of freedmen had to be considered. These and many other

---

[560] See Act of May 20, 1862 (12 *United States Statutes at Large*, 392-394) and Amendatory Act of March 21, 1864 (*ibid.*, vol. 13, pp. 35-36).

things determined the course that Harlan and his con-
fréres, Cooley and Sells, all western men from the single state of Iowa, were bent upon pursuing.

The Fort Smith Council had closed its sessions with
the intention of continuing negotiations later on in
Washington. Only too well did the Indians comprehend that their fate was hanging in the balance. Its
main features had yet to be decided. The loyalists
among them feared the worst, yet had every reason, in
justice and in law, to hope for the best. The secessionists, keener than the rank and file, grasped the situation accurately and prepared to turn it to their own
advantage. Only because of the apostasy of these men
had the present predicament come. If they personally
could emerge from it unscathed, with fortunes relatively unimpaired, they cared little what might befall
their late hostile and now resentful tribesmen. The
Indians in a national way were doomed to suffer and
nobody appreciated that fact more completely than
did those who had made spoliation seem a justifiable
measure.

It was in the spirit of taking time by the forelock
and of seizing an advantage while the loyalists of their
or other tribes were sullenly smothering their indignation at the preposterous demands of Cooley in the Fort
Smith Council that the Choctaws and Chickasaws
selected delegates for the approaching conference in
Washington. They selected them in October,[561] the

561 Telegram, Hunt to Cooley, October 30, 1865, inquiring if he shall
furnish transportation (O.I.A., General Files, *Choctaw*, 1859-1866). The
credentials of the Choctaw delegates bear date, November 10, 1865, and the
signature of P. P. Pitchlynn (*ibid., Choctaw*, 1859-1866). Cooper reported
on the Chickasaw appointments for which the Chickasaw Legislature in its
very brief session had provided (Cooper to Cooley, October 18, 1865, *ibid.*,
C 1629). The Chickasaws presented their credentials, January 18, 1866
(Winchester Colbert and others to Cooley, *ibid., Chickasaw*, C 18 of 1866).

Choctaws through their National Council and the Chickasaws through their Legislature, which as has been already noted, was meeting now for the first time since it passed its secession ordinance in 1861. Ignored in each instance, by Choctaws and Chickasaws alike, was the loyal minority.[562] Robert M. Jones, Alfred Wade, John Page, Allen Wright, and James Riley composed the Choctaw delegation as originally constituted[563] and Colbert Carter, Holmes Colbert and Edmund Pickens, the Chickasaw. Prominent in counsel, indefatigable as ever, was Douglas H. Cooper, ex-United States Indian agent, ex-Confederate States Indian agent and military commander. Officially un-

[562] Evidence of this is seen in the protest and humble petition which certain Choctaws and Chickasaws, "members of the loyal section," presented when the negotiations began in Washington. They begged that "having no representative in the presence of your 'Honorable Body,' the Delegations from these Nations having been selected entirely from the Disloyal or Southern portion," they might have provision made in the proposed treaty for their protection, permanent residence, and "indemnity for losses sustained during the late war." (O.I.A., General Files, *Choctaw*, 1859-1866).

[563] In the later stages of the treaty-making, Pitchlynn was regarded by the Indian Office as one of the Choctaw delegates (Cooley to Pitchlynn, July 17, 1866, O.I.A., *Letter Book*, no. 80, p. 555). He and Winchester Colbert and other people of both tribes appear to have been invited by the government to come to Washington while the negotiations were in progress. They, therefore, claimed their expenses, those "incident to the visit." (Pitchlynn, Colbert, and others to Browning, September 18, 1866, I. D. Files, Bundle, no. 56). Winchester Colbert and Robert H. Love are cited, in the treaty, as additional Chickasaw commissioners (Kappler, vol. ii, p. 918). It would seem that a man, named E. S. Mitchell, was also of the Chickasaw delegation; for, early in the next year, Winchester Colbert put in an itemized bill of expenses for himself, Edmund Pickens, R. H. Love, Holmes Colbert, and E. S. Mitchell. For the journey from Tishomingo to Washington, and covering the period from December, 1865 to January 10, 1866, he asked a total of nine hundred and twenty-five dollars. Colbert Carter, so he stated, "went by the southern route and will present a separate bill." (O.I.A., General Files, *Choctaw*, 1859-1866, C 12). The War Department furnished water transportation to such delegates as cared to avail themselves of the privilege (Cooley to Harlan, June 23, 1866, *ibid., Report Book*, no. 15, p. 335. See also p. 356).

pardoned and not even to be "amnestied" until May 14, 1866,[564] he had already ingratiated himself with the United States authorities, civil and military.[565]

Among the three tribes, Seminole, Creek, Cherokee, that had been more exactly divided by the war into a northern and a southern camp no such eagerness for a re-opening of treaty negotiations was manifested and no such promptitude in the selection of delegates. The inaction, mental and physical, was to be ascribed in large measure to their alarmingly necessitous state. Agent Reynolds, in consort with Lieutenant L. C.

[564] *Johnson Papers*, "Pardon Record," vol. B.

[565] About this time, General J. J. Reynolds addressed Secretary Harlan in the interest of Cooper whom he represented as being anxious "to visit Washington for the settlement of his old account." Reynolds inquired, "Is there any objection to his coming?" (Telegram, dated Little Rock, November 22, 1865, I. D. Files, Bundle, no. 55). In this connection it is interesting to note a letter that Dole wrote to Usher, October 15, 1864 (O.I.A., *Report Book*, no. 14, pp. 29-30), showing how a large number of warrants issued by Cooper were all at once coming in for collection. Not so very long before, Coffin had approached Usher on the subject of securing an order from the solicitor of the Treasury allowing him to take possession of a farm abandoned by Elias Rector, culpable as was Cooper, and described by Coffin as a "a heavy defaulter to the Government." (Coffin to Usher, August 11, 1864, I. D. Files, Bundle, no. 52). The recovered status of Cooper is seen in the following letter, an odd sheet found in *Confederate Archives*, chap. 2, no. 267. The sheet is page 222½ of some as yet undiscovered letter book.

Fort Smith, Oct. 31st/65

Gen'l D. H. Cooper,

Dear Sir:

Your favor has been received and your wishes attended to. Genl Hunt has written to you, enclosing a passport, which however he said was entirely unnecessary. I hope you will conclude to come by Ft. Smith on your way to Washington. Your friends here would be glad to see you before going to Washington.

We have prepared a petition to the President asking a pardon for you which we will have signed as numerously as possible. Your own request for pardon should accompany the petition. This reason if no other should induce you to come by this place.

Yours Fraternally,

G. H. S. Main.

True [566] at the head of a military escort, visited the old Seminole agency in November and discovered there by actual count nigh upon a thousand "former rebel Seminoles" in a "deplorably destitute condition." [567] The poor things had wandered back to their desolated country, literally footsore and weary. Regardless of poverty almost loathsome they had, however, set to work to repair their old dwellings. There was not an Indian, loyal or disloyal, but what had practically lost everything, household effects, farm implements, stock. The agent's orders, obtained from Superintendent Sells, were that he should treat all factions alike.[568] So stricken were they all, indeed, that they had no mind for political differences. All had met the common fate of the Indian in alliance with the white man. It had been all *crow* for the one hunter and all *turkey* for the other.[569] In no mood were the Seminoles to cavil at Reynold's plans and he invited such as cared to make the long journey to proceed to Fort Gibson where a certain amount of supplies – inadequate to be sure but real – was to be had. A similar story of want and suffering was to be told of southern Creeks and Cherokees and, for the latter especially, W. P. Adair, their del-

---

[566] When urged by Reynolds to accompany him, True wrote to Craig, expressing the opinion that it might be well for him to accept so that he might "ascertain all I can in reference to the feelings existing between the Loyal and Disloyal Indians . . . " (True to Craig, November 10, 1865, A.G.O., Archives Division, *Fort Gibson Letter Book.* no. 20).

[567] Reynolds to Cooley, dated Washington, January 13, 1866, O.I.A., General Files, *Seminole*, 1858-1869.

[568] Sells to Cooley, November 17, 1865, transmitting a letter from Agent Reynolds, dated Seminole Agency, Neosho Falls, October 1, 1865.

[569] This has reference to the story of the Indian and the white man who went, on one occasion, hunting together. After the day's sport, the white man divided the game killed, giving the crows to the Indian and keeping the turkey for himself.

egate, solicited immediate relief.[570]   Generals Hunt
and Reynolds interested themselves in the case.   Secretary Harlan brought it, in the course of time, to Johnson's attention and was "authorized by the President
to advise the extension of the same care and protection
to those Indians that they would have been entitled to
had they remained with their respective tribes." [571]

In December, 1865, the Indian Office, impatient of
a too prolonged delay, took steps to secure, under duress
if necessary, the renewal of treaty negotiations.   The
Creeks, instructed from Washington, appointed as delegates three of their head chiefs, Ok-tars-sars Harjo,
or Sands, the successor of Opoethleyoholo, Coweta
Meho (Cow-e-to-me-co) and Cot-cha Chee (Che-
chu-chee).   They were all of them of the northern
persuasion; but, whether selected by accident or by
design cannot be positively asserted, since the Creeks
had ostensibly buried the hatchet.   By the majority
party, at all events, the delegates were regarded, not
as partisan, but as national representatives.[572]   The
Seminoles were similarly summoned to action by the
government and peremptorily.   Their selection was
from chiefs likewise, heads of bands, John Chupco, or
Long John, Principal Chief, Cho-cote Harjo, Foos
Harjo, and John F. Brown.

Among the Cherokees, national affairs were in dire

---

[570] See letter of General Reynolds, October 12, 1865, enclosing a copy
of Adair's petition, setting forth the destitute and despondent condition of
his people (O.I.A., General Files, *Cherokee*, 1859-1865, R 563). See also
Cooley to General Reynolds, October 24, 1865, O.I.A., *Letter Book*, no. 78,
p. 347.

[571] Harlan to Cooley, November 13, 1865, *ibid.*, General Files, *Southern
Superintendency*, 1865.

[572] The treaty conveys an erroneous impression in referring to them as
"delegates at large," and to D. N. McIntosh and James Smith as "special
delegates of the Southern Creeks." (Kappler, vol. ii, p. 931).

confusion. The Indian Office had done nothing to restore rank to John Ross; but the Executive Council, loyal to the aged chief, would not act without him. Accordingly, when in November delegates were appointed "to represent the interest of their Nation before the Government of the United States," John Ross was especially requested and empowered to act with them.[573] This was by regular enactment of the National Council, November 7th; but there the matter rested and the impression obtained at Washington that John Ross was averse to reviving treaty relations with the government. Howsoever that was, Cooley finally felt impelled to force the issue and he did it in the way most obnoxious to Indians, who, like the Cherokees, were jealous of their national character and most tenacious of all that the term, tribal rights, implied. What a ridiculous farce all treaty-making with Indian tribes had become if Cooley's telegram to Agent Justin Harlan, December twenty-second, was to be taken seriously! Its words were serious enough. They were,

"Select three Cherokees who represent the Nation and bring them to Washington at once." [574]

How a mere government agent was to select the national representatives for the Cherokees, the instructions did not disclose. That he could select them constitutionally it would be idle to contend.

As the facts were, however, the Cherokee delegates had been already provided for and that by joint action of the legislative body. They were seven in number, Captain Smith Christie, Captain White Catcher, Daniel H. Ross, a nephew of John Ross, S. H. Benge, ex-chaplain John B. Jones, Captain James McDaniel

---

[573] For a copy of the act, see O.I.A., *Cherokee*, M 390 of 1866.
[574] O.I.A., *Letter Book*, no. 79, p. 51.

and Captain Thomas Pegg. Lewis Downing, acting principal chief, had, on November sixth, handed to them their credentials under which they were "fully empowered to act for and in the behalf of the Cherokee Nation in all questions touching the interests of the same." [575] The credentials were presented to Cooley, January 30th of the next year; but, before that date, certain men representing the Southern Cherokees had made their own presence officially known in Washington.[576] For the most part, to avoid the charge of being self-constituted as in reality they were, they claimed to be acting in virtue of appointment by General Stand Watie under authority of the General Council which had been convened at Armstrong Academy the previous summer.[577]

The southern contingent of each of the three tribes just discussed had no idea of being counted out when the business of treaty-making should begin. In the

[575] O.I.A., *Cherokee*, C 86 of 1866.

[576] W. P. Adair presented his credentials, January 16, 1866, O.I.A., *Cherokee*, A 18 of 1866.

[577]   "EXECUTIVE DEPARTMENT,
                "Cherokee Nation (South), Armstrong Academy, C.N.
                              "November 13th, 1865.
    "COL. W. P. ADAIR
    Will proceed at his earliest convenience to the City of Washington, D.C., as one of the Commissioners with full powers, from the Cherokees south, and assist in entering into full and final negociations at that place between the Cherokee Nation, – "the United States Indian Nations," and the Govt of the United States, through their commissioners, which will be in accordance with Resolutions of the Grand Council of the United Indian Nations, passed in June last, at Armstrong Academy, C.N.
    "Also in accordance with a nomination from this Department, confirmed by action of the Cherokee National Council of the date of 28th June last – copies of which are herewith transmitted – and
    "Also in accordance with the adjournment of the late Indian Council, held and adjourned at Ft. Smith, Ark., *sine die* – for the purpose of convening at Washington City, D.C., to make Indian treaties.
    "Col. Adair will receive as compensation for his services such pay

sequel, indeed, the situation was to be anything but that. Their influence was to preponderate and it was to preponderate because they, sooner or later, were to intimate a willingness to fall in with some or all of Harlan's proposals. The principal member of the southern Cherokee contingent was E. C. Boudinot, who, in early October, had evinced an intention to visit Washington "on business for his people," and had been introduced by letter to Harlan as one who would be found to favor the project for a railroad from St. Louis to Galveston "by way of Fort Gibson through the Indian Country." [578] The railroad project the writer of the letter, S. M. Coleman, commended to Harlan's favorable consideration. Whatever Boudinot's business for his people may have been – and its nature can be safely inferred – it was soon transacted and, in the first week of November, he was hurrying back again to Indian Territory on "special business."

and allowance per day during his mission as the U.S. Govt shall provide in such cases.

"Given under my hand and private seal (there being no seal of office) the day and date above written.

(L. S.)

"STAND WATIE, P¹ Chief."

(O.I.A., *Cherokee*, A 18 of 1866. Enclosure, no. 3. Enclosure no. 1 is a copy of the Resolutions of the Grand Council, June 28, 1865; Enclosure no. 2, a copy of the Action of the Cherokee National Committee (or Council) confirming the appointment of commissioners to visit Washington. A copy of a document, on file in the Indian Office, signed by Stand Watie and addressed to Boudinot, Adair, Vann, Fields, J. P. Davis and Smallwood, bears date August 1, 1865 and testimony that these men were appointed delegates in June).

[578] S. M. Coleman to Harlan, October 20, 1865, I. D. Files, Bundle, no. 55. Who Coleman was I have not been able to discover. He may have been a relative of Agent Coleman whose name is variously spelt. It occurs as *Colman* and as *Coleman* in the records. Agent Coleman had been one of the few agents of the old régime reappointed (Acting Chief Clerk, Interior Department, to Commissioner of Indian Affairs, June 15, 1865, O.I.A., General Files, *Choctaw*, 1859-1866).

Cooley asked of General Reynolds the favor of speeding him on his way.[579]   Evidently the special business was quite urgent.   When in Little Rock, on this return journey, Boudinot fell in with Pitchlynn, bound for Washington, and he straightway notified Cooley that Pitchlynn was of one mind with him.   The mind of the two men is revealed in Boudinot's letter,

> Gov. Pitchlynn of the Choctaw Nation is here on his way to Washington; he agrees with me in his views of Mr. Secretary Harlan's bill for consolidating the Indian nations into one Territory; he says, though, that his people generally were opposed to it.   I hope the Gov't will not despair of obtaining the assent of the great body of the Indians to it.   Each of the treaties should contain an article recognizing the right of the Gov't to organize such territory whenever in the judgment of Congress it seems expedient.   The Cherokee delegation opposed to Ross, I am confident, will cheerfully accede to such a stipulation; and I believe if properly explained all other parties in the territory will go for it.   I hope nothing will be done towards the making of treaties until all the delegates are present; that is Pitchlynn's desire and it looks to me as the best course   .   .   .[580]

The propaganda for Harlan's measures had other than Indian advocates to support it and certain suggestions of General Sanborn's have, in this connection, considerable significance.   They formed a part of his final report on the freedmen and included territorial organization, the location of southern and affiliated tribes on reservations of limited area, sectionization and inalienable allotment in severalty, homesteads of one hundred and sixty acres for freedmen and for single freedwomen with offspring, liberal grants of land in alternate sections to railway companies, and the

[579] Cooley to Reynolds, November 6, 1865, O.I.A., *Letter Book*, no. 78, p. 401.
[580] Boudinot to Cooley, dated Little Rock, November 22, 1865, O.I.A., General Files, *Southern Superintendency*, 1865.

opening up of surplus land to white settlement.[581]
From a standpoint other than the previously conceived
welfare of the Indian, as he of the Ross variety saw it,
the suggestions of Sanborn were the fullest and most
radical yet presented. Could they be divested of all
suspicion of being concocted, not primarily in the interest of the red people, but of the white, they might
be acknowledged to have genuine merit. It would
seem, however, that they constituted advice purely
gratuitous. The subject of railway construction was
not within Sanborn's known terms of reference; but,
perchance, he had received verbal instructions not
recorded. At all events, the conclusions he reached
bear a striking resemblance to the Harlan-Cooley-Sells
views and may originally have been drafted under their
inspiration. The question that must be left to the
reader's inference is, did they form a basis for the
negotiations about to be undertaken?

Harlan's own spirit in the conduct of the negotiations may be gauged from his annual report, one of
the most uncandid upon record. Its half-truths, its
disingenuous presentation of facts, its concealment of
all extenuating circumstances, its dissimulation, and its
brazen reference to Indian misfortunes as if retributive
mark it for absolute condemnation. It was designed
to create a prejudice against a most unfortunate people;
in order that the ends of the white man's material advancement might be the more easily secured. These
are the passages to which the historian has a right to
take exception:

"The number of Indians residing within the jurisdiction of the United States does not probably exceed
350,000, a large majority of whom maintained during

---

[581] Commissioner of Indian Affairs, *Report*, 1866, p. 286.

the past year peaceful relations. Some of them have made gratifying progress in civilization and manifested, during the late war, a steadfast loyalty to our flag worthy of emphatic commendation. Civilized and powerful tribes, however, residing within the Indian territory, united early in the year 1861 with the Indians of the prairies immediately west and north, for hostile operations against the United States. In flagrant violation of treaties which had been observed by us with scrupulous good faith, and in the absence of any just ground of complaint, these confederated Indians entered into an alliance with the rebel authorities and raised regiments in support of their cause. Their organized troops fought side by side with rebel soldiers, and detached bands made frequent assaults on the neighboring white settlements, which were without adequate means of defence, and, on the Indians, who maintained friendly relations with this government. This state of things continued until the surrender of the rebel forces west of the Mississippi. Hostilities were then suspended, and, at the request of the Indians, commissioners were sent to negotiate a treaty of peace. Such preliminary arrangements were made as, it is believed, will result in the abolition of slavery among them, the cession within the Indian territory of lands for the settlement of the civilized Indians now residing on reservations elsewhere, and the ultimate establishment of civil government, subject to the supervision of the United States.

"The perfidious conduct of the Indians in making unprovoked war upon us has been visited with the severest retribution. The country within the Indian territory has been laid waste, vast amounts of property destroyed, and the inhabitants reduced from a prosperous condition to such extreme destitution, that thousands of them must inevitably perish during the present winter, unless timely provision be made by this government for their relief." [582]

In official communications, Commissioner Cooley was almost equally adept at withholding unpleasant but essential facts, essential to the historian and the statesman, if not to the special pleader, the politician, the lawyer, the casuist. Cooley was reticent as to facts that would have placed the Indian case, at the outset, in the right light and in its true proportions; but, nevertheless, his purpose once accomplished, he did have the grace to state precisely for the information of congress and particularly for the senate, before which the treaties were to come for ratification, the four principal points that had presented themselves for settlement, *to wit,*

> The proper and just method of adjusting affairs between the loyal and disloyal, this point applying especially to the Cherokees, where confiscation laws, passed by the national council, had taken effect upon the property of those who were disloyal.
>
> The proper relations which the freedmen should hereafter hold towards the remainder of the people.
>
> A fair compensation for losses of property occasioned to those who remained loyal by the disloyal party.
>
> Cession of lands by the several tribes to be used for the settlement thereon of Indians whom it is in contemplation to remove from Kansas.[583]

In the foregoing, there is no unnecessary mention – unnecessary, that is, from Cooley's point of view – of the loyal Indians's argument that the tribe was acting ab-

---

[582] Secretary of the Interior, *Report*, 1865, *House Executive Documents*, no. 1, 39th cong., 1st sess. (serial no. 1248) p. vii.

[583] Commissioner of Indian Affairs, *Report*, 1866, p. 8.

solutely within its rights in enacting confiscation laws. If rebellion against the United States had been, indeed, so serious an offence, why was not the tribal punishment of the offenders endorsed by the Indian Office? Why was it regarded as further occasion for spoliation? Moreover, why did Cooley seek to convey the impression that losses of property were attributable to the actions of Indians only and that no claim for indemnity could be justifiably lodged against the United States? As a matter of fact, the points for settlement, as the commissioner stated them, were for public consumption as much as for congressional. Phrased as he phrased them, they could not fail to win popular assent. Only on the frontier was their fundamental insincerity likely to be known and, since the frontier was to prove the beneficiary, no protest need be expected to come from it. The Indian then as always lacked the where-with-all for articulate expression.

It is interesting to observe that in negotiating its reconstruction treaties, the Federal government did not scorn to avail itself, and that almost too quickly and too readily, of the services of ex-Confederate agents,[584] the

---

[584] While R. W. Johnson was not exactly one of the agents of the Confederacy, he, too, had had much to do with the opening up of treaty negotiations with the slaveholding tribes, he having been Secretary of State in President Davis' cabinet at the time he secured for Albert Pike his commission. Among the *Johnson Papers* in the Library of Congress are some interesting letters showing the very personal way in which men like R. W. Johnson approached the executive head of the United States government in their endeavor to get themselves reinstated. On the fourth of September, 1866, R. W. Johnson wrote to President Johnson acknowledging his "signature which acquits me of my unfortunate political offences, which releaves me of the penalties of secession and protects me against the dishonest exageration of Radical vindictiveness, and arrests the confiscation of my property, *all* of which will be needed to pay up large debts to a few creditors who have acted a forbearing & friendly part towards me . . .

"I send my acceptance of the pardon . . . Mrs. Johnson begs to present her very kindest regards to Mrs. Patterson, who was a much loved

very men, in point of fact, who had, in the first instance, been the persons most responsible for Indian defection. Reference has already been made to the ingratiating demeanor of Douglas H. Cooper and to its success in disarming erstwhile opponents. It was the same with Albert Pike. People like Cooper and Pike were surely agents of the Confederacy within the meaning of Johnson's amnesty proclamation and, by express phrasing, excluded from its clemency in default of special application. Their responsibility for the Indian treaties of secession was well-known and, by none, disputed.[585] Almost inexplicable is it not then that they should have been accepted as counsellors by the Indian Office when the men whom they had deceived, cajoled, deluded were debarred a fair hearing? The weight of their testimony was to be thrown against the Indians who had tried, although ever so feebly, to be loyal. Therein lies the explanation of the mystery.

It was in connection with the project for territorial organization, Secretary Harlan's prime interest, that the services of Pike were first solicited. In November, before Pike had made any attempt whatsoever to have his "political disabilities" removed,[586] Harlan was ad-

schoolmate of my sister Irene . . . " (*Johnson Papers*, vol. 101). On the twenty-first of the same month, Johnson wrote again, in order to intercede for Dr. Luke Blackburn and sounded once more the note of an old friendship with sister Irene (*ibid.*, vol. 102). By the twenty-seventh, he had become very confidential and addressed the president privately in order to prevail upon him to confer with Judge George C. Watkins about affairs "here." (*ibid.*).

[585] A possible exception to this might be found in some of the *ex parte* documents among the Choctaw and Chickasaw files.

[586] On the subject of Pike's eventual application for pardon, there is a modicum of information in the *Johnson Papers*. On the second of September, 1866, he wrote to the president pleading that his property had been taken by private persons and he had not the means to pay the cost of its recovery. He was then in receipt of a provisional pardon; for he said,

"I sometime since received, with gratitude for your kindness, your

vised not to proceed towards a final settlement of Indian affairs before he could be communicated with.[587] The advice was taken seriously, Pike was accorded an interview, Harlan's bill [588] was submitted to him, and, in five weeks thereafter, it was returned to Harlan with a general endorsement of its main ideas and a few helpful suggestions as to details.[589]   The treaty negotia-

warrant of Pardon for acts done by me during the late Civil War.

"It is proper that I should inform you of the reasons why I have not yet notified the Department of State of my acceptance of its conditions. It is the more proper, because those reasons are somewhat of a public nature, and, as I think, in some degree affect the character of the Nation and its present Chief Magistrate, to whose sense of justice I am glad to be able to submit them.

"In 1864, in the summer, libels were filed in the District Court at Little Rock against property of mine in that town, of the value of $30,000 . . . " (*Johnson Papers*, vol. 100).

Judged in the light of the foregoing, the statement of Horace Van Deventer concerning Pike's position and property is a little misleading. " . . . After the war President Johnson offered to remove his political diabilities, but coupled the offer with such conditions that he could not accept it, and his estate in Arkansas, which was confiscated by the United States, and was about the time of his death valued at $30,000.00, remained in the possession of the Government until since his death, when it was turned over to his children." (*Albert Pike, a Biographical Sketch*, p. 32, in Scottish Rite Temple, Washington, D.C.)

[587] "I have seen General Albert Pike on many occasions recently and he seems to know more about the Indian affairs than any other man.

"He will be in Washington in a few days and I hope to be there at the time. When there I will be pleased to present him to you and and you will be able to profit much by what he will tell you.

"If necessary, it might be well to let the President know that General Pike will be in Washington in a few days that he might not commit himself on the Indian affairs in advance of information.

"There seems to be considerable desire to effect some political objects by Indian politicians. I can promise you full advice from Genl Pike." (Tal. P. Shaffner to Harlan, dated 79, John St., N. Y., November 1, 1865, *I.D. Files*, Bundle, no. 55).

[588] S 459, 38th congress, 2nd session. A copy of this bill is filed with Pike's letter, O.I.A., General Files, *Southern Superintendency*, 1865, P 499.

[589] "My first duty to you is to thank you for your courtesy and kindness to myself in the brief interview with which I was honored five weeks since.

"My next is to thank you, in the name of a brave and unfortunate

tions had not yet been opened up but they were being prepared for. Boudinot, Pitchlynn, Pike, Cooper and many another man of influence but of questionable previous record had taken his stand on the side of the government.

race, for the kindly sympathies which actuate you in respect to the Indian tribes. They do you honor and must earn you the favor of Heaven, if not of men.

"It was said of me by the Confederate officials that I cared only for the Indians. In the positions I held under that Government, that was true, and my interest in the race remains undiminished.

"I return herewith the copy of your bill, with an annotation here and there, to which I invite your attention.

"Title in fee to their lands, and citizenship are, in my view, indispensable to the safety of the Red Men. In this I hope you may agree with me.

"You now have the power to dictate terms to the Indians. You may use this power in such manner as to make it the means of blessing to them. It could be used to their destruction.

"There will be no energy or continuous industry and true progress among the Indians, so long as there is no individual title to land. At the same time, when they hold in severalty, stringent laws should prohibit purchases from individuals, or long leases by white men. In other words, if the Indian tribes divide and sell part of their lands, the portion allotted in severalty to individuals should be inalienable, by voluntary or forced sale, for forty years.

"I am not sure but that too much power of legislation is proposed to be given to the Legislative Council, in which many small and barbarous bands will be represented. My impression is, also, that it would be well for power to be given the Governor and Judges to adopt the first domestic and municipal code.

"Would it not be well, as the Cherokees and the Choctaws and Chickasaws have *two* houses of the Legislature, to establish an upper house, of not more than fifteen members, in which the smaller bands would be collectively represented.

"Why not, to conciliate the large tribes, have a Lieutenant Governor, appointed by the President, he being a member of one of the large tribes, who should preside over the Legislative Council.

"As far as it may be in my power, I should be rejoiced to aid in bringing about the organization proposed by you. But, being unpardoned and moneyless I am and am likely to be helpless to assist in the matter." (Pike to Harlan, dated Memphis, Tennessee, December 6, 1865, O.I.A., General Files, *Southern Superintendency*, 1865, P 499; I.D., *Register of Letters Received*, "Indians," no. 4, p. 435. Pike's letter was replied to, December 12, 1865).

The negotiations, when once begun, continued through several months and, in the case of some of the tribes, almost without intermission. The Seminoles were the first to capitulate.[590] Weak and impoverished as they were, they were no proof against intimidation. In them the hope of the extortionists was abundantly realised. The measure of the intimidation can be found in the preamble of their treaty,[591] in which the commissioners, Cooley, Sells, and Parker, reminded the Seminoles that by throwing off their allegiance they had "incurred the liability of forfeiture of all lands and other property held by grant or gift of the United States." Strictly-speaking the Indians held nothing by grant or gift, as the phrase is popularly understood, and the insinuation that they did was in itself *prima facie* evidence of the essential unfairness of the commissioners. The existing tribal property of the Seminoles represented a series of business transactions dating back to the infamous treaty of Camp Moultrie,[592] forced sales in which, so far as the Indians were concerned, value received had never yet balanced consideration rendered; for there had always been a large profit accruing to the white man. By the Treaty of

[590] The treaty was concluded in March (Cooley to Harlan, April 2, 1866, O.I.A., *Report Book*, no. 15, p. 175); but the southern Seminoles objected so strenuously to some features of the original draft (Cooley to Sells, April 24, 1866, O.I.A., *Letter Book*, no. 80, p. 83) that "corrections" had to be considered and made (Cooley to Johnson, June 30, 1866, O.I.A., *Report Book*, no. 15, p. 359). The treaty was ratified, July 19th, and proclaimed, August 16th; but there was great delay in its execution (Taylor to Otto, May 29, 1867, O.I.A., *Report Book*, no. 16, p. 345).

[591] Kappler, vol. ii, pp. 910-915.

[592] The Seminoles had a long memory. As late as 1879, those that still lived in Florida spoke of this treaty particularly, but of its successors also, with great bitterness. Their distrust of the general government had grown with the years and they wanted "no Washington talk." The Indian Office was, at the time, being besieged with requests for their removal to Indian Territory.

Payne's Landing, the Seminoles had obligated themselves through a few of their chiefs, individually compensated, to remove from their original Florida home and had ceded their remaining lands there for an acreage proportionate to their numbers in the West. Some of their annuity rights were based upon that same treaty and more upon the later treaties of Fort Gibson and Washington, both of which had been exacted from the government when the Indians had come to realize, by bitter experience, the inadequacy, the duplicity, and the injustice of earlier conventions. To call their western home a gift was a mockery. A grant it was only in the sense that it was held by title from the United States given in exchange for a better and more ancient claim. How much the new title was worth as against the old title of ancient occupancy the Indians were soon to know to their cost.

Misrepresentation as to the nature and source of Seminole property rights was not the only or the most serious offence of the sort of which the commissioners were guilty. At the beginning of the preamble, they cited the *liability* to forfeiture and, towards its close, the *liabilities* in satisfaction of which a cession of lands might be demanded. To understand the criminal intent of the authors, their two citations must be brought into the closest juxtaposition possible. "Whereas the Seminole Nation made a treaty . . . and thereby incurred the liability of forfeiture of all lands and other property . . . and whereas the United States, in view of said treaty of the Seminole Nation . . . and the consequent liabilities of said Seminole Nation . . . " The two references were to one and the same delinquency; but whereas, *liability* in the sense in which it was used in the phrase, "liability to forfeiture" betokened exposure only, a more or less probable contingency, *liabilities* implied debts actually contracted.   Now the commissioners had no legal basis whatsoever for the impression of culpability which they were intending to convey.   Congress had indeed enacted that should the president see fit he might by proclamation declare the lands of the secessionist Indians forfeited; but neither Lincoln nor Johnson had moved in the matter, most likely because of the overwhelming evidence obtainable that the Indians had been imposed upon and had never, at their worst, acted as unified bodies.   They owned their lands, not as individuals, but as tribes.   Lincoln, at least, would have appreciated the crass injustice of invalidating the title of an entire tribe when half or more than half of its members had, to the best of their ability, been loyal. In the absence of a presidential proclamation of forfeiture, the title of the Indians remained as good and as complete as it had ever been.

But, as the commissioners frankly stated, the United States was conscious of an urgent necessity for land in the Indian Territory upon which to place tribes that were an encumbrance elsewhere.   The time had come when it could no longer, because of pressure from political constituencies, hold fast to the promises of title in perpetuity which it had, in all solemnity, made to the slaveholding tribes at the time of their removal from the South.   Political expediency necessitated a sacrifice of national honor and good faith.   As a salve to tender conscience, however, the lands might be taken under color of confiscation, the recognized penalty for disloyalty.   In such wise, might the government conceivably take possession of the whole of Indian Territory; but, in its great magnanimity, it had resolved to take only a part and, for that part, in what might well be thought by some to be an excess of magnanimity, it would pay. Very true the price it would pay would be small, so small, in fact, in comparison with the market valuation, as to be but nominal; but, surely, that circumstance ought not to be allowed to obscure or to detract from the intrinsic generosity of its action.

As a way, therefore, out of its own difficulties, the government proposed to take advantage of the southern Indian predicament and, in the case of the Seminoles, to compel a relinquishment of the entire tribal tract, estimated at two million one hundred and sixty-nine thousand acres. The tract was the same that had been conveyed to the Seminoles by joint treaty arrangement with the Creeks in 1856 and secured by patent. It lay between the Canadian River and its North Fork from the ninety-seventh parallel westward. Fifteen cents per acre was the munificient sum that was to be allowed for the cession. A new home [593] for the Seminoles was to be provided out of the country which the United States intended to get from the Creeks and for which it had offered to pay thirty cents an acre. This tract of land was to the eastward of the ceded Seminole reserve and was to be sold to the Seminoles for fifty cents an acre. By a single transaction, therefore, a beneficent government was able to realise a gain of forty per cent and, by another, for the Seminole lands were conceded to be quite as valuable as the Creek only more remote than, fifty per cent. Henceforth, the Seminoles who had occupied a reservation of over

---

[593] Concerning the Seminole settlement upon Creek land, see E. P. Smith to Shanks, March 18, 1875, O.I.A., *Letter Book,* no. 122, pp. 522-523. There is some evidence that the Seminoles themselves desired to move farther east upon the Creek lands. See Geo. A. Reynolds to Cooley, December 5, 1865, *ibid., Southern Superintendency,* S 13.

two million acres were to try to content themselves on one of approximately two hundred thousand. The treaty of 1856 had been necessary because they had found that they could not live harmoniously at close quarters with the Creeks but now they were once more made their very near neighbors. Could any better proof be required of a vacillating governmental policy?

Not a hint was allowed to appear in the Seminole reconstruction treaty as to the obligation resting upon the United States to protect its wards against hostile invasion and to indemnify them out of its own treasury for injury done. The treaty did provide, however, that, for the future, the Seminoles would "remain firm allies of the United States, and always faithfully aid the Government thereof to suppress insurrection and put down its enemies." The shifting of the assistance promised from the strong to the weak power is very interesting. In return for this prospective help, the United States gave the familiar guarantee of quiet possession of their country; but for how long was not stated. It limited the protection, which it reciprocally pledged itself to extend, to a protection against hostilities on the part of other tribes and obtained, for the purpose, the right to make a military occupation of the Seminole country at its own option and expence. Never again would it be possible, in the event of an American civil war, for the Indian nations to contemplate the maintenance of a neutral attitude or claim a protection against the assault of either contestant; but what mattered that since the old guarantee had availed them nothing?

With regard to the amnesty provision which the commissioners embodied in the treaty they were consistent enough to explain that it was an amnesty extended by

the United States to individual Indians. It would
have been little short of ridiculous to have allowed an
amnesty to the tribe as such to appear alongside of the
many clauses that bespoke a punishment. In their
turn, the Seminoles agreed to extend an amnesty to
their secessionist members, to proscribe none of them,
and to refrain from enacting forfeiture and confiscation
laws. If any such had already been passed, they were
to be inoperative. The Indians were compelled to be
magnanimous but were given no model of magnanimity. The tribe as a whole paid for the defection of a
part but it paid to the United States and it was forbidden by that same United States to fix responsibility upon individuals for a crime, which, judged by its punishment, was of surpassing magnitude.

And the forced sale of their home at a relatively
insignificant price fixed by the buyer was not all of
their punishment. Slavery was declared abolished as
was to have been expected and the Seminole ex-slaves,
likewise all other freedmen who might be admitted
into the country, were to be adopted fully and completely into the tribe. That meant, of course, that they
were to share with the Indians in all tribal benefits,
were to occupy the lands, receive a *pro rata* allowance
of the annuities, enjoy the educational facilities, participate in the government, and, when the time for allotment in severalty should come, as come it must, obtain
the individual title to a farm, not the meagre forty
acres that the North advertised and the South was to
be mulcted for, but the more princely holding that the
Indians, once their masters but now their peers and
their peers only, politically, socially, economically,
would eventually get. Under such circumstances, it
was to be anticipated that the two races would inevit-

ably become mixed [594] and all the more so because the land to the westward just ceded by the Seminoles was to become the home, not only of other Indians, but of other freedmen.[595]   There the United States or some of its statesmen hoped to begin the big experiment of negro colonisation.

In respect to the purchase money that would be due from the United States for the Seminole cession, the commissioners arranged an interesting distribution. Not a penny apparently was actually to pass into the hands of the late owners.   The sum realized from the sale, the tract being huge though the price was small, would total three hundred and twenty-five thousand, three hundred and sixty-two dollars.   Out of it was to be deducted, first of all, the purchase price of the new reserve, one hundred thousand dollars, and then all charges for Seminole reconstruction work, for the rehabilitation of that which other hands than their own had destroyed.   Farms were to be re-stocked, a mill purchased.   A sum of seventy thousand dollars was to constitute a permanent trust fund out of which schools were to be supported and the running expenses of the tribe met.   The disbursement of the surplus, ninety thousand, three hundred and sixty-two dollars, was the crowning feature of this most remarkable treaty.   Almost half of the amount was to go for relief and the remainder to be used to reimburse the so-called loyal-

---

[594] In the autumn of 1878, Special Agent, A. B. Meacham reported at great length on the condition of Seminole freedmen (Letter, dated, Muskogee, November 20, 1878).   It was then very evident that the Seminoles were not reconciled to the exactions made upon them in 1866.   Their freedmen were not yet assimilated and they themselves were socially and politically demoralized.

[595] For an official opinion on the right of freedmen generally to settle upon the Seminole ceded land, see E. S. Parker to J. D. Cox, May 21, 1869 (O.I.A., *Report Book*, no. 18, p. 352).

ists for the losses they had sustained. The claimants were to be understood as including loyalists irrespective of race, color, or previous condition of servitude and every one of them was to be required to furnish a board,[596] created for the purpose, with satisfactory evidence "that he has at all times remained loyal to the United States, according to his treaty obligations." Were the limiting clause to be taken seriously, the freedmen would, perforce, possess an exemption, denied to the Indians, since no treaties had ever been made with them.

The concluding provisions of the treaty were of major and minor importance. One of them stipulated that the Seminoles should grant a right of way and other concessions to any railway company authorized by congress. This was distinctly a major provision. Its counterpart, with modifications, is to be found in every one of the reconstruction treaties of 1866 and the general criticism, applicable to all, may as well be made once for all. Had the United States, early in its career, formulated an Indian policy, worthy of a great nation, had it been conscious of its duty to a subject race and made its plans accordingly, by 1866, if not before, the highly-developed southern tribes would

[596] J. Tyler Powell and J. W. Caldwell were appointed commissioners of claims under this provision. They conducted their examination at Wewo-ka, in the Seminole Nation, from September 13 to October 31, 1867. For material bearing upon their findings and report, see Mix to Browning, December 10, 1867, O.I.A., *Report Book*, no. 17, p. 48, also *idem.*, p. 253; Powell to Commissioner of Indian Affairs, March 7, 1868, P 279, *Special File*, no. 87; G. A. Reynolds to same, July 1, 1872, p. 207, *idem.* The report itself on "Loyal Seminole, Rolls and Losses" is published in Senate Documents, no. 72, 55th congress, 3d session. Some of the Seminoles who had been employed as scouts were still in Texas in 1874 (E. R. Smith to H. M. Atkinson, December 19, 1874, O.I.A., *Letter Book*, no. 122, pp. 94-95). As late as 1870, there were "Seminole negro-Indians" in Mexico and anxious to return (H. R. Clum to Otto, October 3, 1870, *ibid.*, no. 20, p. 21).

have been more than ready for the material civilization that has marked everywhere the Anglo-Saxon's progress. Unfortunately, the Indian policy has never been
permitted to be a matter of organic development. It
has never been the subject of, or study by statesmen. Its
best features have been ephemeral and it itself inspired
by the expediency of the moment. Isolation on the
frontier or confinement to a constantly decreasing area
has been the Indian's lot. United States citizenship [597]
was not ordinarily or immediately in prospect for him.
To the advantages of individual ownership he was not
introduced until, in the very nature of things, his community holding was likely to become so small in size
that his old pursuits would be impossible. The coming of the railroad was to him a knell of doom; for it
meant that the isolation, which his guardian had prescribed for him earlier, was now, because it suited the
interests of the white man, to be denied. Every railway provision in the reconstruction treaties of 1866 was
a concession to capitalists and a betrayal of trust.
Every one was an entering wedge to the final ousting
of the Indian reservist. Railway construction and territorial organization were parts of the one great
scheme. Both were steps in the formation of the State
of Oklahoma, which is not an Indian State in the

[597] Because of his participation in the late world war, United States
citizenship is now being spoken of for the Indian generally. Prior to the
formation of the State of Oklahoma, it had been granted on occasions and
in irregular ways, sometimes by treaty as, for instance, in the case of the
Wyandots (Kappler, vol. ii, p. 677). Commissioner Smith, reporting to
Representative Lorenzo Crounse, July 6, 1876 (O.I.A., *Letter Book*, no. 130,
p. 412) said, "I have to state that there is no general law by the terms
of which an Indian can become a citizen of the United States. By treaties
and legislative enactments members of several tribes have been admitted to
citizenship . . . " For an opinion as to the effect of the Fourteenth
Amendment upon the question of Indian citizenship, see *Senate Report*, no.
268, 41st congress, 3rd session.

American Union and yet its limits are coterminous, identical, with those of the country that was promised to the southern exile so long as the grass should grow and the water run.

Inserted in the Seminole treaty were two provisions looking towards, but not expressly arranging for, territorial organization. One of them stipulated that the Seminoles would consent in advance to any legislation that congress might devise for the better government of Indian Territory provided tribal organization were not interfered with; the other recognized the constitutionality of an inter-tribal council. The full details of of this institution were not developed for inclusion in the Seminole pact and are reserved for later discussion.

At this point, by way of furnishing an anti-climax, a single small benevolent action of the Indian's Great Father may conveniently be noticed. The government agreed to construct, but at no greater cost to itself than ten thousand dollars, agency buildings on the new reserve.

The treaty with the Choctaws and Chickasaws [598] was

---

[598] Some explanation, other than that furnished by the fact that their fortunes had been connected for many years antedating the war, may be required for a right understanding of why these two tribes negotiated in unison. Among the "Papers from the Committee on Indian Affairs" (*House Files*, Box xix, 40th congress) are several documents bearing upon the treaties of 1866. In the present connection, those marked, C, D, and E, are especially valuable. C proved to be the "Instructions, Public and Private, to Delegates Sent to Negotiate Treaty;" D, "Resolutions Passed by Both Houses, October 17, 1865;" E, a copy of "Resolutions of the General Council of the Choctaw Nation passed in executive session for the guidance of the Choctaw Commissioners in the further prosecution of negotiations with the U. S. Government." The date of document E is October 19, 1865. Article 2 of Document D stipulated that the five Choctaw commissioners should proceed to Washington along with commissioners from the Chickasaw Nation. The following have been copied from Document E, itself not the original:

By the second resolution, the Choctaw commissioners were to have plenary powers subject to certain restrictions; viz.,

1. That the Choctaw Commissioners, previous to the resumption of

the second of the reconstruction series to be nego-

negotiations with the Government of the United States, shall invite the Chickasaw Commissioners to meet with them and agree upon some mode of operation . . .

2. That it is the settled policy of this Nation neither to sell, barter, exchange or in any wise dispose of the country now occupied by the Choctaw and Chickasaw nations; that they would sooner yield all claim to any funds due to the nations on the part of the U. S. Government than to be induced or forced to sacrifice any principles of honor which is due their people and posterity, in regard to the territory which is so dear to them, and that all questions affecting the sovereignty of each nation, or in any wise diminishing the extent of their common country must be referred to the people for ultimate decision.

3. The failure of the U.S. permanently to settle the Witchita and other Indians as was agreed under the 9th article of the Treaty of June, A.D., 1855, remands the sole jurisdiction of the leased territory or district to this Nation. This Nation will not however hesitate to make arrangements for the permanent settlement of the Kansas and other Indians in the so-called leased district, Provided, reasonable compensation be paid for the same.

4. That rather than sell any portion of the country east of the 98th degree west longitude, the Commissioners are authorized to open the whole of the leased territory for the U. S. to settle therein free of compensation any or all tribes of Indians they wish – this nation claiming their right and interest to the soil of said leased district as expressed in the treaty of June 22nd, 1855.

The Choctaw Commissioners will exercise their best judgment whether it would be better even to relinquish those rights or to admit Kansas & other Indians into the territory east of the 98th degree, with or without their tribal rights under such restrictions as will be least objectionable to the Choctaws and Chickasaws.

5. No part of the lands east of the 98th degree West Longitude and belonging to the Choctaw and Chickasaw Nations will be ceded or sold at any price, and if the United States insist on such cession or purchase, then the Choctaw Commissioners shall request the U.S. Government to send a Commissioner or Commissioners to treat with the people directly on that point.

6. The Choctaw Commissioners are hereby empowered to demand remuneration for slaves emancipated in the Choctaw Nation by the fortunes of war and belonging to citizens or persons who were lawfully residents there at the time of the war and have continued to reside therein to the present time, on the ground that the Proclamation of President Lincoln did not apply to the Indian Territory, and that the Choctaws were not parties to the late war for the purpose of sustaining the institution of slavery. But by the condition in which

tiated.[599] As a reflection upon the United States' Indian policy of the day, the contrast which it presents to the Seminole is of greater historical import than the similarity. The Red River tribes had been in the vanguard of the secession movement and, with some slight wavering, had adhered to the Confederacy unto the end. They were a powerful group, their leading half-breeds shrewd politicians. In those two facts must the key to the enigmas of their reconstruction treaty be sought for; inasmuch as it was the least reconstructive of the entire series.

The treaty bore the official designation, *Articles of Agreement and Convention.* It contained no pream-

they found themselves placed at the beginning of the war they took sides with the South, believing that to be the only mode by which they could prevent their country from falling into the hands of ruthless men and by which they could maintain their occupation, rights and interests to the soil of the country which they now occupy. If however this Nation must bear a share of the confiscation of the Congress of the United States, as well as that of the "Emancipation Proclamation," the U.S. Gov't should at least leave undisturbed the interests of the Choctaw Nation in the lands within the limits of their Nation, east of the ninety-eighth Degree of West Longitude, as she has, by the exercise of the pardoning power, restored her own citizens who were prime instigators of the so-called "rebellion" to their landed rights and interests.

7. Amendments should be proposed to the Territorial Bill, denominated Senate Bill, 459, so as to make the provision a permanent one instead of temporary, and so that the Governor thereof might be chosen by the tribes located within the proposed territory, from one of their own number, in the same manner as provided for a delegate to Congress.

8. The 1st, 2nd, 7th, 8th, 9th, & 10th articles are agreed to. The 3d, 4th, 5th, 6th & 11th articles are open to discussion.

[599] Jno H. B. Latrobe of Baltimore posed as counsel for these Indians in the negotiations. He charged them an enormous contingent fee, although Cooper, writing as his friend, August 2, 1866 (O.I.A., General Files, *Choctaw,* 1859-1866) assured Cooley that the story that Latrobe was to get twenty-five thousand dollars from the Choctaws and Chickasaws was untrue. In the Library of Congress, there is a pamphlet, written by Latrobe, June 19, 1873, in vindication of the part he played in the negotiation of the Choctaw and Chickasaw treaty of 1866.

ble and, therefore, no charge of liability to forfeiture, no statement of indebtedness, no presumptive evidence of guilt. It acknowledged the abolition of slavery as also an obligation on the part of the two tribes "to use their influence and to make every exertion to induce Indians of the plains to maintain peaceful relations with each other, with other Indians, and with the United States." A precautionary measure of the kind would become most necessary should the scheme for colonisation be set on foot. For good or ill, as judged by recent events, no southern tribe or tribes could possibly exercise more control over the wild bands than the Choctaws and Chickasaws. The wildest of the wild bands were in close proximity to the Leased District, which they, heretofore, had frequently overrun. It had consequently formed, since its first organization, a sort of buffer state between the Chickasaws and the hunters of the plains.

This self-same Leased District was now, under the treaty, to be differently disposed of and to be disposed of in such a way as to be bound up indissolubly with the future of the freedmen. Its legal owners, the leasors not the occupants, must have long since relinquished all hope of ever being able again to re-possess themselves in actuality of it. For that reason, no doubt, they readily consented to its sale, notwithstanding that the loss of its huge extent, beyond the ninety-eighth parallel, would cut a big hole in the Choctaw-Chickasaw domain. The price to be paid for the Leased District was three hundred thousand dollars, the same to constitute a trust fund and to be held by the United States under the following regulations: The money was to be held in trust for the Choctaws and Chickasaws at an annual interest of five per cent. For two years during which time the two tribes were to be privileged to make provision for their freedmen by conferring upon them a pre-emptive title to forty acres of land, a fair acreage for residence and cultivation, and certain civil and political rights, inclusive of the electoral franchise.[600] These Indians, however, were specifically excused from adopting the freedmen as *bona fide* members of the tribes and from admitting them as community sharers in tribal lands, annuities, and other monies.

At the expiration of the period stated, one of two arrangements was to be made with respect to the three hundred thousand dollar trust fund. If the Indians had provided for their freedmen, according to the scheme outlined, then the money was to be paid over to them as the purchase price for their lands; but, from it, was to be first deducted enough to allow one hundred dollars for every freedman that had actually removed

---

[600] "Neither of said nations adopted the requisite laws, rules, . . . " and an interesting and highly controversial question arose in consequence as to the economic status of their freedmen. For particulars of the later developments, see *Senate Document*, no. 257, 50th congress, 2nd session. Among the *Freedmen Files* in the Indian Office is a most elaborate statement, prepared "to accompany a letter, written by the Commissioner of Indian Affairs on the 20th of January, 1872, to the Honorable Chairman of the Committee on Freedmen's Affairs of the United States House of Representatives." It has to do mostly with conditions among the Choctaws and Chickasaws. The following letters and reports furnish corroborative or additional information: N. G. Taylor to Browning, July 20, 1868, O.I.A., *Report Book*, no. 17, p. 378; L. N. Robinson to Charles E. Mix, September 26, 1868, *ibid.*, *Southern Superintendency*, 1867-1868; Taylor to Browning, March 2, 1869, *ibid.*, *Report Book*, no. 18, p. 219; E. S. Parker to J. D. Cox, April 26, 1869, *ibid.*, no. 18, p. 315; Walker to Delano, May 8, 1872, *ibid.*, no. 21, pp. 438-439; A. Parsons to E. P. Smith, February 6, 1874, *ibid.*, *Choctaw*, 1873-1876. In this last-named year, the Choctaw delegation in Washington submitted a formal remonstrance against the pressure being brought to bear upon their people to admit the freedmen to full citizenship rights (*House Miscellaneous Documents*, no. 294, 43rd congress, 1st session). For an excellent account of the Choctaws and their freedmen, see *Council Fire and Arbitrator*, 1883-1884, p. 85.

himself beyond the limits of the Choctaw-Chickasaw domain. If, on the other hand, the Indians had not made, within the two years, the requisite provision for their freedmen, the three hundred thousand dollars was to cease to constitute an exclusively Choctaw-Chickasaw trust fund; but was to continue to be held by the United States and under new regulations. It was to be held primarily for the use and benefit of such persons of African descent as the United States could induce to remove from the Choctaw-Chickasaw country within ninety days from the expiration of the two years. Freedmen that returned or remained subsequent to that time were to be denied its benefits and were to be henceforth "upon the same footing as other citizens of the United States in the said nations." What residuary interest the Choctaws and Chickasaws could claim to have in their former trust fund, the purchase price of their ceded lands, the treaty failed to specify and the ambiguity proved a fruitful occasion for controversy and litigation in after years.[601]

Concerning the Choctaw-Chickasaw country to the eastward of the ninety-eighth parallel, the treaty had much to say; but it left its title intact. Sectionization,[602] by which was meant the division and survey of

---

[601] See *Senate Document*, no. 257, 59th congress, 2nd session, *op. cit.*

[602] Sectionization was, in general, approved by the Chickasaws and opposed by the Choctaws. On March 14, 1868, Holmes Colbert reported to Commissioner of Indian Affairs, N. G. Taylor (O.I.A., Land Files, *Choctaw*, 1846-1873, Box 38) that the Chickasaw Legislature had passed an act "giving its assent to the sectionizing and allotting of Chickasaw lands." April 19, 1870, Agent George T. Olmsted informed Parker (*ibid.*) that the Choctaws intended to resort to a referendum. The opposition of the Choctaws may have had something to do with the circumstance that, when the Chickasaw Legislature met in the autumn, it refrained from considering "the subject of a subdivisional survey of lands according to the 11th article of the treaty" (Olmsted to Parker, November 29, 1870, *ibid.*). Two years later, it passed resolutions, approved by Governor C. Harris, September 24, 1872, relative to the disposition of lands held in common by

the land according to the method of the General Land Office, had been much advocated in recent years even before the breaking out of the war and it was now urged upon the Red River tribes and inserted as a possibility into the treaty. Alongside of it, were its necessary concomitants, allotment in severalty and the capitalization of public funds, the whole procedure so much of an anticipation that its details need not be permitted to cumber the present narrative.

Within this reserved territory lying east of the ninety-eighth parallel, the Choctaws and Chickasaws agreed to receive Kansas Indians, not exceeding ten thousand in number, and to grant to them, in general, the same civil, political, and economic status as was to be confered upon the freedmen. They were to be allowed to enter the nation without waiting for the expected survey to take place, the United States agreeing to pay for the land they occupied at the rate of one dollar an acre.

the Choctaws and Chickasaws. One of these recommended that, in case the Choctaws continued to oppose sectionization and allotment, the Chickasaw landed interests should be severed from theirs (O.I.A., Land Files, *Choctaw*, 1846-1873, Box 38, G 183 of 1872). In no wise did this procedure act as a deterrent to Choctaw opposition and, in January of 1874, the Choctaw General Council met in extra session and passed resolutions "protesting against the allotment of lands in the Chickasaw District" as had been provided for by the resolution of 1872, and also protesting against any movement to extend a territorial form of government over the Choctaw people without their consent. The resolutions of protest were transmitted direct to President Grant under cover of a letter to him from Principal Chief, William Bryant, February 17, 1874, and, by Grant, referred to the Interior Department, March 6th (*ibid., Choctaw*, 1874-1876, Box 39, P 167). Secretary Delano looked into the matter and later, March 13th, expressed the opinion that the Chickasaws were powerless without the co-operation of the Choctaws. It is interesting to observe that Albert Pike was suspected of bolstering up the Choctaw obstinacy and that he was doing it in the interests of the railroads (Agent A. Parsons to E. P. Smith, dated Boggy Depot, October 16, 1873, *ibid.*, Box 38). P. P. Pitchlynn issued pamphlets against sectionization, of which Pike was reputed to be the real author.

The idea of an ultimate territorial organization received larger amplification in the Choctaw-Chickasaw treaty than in any other of the reconstruction series. The tribes agreed, as had the Seminoles, to such prospective congressional legislation as might be presumed to be for the benefit of the Indian country, saving, of course, all tribal rights and privileges. They accepted the idea of a general, or inter-tribal, council, meeting annually under the presidency of the Superintendent of Indian Affairs, and representative of tribes, "lawfully resident." Special sessions might be called under authority of the Secretary of the Interior and an upper chamber added should circumstances later on appear to warrant it. It was not, however, in the machinery of the council that Harlan's pet project found its chief expression. It was in one of its functions, in the suggestion, in fact, that should congress see fit to "authorize the appointment of a Delegate from said Territory," he should be elected in the council. The regular organization of Indian Territory had never yet been provided for by law and was not in this instrument, nevertheless, from this point, the Choctaw-Chickasaw treaty proceeded as if it were a *fait accompli*. The reference to the territorial delegate was commonplace, yet subtle, and so normally dragged in that the ordinary Indian scanning the treaty would not be justified in having his prejudices or his fears aroused. The existence of a delegate presupposes the existence of an organized territory and hence, without definitely mentioning organization, the treaty provided, among other things, that the executive of "said Territory" should be the Superintendent of Indian Affairs "with the title of 'governor of the Territory of Oklahoma'." The affair was most adroitly managed; but into no other of the reconstruction treaties did the objectionable details obtrude themselves.

Almost buried among the multiform provisions of the Choctaw-Chickasaw treaty was an understanding reached by the high contracting parties that fully substantiates the claim that, in all essentials, the second of the series was the least reconstructive. It was a provision that acknowledged the binding force of all pre-war agreements between the Red River tribes and the United States. Pre-war guaranties and obligations had apparently suffered no impairment, except that the United States made no offer to reimburse the tribes for their funds lost during the war. By act of congress, payment thereof had been suspended or the funds themselves diverted to other purposes. The record of the war, in this respect, was evidently to be obliterated.

Among the concluding treaty provisions calling for particular comment stands prominently that of amnesty. The provision is a peculiar one and faintly suggestive of the loyalist and debt-paying obligations of the treaty that closed the Revolutionary War. The United States, in 1866, had just emerged from a bloody struggle in which it had, by force of arms alone, vindicated its doctrine of federal supremacy. None the less, in concluding its arrangement with the Red River tribes, it revealed either its impotence or its own fundamental adherence to the opposing doctrine of state rights. This it did by stipulating that it would itself grant amnesty to the individual Indians and would "especially request the States of Missouri, Kansas, Arkansas, and Texas to grant the like amnesty as to all offences committed by any member of the Choctaw or Chickasaw Nation." The Indians were not asked to reciprocate in this particular; for that would have been a damaging admission that white men and their states had wronged them; but they were required to concede amnesty to their own people.   Considering that practically the entire population of the two tribes had seceded, the arrangement was a foregone conclusion.

Claimants [603] for indemnity were necessarily few in number among the Choctaws and Chickasaws, so few that it was an easy matter to provide for them.   The language in which the provision is couched is more interesting by far than the provision itself.   A commission was to be appointed to "take into consideration and determine the claim of such Choctaws and Chickasaws as allege that they have been driven during the late rebellion from their homes   .   .   .   on account of their adhesion to the United States, for damages, with power to make such award as may be consistent with equity and good conscience, taking into view all circumstances, whose report, when ratified by the Secretary of the Interior, shall be final, and authorize the payment of the amount from any moneys of said nations in the hands of the United States   .   .   .   "

A more extensive charge upon the tribal funds than the foregoing was likely to be was the claim of licensed traders,[604] who, by the fiftieth article of the treaty were

---

[603] James G. Blunt became attorney for these claimants and, on April 10, 1866, he submitted to Harlan a statement setting forth their grievance (O.I.A., General Files, *Choctaw*, 1859-1866, B 119). Agent Isaac Colman had, January 12, 1866, testified that they were "heads of loyal Choctaw families." Latrobe was chosen by the two nations to represent their interests. E. W. Rice of Iowa and A. H. Jackson of Nebraska constituted the claims commission (*ibid., Letter Book*, no. 81, pp. 72-74).

[604] On January 19, 1866, Agent Colman reported to Cooley on the subject of these licensed traders and said,

"There are now residing in the Choctaw & Chickasaw country citizens of the United States who were there previous to the Rebellion as Indian agents, licensed traders, &c. who at the commencement of and during the Rebellion exercised their controlling influence, headed

empowered to present their cases to a special commission. Chief among the traders were two citizens of Massachusetts, Joseph G. Heald[605] and Reuben Wright. The attitude of these men towards the war had not always been above suspicion; but that did not prevent due credence being given to their exorbitant claim for damages. The aggregate of the claims was not to exceed ninety thousand dollars and Heald and Wright managed so to marshal theirs that they covered it all. In this matter, as in that of the grant of a right of way to railways, Indian politicians and Indian political schemes figured largely.[606]

& led on the Indians in acts of unusual atrocity. Some of such persons have been adopted as citizens by the Choctaw & Chickasaw Councils and by virtue of such adoption have exercised their acquired knowledge of the country in selecting the choice locations of the country for their future homes, such places as comprise Oil Springs, Salt Springs, Coal Mines &c. Some of these traders have since the close of the Rebellion been engaged in introducing goods into the Indian Country, trading for and driving stock out of the Nation by virtue of their claim to be and remain in the Indian Country, particularly does this statement apply to Eli Mitchell who I understand visits Washington in company with the Choctaw & Chickasaw Delegation."

[605] J. G. Heald, whom Dole recommended to Blunt, May 21, 1862, "as a thoroughly reliable New England man," (O.I.A., *Letter Book*, no. 68, p. 256) was one of the sources upon which the Indian Office relied to get its information regarding conditions in the Indian Territory at the commencement of the war. Heald's letter to Dole, dated Pepperell, May 17, 1862 (O. I. A., General Files, *Southern Superintendency*, 1859-1862) gave the strength of the Pike military forces at the time Heald left the Choctaw Agency, April 10, 1862.

[606] The claim of Heald and Wright came before the Jackson-Rice commission, which was appointed in July (Cooley to Jackson and Rice, July 30, 1866, O.I.A., *Letter Book*, no. 81, pp. 72-74). There is a voluminous amount of material on the subject of the two kinds of claims, the loyal Indian and the licensed trader. The published report, *House Executive Documents,* no. 204, 40th congress, 2nd session, gives, of course, much of it in a nutshell. Many unpublished documents are, however, to be found in "Papers from the Committee on Indian Affairs," *House Files,* 40th congress and in Indian Office *Special Files,* nos, 134, 142, 245. In Indian Office *Report Book,* no. 20, p. 120, the claim of Reuben Wright for depredations committed by the Chickasaws is set forth. The whole subject of the settlement of claims under

The treaty with the Creeks was more difficult of procurement [607] than had been either of the others and it

the forty-ninth and fiftieth articles of the Choctaw-Chickasaw Treaty of 1866 is too intricate, too much bound up with charges of fraud and corruption to be dealt with adequately here.

[607] In its original form, the Creek treaty was apparently one of the very first to be drafted. The delay in its definite procurement was chiefly caused by differences between the northern and southern representatives. The northern refused to recognize the southern as in any sense official and Agent J. W. Dunn, who with other agents like Harlan and Reynolds had been in Washington since January engaged in the business of treaty-making (Cooley to R. W. Taylor, First Comptroller of the Treasury, August 27, 1866, O.I.A., *Letter Book*, no. 81, p. 262), endorsed their view (Dunn to Sells, May 10, 1866, O.I.A., General Files, *Creek*, 1860-1869). Prior to the time when the Indian Office summoned the tribe to send delegates, a meeting had been held "on Scipio place" on which occasion Sands, the recognized leader of the loyal element, was authorized to go to Washington at the head of a delegation (Loyal delegates to Cooley, April 21, 1866, *ibid.*). This was on November 5, 1865. Later, in December, came the order from Washington and the full delegation was selected. In February, when Dunn with this delegation was in Fort Smith, *en route* for Washington, he telegraphed to Cooley, inquiring if he should furnish transportation to D. N. McIntosh and James M. C. Smith, who were intending to be present at the negotiations (Dunn to Sells, May 10, 1866, *ibid.*). He was answered in the affirmative; but the circumstance "was not intended to be interpreted that they were looked upon as official delegates."

Almost at the outset, however, the southern men made their presence felt and interjected their opinions into the treaty discussions. March fifth, they asked for an opportunity to read the treaty as drafted on the third in order that they might see how it affected the rights of the secessionists (McIntosh and Smith to Cooley, March 5, 1866, *ibid.,*). The request was complied with and in a manner and with a result such as can be gleaned from the following letter from Dunn to Cooley, March 15, 1866 (*ibid.*):

"On the 9th inst you furnished me a copy of the treaty lately concluded between the U. S. Government and the Creek Nation for the inspection of Col. McIntosh and Capt. Smith, who had lately arrived here as delegates from the disloyal portion of said Nation and who were anxious to make amendments to the treaty provided it could be done with the consent of those who had made it

"Messrs McIntosh, Smith & myself met the delegates who had made the treaty at their rooms at the Union Hotel at the date aforesaid when the parties had a free & friendly talk in relation to the treaty and their troubles for the last four years.

"The delegates who had made the treaty refused the right of McIntosh & Smith to act with them, saying that they alone were authorized to make a treaty, that they had made one, the best that

was the claim for indemnity that proved the great stumbling-block in the course of its negotiation. The treaty was defined as one of "cession and indemnity."

could be made situated as they were, that they were satsfied with it, and that they presumed the U. S. Government was, and that they would regard any interference in what had been done on the part of McIntosh & Smith as unkind & without authority – And here the conference ended . . . "

Their purpose defeated, McIntosh and Smith addressed themselves directly to the United States commissioners, Cooley, Sells, and Parker, and enumerated their objections to the treaty as it then stood, March 18, 1866. In brief, they opposed more particularly these matters: their own exclusion from the treaty-making, the confiscation of property, the recognition of former negro slaves as the equals of the Creeks politically, and the jurisdiction of congress. With regard to the last-named, they were ready to say that they were "not opposed to a proper and safe organization of the Indian Country into a Territory, giving due consideration and weight to the rights and welfare of the Indians." The same objections, a little better stated, perhaps, were, on March 31, 1866, embodied in an address to the president.

It would appear, although the dates of some of the documentary evidence is a little confusing, that a new draft of the Creek treaty was made and, on May 8th, submitted to McIntosh and Smith; but it failed to meet with their approval (McIntosh and Smith to Cooley, May 9, 1866, O.I.A., General Files, *Creek, 1860-1869*; Cooley to Harlan, May 18, 1866, *ibid., Report Book*, no. 15, p. 286). On the eleventh, Harlan himself wrote to them, asking if they would be willing to sign if the preamble be changed. Their reply was,

" . . . Our chief objection to that treaty grows out of the fact that in the title and in the body – not in the Preamble – of that instrument, the majority of the Creek people are practically ignored and their rights confiscated, and as that objection, in our opinion, was paramount to all others, we considered it – and still consider it – useless to attempt to discuss minor details, until the main difficulty is disposed of by the recognition of the great body of the Nation, and of their right to be heard in the settlement of questions affecting their very existence . . . " (McIntosh and Smith to Harlan, May 14, 1866, I.D. Files, Bundle, no. 56).

Another attempt to re-draft the Creek treaty was made in June and completed June 14th (Cooley to Otto, June 14, 1866, O.I.A., *Report Book*, no. 15, p. 325); but, in the great essentials the old remained unaltered. In the case of the Creeks, the government had found the unionist element the more pliable and had worked with it to the undoing of the tribe. In the next few years, Creek troubles multiplied enormously and they traced themselves, upon investigation, to the reconstruction treaty of 1866.

For once the Indians were striving for exactness in terminology. In most respects the provisions of the treaty were made to resemble rather closely those of the Seminole. They registered the same insistence upon the thought that the Creeks had incurred liability of forfeiture because, in entering into an alliance with the Confederate States, they had "ignored their allegiance to the United States and unsettled the treaty relations" with that government. The confounding of liability to forfeiture with liabilities made its appearance again despite the fact that Cooley had had his attention called to the very evident discrepancy between the two, the former indicating a contingency, the latter, an accomplished fact.

By the now familiar device, the omission of a guaranty clause, the United States commissioners cleverly avoided fixing upon their country the responsibility for protection should another civil war occur. They forced the acknowledgment of tribal amnesty and pledged to individual Indians the benefaction of federal. As was the case in all the other treaties, the very words of the Thirteenth Amendment to the United States constitution were inserted into the treaty, which meant that the institution of slavery together with any other form of involuntary servitude except as a punishment for crime was to be forever abolished. The cause, invariably found attached, "whereof the parties shall have been duly convicted," had an interesting addition, "in accordance with laws applicable to all members of said tribe." It was undoubtedly intended as a protection for the freedmen against civil and judicial discrimination. Other safeguards for the freedmen there were and not the least of them the provision exacted of the Seminoles that the blacks, whether ex-slaves or new immigrants, should be eligible to full membership in the tribe, be regularly adopted by it, and made competent to participate with native citizens in all its rights and privileges, "including an equal interest in the soil and national funds."[608]

The land cession made by the Creeks on this occasion was an extensive one, approximately three million two hundred and fifty thousand five hundred and sixty acres. It comprised the entire western half of their tribal domain. Out of its extreme southeastern corner, the Seminoles had already been provided for, a tiny section of the whole. The retained eastern half of

---

[608] Against this provision in all its stages, the southern Creeks most vigorously protested. McIntosh and Smith, in a letter to Harlan, May 22nd, said,

"We cannot but think that you are disposed to require more for the freedmen than is just or reasonable – more than the whites have done or propose to do anywhere – and more than has been required of the Choctaws and Chickasaws in their behalf.

"We feel certain that to give them an equal interest in either annuities or soil would be an ill-advised step, calculated to create a prejudice against them in the minds of our people. So far as we are concerned, we are willing to give them all the rights, privileges, and immunities of our own citizens – with the right to occupy and cultivate forty, or even 80 acres of land – in other words, that quantity to be held on the same terms under which our own people hold their possessions . . . " (O.I.A., General Files, *Creek,* 1860-1869).

The Creeks did not altogether live up to the agreement regarding the freedmen, which was not surprising, especially when the fact be realised that the Indian Office and the Interior Department made very peculiar rulings in the premises. For instance, the Commissioner of Indian Affairs, on one occasion, ruled that "negroes who become citizens of the Creek nation, under the provisions of the Creek treaty of 1866, are not Indians within the meaning of the Intercourse Act and are subject to the jurisdiction of the U.S. courts." (O.I.A., *Report Book,* no. 20, p. 350). Secretary Delano reversed this decision (Delano to the Commissioner of Indian Affairs, February 2, 1872, O.I.A., Land Files, *Creek,* Box 45). A clause in the Indian Appropriation Act for 1868 authorized the withholding of Creek money until the freedmen should be provided for (See Taylor to Browning, August 10, 1868, O.I.A., *Report Book,* no. 17, p. 406. On the same subject, see *Report Book,* no. 18, pp. 16, 17).

their old reserve the Creeks were assured that they might hold henceforth in perpetuity. Probably, upon no other condition, could they be prevailed upon to surrender anything. The sale price of the cession was fixed at thirty cents an acre and, out of the amount realised, that is, out of the Creeks' own funds, the United States government generously undertook to pay two hundred thousand dollars per capita unless the President should otherwise direct, for reconstruction work "to enable the Creeks to occupy, restore and improve their farms, and to make their nation independent and self-sustaining." In much of this there was the spirit of a self-denying ordinance; but just the same the Creeks would have been better pleased had their Great Father undertaken a little reparation work on his own account. He might, for example, have advanced the comparatively small sum, two thousand dollars or less, with which the losses sustained by missionary establishments were to be made good. Obviously, the payment to soldiers of the Home Guard should have constituted a just charge upon the United States treasury; but that was not the opinion of Cooley and his associates. A sum of one hundred thousand dollars was by them set aside to be apportioned among "soldiers [609] that enlisted in the Federal Army and the

[609] In the matter of the claims of Creek Indians who served in the Federal army, *Senate Document*, no. 67, 55th congress, 1st session is important. The claim of the Home Guards to the bounties and pensions granted to white soldiers, under the various acts of congress (Glasson, *History of Military Pension Legislation*, pp. 70-87), was for long a matter of dispute between the War Department, arguing in the negative, and the Department of Justice, in the affirmative. When finally allowed, it gave the usual occasion for fraud. Scarcely had the first regiment been mustered out, when a pension agent, John W. Wright, appeared at Fort Gibson and opened an office. For details of his activities, see *Report of J. G. Blunt*, who acted as attorney for the Creek soldiers (A.G.O., Old Files Section, B 1013, V.S., 1863, Jacket 15 of 15); *House Report*, no. 96, 42nd congress, 2nd session;

loyal refugee Indians and freedmen [610] who were driven from their homes by the rebel forces." The disbursement of the remainder of the nine hundred and seventy-five thousand one hundred and sixty-eight dollars, which was to come to the Creeks for their cession, is for the present purpose immaterial. A claims commission was to be appointed. The treaty now made was to be understood as a full settlement of all Creek [611] claims against the United States. The old treaties, in so far as they were not incompatible with the new document, were to be restored and renewed payment of the old annuities was to begin from the opening of the next fiscal year. The special measures of a general council, premature endorsement of congressional legislation, a grant of right of way to railroads were presented in the Creek treaty as in the Seminole.

Interior Department Files, 1852-1868. Wright's "Argument to the Secretary of War," E. M. Stanton, is most instructive as also, in repudiation of the charges against himself, his "To the Public," which was published in May of 1869. Wright contended that those opposed to him were "the regular Indian Ring, who, finding their power obtained under the late Administration quite gone, seek to put on an honest face and gain favor with the powers that be."

[610] In Indian Office *Special Files,* no. 284 are several documents, bearing upon the Creek claim for reimbursement because of money paid out of Creek funds to negroes who were not Creek, but wholly or in part, Cherokee freedmen.

[611] The loyal Creek claims are the subject matter of inumerable documents filed among the *Special Cases* in the Indian Office. Special Case, no. 52706 of 1906 is the general file number for many of them. In General Files, *Creek,* 1860-1869, are papers dealing with the Creek Orphan Fund, which, subsequent to the negotiation of the treaty of 1866, became the occasion of a more or less acrimonious correspondence.

X. NEGOTIATIONS WITH THE CHEROKEES

As was to have been anticipated, the most serious opposition as well as the greatest degree of obsequiousness came from the Cherokees and, consequently, the negotiations with them were the most prolonged. Since the adjournment of the Fort Smith Council, the Cherokee Nation, by which must be meant, that part of the tribe that had, in 1863, repudiated its treaty with the Southern Confederacy, abolished slavery, and, in the spring of 1865, so far registered its confidence in its aged chief, John Ross, as to receive him once again as its Principal Chief,[612] had not been inactive.   Through its National Council, it had unanimously entered a solemn protest against the official degradation which Cooley and his associates had meted out to Ross at Fort Smith.   Armed with that protest, the Cherokee delegates came on to Washington to renew negotiations with the United States government in 1866; but they had been charged and were resolved not to proceed in those negotiations until rank and prestige had been restored to their stalwart defender, who, with spirit undaunted, had travelled eastward, at the special request of the National Council, to conduct one last campaign in defence of the rights of his people.   He was to die

---

[612] On April 5, 1865, John Ross had submitted to the Indian Office his oath of office as Principal Chief of the Cherokees and he had taken then the opportunity to call attention to the pledge of allegiance to the United States constitution and laws which it, by express reference, involved (O.I.A., General Files, *Cherokee*, 1859-1865, R 479).

before the struggle was entirely over; but he lived long enough to know to his sorrow, as he had known in the fateful years leading up to removal, that the worst enemies of the Cherokee tribe were in its own camp.

With their special mission before them, the Cherokee delegates, on January 24, 1866, addressed to the President, the Senate, and the House of Representatives a memorial [613] in which they had reviewed the history of the past four years, had explained their relations with the Confederate States as also with the United States and had put up a strong and impassioned plea for justice. To remove the stigma of disloyalty from their nation was their paramount object and, for its accomplishment, must come, before everything else, the reinstatement of John Ross. Upon his impeccability and upon the integrity of his motives, they rested their entire case.

A further discrediting of John Ross had, however, already been attempted. Earlier in the month of January, Boudinot and Adair had made inquiry [614] of Cooley, but not because they expected him to have on file, in his office, the information, "in regard to the distribution of money paid to Mr. John Ross, or the 'constituted authorities' of the Cherokee Nation, by the late so-called Confederate States, in the year 1861, or

[613] The text of this memorial I have never yet been able to locate notwithstanding that I have made diligent search therefor. Its contents I have inferred from the various answers that were made to it.

[614] E. C. Boudinot and W. P. Adair to Cooley, January 12, 1866 (O.I.A., *Cherokee*, B 22 of 1866). In the brief on the outside of this communication, these two men are cited as Cherokee representatives. Apparently they were the only ones of the southern delegation yet on hand, and they must have been in straitened circumstances for, on the sixteenth, when he presented his credentials formally to Cooley, Adair begged for an advance of twenty-five dollars to apply on his salary as delegate. He had been confined to his bed with sickness he said (Adair to Cooley, January 16, 1866, *ibid., Cherokee*, A 18 of 1866).

1862." Some data on the subject of the money they had themselves and they furnished it to Cooley. The amount was "Near the sum of Two Hundred and Fifty Thousand Dollars," and it had been "paid to these 'constituted authorities,' and received by their treasurer; and it is equally certain that none of the 'disloyal' Cherokees were beneficiaries." Had Pike been the one to furnish this particular scent? [615] And what was the role that Boudinot and Adair were arranging for themselves?

[615] Upon this subject Pike must certainly have been applied to for information although there is no record of any letter having been sent to him. He wrote from Memphis, on the 6th of February, concerning John Ross's relations with the Confederacy and, incidentally, gave specific details regarding the money paid to the Cherokee tribe. Strange to say, his letter was not handed over for filing until September 29, 1866, when it was listed as though just received. In the letter, Pike averred,

"Early in March 1862 I paid Lewis Ross, the Treasurer of the Nation and brother of John Ross, the specie stipulated, and the $150,000 in Confederate Treasury notes, in John Ross' house, John Ross being present, and I have the receipt for both sums. It was supposed that the $150,000 was desired for the purpose, chiefly, of paying scrip of the Nation held to a considerable amount by Mr. Ross and his relatives. Whether it was so applied or not, I do not know." (Pike to Cooley, February 6, 1866, O.I.A., *Cherokee*, P 208 of 1866). In April, John W. Stapler wrote as follows to Secretary Harlan:

"Not having the honor of a personal acquaintance, excuse the liberty of my addressing you.

"Learning from a reliable source that the Department suspected Chief John Ross of having received and used for his own private purposes the $60,000 Gold received by the Treasurer Mr. Lewis Ross from the Rebel A. Pike –

"I am constrained from a sense of duty and justice to him to make known to you – that I can give testimony touching that Gold-derived from personal knowledge which will remove that belief from the most prejudiced mind and exonerate the Chief from the charge.

"The Treasurer Office and Iron Safe we kept in one of the rooms in my Store at Tahlequah the Capitol of the Nation.

"A Citizen of the Nation by marriage having resided there for fifteen years and at the breaking out of the rebellion had a Wife and three small children. We remained loyal – were persecuted – robbed –shot at – and finally when the Union Troops under Col. Cloud penetrated to our Country we fled from our comfortable home.

"We are now residing in Wilmington my native city . . . "

Were they intending to turn state's evidence?   Certain it is that they were bent upon imputing venality as well as disloyalty to the leaders of the faction opposed to themselves in their tribe.   Did they wish to imply also that since their faction received none of the Confederate money, they could not, legally, be held as responsible parties, responsible, that is for Cherokee defection? Their insistence upon "constituted authorities" might suggest that there was method in their madness and that they appreciated to the full the argument of those who were clamoring for the indictment of Jefferson Davis. Moreover, their repeated reference to Mr. John Ross as if he were a private individual instead of then as now the highly esteemed Principal Chief of the tribe, Harlan and Cooley to the contrary notwithstanding, betrayed their contemptible pettiness of spirit.   The use that Cooley intended to make of their letter is significant.   As it appears in the government files to-day, it carries on its envelope this memorandum, which was undoubtedly from Cooley's pen: *File for use in our negotiations with 'Cherokees'.*[616]

A second letter,[617] which Boudinot and Adair addressed to the Commissioner of Indian Affairs in Jan-

(John W. Stapler to James Harlan, dated Wilmington, Delware, April 28, 1866, O.I.A., *Cherokee*, S 233 of 1866).

[616] The so-called *John Ross Papers* were requisitioned for the negotiations of 1866 as for the Fort Smith Council. As they appear in the files to-day, they were evidently prepared for elaborate use in January, 1866. The bundle containing them is labelled, *Loyalty of John Ross, Principal Chief of the Cherokees*. In Indian Office *Special Files*, no. 125, are many documents bearing directly upon the negotiations of 1866 as they affected John Ross and his people. In *Irregularly-Shaped Papers* of the Indian Office are rough drafts of practically all the longer documents prepared during the course of the negotiations. They will be referred to separately as occasion demands. In General Files, *Cherokee*, C 515 of 1866, are about twenty-five documents most of them being copies of the *John Ross Papers*.

[617] E. C. Boudinot and W. P. Adair to Cooley, January 19, 1866, O.I.A., *Cherokee*, B 60. The same day Phillips wrote to Doolittle a letter that was

uary indicated exactly how they had come to regard their own adherence to the Confederacy. They wrote the letter to express umbrage at a certain implication in one of Superintendent Coffin's reports to the effect that government agents, white men of position and character, had been primarily responsible for the

---

of tenor very different. It put the facts as they should have been put by officers higher up in the United States government. It reads as follows:

I regretted extremely that your commision did not come to Fort Gibson, before my command was mustered from the service. After my return I endeavored to see some of the committee, but failed to do so.

There was many matters of grave importance, vitally connected with the interests intrusted to you, and it was impossible to communicate them in writing.

For three years, while military commander in the Indian Territory, I was constantly beset with the difficulties. A combination, as powerful as it was corrupt, threatened alike the interests of the Indians and the government.

In my arduous task I regret to say, that I had but little support from that government. When my temporary removal from command was once or twice affected I was, it is true, ordered back, but my demands for a Court of Inquiry were, if not refused, at least not attended to. My demands for the arrest and trial of persons high in rank, and the request that I be instructed to prefer charges against them, evoked nothing farther than assurance that the evils would be remedied. Occasionally an officer, or guilty official in the other department might be removed, but, I was denied the scrutiny that would have resulted in my complete vindication, and the probable punishment of the guilty.

I cannot cumber this letter with details that ran their astounding course for several years. I will refer briefly to one or two points. In the beginning of 1864, all my cavalry was taken from me, leaving me without a picket, and a system of stealing cattle inaugurated in my rear. For 160 miles the country lay exposed in my rear, and thousands of refugees clustering around my camp at Gibson. A letter, proving the complicity of the officer commanding the south sub-district of Kansas, fell into my hands. I forwarded copies of it to my superior at Ft. Smith and to Gen. Curtis in Kansas, demanding proceedings against the parties, and yet *that officer remained in command up to the close of the war,* and I have reason to fear that at least one of my letters was sent to him.

I staked my character in an endeavor to stop the payment of several fraudulent accounts for supplying refugee Indians, and had the mor-

Cherokee treaty of October, 1861. Coffin had written,
September 24, 1863, that "they" – and he was referring
to the Cherokees – "resisted the insidious influences
which were brought to bear upon them by Rector, Pike,
Cooper, Crawford and other rebel emissaries for a long
time." His inclusion of Cooper in this particular list
was a little unfortunate; inasmuch as it now afforded
to Boudinot and Adair the opportunity they sought to
impeach all such testimony. That Cooper belonged
in the category of Confederate emissaries no one could
gainsay; but he had confined his attentions to the Red
River tribes. Even if he had possessed any influence
over the Cherokees, he could, at that time, have exerted
it only very indirectly.

tification to learn that the only result was that copies of my correspondence had been placed in the hands, or obtained by the band of
thieving contractors.

But I cannot enumerate. I now see that questions of disloyalty are
artfully preferred against the only Indians who have the independence
and intelligence to preserve the rights of their people.

Knowing well, the circumstances under which all of their people
acted – having brought the greater part of them, *in person,* within the
federal lines – during the arduous struggle for power there, I can
fully comprehend the spirit of iniquity, that for its own sinister purposes, uses technicalities and words to accomplish their purpose.

I do not prosecute this matter in any spirit of vindictiveness. It has
been the misfortune of a sacred cause to have its motives impugned,
and, for my part I struggled against these evils without giving them
notoriety, not desiring to be considered turbulent, until their very
magnitude left me no alternative.

Serving my government faithfully I have been treated *as no other
has been treated.* I have been refused Investigation. I have been left
to the mercy of a powerful combination – although I hope I have
not the meanness to fear it, and I have even been denied the privilege
of testifying before your committee. I write to say that while the necessities of the times may require you to do much that may be unsatis-
factory to the civilized Indians yet I entreat you to see that those who
served us so faithfully when our cause was in doubt, *get* Justice.

(Wm. A. Phillips to J. R. Doolittle, dated Topeka, January 19, 1866,
O.I.A., *Southern Superintendency,* I 89 of 1866. This letter is labelled thus:
"Confidentially submitted to Mr. Harlan,

J. R. D."

In January of 1866, individual Cherokees had little to fear by way of punishment for their abandonment of federal allegiance. The United States government needed land and needed it badly; but it could get it in the required amount from a tribe only. The position of the Cherokee Nation, with respect to the Civil War, was, for its purposes exceedingly awkward; but, if it could only hold fast to the doctrine that the "constituted authorities" of that nation had been fundamentally disloyal, their attainment would be easy. This argument Boudinot and Adair had long since ascertained and accepted. With complacency, therefore, they exonerated white men from blame; but, instead of shouldering that blame themselves as the words[618] of their letter might imply they intended, they thrust it upon John Ross and others of the "constituted authorities" of the Cherokee Nation. Was it an accident that some of the white men were close at hand, influential, and ready to serve the Boudinot-Adair interests, if their own were safeguarded? As recognized emissaries of the late Confederacy they were in a far more serious position than was the Indian chief, John Ross; but, could the charge that they were emissaries be once refuted and refuted by men, who knew all the facts and who might be presumed to have something of their own to gain by its substantiation, a long step would have been taken in the recovery of their lost status and, more important that all else, they would have regained the official confidence of the United States Indian Office, with which they hoped to have future dealings of the sort that had proved so profitable to them in times past.

The Cherokee memorial that had been handed in on January 24th was given a fairly wide circulation. In

[618] O.I.A., *Cherokee.*

particular, it was referred, formally or informally, to Boudinot and Adair and to Pike and, naturally, it aroused in the southern delegation a spirit of strong opposition. On the thirtieth, Boudinot and Adair acknowledged its receipt and then set to work to prepare an answer in rebuttal despite the fact that they stigmatized it as "but a tissue of misrepresentations and falsehoods and duplicity from beginning to end." "At any rate," said they, "we do not feel that it is incumbent upon us as a duty to answer it, with a proper regard to your late proceedings at the Treaty-making Council at Ft. Smith, Ark., last September. By those proceedings you representing the U.S. Govt deposed Mr. Ross as Principal Chief of the Cherokee Nation and made Treaties of Amity and Peace with both branches of the Nation – and as we have stated a due regard to these Treaties and *your acts* as Comm[r] of Indian Affairs, seem to require of us no official notice of him or his Dellegation – until this question of his Chieftaincy be settled, as we believe it has been . . . "[619]

The Boudinot-Adair counter-memorial when finished was handed to Albert Pike and he, after studying it in its relation to the one of January twenty-fourth, submitted to Cooley a lengthy letter[620] by way of comment. This was on February seventeenth. Pike's letter is most interesting. It is a general and very verbose statement of his own diplomatic activities but with no unnecessary emphasis upon self-incriminating details. Evidently, he had seized eagerly upon the opportunity, which Cherokee dissensions offered, to recount, in his own way, his official connection with the Confederacy;

[619] Boudinot and Adair to Cooley, January 30, 1866, O.I.A., *Cherokee*, B 49 of 1866.

[620] Pike to Cooley, February 17, 1866, O.I.A., *Ross Papers*, no. 6.

but what is most significant is the relief into which he endeavored to throw the coincident actions of John Ross. His purpose was obvious and it was, in effect, the sustaining of Cooley's contention that Ross's own disloyalty justified completely his dethronement. The sycophancy of men of the Boudinot and Pike stamp could scarcely have brought much gratification to the government officials, who, nevertheless, accepted it.

How much they accepted it can be surmised from the use to which the anti-Ross arguments were put. On February twenty-fifth, after he had had time thoroughly to digest the Cherokee memorial, its accompanying documents, the Boudinot-Adair rebuttal, and the Pike narrative, Cooley sent to President Johnson his own reply;[621] but it was of a character little conducive to the adjustment of conflicting opinions and interests. It had some aspects of a lawyer's brief and that, in effect, it was designed to be. It was a clever contrivance for placing indisputable facts in such relations that they could not fail to work a prejudice against John Ross.

The attitude of Secretary Harlan, at least to the extent that his ulterior motives would permit, was less personal, more statesmanlike and detached. Indeed, it was almost conciliatory. It expressed itself in conversation with the delegates and in a list of suggestions[622] for a treaty that he himself seems to have prepared. With Harlan's suggestions before them, the two groups of Cherokees went to work.[623] Their labors, however,

---

[621] This has been located in rough draft only.
[622] O.I.A., *Papers Bearing upon the Cherokee Negotiations of 1866.*
[623] The northerners gave notice of progress in this wise:

"We have the honor to inform you that, in compliance with your suggestions, we are engaged in considering provisions for a new treaty with our people; & that in a few days we will be prepared to present a draft of one which will be acceptable to the Cherokee Nation" (John Ross, Principal Chief, S. H. Benge, White Catcher,

accomplished nothing in the direction of bringing them closer together.   They pushed them, if anything, more widely apart; for each group seized the opportunity to prepare an *ex parte* document.[624]

Meanwhile, a new feature of the Cherokee case was assuming great prominence.   It was to be eventually the crux of the whole matter.   What the secessionists wanted was political separation, segregation, the assignment to them, by title in perpetuity, of a proportionate share of the tribal domain.   It was what the elder Ridge had contended for, as leader of the Treaty Party, years previous and what President Polk, with the facts all before him, had positively refused to grant.   Strange that at this particular time, when a war against secession had just been concluded, the thought of such a thing should have been entertained for a single moment by the United States government.   And yet it was entertained and entertained seriously.   The southern representatives included it in their reply to Harlan's suggestions.   Their differences with the Ross faction, the Non-Treaty Party of an earlier day, were held to be incapable of adjustment and, upon that supposition, Cooley proceeded to make inquiries far and wide.   He was seeking confidential information respecting domes-

Thomas Pegg, James McDaniel, Daniel H. Ross, J. B. Jones and Smith Christie, Delegation of the Cherokee Nation, to Secretary Harlan, dated Corner 8th & Pa. Ave., Washington, March 7, 1866, O.I.A., *Cherokee*, R 46 of 1866).   Either the writers were ignorant of the fact that the others were being communicated with also or they chose to ignore it.   Note the citation of John Ross as Principal Chief.   He signed the letter with his own hand.

[624] The two documents are not regularly filed in the Indian Office; but they are there with other rough and shapeless papers that bear upon the negotiations of 1866.   The project for a treaty prepared by the official delegates is dated, March 15, 1866 and labelled *Proposed N. Cherokee Treaty*.   The response of the secessionists is no. 9 in the series, *Papers bearing upon the Cherokee Negotiations of 1866*.

tic affairs within the Cherokee country; but he applied
for it to people who were known to be amenable to suggestion from him or hostile to John Ross.   He applied
to Sells, to Blunt and to one, J. M. Tebbetts,[625] a citizen
of Arkansas, who had just been refused permission to
drive cattle through the Indian Territory.

The upshot of Commissioner Cooley's inquiries
would seem to have been a decision to prepare his own
project of a treaty,[626] which he forthwith did.   It was
entrusted to Agent Harlan for delivery to the delegates
and the day following brought from them a protest.
They had taken great offence at the complete ignoring
of their draft, which they professed to have developed
along the lines laid down by Secretary Harlan.   It was
intended by him, so they had understood, as a basis for
negotiation and they would, therefore, respectfully suggest that it be treated as such and that all modifications be dealt with as amendments to it and to it alone.[627]

A serious dilemma had been created.   Feeling between the two groups of Cherokees was running high;
for the secessionists hesitated not to insinuate and to
assert that the unionists were cut-throats and assassins.[628]

---

[625] Tebbetts' reply was of date, March 30, 1866, Agent Harlan, applied
to also, reported on the subject to Sells, March 28, 1866, O.I.A., *Cherokee,*
S 171 of 1866.

[626] Cooley's draft is on file; but is not copied here because it is substantially identical with the treaty finally adopted.

[627] John Ross, Principal Chief, and others to Harlan, March 22, 1866,
O.I.A., *Cherokee,* R 57 of 1866.

[628] This sort of abuse was indulged in until the very close of the
negotiations.   See especially document, no. 11 in *Papers bearing upon Cherokee Negotiations of 1866.*   It contains several enclosures all of which have
to do with the necessity for protection in the Cherokee country.   On that
matter see also *Cherokee,* I 318 of 1866; I 415 of 1866; R 93 of 1866.   The
last-named is interesting for another reason.   It is a letter from John R.
Ridge to Cooley, May 17, 1866 revealing great anxiety lest unguarded
language used by him in conversation with the president "yesterday" may
have been misapprehended.   "I am satisfied," wrote Ridge, "upon reflection

In their reply to Harlan of March fourth they had ventured to say as much and they had also artfully contrived to represent themselves as victims of un-paralled oppression. How could they, they had even the temerity to ask, have remained loyal when, in fight-ing with the so-called Confederacy, they were but obey-ing the laws which the Ross administration had passed? Presumably, Boudinot had quite forgotten his activities in the Arkansas secession convention and the others their acceptance of military position long before Chief Ross had convinced himself that, for the Cherokees, neutrality and inactivity were impossible. They had also forgotten certain other things, among them the circumstance that they had continued to adhere to the Confederacy long after Chief Ross had officially re-stored his tribe to its position of allegiance towards the United States government. That Boudinot and his associates – there were five of them now – were ever permitted to place their contemptible charges and al-legations upon record and almost encouraged to con-tinue their production is something to be marvelled at at this distance of time.

Despite the terrible injustice of his procedure, Cooley persisted in dealing with the two groups of Cherokees as if they were of equal diplomatic standing

that the President did not receive correctly the idea which I intended to convey when I spoke of the bloodshed which would ensue in the Cherokee Country, if the Government delivered us over into the hands of the Ross dynasty. I did not mean – and did not say – that *we*, the Ridges, Boudinots and Waties, would raise the flag of war and *begin* difficulties, but that the Ross power would certainly renew upon *us* the oppressions of old and dig graves for us as they did for our immediate ancestors, or try to dig them; and that in that case, we were men enough to resist, and that we *would* resist, if it drenched the land in blood. I thought this observation was just, manly and true, but not as it was probably understood by the Pres-ident . . . " The letter of Adair to Cooley, June 22, 1866 (*Cherokee, A 214 of 1866*) is on the same order as the foregoing.

and untrustworthiness. In his eyes, the secessionists seemed deserving of the greater consideration. On March thirtieth,[629] he had a conference with the legal representatives of the two groups, General Thomas Ewing having been retained by the unionists and Daniel W. Voorhees by the secessionists. It was the old story repeated. Ross was still in disgrace[630] and

---

[629] *Papers Bearing upon the Cherokee Negotiations of 1866.*

[630] Between the two dates when formal conferences were held in the Indian Office; that is, between May 3rd and May 11th, some communications of vital importance to Ross were sent to Cooley. One of date, May 4th, was sent by Ross himself and was in the nature of proof that a certain charge to be found in the commissioner's annual report, 1864, p. 343, was grossly false. It was a charge of profiteering against John Ross "and all the Ross family" (*Cherokee*, R 92 of 1866). The second communication, indicating that John Ross was in a peculiar position officially, was of date, May 8th, and was as follows:

"In behalf of the Cherokee Nation, We herewith file with you the Act of the Cherokee National Council, directing John Ross, Principal Chief of the Nation, to act with the Cherokee Delegation. The reason why this is formally delivered to you is that, during negotiations with your department, statements are occasionally made, or permitted, which would seem to imply that charges had been laid against Mr. Ross, or entertained, by your department, At the same time communications addressed to him officially from the Secretary of the Interior leave the matter in doubt.

"Nothing, of course, can be assumed, on mere charges, against any one. It is not presumed that the Departments propose to abolish or set aside any constituted part of the Cherokee Government. Should such a design be entertained by any one, it is respectfully requested that the matter take the proper shape. A fair trial or investigation is demanded before anything is determined, and should it be afforded it will offer an opportunity to set aside many cruel and unjust insinuations which we anxiously desire to embrace."

(James McDaniel and others, Cherokee delegation, to Cooley, May 8, 1866, O.I.A., *Cherokee*, M 390 of 1866).

Notwithstanding the unmistakable resentment implied in the letter just quoted, no redress for the wrong done to John Ross was vouchsafed by the Indian Office. Before many days had passed, the aged chief began to sicken. About the middle of the month, a warrant upon the Cherokee treasury to relieve his actual necessities was placed in Harlan's hands (Daniel Ross to Harlan, May 25, 1866, *Cherokee*, R 100 of 1866); but, by no means immediately honored. Affairs dragged on, Ross rapidly failing. In July, his daughters made a personal appeal to Johnson in his behalf;

his opponents were still insistent that the principle of self-determination be applied in order to relieve them from intolerable wrong. The issue, lost in the American Civil War, was to be given as a boon for Indian disloyalty.

On May third,[631] there was another conference in the Indian Office and, on the eleventh,[632] another, both delegations being present on each occasion. The lawyers presented their facts as before; but it was in the presence of no impartial judge and General Ewing's arguments made little or no impression. In the earlier of the two meetings, Cooley had demanded that, in all future discussions, certain propositions be regarded as an ultimatum. To his credit be it said, the absolute separation of the two factions, politically and territorially, was not among them. The two factions were to live apart, it is true, if they so desired and, to the secessionists, the Canadian District so-called was to be assigned; but as a residence only. In its relations with the United States government, the tribe was to be a political unit as before. The other propositions were to all intents and purposes the same as had been exacted of the tribes already considered.

The arrangement pleased nobody except its maker.[633] Some public indignation had by this time been

---

for the injustice that had been meted out to him was preying upon his mind (*Cherokee*, R 135). They begged he be exonerated that he might die in peace. Their prayer was finally answered. On the settlement of his affairs, see *Cherokee*, C 383, I 513, S 443, S 446, M 80, I 570, I 603.

[631] See *Papers Bearing upon the Cherokee Negotiations of 1866.*

[632] *Idem.*

[633] The Secessionists refused to admit that the conceding of them a home in the Canadian District amounted to anything (Communication to Cooley, April 27, 1866, no. 10 of *Papers bearing upon Cherokee Negotiations of 1866*). About the time of the conferences they seem to have prepared a project of a treaty to suit their own views. It is on file in the aforementioned series.

aroused [634] at the way things were going but Cooley pursued the course he had, from the beginning, entered upon, unchecked. On May twenty-first, the opposition of the loyal Cherokees to his procedure took tangible shape in the form of an elaborate memorial [635] in which their rights and their wrongs were ably set forth. The memorial the delegates had printed, so they informed Cooley on the occasion of its transmission to him, "for more convenient examination." [636] The futility of the effort might have been easily prognosticated.

As summer advanced, new troubles came upon the Cherokees. Their old chief, worn out with the labor of years and accumulated sorrows, was evidently dying. In April, had passed away Judge Thomas Pegg of the delegation. [637] His colleagues had mourned his loss; but infinitely more they now, in anticipation, mourned the approaching end of their outraged chief, whose daughters were interceding with President Johnson for the vindication of his honor. [638] It came but almost too late and not even it was adequate to prevent the successful termination of Cooley's scheme. On June fourteenth, he had reported articles of agreement be-

[634] On May 16, 1866, J. S. Backus, secretary of the American Baptist Home Mission Society, wrote to Seward expressing the hope that in the matter of the treaty with the Cherokees the president would favor the policy of Colonel W. A. Phillips and General Ewing, "who represent," said he, "the loyal party, and who as we believe can be relied on as representing the great body of the Cherokee Nation. We have great fear that the disloyal party are sacrificing the interests of their nation to the interests of speculators." (I. D. Files, Bundle, no. 56) Enclosed with the letter was a copy of one written by Phillips to Johnson, May 4, 1866, which he sent in duplicate to Seward.

[635] O.I.A., Land Files, *Treaties*, Box 3, 1864-1866, M 392.

[636] — *Ibid.*

[637] O.I.A., *Cherokee*, R 72 of 1866.

[638] — *Ibid.*, R 135 of 1866, *op. cit.*

tween the United States and the "Ridge and Watie party of the Cherokee Nation, commonly known as the 'Southern Cherokees'." [639]   Negotiations had to continue, however; for the Ross party had not yet exhausted its powers of resistance.   July nineteenth it yielded consent to a compromise treaty. [640]   It was then the turn of the southerners to be dissatisfied and they let it be known that only with the addition of certain amendments would they consent to the substitution of the "Treaty of the Ross Delegation" for that of the Ridge.   Their proposed amendments included a recognition of themselves as official representatives of the tribe and the inclusion of an article "providing that the Northern Cherokees shall account for all monies received by them from the so-called Confederate States and that so much thereof as can not be legally accounted for by them shall be deducted from their monies due under this Treaty." [641]

Then began another round of discussions.   Eventually, the Ridge delegation, for so it might as well be designated, had its wounded feelings assuaged by the promise of a monetary compensation to meet the heavy expenses which it claimed to have incurred. [642]   In the

---

[639] Cooley to W. T. Otto, acting secretary of the Interior, June 14, 1866, O.I.A., *Report Book*, no. 15, p. 324.   The agreement is on file in the *Papers bearing upon the Cherokee Negotiations of 1866*, being document no. 8.

[640] Cooley to Harlan, July 19, 1866, O.I.A., *Report Book*, no. 15, p. 375.

[641] Communication, August 1, 1866, *ibid.*, *Cherokee*, P 176 of 1866.

[642] The language, in which this promise was couched, was a trifle deceptive.   The money was to be paid to meet "the expenses of the delegates and representatives of the Cherokees invited by the Government to visit Washington for the purpose of making this treaty . . . " (Article 29, Kappler, vol. ii, p. 950).   Peace had been made with the Cherokees at the Fort Smith Council.   That peace ought to have been made with the surrendered forces; and the treaty of 1866 with the nation in its official capacity. Boudinot and his associates were not a national delegation.   They had insisted, however, that the word, "Cherokees," should be substituted for "Cherokee Nation," since no one could dispute their being representatives of

long run, the provision divided the delegation against itself, Boudinot going so far as to charge that his colleagues had grossly swindled him.[643]

In all essentials, the treaty that the Ross delegation consented to, on July nineteenth, was the one finally ratified. Much had been conceded to Cooley and yet much saved to Cherokee national dignity. The Indians had secured, for instance, a recognition of John Ross as Principal Chief[644] and of the fact that the Cherokees had repudiated, on their own initiative entirely, their treaty with the Confederacy. They consented to no partition of their tribal domain; but they did agree to repeal their confiscation laws and to restore the secessionists to full rights. The Canadian District was to be established and, should occasion for arise, its boundaries be enlarged. The freedmen were to be provided for but not to the extent of incorporation. In most other respects, the Cherokee treaty coincided almost exactly with the Choctaw and Chickasaw, previously analyzed. It had the provision for a general council, for a right of way to railroads, and for things of lesser moment.

Its provision for the reception of other Indians, who, if received, were to become part and parcel of the Cherokee Nation, contributory and receptive, was somewhat unique; but, as events turned out, it made for great confusion. The provision for the sale of land

"Cherokees." It would seem that the true delegation did not comprehend the true significance of Article 29; inasmuch as the Indian Office had later to insist that the others were beneficiaries under it. There are numerous communications on file respecting the matter.

[643] Boudinot to Browning, November 15, 1899, O.I.A., *Cherokee*, B 308. See also B 309, B 329.

[644] This is to be found in the naming of the treaty (Kappler, vol. ii, p. 942) "John Ross, principal chief of the Cherokees," was spoken of as "being too unwell to join in these negotiations."

had been, of course, with Cooley and Harlan a *sine qua non*. It was quite comprehensive. The *Neutral Lands* [645] in Kansas and the *Cherokee Strip* were to be ceded in trust and any lands that might be yet remaining to the Cherokees in Arkansas surrendered. Beyond the ninety-sixth parallel extended the *Cherokee Outlet* [646] and there the United States was given permission to settle civilized Indians, the lands to be sold as occupied.

The ratification of the treaties of 1866 concluded the formal reconstruction of the great slaveholding tribes. The re-adjustment of their relations with the United States government had at last been accomplished. To all intents and purposes, their huge domains, collectively considered, had been dealt with as conquered soil. Misguided originally, the Indians had learnt a bitter lesson and they had paid dearly for the teaching it involved. They were soon to learn, moreover, that the settlements of 1866 were but the beginning of new and bigger and never-ending troubles. Their boundaries were interdicted lines no longer. The first to cross the old-time barrier was the civilized Indian, non-southern, the next, the uncivilized, and then the white man.

---

[645] The sale of the Neutral Lands, as arranged for by Harlan with the American Emigrant Company, a Connecticut corporation, was set aside later as fraudulent (Abel, *Indian Reservations in Kansas and the Extinguishment of Their Titles*, pp. 106-107). The Indians of both factions were ready to sell the Neutral Lands; because the government had abundantly proved its utter inability to keep out intruders. Since the close of the war, "discharged soldiers, on the assurances of the agents of a R. R. Company and other interested parties that the land would certainly be treated for during the present session of Congress, had settled there in large numbers (I.D. Files, Bundle 56). For other information about the Neutral Lands at this stage of their history, see O.I.A., *Cherokee*, C 325, C 412, I 447, I 646, M 465, S 241 of 1866.

[646] In negotiating with the Kiowas and Comanches, the United States encroached upon Cherokee rights in this region (*Cherokee*, F 69 of 1866).

Reconstruction work, in the true sense of the term, was a slow process in Indian Territory. The havoc wrought by the war had been terrible. The rebuilding came to be associated with the running of railroads, the convenient guise of civilization, and the Indians, or such of them as were not financially interested, resisted it with might and main. It was then that they real- ized, in their despair, what the reconstruction treaties actually meant, not amnesty as purported, but the con- fiscation of rights that the Indians, in their innocence and in their refusal to profit by experience, had deemed inalienable.

SELECTED BIBLIOGRAPHY

I. GENERAL ACCOUNT OF DOCUMENTARY SOURCES

For this volume, as for the preceding volumes of the *Slaveholding Indians* series, the records of the Indian Office, of the Adjutant-General's Office, and of the Interior Department have constituted the chief sources of information. An examination was made, but without the large results expected, of the *Johnson Papers* [647] in the Library of Congress and of the *House Files* [648] in the Capitol. The former yielded practically nothing of prime importance and the latter not enough to make a similar perusal of the *Senate Files* seem incumbent upon the investigator. In the present connection there is nothing to be added to what has already been said in earlier volumes of this series of the Interior Department records and only a very little of the Indian Office. Of Files, the *Cherokee Citizenship*,[649] the *Freedmen*, the *Inspectors*,[650] and the *Old Settler Cherokees* are especially to be noted; of Collections, the *Bussey Correspondence*, the *Council of Fort Smith Papers*, and *Papers Bearing upon the Loyalty of John Ross*; of Rolls, *Freedmen* and *Citizenship*; and of Books, the following:

FROM THE CENTRAL SUPERINTENDENCY,

"Letters to Commissioner, 1859-1863." The letters herein are

---

[647] Volumes 58 to 107, covering the period from March 13, 1865 to January 4, 1867; *Letter Press Books*, October, 1865 to February, 1869; *Telegrams*, September, 1865 to December, 1866; *Telegram Press Book*; *Pardon Record*, three folio volumes; *Register of Appointments*, two volumes.

[648] To a large extent the *House Files* yielded the text of bills introduced, petitions, data furnished in the course of investigations, most of which can be found in published form in congressional documents.

[649] The *Cherokee Citizenship Files*, the *Freedmen Files* and *Rolls*, the *Old Settler Cherokee Files*, and the *Citizenship Rolls* were all originally a part of the records of the *Land Division* of the Indian Office.

[650] After 1878, the Inspectors' reports were filed no longer separately but with *Miscellaneous Files*.

dated from St. Louis, St. Joseph, etc., November 1, 1859 to February 5, 1863, and deal mostly with fiscal matters.

"Letters to Commissioner, Records." February 14, 1863 to June 6, 1868.

"Copies of letters sent from office of Superintendent at St Joseph, Mo., Atchinson, Kansas and Lawrence, Kansas from May 23, 1861 to July 1, 1871." This book contains letters to agents and to others than the commissioner. The subject-matter of the letters is chiefly fiscal.

"District of Nebraska," "Letters Sent," vol. i, December 12, 1867 to August 22, 1871. The letters were from the superintendent to agents. After August 22, 1871, so the record says, "all official letters to agents were copied by Press and not by hand."

"District of Nebraska," "Letters to Commissioner, 1868-1871." vol. i. It comprises letters from the superintendent to the commissioner and also the annual reports of the superintendent.

FROM THE SOUTHERN SUPERINTENDENCY,

"Letters to Comʳ. E. S. Parker and Others, 1869-1870." Upon examination the book discloses the following as its contents:

pp. 4 to 58, inclusive, copies of Letters sent.

pp. 202 to 268, inclusive, copies of Letters Received.

pp. 59 to 201, inclusive, blank.

The earliest date of the letters is, October 12, 1869 and the latest, August 9, 1870. The correspondence was chiefly that of Wm. B. Hazen, Colonel 6th Inᵗʸ., Southern Superintendent, and of S. P. Jocelyn, 1st Lieut. 6th Inᵗʸ., Ass't Sup't.[651]

Very valuable additions to bibliographical and historical knowledge came from the Adjutant-General's Office and came from the practice, otherwise deplorable, of changing the resting-place of the national archives and depositing them where, because of local conditions, the ban upon free accessibility had to be removed and the obnoxious red tape of officialdom eliminated.

During the all too brief participation of the United States in the late world war, a stupendous need for office room in the capital city was created and this necessitated many and, in some instances, frequent transfers of the government records,[652] particularly of such as are no

[651] For an account of the *Bussey Correspondence* so-called, see ante p. 144.

[652] It was only very recently that the Indian Office found lodgment in the

longer required regularly in the transaction of current business. For such, of course, a Hall of Records ought long since to have been erected.

To the War Department the transfer of records, occasioned by the war, came as a somewhat novel experience. A few years ago it would have been presumptuous to have hazarded the opinion that a time would ever come when the archives, which General Ainsworth,[653] proprietor-like, guarded so jealously as almost to preclude thorough-going historical research, would be removed from the pretentious State, War and Navy structure to a humble garage; but so it was. The garage was a huge affair, reasonably clean and fireproof, at the corner of twenty-fourth and M streets, N.W. and in it the *Records Branch*[654] and also the *Archives Division* of the Adjutant-General's

new Interior Department Building and yet even its records, the older files that is, had to make way for the new clerical forces. They were shifted in whole or in part no fewer than ten times, mostly from room to room, it is true; but shifted, none the less, and dislocated and, by totally inexpert hands, re-arranged. In the course of their peregrinations, some of them travelled back to the old familiar but unsafe abode on E street, the Pension Office Building. There they will doubtless be left until forgotten and when forgotten soon destroyed, since there is nobody there who is officially responsible for them.

[653] It is believed by those who worked under General Ainsworth that he resented and resisted to the utmost an invasion of his office by the historical investigator because he hoped that Congress would eventually authorise the publication of another such series as the *Official Records of the War of the Rebellion.*

[654] The *Records Branch* is to be distinguished from the present *Old Records Division*, which was formerly and before a consolidation with the *Correspondence Division* had taken place, the *Regimental Records Division*. It is located in the Old Postoffice, or General Land Office Building, on Seventh and F. streets. Its records are of such a nature as to imply that, *Records of Old Wars*, would more appropriately describe its character. The records include the original muster rolls of Indian wars, of the Mexican War, and of the Union side of the Civil War, also all papers, antedating October, 1912, of military organisations prior to a brigade formation; that is, regiments, companies, etc. The records of volunteers and regulars, since the date mentioned, are handled by the *Demobilized Records Division*, located at Sixth and B. streets. In the Tenth Street Branch of the Adjutant-General's Office, which has been housed in Ford's Theatre ever since that building was taken over by the government, are to be found cards of the muster rolls of the War of 1812, of the Confederate side of the Civil War,

Office reposed peacefully for a little over a year. In midsummer of 1919, they were removed, at the usual enormous cost in time and money and at the usual risk of displacement and loss of files, to the place where they are at present, concrete building, No. E.[655] How long they will be allowed to remain there it would be foolish to conjecture. Migrations once begun are likely to continue until they become habitual. Rumor has it that the fiat has already gone forth for the removal of the *Records Branch*.[656]

THE RECORDS BRANCH, known in Office parlance as "Old Files," [657] comprises the records proper of the Adjutant-General's

---

of the Spanish-American War, and of the Philippine Insurrection, also the Finger-Print records of America in the World War. Of this division Mr. Jacob Freech is Chief Clerk and, of *Old Records*, Mr. David Currier, former head of the *Correspondence Division*. Mr. H. A. Johnson, ex-chief of *Old Records*, is his assistant.

[655] An exception to this is to be found in the case of the records relating to colored troops. Such records were taken back to the State, War and Navy Building.

[656] Some of the records of the *Archives Division*, those of apparently no statistical or historical value, have already been packed in cases and sent elsewhere for storage. In the course of the recent war, the *Records Branch* was obliged to take on Demobilization, War Risks, and various other matters somewhat foreign to its earlier interests. It is now so large, from the standpoint of current business that it cannot long stay undivided. Most likely, in the near future, the strictly *Old Files Section* will be consolidated with the *Archives Division*. A logical proceeding would be for the genuine archives to be merged with all the old files of the Adjutant-General's Office and that ought to be done before there is any possibility of a certain supposition that now exists being verified; viz., the supposition that "Old Files" are soon to be permitted to occupy the Library on the fifth floor of the State, War and Navy Building. All contemplated removals of archives ought to be deserving of a long, long thought.

[657] The sobriquet of "Old Files" is a relic of the past and dates from the time when the *Records Branch* was a constituent element of the *Mail and Record Division*, the *Old Files Section* of the same. Mr. Thomas Carmick, who has been connected with the Adjutant-General's Office since 1875, is the Chief Clerk in charge of "Old Files." In 1894, he prepared, in typewritten form, an elaborate inventory, which, in effect, constitutes, not simply an index, but a complete history of a very important piece of governmental machinery. It is entitled, "Key to the Records of the Adjutant General's Office," and, presumably, will soon appear in print as the major part of the report of the Efficiency Board that lately borrowed it. Its value to clerk and to outside investigator is incalculable. In reality, it deals, not only with the records proper of the Adjutant-General's Office, but also with

Office,[658] the incoming and the outgoing mail that has accumulated in the long years since the United States government was first organized.[659] Undoubtedly, its books and files are as nearly intact as any in the government service and they hold the history of all the high commands, the brigade, the division, the corps, and the department, also military divisions, regional in character, and army headquarters. It was in the *Records Branch* that most of the material on the Indian Home Guards was found.

THE ARCHIVES DIVISION, in general, contains the papers of discontinued commands and it is by the name of *Discontinued Commands* [660] that it is more popularly known. These papers include the

"such other records as have been at any time in charge of the Adjutant-General or are closely connected with the records of his office."

[658] The organisation of the Adjutant-General's Office into divisions came as a result of the large increase of business incident to the breaking out of the Civil War. To each division a particular portion of that business was assigned. At intervals, since the close of the Civil War, the number and names of divisions have undergone change according to circumstances. Initials have usually been adopted to designate divisions. Thus all records of the *Appointment, Commission and Personal Branch* are labelled, A.C.P.; of the *Principal Record Division, P.R.D.*; of the *Volunteer Service*, V.S. Some divisions have had no office mark, notably, the *Volunteer Rolls Division*, and, naturally, the *Confederate Archives Division*. In illustration of changes of location, these facts may be cited in support of those already instanced: the *Miscellaneous Branch* of the ante-bellum office became merged in the *Principal Records Division*, the *Discontinued Commands Division*, organised in 1866, was for a time transferred to the *Record and Pension Office* and later to the *Mail and Record Division*. For a brief period years ago there was a *Military Reservation Section* and there is now on file, a Military Reservation Book.

[659] Supplementary to the records of the Adjutant-General's Office are the Army Post retained records, records of abandoned posts and discontinued commands that have not found their way to Washington but have been sent to central or to departmental headquarters; regimental records; and, finally, the records kept in the Secretary of War's own office. At the moment these last-named are confided to the care of Mr. John Randolph. Regimental records are officially a part of the Adjutant-General's files. So also, originally, were the records of other bureaus, now distinct. Up to 1857, apparently, the Adjutant-general and the Inspector-general were one and the same; but for over half a century now there has been a separate inspector's bureau and, therefore, a separate file. The commissary and quartermaster's records and likewise the engineers' are similarly to be differentiated from all yet described.

[660] Under an earlier organisation of the Adjutant-General's Office there

records of abandoned posts, of old frontier forts and have much to do with Indian wars, with Indian scouts, and with the wild life of the old West.[661] Among them are to be found the *Confederate Archives,* so extensively used for volume ii of the *Slaveholding Indians* series. For volume iii, the records of the old *Discontinued Commands Division* itself seemed most promising but the material derived from a close examination of them proved but fragmentary. The really valuable were the *Fort Gibson* books and files. Of the former, an office index takes notice of one hundred and nineteen volumes but not all of them were located. The volumes are not numbered in chronological order. Some of the most interesting of them deal with the old dragoons and go back, historically, to the first days of the post. The eight *District of Indian Territory* books were all consulted but to little purpose. *Morning Reports, Guard Reports*, and *Endorsements and Memoranda* books were almost invariably of no account. The books of places like *Camp Wichita, Camp Supply,* and the like were usually of too late date and of greater value for material relating to the tribes of the plains than for those who more regularly participated in the Civil War.

---

was a *Discontinued Commands Division*, which was later taken over by the Archives Division, consolidated with it, in fact, as was also the *Confederate Archives Division* with its twelve chapters, the whole having formerly been a part of the *Record and Pension Office*. Each of the twelve chapters of the *Confederate Archives* represents a particular branch of the old southern service. There is in existence a complete index to the same and it is to be found at the desk of Sanford W. Smith.

[661] This statement by no manner of means exhausts the content of the *Archives Division*. From memoranda, possessed by Mr. Edwin Williamson, Chief Clerk, it appears that the content embraces data, more or less valuable, of nearly all the wars in which the United States has been engaged, inclusive of the War of Independence and the recent World War. Much of the data is in the shape of muster rolls; and, for the World War, there are records of recruiting stations, training camps, hospitals, casualties in France, etc. For the reconstruction period of United States history, it has the records of the *Bureau of Refugees, Freedmen, and Abandoned Lands*, also of the *Freedmen's Bureau* of the Adjutant-General's Office and of the five military districts of the southern states. Moreover, among its miscellaneous files are the documents bearing upon the Philippine Insurrection, the China Relief Expedition, and the Cuban Pacification. The correspondence, books and papers, of the secretary's office, from 1800 to 1866, are its possession.

II. ALPHABETICAL LIST OF PRINTED SOURCES

BOARD OF INDIAN COMMISSIONERS, Annual reports of (Washington, 1869-1876).

BOWLES, SAMUEL. Across the continent: A summer's journey to the Rocky Mountains, the Mormons, and the Pacific States with Speaker Colfax. (Springfield, Massachusetts, 1865).

BUCHANAN, JAMES. Works collected and edited by John B. Moore (Philadelphia, 1908-1911) 12 vols.

CHEROKEES. Laws of, passed 1839-1867 (*St. Louis Democrat* print).

COMMISSIONERS OF INDIAN AFFAIRS. Annual Reports of (Washington, D. C., 1860-1868).

COOLEY, DENNIS N. The Cherokee Question: Report of the Commissioner of Indian Affairs to the President, June 15, 1866, being supplementary to the Fort Smith Report (Washington, 1866) pamphlet.

GLADSTONE, THOMAS H. Kansas, or Squatter Life and Border Warfare in the Far West (London, 1857).

GRAFTON, B. F. Argument of, as counsel for the Indians before the Committee on Territories, H. R., January 26, 1878, against House Bill, no. 1596, for organizing the Territory of Oklahoma (Washington, D.C., 1878) pamphlet.

GREELEY, HORACE. The Overland Journey from New York to San Francisco (New York, 1860).

HOWARD, GENERAL OLIVER O. Proceedings, findings, and opinion of the Court of Inquiry, convened under the Act of Congress of February 13, 1874, in the case of (Washington, D.C., 1874).

HUTCHINSON, C. C. Resources of Kansas (Topeka, 1871).

JONES, EVAN. Statement of, respecting the condition of the loyal Cherokee Indians. Prepared under the direction of John Ross (Washington, 1863) pamphlet.

KAPPLER, CHARLES J. Compiler and editor, Indian affairs – laws and treaties. United States Senate Documents, 58th congress, second session, no. 319, 2 vols. Supplementary volume, United States Senate Documents, 62nd congress, second session, no. 719.

LATROBE, JOHN H. B. Opinion of, on the effect of the tenth article of the Choctaw and Chickasaw treaty of 1866 (Baltimore, 1869) pamphlet.

LEHMAN, E. W.   Answer in chancery of, to the bill of complaint of L. S. Lawrence in the district court for the city and county of Philadelphia, in Equity, September, 1862 (House Files, Box, labelled, "40th congress, papers from Committee on Indian Affairs – Pacific R. R.") pamphlet.

McDANIEL, JAMES and others, Cherokee delegates.   Reply of, to the demands of the Commissioner of Indian Affairs, May, 1866 (Washington, 1866) pamphlet.

McPHERSON, EDWARD.   Political history of the United States of America during the Great Rebellion (Washington, 1864).

—— Political history of the United States during the period of reconstruction (Washington, 1871).

OKMULGEE.   Journal of the Second Annual Session of the General Council of the Indian Territory, meeting in, June 5th to 14th, 1871 (Lawrence, Kansas, 1871) pamphlet.

PIERCE, EDWARD L., editor.   Memoir and Letters of Charles Sumner (Boston, 1893).

PIKE, JAMES S.   The prostrate state (New York, 1874).

POLLARD, EDWARD A.   Southern history of the war (New York, 1866).

—— The lost cause (New York, 1867).

—— The lost cause regained (New York, 1868).

REAVIS, L. U.   Life and military services of General William Selby Harney (St. Louis, 1878).

RICHARDSON, JAMES D., editor and compiler.   Messages and Papers of the Presidents, 1789-1897 (Washington, 1896-1899) 10 vols.

SANBORN, JOHN B.   Regulations of, issued from army headquarters, 1866, for determining relations between the freedmen of Indian Territory and their former masters (Fort Gibson, 1866) leaflets.

SCHUCKERS, J. W.   Life and public services of Salmon Portland Chase (New York, 1874).

SECRETARY OF THE INTERIOR, Annual reports of, 1864-1868 (Washington).

SEWARD, WILLIAM H.   Works, edited by G. E. Baker (New York, 1853-1884) 5 vols.

TUTTLE, CHARLES R.   A new centennial history of the state of Kansas (Madison and Lawrence, 1876).

UNITED STATES LAND LAWS, Local and Temporary. (Washington, 1880) 2 vols.

WILDER, DANIEL W. Annals of Kansas (Topeka, 1875).

III. ALPHABETICAL LIST OF AUTHORITIES

ABEL, ANNIE H. Indian reservations in Kansas and the extinguishment of their titles (Kansas Historical Society, *Collections*, vol. viii, 72-109).

—— Indians in the Civil war (American Historical Review, vol. xv, 281-296).

—— Proposals for an Indian State in the Union, 1778-1878 (American Historical Association Report, 1907, vol. i, 89-102).

—— Slaveholding Indians: vol. i, American Indian as slaveholder and secessionist (Cleveland, 1915); vol. ii, American Indian as participant in the Civil War (Cleveland, 1919).

—— Official correspondence of James S. Calhoun (Washington, 1915).

—— A new Lewis and Clark map (Geographical Review, vol. i, 329-345).

ADAIR, WILLIAM P. and others, Cherokee, Creek, and Choctaw delegates. Memorial against the passage by congress of an act providing for the organization of a United States territorial government over the Indian country (Washington, 1880) pamphlet.

ANDERSON, MABEL WASHBOURNE. Life of General Stand Watie (Pryor, Oklahoma, 1915).

BARRON, SAMUEL BENTON. Lone star defenders (New York and Washington, 1908).

BLACKMAR, FRANK W. Life of Charles Robinson (Topeka, 1902).

BONAPARTE, CHARLES J. and WOODRUFF, CLINTON ROGERS. Report of, on alleged abuses and irregularities in the public service of the Indian Territory under the control of the Department of the Interior (Washington, 1904) pamphlet.

BRIGHAM, JOHNSON. James Harlan (Iowa City, 1913) Iowa Biographical series, edited by B. F. Shambaugh.

BROWN, GEORGE W. Reminiscences of Governor R. J. Walker (Rockford, Illinois, 1902).

—— John Henry. History of Texas, 1865-1892 (St. Louis, 1893) 2 vols.

CASE, NELSON. History of Labette County, Kansas (Topeka, 1893).

CHADSEY, CHARLES ERNEST. Struggle between President Johnson and congress over reconstruction (New York, 1896) Columbia University Studies in History, Economics, and Public Law, vol. viii, no. i.

CHEROKEE NATION Memorial of the delegates of, to the President, Senate and House (Washington, 1886) *Chronicle* print.

CLARK, DAN ELBERT. Samuel Jordan Kirkwood (Iowa City, 1917) Iowa Biographical series.

CONNELLEY, WILLIAM E. A standard history of Kansas and Kansans (Chicago and New York, 1918) 2 vols.

CURTIS, SAMUEL PRENTIS. The Army of the Southwest and the First Campaign in Arkansas. Annals of Iowa, vols. iv, v, vi, vii.

—— Campaign against Price. Annals of Iowa, vol. viii.

CRAWFORD, SAMUEL J. Kansas in the Sixties (Chicago, 1911).

CUTLER, WILLIAM G. History of Kansas (Chicago, 1883).

DANA, CHARLES A. Recollections of the Civil War (New York, 1898).

DAVIS, JOHN M. Elijah Sells, Annals of Iowa, Third series, vol. ii, pp. 518-530.

DAVIS, JOHN P. Union Pacific Railway (Chicago, 1894).

DAVIS, WILLIAM W. Civil War and Reconstruction in Florida (New York, 1913) Columbia University Studies, vol. liii.

DUNNING, W. A. Essays on Civil War and Reconstruction (New York, 1898).

—— Reconstruction, Political and Economic, 1865-1877. American Nation series (New York) vol. xxii.

EATON, RACHEL CAROLINE. John Ross and the Cherokee Indians (Menasha, Wisconsin, 1914).

EBBUTT, PERCY G. Emigrant Life in Kansas (London, 1886).

ECKENRODE, HAMILTON JAMES. Political history of Virginia during the Reconstruction (Baltimore, 1904).

ENYART, O. M., compiler. Biographical congressional directory House Document, no. 458, 57th congress, 2nd session (Washington, 1903).

FERTIG, JAMES WALTER. Secession and reconstruction in Tennessee (Chicago, 1898).

FICKLEN, JOHN ROSE. History of reconstruction in Louisiana (Baltimore, 1910) Johns Hopkins University Studies in History and Political Science, series xxviii, no. i.

FISH, CARL RUSSELL. Civil Service and the Patronage (New York, 1905) Harvard Historical Studies, vol. xi.

FLEMING, WALTER L. Civil War and reconstruction in Alabama (New York, 1905).

GARNER, JAMES WILFORD. Reconstruction in Mississippi (New York, 1901).

GITTINGER, ROY. Formation of the state of Oklahoma (Berkeley, 1917) University of California Publications in History.

GLASSON, WILLIAM HENRY. History of military pension legislation in the United States (New York, 1900) Columbia University Studies, vol. xii, no. 3.

GLEED, CHARLES S., editor. The Kansas memorial: a report of the old settlers' meeting held at Bismarck Grove, Kansas, September 5 and 6, 1879 (Kansas City, Mo., 1880).

GRANT, MADISON. The Passing of the Great Race (New York, 1916).

HALLUM, JOHN. Biographical and pictorial history of Arkansas (Albany, 1887).

HAMILTON, JOSEPH G. Reconstruction in North Carolina (Raleigh, 1906).

HASTINGS, ROSETTA B. Personal recollection of Pardee Butler (Cincinnati, 1889).

HEITMAN, FRANCIS B., compiler. Historical register and dictionary of the United States army, 1789-1903 (Washington, 1903) House Document, no. 446, 57th congress, 2nd session, 2 vols.

HINSDALE, MARY L. History of the president's cabinet (Ann Arbor, 1911).

HODGE, DAVID M. Argument of, before the Committee on Indian Affairs of the United States Senate, March 10, 1880, in support of Senate Bill, no. 1145, providing for the payment of awards made to the Creek Indians who enlisted in the Federal Army, Loyal Refugees, and Freedmen (Washington, 1880) pamphlet.

—— and others, Creek delegates and agents. Appeal to the Committee on Indian Affairs of the House of Representatives of the 51st congress in the matter of the claims of the Loyal Creeks for loss of property taken by and for the use of the United States military authorities (Washington, 1890) pamphlet.

HOLLIS, JOHN PORTER. Reconstruction in South Carolina (Baltimore) Johns Hopkins University Studies, vol. xxiii, nos. i and ii.

HOUGH, EMERSON. Passing of the Frontier (New Haven, 1918) Chronicles of America series, vol. xxvi.

HOWARD, O. O. My life and experiences among hostile Indians (Hartford, 1907).

HULBERT, A. B. Historic Highways of America (Cleveland, 1902-1905) 16 vols.

HUMPHREY, SETH K. The Indian dispossessed (Boston, 1906) revised edition.

JACKSON, HELEN. A century of dishonor (Boston, 1895).

JULIAN, GEORGE W. Speeches on political questions (New York, 1872).

—— Political recollections, 1840-1872 (Chicago, 1884).

LEARNED, HENRY BARRETT. The president's cabinet: studies in the origin, formation, and structure of an American institution (New Haven, 1912).

LOWREY, LAWRENCE TYNDALE. Northern Opinion of approaching secession, October, 1859 – November, 1860 (Northampton, Massachusetts, 1918) Smith College Studies in History, vol. iii, no. 4.

LYNCH, JAMES DANIEL. Bench and bar of Texas (St. Louis, 1885).

McCALL, GEORGE A. Letters from the frontier, written during a period of thirty years' service in the United States army (Philadelphia, 1868).

McCARTHY, CHARLES HALLAM. Lincoln's plan of reconstruction New York, 1901).

McCULLOCH, HUGH. Men and measures of half a century (New York, 1888).

McLAUGHLIN, JAMES. My friend, the Indian (Boston and New York, 1910).

MANNING, EDWIN CASSANDER. Biographical, historical, and miscellaneous selections (Cedar Rapids, 1911).

MATHEWS, JOHN MABRY. Legislative and judicial history of the fifteenth amendment (Baltimore, 1909) Johns Hopkins University Studies, vol. xxvii, nos. 8-12.

O'BEIRNE, HARRY F. and Edward S. The Indian Territory: Its chiefs, legislators, and leading men (St. Louis, 1892).

OBERHOLTZER, ELLIS PAXSON. History of the United States since the Civil War (New York, 1917), 5 vols.

OLDT, FRANKLIN T., editor. History of Dubuque County, Iowa (Chicago).

PUMPELLY, CHARLES WILLIAM. Reminiscences (New York, 1918), 2 vols.

RAMSDELL, CHARLES WILLIAM. Reconstruction in Texas (New York, 1910) Columbia University Studies, vol. xxxvi, no. i.

RANDALL, JAMES G. Some legal aspects of the confiscation acts of the Civil War. American Historical Review, vol. xviii, 79-96.

—— Captured and abandoned property during the Civil War. American Historical Review, vol. xix, 65-79.

REAGAN, JOHN H. Memoirs of (New York and Washington, 1906) edited by W. F. McCaleb.

REYNOLDS, JOHN HUGH. Presidential reconstruction in Arkansas. Arkansas Historical Association *Publications*, vol. i, 352-361.

—— J. S. Reconstruction in South Carolina.

RHODES, JAMES FORD. History of the United States from the Compromise of 1850 (New York, 1893-   ) 8 vols.

ROBINSON, CHARLES. The Kansas conflict (New York, 1892).

ROCK, MARION TUTTLE. Illustrated history of Oklahoma (Topeka, 1890).

ROOT, FRANK A. and CONNELLEY, WILLIAM E. Overland stage to California (Topeka, 1901).

ROSS, MRS. W. P. Life and times of the honorable William P. Ross (Fort Smith, 1893).

ROYCE, C. C. Cherokee Nation of Indians. Bureau of Ethnology Report, 1883-1884.

SHINN, JOSIAH H. Pioneers and makers of Arkansas (Washington, 1908).

SMITH, WILLIAM HENRY. Political history of slavery (New York, 1903), 2 vols.

SPEER, JOHN. Life of General James H. Lane (Garden City, Kansas, 1896).

TAYLOR, RICHARD. Destruction and reconstruction (New York, 1903).

THOMPSON, C. MILDRED. Reconstruction in Georgia, economic, social, political, 1865-1872 (New York, 1915) Columbia University Studies, vol. lxvi, no. i.

VIOLETTE, EUGENE MORROW. History of Missouri (New York, 1918).

WILLIAMS, R. H. With the border ruffians: memoirs of the Far West, 1852-1868 (London, 1908).

WOOLLEY, E. C.   Reconstruction of Georgia (New York, 1901), Columbia University Studies, vol. xiii, no. 3.

WOOTEN, DUDLEY G., editor.   Comprehensive history of Texas, 1865-1897 (Dallas, 1898), 2 vols.

INDEX

ABBOTT, JAMES B: calls meeting of Shawnee Council to consider representation at Fort Smith Peace Council, *footnote* 392; attends Fort Smith Peace Council, 182

Abel, Anne Heloise: works of, cited, *footnotes* 459, 460, 493, 497, 502, 645

Abolitionists: Choctaws not ready to unite with, 13; Gen. Paine, an old leader of, *footnote* 514

Abraham, R. H: and others urge Crawford to seek coöperation of federal government in suppression of illicit traffic in cattle, 92, *footnote* 205

Adair, Washington: *footnote* 539

Adair, W. P: *footnote* 275; appointed on Cherokee peace delegation, *footnote* 317; letter of, to Veatch, *footnote* 337; solicits immediate relief for destitute southern Cherokees, 305-306, *footnote* 570; presents credentials, *footnote* 576; Boudinot and, received by Cooley as "representatives" of the Cherokees, *footnote* 611; letter of, to Cooley enclosing explanation of incendiary language used by John R. Ridge, *footnote* 628

Africans: see *negroes, freedmen*

Ainsworth, J. G: 18

Albin, William M: *footnote* 155

Allen, Henry W: *footnote* 275

Allston, Ben: *footnote* 257

American Baptist Home Missionary Society: *footnotes* 117, 634

American Emigrant Co: Harlan's sale of Cherokee Neutral Lands to, set aside, *footnote* 645

Anderson, Captain: *footnote* 132, 276, 279

Annuities: Doolittle's amendment substantially confiscation of, *footnote* 134; applied to relief of refugees, *footnote* 496; payment of, to Creeks to begin from opening of next fiscal year, 343

Anthony, D. R: *footnote* 201

Anthony, Henry B: votes against Harlan Bill, *footnote* 512

Arapahoes: Sanborn negotiated treaty with Cheyennes and, *footnote* 520

Arkansas: 20, *footnote* 32, 49, *footnote* 130, *footnote* 177, *footnote* 230, 119, *footnote* 258, 130; Gov. Flanagin of, attends conference of governors, *footnote* 275; secession convention of, 137; Harney's name has power in, *footnote* 373; John Ross testifies that he did all he could to resist pressure from, *footnote* 431; men of, interested in development of I. T., 228; economic relation of I. T. to, according to Gov. Walker of Kan., 231; U. S. will request, to grant amnesty to Indians, 335; J. M. Tebbetts, a citizen of, denied permission to drive cattle through the Indian country, 355; any Cherokee lands in, to be surrendered, 362

Arkansas River: 39, 47, 49, 61, *footnote* 131, *footnote* 132, 75, *footnote* 233, 116, *footnote* 281, 292; Col. Garrett in command at Fort Gibson insists that Stand Watie's delegates cross to other side of, 156;

by treaty to act in concert, *footnote* 362; loyal, among the first to sign the Fort Smith peace treaty, 197; secessionist Choctaws and, courageously take upon themselves the responsibility for their alliance with the South, 211; Rector would give to Choctaws and, a congressional delegate, 229; number of, *footnote* 476, *footnote* 480; United States not bound to regard treaties with the, any longer, 257; said to be ill-treating the negroes, 273, *footnote* 518; delegates from, present credentials, *footnote* 561; ignore loyal minority, 303, *footnote* 562; reconstruction treaty with Choctaws and, 327 *et seq.*; in general approve of sectionizing land, *footnote* 602

Chief Joe: *footnote* 248

Childress, Daniel: makes affidavit against Phillips, *footnote* 176

Chipman, N. P: *footnote* 200

Chippewas: *footnote* 480

Chisholm: *footnote* 306

Cho-cote Harjo: Seminole delegate, 306

Choctaw country: William Weir greatly excited over prospective Indian gathering in, *footnote* 356; maize purchasable at one dollar a bushel in, 294, *footnote* 548; claims of licensed traders in, 336-338, *footnote* 604

—— General Council: passes resolutions against allotment of land in the Chickasaw District, *footnote* 602

—— Nation: 22, 23, pledge of the U. S. to, *footnote* 141; Herron's headquarters not far from, 146; Matthews' truce with governor of, *footnote* 339; Armstrong Academy, the capital of, 166; delegates of, can be appointed constitutionally at capital of only, *footnote*

362; title of, to land in I. T., *footnote* 495; instructions to delegates of, *footnote* 598

Choctaws: 11, 13, 14, *footnote* 6, 15, 18, 19-21, 25, 27, 28, *footnote* 36, 29, 36, *footnote* 82; statistics concerning refugee, *footnote* 139; grievance of other Indians against, 77; delegation of, Armstrong Academy for Fort Smith, 143; Capt. G. Wilcox and a delegation of, arrive at Fort Smith, *footnote* 318; have not appointed their peace commissioners, *footnote* 339; and Chickasaws bound by treaty of 1855 to act in concert, *footnote* 362; reject Colbert's suggestion that Boggy Depot be a meeting place for delegates *en route* to Fort Smith, 171; treaty of, with Confederacy, 188; approval of Cooley's proposals by loyal, of little consequence, they being so few in number, 190; secessionist, gallantly take full responsibility for defection, 211; Rector proposed for, and Chickasaws a delegate in congress, 229; number of, *footnote* 476, *footnote* 480; U. S., says Doolittle, is no longer bound by treaties with, 257; said to be vindictive towards, 273, *footnote* 518; legal status among, of the offspring of negro women and of Indian women respectively, 298; select a Washington delegation, 302-303, *footnote* 561; ignore loyal minority, *footnote* 562; reconstruction treaty with, and Chickasaws, 327 *et seq.*; in general, oppose sectionization, *footnote* 602

Christensen, C. T: *footnote* 324

Christie, Smith: *footnote* 96, *footnote* 129; objects to Blunt's order, 85-86, *footnote* 180, *footnote* 182; appointed to confer with Stand Watie's delegation, *footnote* 346; signs

Cherokee protest against Cooley's refusal to recognize John Ross, 214; selected as one of Cherokee delegates, 307; and others of Cherokee delegation report progress, *footnote* 623

Chupco, John: see *Long John*

Chuste-Nallah: battle of, *footnote* 290

Claremore's Mound: 34

Clermont: *footnote* 400, *footnote* 449

Clark, Daniel: 259

Clark, James H: *footnote* 218

Clarke, Sidney: nominated for congress, *footnote* 184; writes to Harlan about Supt. Coffin, *footnote* 201; written to, regarding Indian peace council at Fort Smith, *footnote* 356; wants Cherokee colored people removed to their homes in I. T., *footnote* 540

Clinton: *footnote* 161

Cloud, George: *footnote* 435

Cloud, Colonel: at head of union troops penetrates Cherokee country, *footnote* 615

Clum, H. R: *footnote* 596

Cochrans: *footnote* 268

Coffin, A. V: *footnote* 108

Coffin, William G: 27, *footnote* 34, 30, 31, 37, *footnote* 51, 38, 41, 42; suspected of dishonesty, 43, *footnote* 70; finds removal of refugees difficult, 56; seeks Creek consent to senate amendments to treaty of, 1863, *footnote* 117; objects to the furnishing of funds to Cherokee delegation, 66; suspicion of, *footnote* 142; recommends A. G. Proctor as special agent, *footnote* 184; and other agents make a pretense of destroying illicit traffic in Indian cattle, 89, *footnote* 194; Indian agents rise to support of, 91, *footnote* 200; called upon to render an account of supplies furnished to the refugees, *footnote* 201; su-

perseded by Elijah Sells, 93; Sells asks that ownership of cattle in possession of, be inquired into, *footnote* 218; seeks an order permitting him to take possession of a farm abandoned by Elias Rector, "heavy defaulter to the Government," *footnote* 565; classifying by, of Cooper with Crawford, Rector and Pike unfortunate, 350

Coffy, J. A: *footnote* 526

Colbert, Holmes: Chickasaw delegate, 303, *footnote* 602

Colbert's Mills: *footnote* 268

Colbert, Winchester: 23, governor of Chickasaw Nation, 143-144; asks for safe conduct to Washington of Indian peace commissioners, 144; communications from, carried by Wilcox to Bussey, *footnote* 318; Matthews opens up correspondence with, 148; communication of, to Bussey, 149; truce of, with Matthews, 151, *footnote* 336; some property of the Confederate States still in possession of, *footnote* 339; reports Fort Washita burned on night of August 1, 1865, *footnote* 339; is asked to notify tribes of approaching peace council, *footnote* 360; must have been ignorant, when he wrote to Bussey, of certain provisions in truce, *footnote* 362; undertakes to invite Reserve Indians to peace council, *footnote* 363; persuades Chickasaws, Creeks and Cherokees to meet at Boggy Depot, 171; revives idea, because of difficulty with Choctaws, of holding peace council at Armstrong Academy, *idem*; suggests that Grand Council convene at Armstrong Academy and then adjourn to Fort Smith, *idem, footnote* 366; signature of, attached to resolutions of Grand Council, *footnote* 400; will not arrive at Fort

footnote 370; presides over Peace Commission, 179; submits to colleagues the draft of an address, 180; wires Harlan for further instructions, 182-183; prepares an address applicable to situation of secessionist Indians only, 183; informs Indians they must be prepared to sign treaties, forthwith, 184; address of, 187-190; seeks to explain away his first interpretation of law of congress, 193; pretends to be unaware that Cherokees had long since repudiated their treaty with the Confederate States, 194; objects at first to loyal Creek reservation with respect to signing of Fort Smith peace treaty, 198; renews his attack upon John Ross, 199; decides that refusal to recognize is preferable to deposition, *footnote* 427; reports to Sec. Harlan that John Ross "has been in our way" and that he and his fellow commissioners have unanimously decided not to recognize him as Chief of Loyal Cherokees, *footnote* 428; warns E. C. Boudinot that object of Peace Council is not to stir up bad feeling, *footnote* 431; Southern Creeks report upon propositions of, *footnote* 443; reports that he and his colleagues have been strengthened in their suspicion and distrust of John Ross "by accumulating evidence," *footnote* 449; physically indisposed, 216; adjourns Fort Smith Peace Council *sine die*, 218; Harlan agrees with, that Cherokee freedmen ought to have same rights and advantages as Indians, *footnote* 522, 290; Colbert and Pitchlynn complain to, of lawlessness in southern part of I. T., *footnote* 526; makes arrangements for special agents to relieve distress of

indigent Indians, 293, *footnote* 541, *footnote* 542; instructs Agent Harlan to select Cherokee representatives, 307; withholds knowledge of essential facts, 313; consents to receive McIntosh and Smith as unofficial Creek delegates and pay their expenses, *footnote* 607; Boudinot and Adair seek certain information of, with a view to the further discrediting of John Ross, *footnote* 614; labels documents prejudicial to case of John Ross, 348, *footnote* 616; sends to President Johnson his own reply to various documents bearing upon the John Ross case, 353; seeks information from prejudiced parties, 355; prepares draft of a treaty for the Cherokees, 355, *footnote* 626; demands that certain propositions be regarded as an *ultimatum*, 358; loyal Cherokees present memorial to, May 21, 1866, 359; reports articles of agreement concluded with the "Ridge and Watie party of the Cherokee Nation," 356-360; cession of land by Cherokees had been with Harlan and, a *sine qua non*, 361-362

Cooper, Douglas H: *footnote* 11, 28, *footnote* 257; in full charge of secessionist Indians, 128; surprise of, at Kirby Smith's surrender, 131; precautions taken by, against disorder in I. T., 132-134; advances project for sending a mission to the wild tribes, 134; headquarters of, the scene of discussion as to plans for a raid into Kans., 136; decides to leave Indians unrestrained, 137; hears rumors that Indian annuities are to be paid in cotton, *footnote* 303; considers expediency of calling Grand Council at Armstrong Academy, 141; Wilcox reports to Bussey that, ig-

196; refuse to sign Fort Smith treaty unless statement exonerating them be accepted for filing by Peace Commission, 198; John Ross denies having used influence with, against the interests of the U. S., *footnote* 431; southern, impugn motives of Opoethleyohola, 208; factional strife among, 210; attitude toward negro incorporation, 210, 297; indemnity from U. S. hoped for, *footnote* 443; unprepared for treaty-making at Fort Smith, *footnote* 452; congressional delegate for, and Seminoles, 229; number of, *footnote* 476; *footnote* 480; intermixture of, with negroes, *footnote* 498; reconstruction treaty with, 338 *et seq.*; treatment of freedmen by, *footnote* 608; claims of loyal, 343, *footnote* 611

Crosby, J. S: *footnote* 313

Crounse, Lorenzo: *footnote* 597

Curtis, Samuel P: *footnote* 24, *footnote* 27, *footnote* 35, 49, *footnote* 97, 54, 55, *footnote* 130; *footnote* 132; *footnote* 154, 81; charges referred to, for investigation, 84; report of, *footnote* 176; opinion of, 86; coöperation of, secured by Coffin, *footnote* 194; believed to condone cattle-thieving, *footnote* 200; possible letter of, wanted by Cooley, *footnote* 411; Phillips sends letters to, preferring charges against government officials, *footnote* 617

——, H. Z: *footnote* 411

Cutler, George A: *footnote* 132

——, H. D. B: *footnote* 221, *footnote* 342, *footnote* 518

DAILY CONSERVATIVE: cited, *footnote* 239

Dakota: pacification of tribes in, to be undertaken, *footnote* 439

Dana, C. A: *footnote* 180, *footnote* 199, *footnote* 245

Dancing Rabbit Creek: treaty of, *footnote* 141, *footnote* 495

Daniel, Jones C. C: *footnote* 346

Davis, Garrett: *footnote* 492

——, Jefferson: 130, *footnote* 274; proposed trial of, *footnote* 514; R. W. Johnson in cabinet of, *footnote* 584; basis of indictment of, 348

——, John M: work of, cited, *footnote* 371

——, J. T: appointed on Cherokee peace commission, *footnote* 317, 155, *footnote* 346; credentials of, *footnote* 577

Dean, Charles W: 229

Deitzler, George W: authority upon which Phillips based his accusation against Lane, *footnote* 220

Delahay, M. M: writes to Lincoln in behalf of Blunt, *footnote* 236

Delano, C: *footnote* 600, *footnote* 602; reverses decision of Indian Office regarding status of Creek freedmen, *footnote* 608

Delashnutt, John: *footnote* 225

Delawares: 33, 77, Agent Pratt inquires if Cooley wants chief of, to attend peace council, *footnote* 357; representation of, at Fort Smith, *footnote* 391; treaty of Wichitas and, with Confederacy, 188; number of, *footnote* 480; may go to I. T., 251

Department of Agriculture: 39

—— of Ark: I. T. included in, *footnote* 99; Reynolds assigned to, *footnote* 314

—— of Interior: 39, Phillips sends information of corrupt practices direct to, 90, *footnote* 198; discretionary power given over sale of Indian stock, 93; responsibility of, with respect to refugees, *footnote* 244; Bussey awaits instruc-

of, into Union expressly protected Indian rights, *footnote* 508; in districting, Indian prior rights ignored, *footnote idem*; Ga. imitated by, *idem;* negroes from I. T. in, *footnote* 539; people of, importunate for removal of all Indian freedmen from, *footnote* 540; tribes from, to be allowed to settle on Choctaw-Chickasaw cession, 333; U. S. will request, to grant amnesty to Indians, 335

Kansas-Nebraska Act: 24, 80-81, 227, 228, *footnote* 507, 260, *footnote* 508

Kappler, C. J: work of, cited, *footnote* 19, *footnote* 141, *footnote* 155, *footnote* 417, *footnote* 495, *footnote* 503, *footnote* 591, *footnote* 597, *footnote* 642

Kaskaskias: *footnote* 38, 67, *footnote* 480

Kaws, Kansa, or Kansas: *footnote* 37, *footnote* 480

Keith, Charles B: *footnote* 155

Kellenberger, John H: *footnote* 529

Kendall, Captain: *footnote* 258

Keokuk: *footnote* 37

Ke-too-wha: *footnote* 96

Kickapoos: 36, *footnote* 155, *footnote* 157, *footnote* 480

Kiowas: *footnote* 131, 81, 135, *footnote* 520, *footnote* 646

Kirkwood, S. J: cited, *footnote* 332

"Knights of the Brush": 97

Koch-e-me-ko: *footnote* 76

LANE, HENRY S: votes for the Harlan Bill, *footnote* 511

——, James H: 49, *footnote* 97, *footnote* 117; name of, connected with contract frauds, *footnote* 220; innocence of, testified to by MacDonald and by Fuller, *footnote* 220; writes in interest of Blunt, *footnote* 236; warning of to Wyandots, 185; proposals of, for relieving Kansas of Indians, *footnote* 479; succeeds

in getting law passed for removal of Indians from Kans., 240-241, *footnote* 481; renews effort to relieve Kans. by organization of I. T., 241-242; member of Senate Committee on Indian Affairs and of Committee on Territories, *footnote* 491, *footnote* 492; mis-statement of, respecting charge upon the government for relief of refugees, 250-251; advocates amalgamation of Indians and negroes, 253-254, *footnote* 500; votes for the Harlan Bill, *footnote* 511

Land: allotment of, 333; confiscation of, 23, *footnote* 32, 185, 188, 193, 320 *et seq.*; sectionization of, 332-333, *footnote* 602

Lanniwa: proposed territory of, 236

Latrobe, John H. B: *footnote* 599, *footnote* 603

Lawrence: *footnote* 356

Leased District Indians: 36, *footnote* 43, 56; engaging in cattle stealing, *footnote* 155, *footnote* 156, 82; camping near the Old Cherokee Village on the Washita, *footnote* 363; not represented at first meeting of Fort Smith Council, 181; treaty of, with Confederacy, 188; pledged by Gookins, 190; sign peace treaty with reservations, 198; belong to Tex., 257; bearing of Choctaw and Chickasaw instructions upon, *footnote* 598; sale of the land occupied by, proposed, 330 *et seq.*

Leavenworth, J. H: *footnote* 131, *footnote* 267, *footnote* 306, *footnote* 439

Leavenworth Daily Times: cited, *footnote* 117

Lecompton: 262

Ledger, Captain: *footnote* 132

Lee, Albert L: *footnote* 236

——, Robert E: 129, 132, *footnote* 278

southern superintendency, 93; had
been Third Auditor of Treasury,
footnote 212; has much to say on
cattle-thieving, 96, *footnote* 219;
vigorous measures of, *footnote*
244; appointed on Peace Commission, 175; interested in Harlan's
appointment, *footnote* 371; calls
for information from Mix, 180;
secures from Creeks seemingly incriminating evidence against John
Ross, 195; joins with Agent Harlan in recommending deposition of
Ross, 199-200; signs resolutions
justifying humiliation of Ross,
footnote 424; present when Black
Dog informed against Ross, *footnote* 449; admonished, 294, *footnote* 547; instructs Agent Reynolds
to treat all factions alike, 305;
Cooley seeks information from, regarding Cherokee factional strife,
355

Seminoles: 23, 27, 32, 33, 36, 44-45,
footnote 76, *footnote* 77, 57, *footnote* 113; famishing at Neosho
Falls, 67; statistics of refugee,
footnote 139; pledge of U. S. to,
footnote 141; and Indian Brigade,
footnote 231; Cooper's orders respecting, *footnote* 281; Downing
forwards invitation to, to attend
peace council, *footnote* 363; loyal,
refuse to confer with disloyal,
164; treaty of, with Confederacy,
188; idea of negro colonization or
absorption into tribe repugnant to,
192; opposed to general colonization of negroes within Indian
country, 192-193; loyal, among the
first to sign peace treaty, 197; secessionist, sign prematurely, *footnote* 434; secessionist, ask leave
to reconsider decision and thereupon disapprove of certain features, *footnote* 435; agree to bury
the hatchet, 210; seem somewhat

more friendly towards idea of receiving Indians from Kans., 210;
Rector favored giving a congressional delegate to Creeks and, 229;
number of, *footnote* 476, *footnote*
480; title of, to land, *footnote* 495;
Sanborn of opinion that Creeks
and, would not object to incorpor-
ating negroes into tribe, 297; Reynolds and True find conditions at
old agency of, deplorable, 309; the
first to agree to a reconstruction
treaty, *footnote* 590; long memory
of, *footnote* 592; cession of, 321;
settlement of, upon Creek lands,
footnote 593

Senecas: *footnote* 38, 33, 36; Ely S.
Parker, one of, 176; treaty of, with
Confederacy, 188; outline their
own case, 191; number of, *footnote*
476, *footnote* 480

Senecas and Shawnees: treaty of,
with Confederacy, 188

Senate Committee on Indian Affairs:
48, 50, *footnote* 122, *footnote* 477,
242, *footnote* 491

Seorah: *footnote* 439

Seward, W. H: *footnote* 229, 234,
footnote 634

Shaffner, Tal. P: *footnote* 587

Sharps Creek: *footnote* 38

Shawnee Council: *footnote* 392

—— County: *footnote* 218

Shawnees: 33, 36, *footnote* 155, 77,
181-182, *footnote* 392, 188, 198,
footnote 476, *footnote* 480

Sheridan, General P: distrusts Kirby
Smith, *footnote* 285

Sherman, General: *footnote* 357

——, Senator: observation of, on
Indian policy, 71; opposed to
further treaty-making with Indian
tribes, 260

Shon-tah-sob-ba (Black Dog): talk
of, *footnote* 449

Shreveport: 55, *footnote* 321, 150

Silverheels, Moses: *footnote* 392